CORPORATE DISCLOSURE

Literature review and implication

Yungwan, Suh

Copyright © 2021 Yungwan Suh

All rights reserved.

In dedication to

my parents and family

CONTENTS

Title Page	1
Copyright	2
Dedication	3
Preface	7
1. Market efficiency and disclosure	
2. Voluntary disclosure	
3. Disclosure regulation	
4. Disclosure enforcement	
5. Demand-side approaches	
BIBLIOGRAPHY	342
Footnotes	366
About The Author	407

PREFACE

The role of information in capital market is of great significance, and thus a better understanding of disclosure is essential in promoting market efficiency. So far as disclosure issues are matters of economics, those can be well explained and presented by using economic concepts. This book is intended to introduce many pieces of academic researches along with the concepts of microeconomic theory. There is voluminous literature regarding corporate disclosure, but no book seems to provide beginners with comprehensive summary. This book is to introduce many researchers' various theories and empirical evidence.

You may use this book as a guide map to understand what types of studies have been covered so far. However, this book is very limited because of the lack of my ability and efforts. I focused selectively on some literature that might be useful to cover concerning topics. Rather than introducing the details of the existing literature, I aimed to draw your attention to research trends and basic understanding.

As English is a foreign language to me, writing a professional book in English was very challenging. I sometimes felt stuck in the middle of a minefield, and thus I just aimed to get out of it.

Most of key points in this book reflect the original authors' wisdom, and thus I have no ground to claim that I identified any issues or achieved certain analyses. I cannot say thank you enough to those researchers who reported such wonderful literature. I hope my poor understanding and writing would not obscure the literature that are cited or summarized. I would be as happy as ever if this book could contribute the researchers who are interested in corporate disclosure.

1. MARKET EFFICIENCY AND DISCLOSURE

11. Market efficiency
12. Counteracting measures
13. Theory of non-disclosure
14. Theory of voluntary disclosure
15. Investor's welfare effects of disclosure

11. Market Efficiency

111. Efficiency

Economists tend to assess economic performance with key standards such as efficiency, equity, and growth. Especially, efficiency is to evaluate "static performance" while growth is to "dynamic performance." Disclosure is one of the most significant economic issues in capital market as it influences the efficiency of capital market.

As capital market is multi-dimensional, the efficiency should be defined depending on the context it is used. Economists explain economic efficiency with three forms of economic efficiency, such as operational efficiency, informational efficiency, and allocational efficiency.

A market that satisfies allocational, operational (or transactional), and informational efficiency is said to be a "perfectly efficient market." Operational efficiency is to measure transaction cost, such as tax and commission. A capital market is informationally efficient when market price reflects all available information. Allocational efficiency is satisfied when resources are assigned to projects with the highest profitability in the precise amount that is needed. Informational and operational efficiency are prerequisites of allocational efficiency, which means that the level of allocational efficiency depends on the level of informational and operational efficiency. Thus, the market is no more in an efficient status in terms of allocational efficiency when disseminated information misleads investors, or transaction costs are high.

112. Capital Market Efficiency

The dawning of informational efficiency

Information is the most important parameter for investors to trade risky assets in uncertain markets. A French mathematician Louis Bachelier (1900) is known to be the first who introduced the primitive concept of informational efficiency. In the "Theorie de la Speculation", Bachelier observed that *"The influences which determine the movements of the Stock Exchange are innumerable. Events past, present or even anticipated, often showing no apparent connection with its fluctuations, yet have repercussions on its course. ... It is evident that a gambler will be neither advantaged, nor disadvantaged if his total mathematical expectation is zero. The game is then said to be fair."* When a market reflects a 'fair game,' there is no arbitrage opportunity, and the market is called efficient. (1)

Efficient Market Hypothesis (EMH)

Fama (1965, p.3~4) defined an efficient market as *"a market where there are 'large numbers' of rational profit maximizers actively competing, ..., and where important current information is almost 'freely available' to all participants."*(2) In capital market contexts, the concept of "market efficiency" generally means the "informational efficiency" that is concerned with the relationship between stock price and information. Markets are said to be informationally efficient to the degree that stock price is adjusted to information. Assumptions for an efficient market may be summarized as below: rational price-taker, symmetric information, and investor's adequate reaction. (3, 4) For example, it can be an efficient market if a large number of rational investors actively participate in the market, irrational investor's trades are random and cancel each other out, or those are met by rational arbitrageurs who eliminate their influence on stock prices, investors react quickly to additional information and adjust stock prices, and information is randomly generated and widely dispersed for free to investors at the same time.

Three forms of EMH

Fama (1970, p.383) defined an efficient market as *"a market in which prices always 'fully reflect' available information"* and classifies market efficiency into three types of relevant information subsets: weak form, semi-strong form, and strong form.(5) If a market is efficient relative to "historical" information set, any investor with historical information cannot make abnormal returns by trading on that information, which refers to the "weak" form efficiency. Under the semi-strong form efficiency, price always fully reflects available "public" information (e.g., annual reports), so fundamental analysts cannot find undervalued stocks. Under the strong form efficiency, price always fully reflects "all" types of information, public or private, so any investors cannot beat the market.

Empirical evidence

Some pieces of evidence seem to show that capital markets are efficient in semi-strong form, while others reveal strong efficiency or strong inefficiency. Regarding the semi-strong form, Fama, Fisher, Jensen, and Roll (1969) indicated that the stock splits are fully reflected in the stock price almost immediately after the announcement date.(6) Regarding the strong-form, Jensen (1968) supported strong-form with evidence that mutual funds, on average, neither outperformed a buy-the-market-and-hold policy nor recouped even their brokerage expenses.(7) On the contrary, Finnerty (1976) found that the insiders can outperform the market supposedly based upon informational advantage.(8)

Limitations of EMH

EMH is a meaningful standard and useful benchmark of informational efficiency. The "efficient market" does not mean the "perfect market" of economic literature since it lacks an essential market equilibrium concept.

EMH neither assumes investors are "absolutely" rational nor that information should "always" fully reflect market prices. On the other hand, EMH is also challenged by empirical researchers with numerous shreds of evidence of market anomalies and behavioral biases.(3) Warren Buffet has developed a long-standing reputation for being a sage of Omaha by adhering to the value investment and was tracked by many investors in the world, which also challenges EMH.

Rational expectations equilibrium (REE)

In the Walrasian general equilibrium theory, market price clears the market by matching demand and supply when market participants are price takers and informationally homogeneous. Under the rational expectation theory, rational market participants form expectations about future stock prices based on available information. The market price reveals and aggregates information. Thus, uninformed market participants try to embed the current price into their decision. In equilibrium, all market participants do not have to adjust their investment decision.(9)

113. Information Failure

1131. Omni-present information failure

Information failure can be recognized as a significant market failure that can be found in any market when some players do not have perfect knowledge, or one knows more than the other. As there is no informationally perfect market, information failure is a matter of degree not existence. There are various examples of information failure in many market contexts. In financial markets, investors are not fully aware of the amount of risk. In pension markets, pension sellers mislead pension buyers. In job markets, job applicants sometimes fail to signal their particular skills. In real estate markets, a buyer does not have information about problems. In product markets, a firm does not inform the consumer of the risk.

1132. Information asymmetry

History of terminology

Before Akerlof (1970, p.489) firstly used the term "information asymmetry" for the used car market, Arrow (1963, p.965) studied insurance market failure by using the term "information inequality" between physician and patient.(10, 11)

Symmetric information vs. Asymmetric information

Symmetric information signifies a situation that any player can observe facts or behaviors of the other players because they are provided with homogeneous information. Asymmetric information refers to a situation in which both parties face heterogeneous information, and one party has better information than the other.

General effects of information asymmetry

Information failure can be caused by information asymmetry from supply side (e.g., lack of supply, complexity) and demand side (e.g., lack of awareness). Although all the information shares basic attributes in common, impacts on market efficiency may vary according to the situation where market participants face. Information asymmetry is a significant economic problem because one party can exploit the opponent party by using information advantage, and thus market efficiency would not be reached. Even a small portion of asymmetric information could have significant effects on market equilibrium, market efficiency, and social welfare.

Effects of ex-ante versus Ex-post asymmetry

Information asymmetry can be classified by ex-ante and ex-post asymmetry according to the situation that players face. Ex-ante information asymmetry exists before both parties enter into a contract. If a potential investor does not have information about the characteristics or type of listed firm, the potential investor is exposed to a selection problem, and this may result in adverse selection. Ex-post information asymmetry exists after both parties enter into a contract. If a shareholder cannot observe manager's behavior, the shareholder is exposed to hidden action problem, and this may result in moral hazard.

1133. Adverse selection

Lemon problem

Akerlof (1970), modifying Gresham's law that is widely known by "*Bad money drives out good money*," explored the adverse selection problem in a second-hand car market. It is also known as "lemon problem." In the market under information asymmetry, bad cars sell at the same price as good cars since a buyer cannot distinguish good cars from bad cars. He warned that good cars might be driven out of the market by the bad cars (lemons), as a result of a continuous sequence of driving out process, no market exists at all.(11)

Adverse selection example in capital market

To evaluate the fundamental value of a stock, detailed information should be provided. As the asymmetric information on the quality of used cars can bring a market break down, so the lack of information that is essential for investment decisions can give rise to adverse selection problem. When it is asymmetric, any information that is essential for decision making can cause adverse selection. For example, let us assume all the conditions, but the risk premium is equal among firms. Under the asymmetric information of the lemon market, it is the best way for the uninformed investors to make a decision based on stochastic estimates, such as average risk premium. They cannot perceive the individual firm's risk premium while the informed (i.e., firm) can behave based on the true firm-specific risk premium. As a result, the risk premium gap appears between investors and the firm. High-type firms (i.e., apple) that are evaluated in the market at higher risk premium than its true firm-specific risk premium would cease to raise funds and exit to the other apple markets that ask relatively lower risk premium.

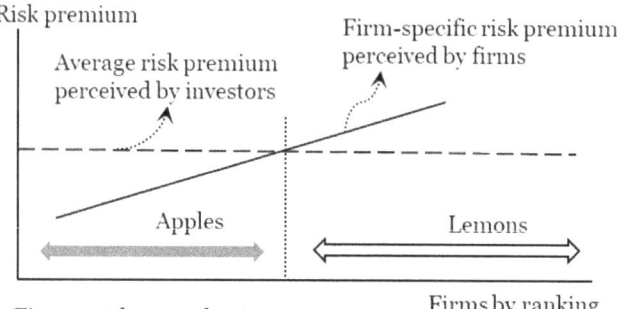

Figure 1 Adverse selection

However, the lemon firm that is asked lower risk premium than its real premium would make the best use of the asymmetric situations by raising as many funds as they can do. The lemon is willing to pay even additional cost to hire a professional consultant for its utmost exploitation. Due to the involvement of professional intermediaries, the lemon problem would become endemic, thereby provoking many apples to exit the current market. To make matters worse, some rational investor who acknowledges such an overvaluation will also exit the market. In the end, only lemon firm and lemon seeking investors will remain in the lemon market. The lemon market may seemingly provide a price discovery function, but it is just in a continuous sequence of driving out apples, thereby forcing the market to break down.

Adverse selection cost; Loss-recoup hypothesis

Bid-ask spread is suggested to consist of order processing cost, inventory holding (control) cost, and adverse selection cost. Informational source of the bid-ask spread, that is adverse selection cost, has been suggested by many researchers who modeled the adverse selection component of bid-ask spreads when investors have asymmetric information. It will cause a decrease in overall return for market markers in trading with informed investors since informed investors will trade only when they are expected to earn profits from trading. Market makers who understand this possible loss will increase the size of the bid-ask spread to recoup expected losses based on the probability of trading with the informed investors.(12-15)

Empirical results of adverse selection costs

Stoll (1989) showed that the quoted spread is related to the characteristics of securities: the volume of trade, the stock price, the number of market makers, the risk of security, and other factors. The quoted spread of NASDAQ/NMS that is a dealer market may be decomposed into the following three components; adverse information costs 43%, inventory holding cost 10%, order processing costs 47% of the quoted spread. (16) [1]

1134. Moral hazard

Concept

The concept of moral hazard has become a central topic since the 1960s. It has been used to explain market inefficiency that arises from hidden action under asymmetric information. Arrow (1963, p.961) emphasizes the possibility of moral hazard in an insurance market, explaining that *"What is desired in the case of insurance is that the event against which insurance is taken be out of the control of the individual. Unfortunately, in real life this separation can never be made perfectly."* (10) [2]

Moral hazard occurs under information asymmetry when one party with more information takes more risks that can be the cost of the others who are with less information. Moral hazard can also arise from the principal-agent problem, where an agent with more information is expected to act on behalf of the principal but act inappropriately against the principal when the agent is not completely monitored.

The information that increases the quality of decision acts as an asset and can be traded in a market. "Uncertainty or risk" can be translated as the contrary concept of information: a state of "the lack of information". Thus, the uncertainty decreases the quality of decision, and it can be "transferred or shifted" to the other party through a contract. For example, managers may be less cautious in making an investment decision because the negative consequences of investment are not be borne by the managers but fully shifted to the shareholders. The insurance company assumes the uncertainty in return for the insurance premium. If the incentive or risk-sharing is inadequately designed, then the informed agent may deliberately exploit the uninformed principle for his private advantage.

Moral hazard arises from a principal-agent relation, where an agent acts on behalf of a principal. An agent has more information about his actions than a principal because a principal cannot wholly monitor the agent's action. As a result, an agent may be incentivized to act adversely against the principal since the interests of both are not aligned. The principal-agent problem is associated with the separation of management control from ownership. The manager (i.e., agent) who has different interests from the owner (i.e., principal) has an incentive to act on his interest under the asymmetric information condition.

Conditions of moral hazard

The possibility of agents' opportunistic behavior may increase a) when agents' inappropriate behaviors are not likely to be found out because those are neither easily observable nor cheaply verifiable, b) when agents think they can evade from principal's monitoring, or c) when they are insured against the damage and loss associated with their behavior.

Economic consequences of moral hazard

Moral hazard creates not only efficiency problems but also equity problems since the informed agent is opportunistically exploiting the uninformed principal. Under the perfect information environment, the principal can monitor the agent's moral hazard. Moral hazard that has arisen from information asymmetry may become a serious issue in capital market when it is coupled with the principal–agent problem. Especially, the transaction amount in the capital market is so vast as to transfer enormous benefits inappropriately from the principle to the agent.

12. Counteracting Measures

121. Introduction

Principals (e.g., investors), agents (e.g., managers), and regulators have incentives of responding to information asymmetry with counteracting measures to minimize adverse impacts on individual and social welfare. Investors respond to protect their profits, managers to maximize firm value, and regulators to protect investors. In either case, to properly implement counteracting measures, the expected benefits of measures should exceed the costs. One may borrow the measures from commodity market (e.g., guarantee, brand, chain, or franchise) to the capital market. These mechanisms offer consumers with quality, sellers with reputation, and markets with growth. However, measures of commodity market cannot be directly applicable to the capital market since there are considerable differences in characteristics. Besides, there is no "one size fits all approach" to solve information failure. Considering the different incentives of market participants to mitigate the information asymmetry, it is meaningful to classify measures by subjects; principal, agent, and regulator.(17, 18)

122. Measures Of Principal (Investor)

Once investors face information asymmetry, they try to devise various measures to protect themselves. These measures can be categorized as active and passive strategies. Investors will choose optimized measures by considering the benefits and costs of each strategy. They are required to have a certain level of ability (e.g., cognitive ability, willingness to pay a cost, organizing association) to employ active strategies. Differences of investor's attitudes in choosing measures against information asymmetry will make different impacts on market efficiency. Market efficiency is expected to be more improved by active strategies but might be undermined by passive strategies.

1221. Active strategy

Private information search

Investors may directly search for information to make a better investment decision. Seeking information will result in a higher quality of information in exchange for search cost. Thus, it is natural for the investor to maintain the optimal level of information search. We can put it with the optimization theory of neoclassical economics. An optimal level of the information search is achieved when marginal benefit equals the marginal cost. As a result, the private information search will not only maximize investors' welfare but also increase social welfare by reducing information asymmetry.

Screening

Under imperfect information with respect to the quality of equities, investors who can sort equities as more profitable can obtain a higher profit. Stiglitz (1975) named this process as "screening."(19) Screening may be defined as a mechanism with which the investors identify the characteristics of the firm and manager. Investors can employ a screening strategy on the premise that a certain amount of information is already available at their hands. There are many examples of screening mechanism; screening the characteristics of the previous owner of used cars, screening job applicant's attitudes, screening borrower's financial status to reduce the default risk.

Employing intermediary

To solve information asymmetry, a potential car buyer can hire an analysis service company that provides information about the quality or a dealer who can certify the quality of used cars. In the capital market, investors can also use information intermediary (aka. infomediary; credit rating agency, financial analysts, news media). Recently, there is a drift for the infomediary to take more roles in facilitating credible information flows and in mitigating information problems.

Contractual disclosure

Shareholders can ask the managers to put some voluntary disclosure requirements in the article of association, contract, or covenants. Examples of contractual disclosure include below.

a. Bond covenants: Managers may enter into a commitment contract with bondholders to release information prescribed in contract or covenant.

b. Ownership ratio: An article of association may require any shareholder to disclose when his ownership ratio changes above a certain ratio. In addition, it can proscribe that noncompliance leads to the withdrawal of voting rights.

Incentive contract

It might be worthy of an experiment for investors to create an incentive mechanism to enhance transparency. For example, investors can make managers converge to the interest of investors by constructing incentive mechanisms (e.g., compensation based on disclosure quality index).

Shareholder activism

Shareholder activism refers to a campaign or investment strategy using a fairly small portion of equity stake to put pressure on managers. The goals range from financial issues (e.g., investment, dividend, cost) to non-financial issues (e.g., strategy, transparency). Implementation of shareholder activism focusing on transparency can take various forms: proxy, litigation, negotiations, and advertisement.

1222. Passive strategy

To protect themselves from information asymmetry, investors who do not want to bear the implementation cost of active measures might prefer passive measures: price adjustment, quantity adjustment, and avoidance. The impact of passive measures on welfare is different from that of active measures.

Price adjustment; bid-ask spread

Copeland & Galai (1983) and Glosten and Milgrom(1985) analyzed information effects on the bid-ask spread. Under the asymmetric information context, investors want to be protected from trades with informed traders by adjusting the bid/ask price. They will discount bid price or add a premium on ask price to reduce their losses, which will make the bid-ask spread wider. Thus, the spread depends on the degree of information asymmetry. Investor's price adjustment may reduce liquidity and efficiency. The spread is useful in measuring the degree of information failure since it reflects the attitude of an uninformed trader.(13, 14)

Quantity adjustment; quantity rationing

Jaffee and Russell (1976) developed a model of how imperfect information can lead to credit rationing that can be explained by the principles of moral hazard and adverse selection.(20, 21) In the neo-classical view that assumes symmetric information, the distribution of a scarce resource is made by market prices, which means "price rationing." The price will rise when there are excess demands. In a neo-Keynesian view that assumes asymmetric information, credit lenders (e.g., banks) who are less-informed than borrowers may not want to increase interest rates even though they face excess demands. If lenders increase interest rates, there can be only high-risk borrowers who borrow from the lenders. Therefore, lenders rather fix interest rates and ration credit to minimize adverse selection problem, which means "quantity rationing." The logic of credit rationing can be expanded to the equity market also. In an asymmetric information context, investors prefer well-known firms to less-known firms. When the information environment turns out to be very asymmetric, investors re-allocate their assets by increasing the weight of high-type. Investors can be protected by quantity rationing.

Avoidance; market exit

When the information environment of a specific capital market turns out to be severely asymmetric, investors may try to avoid and exit the market entirely. Avoidance strategy may be said to be an extreme case of quantity adjustment, which may occur only when investors know the severity of asymmetric information in each market.

123. Measures Of Agent (Manager); Signaling

Akerlof (1965, p.499) illustrated signaling strategies that are designed to counteract the uncertainty. Examples of signaling include guarantees, brand-name, chains, and licensing.(11) Managers may choose one of the alternatives considering the benefits and costs of each signaling measure.

Voluntary disclosure

Voluntary disclosure is a key signaling mechanism in the capital market where companies would disclose even more information than required by laws and regulations. The most profitable company sends a signal with more information to attract investments by showing off their superior characteristics. There are numerous signaling examples of voluntary disclosure in other areas such as advertising product quality, releasing test results, showing scanned sample pages in an on-line book market.

Third-party reputation

Third-party reputation mechanisms (e.g., licensing, certification, quality labeling) are designed to provide an objective evaluation from the third party (e.g., bond rating agencies, CPA, underwriters, auditors, or quality testing institutions). Investors would think that it is a high-type firm that seeks certification by the credible and influential third-party institution. Investors who infer the in-house or private certification is less renowned or less costly will hardly respond to such a private certification, whereas credible third-party certification will be associated with better access to the market. Investors will trust disclosure more when verification is easy and cheap, or when it is backed by reputation, warranty, or legal enforcement. As verification is generally costly, firms tend to resort to third-party reputation mechanisms to signal their high quality by contracting auditors and underwriters who can credibly certify the quality. Some empirical evidence shows that value-maximizing managers will choose to employ third party reputation. *"Prestigious underwriters are associated with lower risk offerings."*(22) An inverse relation between auditor reputation and IPO initial return earned by the investor is supported. Hiring a well-known audit firm is related to a less underpricing of an IPO. (23) *"Certification results in a higher price regardless of the seller's reputation."* (24)[3]

In-house reputation

Some firms have developed an "in-house reputation" as a device to assure high quality in the absence of any credible third-party reputation. Well established reputation has a significant impact on firm value. In the commodity market, establishing brand-name or franchising are examples of in-house reputation. In-house reputation mechanism adopted by firms with short history under adverse selection, however, will not be effective in providing enough incentives because reputation will be effective only above a certain degree of transparency.(25)

Warranty and guarantee

In commodity market, adverse selection problems can be mitigated by signaling mechanisms such as warranty and guarantee with which sellers can generate a buyer's potential belief on the quality of products. The guarantee period should be so long enough to create a belief on the quality. The one-week guarantee will be regarded just as a cheap talk. In the capital market, the market price crash below the offering price in the IPO process can lead investors to the lack of confidence. Thus, the issuer may reach a preventive agreement with the underwriter by employing all legal price stabilization measures to keep the price above the offering price. Underwriter's market price stabilization might be taken as a similar mechanism with warranty or guarantee. It will make investors confident of the belief that the offer price will reflect a fair price.

124. Measures Of 3Rd Parties

Third parties such as association, exchange, and regulators can design mechanisms to enhance a firm's transparency and support investor's understandability.

a. Government: Conveying more information by regulation is an immediate approach to solve the asymmetric information problems.

b. Exchange: Despite the key issues on whether exchanges compete for more trading volume or not, most stock exchanges have designed optimal disclosure mechanisms. In case exchanges engage in "race for the top" by adopting higher disclosure requirements, transparency would be enhanced. (26)

c. Association: In many countries, the associations of listed firms or analysts are organized for their goals to improve transparency.

13. Theory Of Non-Disclosure

Laissez-faire

Laissez-faire, "let them do," is an economic concept that private transactions should be free from any intervention (e.g., regulation, subsidy) to enable the wealth of the nation to grow.[4] Adam Smith (1759, 1776) was the first to use the word "invisible hand" that has long been closely related to the doctrine of laissez-faire.(27, 28) Laissez-faire in combination with the invisible hand provides two rationales; caveat emptor and signaling. The classical view seems to have a mindset that "Let investors beware of managers, let managers beware of investors, and managers will signal when it is necessary."

Caveat emptor

In the same vein with laissez-faire, the ancient maxim of caveat emptor, "let the buyer beware," implies that sellers have no duty to disclose information. Instead, buyers are responsible for collecting all information at their own costs. Many people think it as a unidirectional concept but actually it is a bidirectional one because caveat emptor usually includes "caveat venditor," which signifies "let the seller beware". Both concepts mean all parties are responsible for their own decisions in arm's-length transactions.(29)

14. Theory Of Voluntary Disclosure

141. Signaling Hypothesis

Signaling is the strategy that agents (e.g., job applicant, manager, borrower.) choose their action or convey signals to change the belief of principal (e.g., employer, investor.). Signaling can be defined as the voluntary behavior that the agent conveys hidden information about itself to the principal. Informed agents are argued to have enough incentives to construct costly signaling mechanisms for more benefits.(30)[5]

The signaling hypothesis is the idea that agents are motivated to make a decision for a "signaling" purpose rather than for a "fundamental" purpose (e.g., firm value maximization). Avid supporters of the signaling hypothesis think that it is an effective means of mitigating or overcoming the information asymmetry, and a great many phenomena may be explained by the signaling hypothesis.

The signaling hypothesis relies on the assumption that managers will commit to a credible decision, behavior, or disclosure to an adequate degree. The optimal signaling strategy depends on market characteristics. Certification of a respected third party may send the strongest signal in one market, but it may not hold in the other. We need to consider combining various signaling strategies based on the benefits and costs of signaling. The individual signaling equilibria may not be equivalent from the viewpoint of social welfare because private and social welfare may diverge. Individuals can maximize their welfare with signaling but may harm social welfare because of signaling costs.

Evidence of the signaling hypothesis include studies of dividend, debt, and IPO. For example, a sharp increase in dividend tends to indicate the firm's positive future prospects. Managers can make a generous dividend policy not as a value-maximization policy but as a positive signal to the investors. A debt issuance can signal a stable financial condition. On the contrary, it can be a negative signal that the firm is burdened by future interest payments. Market recognize higher ownership ratio as a more favorable signal, and thus the entrepreneurs are motivated to choose a higher ownership ratio.(31)

142. Unraveling Hypothesis

The signaling hypothesis developed in the labor market has been used to explain managers' decisions and voluntary disclosure in the capital market. It can explain why managers voluntarily disclose but does not clarify whether all the managers disclose.(32) The firms would follow a full disclosure policy in equilibrium as long as there are "credible and costless" means of disclosure. It is assumed that investors can verify the disclosed information at a low cost, and they are willing to pay for the perceived value of the firm. A high-type firm would always reveal its value or quality to distinguish itself from other low-type firms, and the silent firm will be perceived as the lowest type. The comparative advantage of being distinguished is a sort of signaling benefits (i.e., disclosure benefit). If any firm is detected to withhold information, then investor adopts a skepticism. They will be suspicious about the value of withholding firms and, as a result, discount the price to the point that managers reveal the true state. Through such a continuous unraveling process, information is fully revealed, and disclosure regulation is characterized by redundancy.(33-35)

Price decline induces the provision of information, which accomplishes market efficiency. Voluntary signaling can also play a meaningful role even under mandatory disclosure context when investors would search for more information than the requirements mandated by laws and regulations. The information, as a signal, reveals the true value of a firm. Thus, managers make disclosure decisions considering the potential impacts of disclosure on the market price. As information arrives, managers compare the two prices: the expected price as a result of disclosure and the expected price as a result of withholding. Managers have an incentive to disclose the good news that is indicating a higher firm value than the current price while they withhold the bad news that is indicating a lower value than the current price.(36)

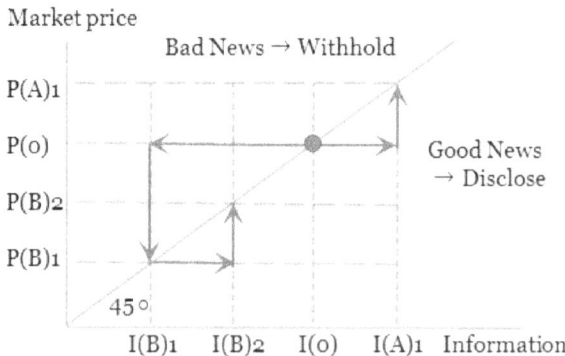

Figure 2 Unraveling process

Figure 2 explains the unraveling hypothesis. Suppose that all firms, including A and B, are endowed with the same information (I(0)) at the initial phase (t=0). At time t=1, firm A receives and discloses new information I(A)$_1$ that represents higher value than the original value (i.e., P(A)$_1$>P(0)), and as a result the stock price rise to the true value P(A)1. However, investors might give a skeptical response to the non-disclosing firm B, conjecturing that the fundamental value of firm B might be $P(B)_1$ far lower than $P(0)$. No sooner than such a severe skepticism brings the stock price of firm B down to $P(B)_1$, firm B will make a reluctant disclosure for the information $I(B)_2$ that has been withheld. The information $I(B)_2$ was then-current bad news but now became good news because the stock price is below $P(B)_2$. Finally, the stock price of firm B will rise to the fundamental value $P(B)_2$.

143. Critics

A signaling hypothesis and unraveling procedure has contributed in explaining the possibility that investor's skepticism can induce full disclosure. On the other hands, there are as many counter-arguments against the signaling and unraveling hypothesis.

a. Benefit: A firm expecting a low level of disclosure benefit may decide not to disclose its private information. Financial signaling such as voluntary disclosure might have low effectiveness since it is almost costless unlike the job signaling of which cost is high. (32)

b. Cost: Unraveling hypothesis assumes that there is no cost. However, it is the stark reality that disclosure cost prevents managers from voluntary disclosure. Trading costs can also reduce the possibility of an investor's skeptic behavior for the non-disclosing firm.

c. Rationality: Even rational investors may well have enough reasons for her non-skepticism. For example, non-disclosing firms did not show particularly poor earnings. Only about 15% of managers provide forecast earnings, and thus rational investors do not mindlessly respond with skepticism for non-disclosure. (37)

d. Cheap talk: Various behaviors may result in information failure when investors misinterpret a signal, or managers convey a dishonest signal. What principals can do is only to make a guess on agents' behavior. This cannot be a solution to information asymmetry because managers may make costless or non-binding cheap talks, which is often defined as a communication that is costless, non-binding, and unverifiable by a third party. (38) [6]

Evidence of partial disclosure

Examples of empirical evidence of withholding or partial disclosure include below. However, some pieces of evidence exist arguing that managers disclose both good news and bad news voluntarily.(39, 40) In a real world, managers do not seem to follow the unraveling hypothesis but their discretionary decision.

Managers withhold bad news and a stock price decline triggers disclosures of previously withheld bad news.(36) Managers delay the bad news announcement and negative items (e.g., asset write-down) to the 4th quarter.(41) Good news tends to be disclosed earlier than bad news.(42) Managers disclose good news forecasts more often than bad news.(37, 43-45) Managers disclose good news as a numeric forecast, whereas bad news as a qualitative announcement that is less distinguishing.(46)

Managers will send a signal when the information seems to distinguish the disclosing firm from the low-type. If the information might not be distinguishing, then it will be withheld or delayed. They will withhold the bad news until the stock price falls. If the stock price falls below the true value, then the bad news is recognized to be a piece of good news. The unraveling hypothesis sounds like a full disclosure process but just a "delayed" disclosure only for the good news at present that had been withheld. Managers will make delayed disclosure only when it becomes good news. However, the concept of full disclosure should naturally include "timely and full disclosure" including bad news.

15. Investor's Welfare Effects Of Disclosure

151. Non-Disclosure Context

Information search

Investors must pay a significant "set-up cost," or a sunk cost, to search and process information. If the minimum required budget to follow exceeds the current budget level of investors, then an investor will not follow the firm, making it neglected stock. Thus, managers voluntarily increase investor relation activities to

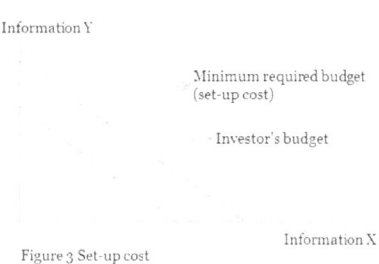

Figure 3 Set-up cost

reduce such a set-up cost, making investors aware of the firm.(47, 48) Conceptual tools of welfare economics can be borrowed to effectively explain the welfare consequences of information disclosure.[7]

Under the non-disclosure context, investors will optimize their voluntary information searching behavior where the budget line is tangent to an indifference curve of the utility function.

Lay Investors vs. Experts

Under the non-disclosure context, investors should make a search for information within a given budget constraint (e.g., resource, ability). Optimum information search level, an equilibrium, is reached at the tangent point of budget line and indifference curve. Analysts with abundant budgets will increase their utility, reaching a higher tangent point while

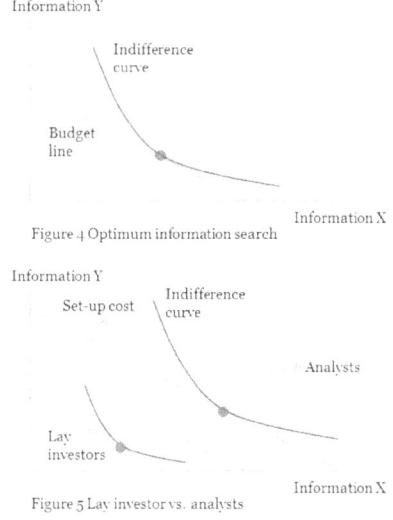

Figure 4 Optimum information search

Figure 5 Lay investor vs. analysts

lay investors with less budget will neglect the stocks because her budget is lower than set-up cost. However, none of the information users can achieve full information. (Figure 5)

152. Disclosure Context

1521. Price subsidy effect

When the information search cost for a specific piece of information (e.g., information X) has been reduced due to development of information technology, information users shift to new optimization equilibrium. The cost reduction due to the development of technology has a similar effect with the "price subsidy." Investors will reallocate their resources within budget constraints, and the allocation ratio between two types of information will be determined by their utility function and new budget line. In case information user's welfare function is stable, a new tangent point of the indifference curve and the budget line will optimize their utility (Figure 6: from (x_1, y_1) to (x_2, y_2)).

However, the degree and direction of impacts on individual information search behavior depend on the characteristics of information and the nature of investors' preferences. In addition, new technological advances can change information user's welfare function (Figure 7, from indifference curve 1 to Indifference curve 2). For example, with the technological advances and its subsequent cost reduction of "quantitative" information analysis, investors might pay more attention on "quantitative" information (Figure 7, (QN_3, QL_3)) while they might divert their attention by allocating more resource in searching and analyzing "qualitative" information which may create more welfare (QN_4, QL_4). The latter signifies that investor's information preference function (i.e., indifference curve or welfare function) is affected by technological advances.

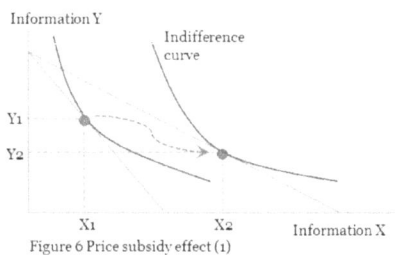
Figure 6 Price subsidy effect (1)

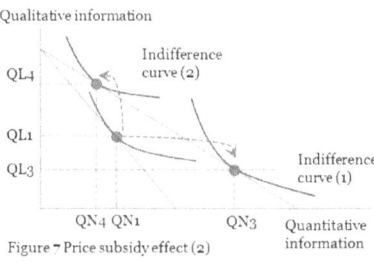
Figure 7 Price subsidy effect (2)

1522. Income subsidy effect

Voluntary disclosure

Voluntary disclosure shares functional resemblances with an income subsidy policy, which makes investor's budget constraints move further and increases investor's welfare. Under non-disclosure contexts, investors optimize their information search at N (Figure 8, (x_n, y_n)). In case information X is voluntarily provided while information Y is withheld, the budget line moves parallel to the direction of

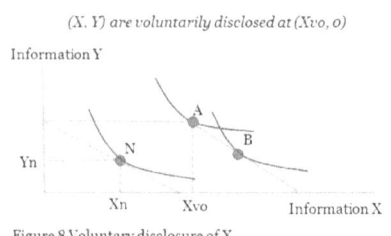
Figure 8 Voluntary disclosure of X

information X by optimizing at A (x_{vo}, y_n), which means investors are subsidized with information X. However, if investors who prefer more information X, he might still voluntarily search more information X by optimizing at B.

In case information Y is also voluntarily provided, the budget line will move upward to the direction of information Y, which means investors are also subsidized with information Y (Figure 9, $C_0/C_1/C_2$). Whichever choice investor make among A, B, C, voluntary disclosure will elevate the budget line and the indifference curve further and enhance information user's welfare.

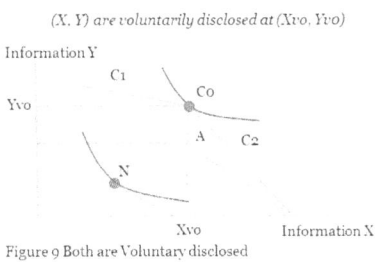

Figure 9 Both are Voluntary disclosed

A: Investors who are satisfied with voluntary disclosure for X will allocate their all resources in searching for information Y.

B: Investors choose to allocate more resources in voluntarily searching X even though information X is already voluntarily provided. Information search (i.e., information consumption) for X will sharply increase with the help of voluntary subsidy and additional resource allocation. Investors would seek more information X, especially when they assume managers do not make credible full disclosure. Furthermore, voluntarily disclosed information that provides some hints for additional information may trigger more active voluntary information search behaviors.

C_0: Investors who are satisfied with voluntary disclosure for both information will stop additional information searching but be optimized at C_0 or they might choose to voluntarily search more information at C_1 or C_2 depending to their own welfare function.

Mandatory disclosure

Coffee (1984) explains a mandatory disclosure as a subsidy policy that reduces investor's information search costs by securing a greater quantity and quality of information. Mainly the securities analysts can perform information search and verification functions at a lower cost. As a result, a mandatory disclosure

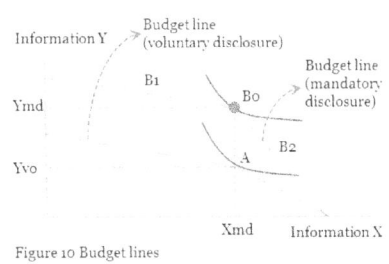

Figure 10 Budget lines

improves allocative efficiency and social welfare.(49) In case firms are mandated to disclose information X_{md} but information Y is voluntarily disclosed at y_{vo} (Figure 10, A), additional mandatory disclosure for both Y will increase investor's welfare further (B_0). Even though disclosure regulation for both information is in place, investors might engage in additional voluntary information searching because mandatory disclosure does not guarantee perfect information (B_1 or B_2).

1523. Sources of welfare enhancement

Information cost savings effect

Diamond (1985) introduces two types of effects to investors from public disclosure; information cost savings effect and risk-sharing effect. Under the non-disclosure policy, each investor has an incentive to acquire information; however, disclosure makes it incentive-compatible to refrain from acquiring private information. An individual investor can be improved in welfare by private information acquisition, but they are worse off collectively. Firms that are pursuing investor's welfare maximization will establish disclosure policies on the information which investors could have acquired at some finite cost. All the shareholders will prefer the optimal disclosure policy that makes all investors better off, which leads firms to pre-commit with voluntary disclosure. The information cost savings effect is the "savings of real resources" which would have been consumed away in private information acquisition with non-disclosure policy. A policy of disclosure makes all shareholders better off, which occurs from information cost savings. Investors have incentives to make information acquisition voluntarily, but it is costly, which makes them demand firms to provide disclosure. The firm's commitments to release information will improve the welfare of all investors who otherwise would acquire costly information in the absence of disclosure. When the information production cost of a firm is no higher than that of investors, there is a firm's disclosure policy that increases investor's welfare. A public disclosure refrains investors from acquiring private information. (50)

Verrecchia (1982) suggests that, in a competitive market, investors can learn both from costly private information and costless price information. If all traders try to acquire costly information, price aggregates all the information, including disclosed and gathered information, and partially reveals it. Price information serves the role of an aggregator of total information. However, since price information reveals information only partially, incentives for private search are not eliminated.(51) Thus, the price revelation effect will additionally contribute to the cost-saving effect of information searching.

Set-up cost reduction effect

Merton (1987) develops a model of incomplete information by assuming that *"investors only know about a small subset of the available securities."* Thus, an investor constructs the optimal portfolio only with securities that she knows about. There is a significant set-up cost of making investors aware of the firm. If an investor does not follow a particular firm, then a disclosed information is not likely to cause trading. The set-up cost determines the "degree of investor recognition" and the "relative size of the investor base."

The set-up cost is a sunk cost for current shareholders; however, potential shareholders may recognize it as a serious recognition barrier. (48) Arbel, Carvell, and Strebel (1983) suggest the "neglected" stocks. If the stock is not followed by large numbers of professional analysts or the number of investors is relatively small, then the security would fit the neglected stock. (47)

Under the non-disclosure context, a higher set-up cost results in higher break-even point, which leads to the neglected stock. Even though investors might achieve the net benefit of analysis by voluntary information search, the amount might be very limited. Besides, they would prioritize the favorite stock selection based on the amount of the net benefit of analysis. As a result, a stock will be neglected if the net benefit of analysis is lower than the absolute threshold level that is required, or they might remove the stocks that are positioned at the bottom of the list.

By the way, disclosure by the neglected firm ($D_1 \rightarrow D_2$) will reduce a set-up cost of stock analysis (Figure 11, $SC_1 \rightarrow SC_2$). Firm's active disclosure will reduce the fixed cost of analysis (Figure 12, $FC_1 \rightarrow FC_2$) and total cost of analysis ($TC_1 \rightarrow TC_2$). Finally, it lowers the break-even point of stock analysis ($BEP_1 \rightarrow BEP_2$). As a result, the number of neglected firms will be reduced, while the number of followed firms be increased.

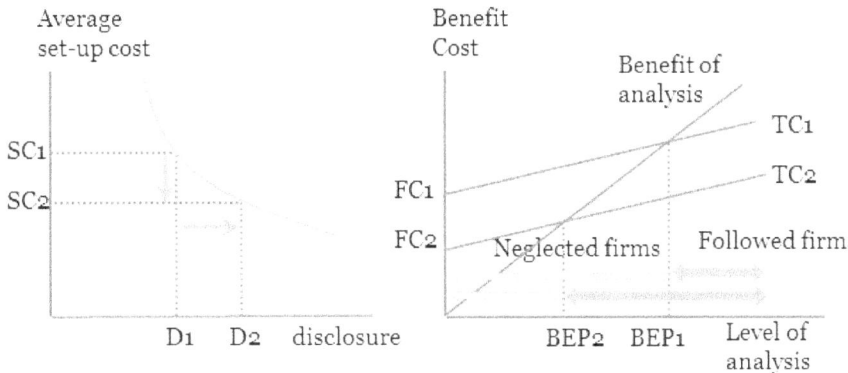

Figure 11 Set-up cost reduction effect (1) Figure 12 Set-up cost reduction effect (2)

2. VOLUNTARY DISCLOSURE

21. Nature of information
22. Disclosure and Valuation
23. Disclosure benefit
24. Disclosure cost
25. Determinants of disclosure
26. Disclosure effect
27. Opportunistic disclosure
28. Disclosure credibility

21. Nature Of Information

211. Concept

Definition

There are numerous definitions of 'information' presented by researchers in various fields, and a comprehensive definition of information that can cover multiple areas is not easily attainable. There can be objective and subjective approaches.

First, according to the objective approach, the most common and traditional view of information is "processed data" for decision-makers' needs. This view involves an implicit assumption that 'data' is objective, so to speak, it has an existence and structure in itself, regardless of information user. The objective approach assumes that objective information exists and produces a similar effect among receivers.(52) Davis and Olson (1985) have defined information as *"data that has been processed into a form that is meaningful to the recipient and is of real or perceived value in current or prospective action or decision."* (53) Descending from 'wisdom' which is located at the top of a hierarchy, there are 'knowledge', 'information', and, 'data' at the bottom. This DIKW(data-information-knowledge-wisdom) views information as 'processed data'.(54)

Second, a subjective approach focuses on the information user side. Each information user will result in different meanings and decisions due to personal values and beliefs.(52) *"Uncertainty is summarized by the dispersion of individuals' subjective probability (or belief) distributions ... Information ... consists of events tending to change these probability distributions."*(55)

Significance of information

Before starting with disclosure, understanding the nature and roles of information might be helpful. Kothari (2006) emphasizes that a capital market is characterized by "dis-intermediation" which enables firms to access abundant capital without traditional financial intermediaries;

> *"The fuel for the disintermediation market has been provided by the capital markets. ... No doubt, securitization adds power to the process of disintermediation, as it moves more and more assets into the capital market directly"*(56)

Due to the vacancy of traditional financial intermediaries, the market protection based on information (i.e., disclosure) has become more fundamental. Information is a central concept in understanding market efficiency and disclosure behaviors. However, just providing information cannot properly reduce inefficiency. To achieve the effectiveness of the capital market, exploring the nature and role of information is essential for a better understanding of market efficiency. The purpose of paying attention to the nature of information is to carry out an in-depth study of disclosure behavior because diverse natures and attributes of information can seriously affect the market participant's decisions.

Flow of information in capital market

Healy & Palepu (2001) provides a diagram (Figure 13) about the flow of capital and information in the capital market to explain the role of disclosure among households, firms, intermediaries, and regulators. Capital flows either directly from households to firms or indirectly through financial intermediaries, and information also can flow either directly or indirectly through intermediaries. (57)

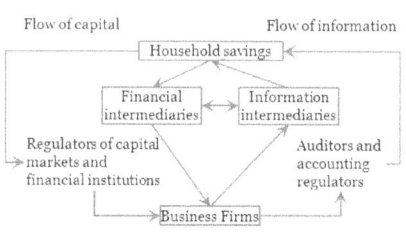

Figure 13. Flows of capital and information
Source) Healy & Palepu (2001, p.408)

212. Violating The Law Of One Price

Jevons (1879) had named the 'Law of Indifference' or the "Law of One price," signifying that there can only be one price or ratio of exchange for the same commodity in the same market. The market for capital is like all other markets, and there can be one price at one time.(58)

The average cost curve of commodity production is U-shaped (Figure 14), but that of information production is continuously declining because information production is independent of scale, and the marginal cost of information is almost zero (Figure 15).[8] Thus, when it comes to information, the 'Law of One price' may not be sustained.

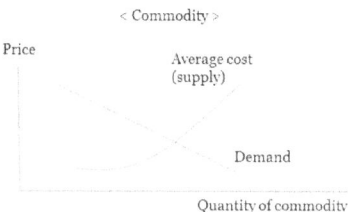

Figure 14 Supply and Demand of Commodity

According to the peculiar cost structure of information, the law of one price can be violated, resulting in two or more prices. It provides some implications. For example, lay investors who cannot afford the expensive red-hot news are likely to wait for delayed information that can be gathered at nearly zero cost. In contrast, institutional investors may be interested in paying high costs. If the information users can be separated, information producer operating closed

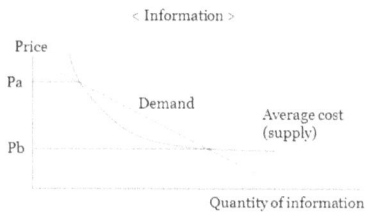

Figure 15 Supply and Demand of Information

membership may distribute real-time information to the members first and then to the internet users on a selective basis sometime later.

213. Information Production

Public goods

The information has some attributes in common with public goods; non-rivalrous and non-excludable. Information is a public good so long as it is non-rivalrous and non-excludable. On the other hand, it can be a private good, so long as it is exclusive where other people can be excluded from access. Information may alternate a private good and a public good depending on its environment.(59) First, regarding non-rivalrous nature, one's consumption does not diminish others' consumption. Once anyone paid for information, others who did not pay for can make free use of it as a "free rider." It is a non-rivalrous resource when the marginal cost of reproduction of information is almost zero. Second, regarding non-excludable nature, once information is released, it is impossible or extremely costly to prevent others from using it. It is a non-excludable resource when the owner cannot prevent others from using it.

	Excludable	Non-excludable
Rivalrous	Private goods	Common resources
Non-rivalrous	Club goods	Public goods

Note) "Rivalrous" nature refers to a nature that one's consumption affects other's consumption, and "excludable" nature refers to the nature that individuals can be kept from consuming.

Underproduction

It is not easy for even information owners to control information due to the non-excludable nature of the information. In many countries, the government establishes statutory mechanisms to promote the production of useful information by protecting the information owner. However, such legal protection is limited since the government cannot protect all types of useful information. As a result, all information producer cannot be protected, which makes the private benefit of information production is lower than the social benefit of information production. If the public goods such as information is left to be priced and produced under the market pricing mechanism, there will be underproduction caused by the lack of incentive. If the marginal cost of information distribution is almost zero, they will wait and see until the price of information significantly drops. Such free-riding will inhibit information production.

Overproduction

If a patent is allowed to information producer as an incentive and protection, they will race for information and, in some cases, may produce a lower quality of information. As the quality of information cannot be evaluated on a subjective basis, they may lower the quality of information only for the patent rights. As a result, we cannot exclude the possibility of deterioration of the information quality. In capital markets, we cannot deny that market rumor is widespread at any time of span.

214. Attributes And Roles Of Information

2141. Basic attributes

Information is a useful asset when it is kept secret from others, but the information owner cannot exclude others from the use after it is released. Information is replicable at low cost, but many copies of the same item of information are not necessarily worth much more than one. Information is easily replicable at low cost and, thus, the released information can lead to severe and widespread competitive disadvantages. Information is self-assembling in its nature by being blended with other information and provides analysts an opportunity to make a guess; the mosaic theory.

Information is highly expandable and is self-generating. It is very easy or less costly to add additional information. However, it does not mean that the value of expanded information is additive.(59) The owner of a large database may be able to achieve substantial economies of scale in producing additional information. Information is highly convertible to its format. To fully achieve the purpose of disclosure, the information should be expressed in many different ways (e.g., language, table, chart, number, etc.).

When new information is connected with old information, it generates verification, confirmation, and comparison, enabling a higher level of consistency and transparency. However, the value of non-complete information is uncertain. Partial information may be worse than no information, because separated or non-holistic information may be distorted or meaningless.

2142. Dependent nature of information

Compared to tangible resources, information has various attributes as below. (60)

a. Source dependency: The quality of information is dependent on the source or producer. Especially analysts who scrutinizes disclosed information are likely to carefully monitor the motives of disclosure. As a result, information that is provided by a less credible source may be discounted by rational and scrutinizing investors and, as a result, the impact of disclosure to the market might be weaker.

b. Media dependency: Regarding the information transmission process, information is dependent on media and source. Due to its formless and intangible nature, information has to be presented by any physical media. The information must also be presented in a way that helps the information users understand in a specific context. As a result, the quality of disclosure media may affect the quality of information.

c. Context and Time dependency: The value of information depends on the context, social culture, market environments. The same information can be interpreted in a different way resulting in asymmetric impacts. Information is valuable to a particular historical time period. Value is negatively associated with time flow.

d. User dependency: Investors subjectively assess the value of information through their perception and interpretation that is based on personal beliefs. The subsequent impact on the market may be dependent upon investor's understandability, degree of rationality, educational background, willingness to use, and the ability of payment. The ability of information analysis among investors may indicate highly skewed distribution. The purpose of gathering information differs from person to person, which implies that certain information can be assessed as highly satisfying for one but cumbersome for another.

2143. Social attributes

The capital market consisted of disclosing firms, analysts, credit rating agencies, regulations should be understood as a huge informational organization that controls information and through which information flows. In markets, each entity releases, disseminates, and assesses information. They respond to maximize their net benefits. Information creates social responses from others, and the flow of information connects each other. Ensuring the virtuous cycle of information in the capital market is a duty of every entity.

2144. Supplementary information

Cumulative attributes of information

When it is accumulated and supplemented, information becomes more valuable, increasing its quality, credibility, and value. The degree of integration determines the magnitude of value. For example, upon the prior disclosure, managers can provide incremental information that is updating, descriptive or explanatory, confirmatory or verifying. The supplementary disclosure increases the degree of information integration for investors. Consolidated information would support investment decisions because information becomes more useful and valuable when it is combined with other supplementary information. However, integration, consolidation, or supplementation beyond a certain level may be counterproductive to information users.(61)

Supplementary disclosure

Managers sometimes supplement prior disclosure with additional disclosure when they think that the prior disclosure is not enough in isolation, or there is a necessity to revise market expectations. Even though the supplementary disclosure does not affect the information content of prior disclosure, the prior disclosure may become more informative and credible when followed by the additional, verifiable, or explanatory disclosure. Thus, researchers need to shed light on the natures of supplementary disclosure, managers' incentives, consequences of supplementation.(45, 62, 63)

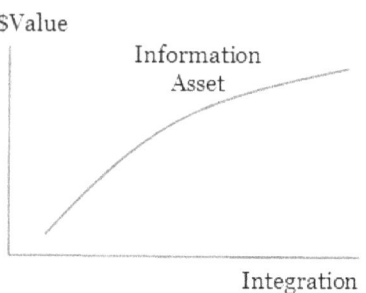

Figure 16 Effect of integration

Source) NewZealand Government (2018)

It is evidenced that only some of earnings forecasts are issued without contemporaneous disclosures in isolation, but most of earnings forecasts are supplemented and bundled with other information (e.g., earnings announcements, dividend, and M&A) as a "disclosure packages."(45) Additional information (i.e., prospective comments and data) that is released concurrently with earnings announcements contains informative content and thus significantly affects the excess returns.(63) Managers are motivated to release other credible information when the earnings forecasts are insufficient to adjust stock prices to the level that is consistent with managers' expectations.(64)

Asymmetric supplementation

One may predict that bad news is more likely to be supplemented because managers want to attribute poor performance to other factors beyond their control. On the contrary, managers are more likely to supplement good news with verifiable information because investors are more skeptical about good news. Hutton, Miller, and Skinner (2003) investigated managers' disclosure incentives to supplement earnings forecasts and found that managers are *"more likely to supplement good news forecasts with verifiable forward-looking statements."* It is supported that supplementary disclosure bolsters the credibility of good news forecasts. Bad news earnings forecasts are found to be always informative even they are released without supplement, but good news forecasts are informative only when they are supplemented by verifiable forward-looking statements.(62) Consequently, supplementary disclosure can be a good choice to enhance the quality of a specific disclosure. However, managers need to devise more systematic approaches for disclosure quality management.

2145. Value of information

Economic goods

The information is not a free-goods but an economic good. It has a value and may be treated as an asset, product, commodity, capital resource, or service. It is produced, acquired or analyzed at a finite and measurable cost. The personal value of information can be maximized when it is exclusively consumed. Once information owner releases the private information to the public, he loses exclusive benefits of private information. The information is more valuable when it is cumulated in a big database. Such nature provides implication to electronic disclosure system and news media.(65, 66)

The essential characteristics of information as an asset are fundamental in understanding a firm's disclosure. The information provides the capability to make effective decisions, and the benefits of information owners may arise from either use or sale of information. The ability of information owners' in denying or regulating determines the extent of benefits. Information as an asset explains the proprietary nature of the information.

Classification

The Congress of the US, Office of Technology Assessment (US OTAC, 1981) classifies three basic values of information: public, private, and commercial. (67)

a. Public value: Many people who stand up for the public value of information argue the free flow of information to the public as the lack of free flow can cause the rich-get-richer and the poor-get-poorer. It is positively necessary to arrange an efficient production and distribution mechanism.

b. Private value: Information owners (i.e., firms) consider important information as a proprietary asset that can be damaged by public disclosure since it is a key determinant of competitiveness. The private value of information is sometimes materialized into property rights.

c. Commercial value: These days, information is deemed a commercial product, and information intermediary (i.e., media) has proliferated. The value of information increases as people rely more on it, especially the commercial value of information becomes more central in the capital market.

Conflicts

US OTAC (1981) dictates that the change of information environment (i.e., technology) changes the relative importance and conflicting relations of these values. Such a conflicting relationship possibly become detrimental to the information quality and the degree of allocational efficiency, thereby harming social welfare.(67)

a. Public vs. private: The public value of information regulated by the government possibly conflict with the private value of information, as mandated disclosure of proprietary information can harm the private welfare. Facilitated by the developments of information technology, the proprietary advantage can be harmed by the mandated disclosure as access becomes easier.

b. Commercial vs. public: As information is becoming more commoditized, commercial value increasingly competes with public value. The public interest of equal access may conflict with the commercial services of the private sector (e.g., media). The relation can also be perceived as a competitive and complementary relation.

c. Commercial vs. private: Commercial use of proprietary information without proper approval from the owner can cause serious conflicts, especially when the information is very poor in quality or damaging proprietary rights.

Economic nature of information

In the perspective of cost, the arguments that the marginal cost of information is almost zero are frequently commented when mentioning "dissemination cost." On the contrary, the marginal cost of creating or "producing new information" is more likely to increase sharply. For example, the required costs of production to gain additional quality of information (e.g., accuracy) is likely to gradually increase.(68) However, the marginal cost of information production will sharply increase when the firm is required to disclose a cash flow statement in addition to a balance sheet.

From the perspective of utility, the repeated provision of redundant information from other sources might create some benefit by confirming that already gathered information is correct. But redundant releases for confirmation would rather create more inconvenience than benefits. In contrast, additional information that can reduce the complexity of existing disclosure will increase investor's welfare.

215. Roles Of Information

The information allows users to communicate thoughts and facts. It represents reality or is used to construct it. When we are deprived of information, the world becomes darker.(69) It should properly represent reality since such proper representation is a prerequisite of other roles of information. Information can alleviate uncertainty and enable efficient decisions when it is interpreted by a rational information user. The information has been regarded as a static resource that has to be accumulated for decision-making. However, recently, as a dynamic driving force, information forces a society or organization to alter current conducts and solve problems. Information can change the society and market through information user's decisions or market price.(70)

Arrow (2012) emphasizes the endogenous nature of the information. The idea that information is endogenous in the market deserves some intense stress. As Arrow (2012) mentioned, *"… Information comes in many shapes and forms, but two important things can be said. One, it plays an essential role in directing the allocation of resources above and beyond the role of the prices of the usual commodities. Two, it is itself a commodity, being both scarce and valuable, but it has properties quite different from the usual."* Information, itself a scarce and valuable commodity, plays an essential role in the allocation of resources. Information becomes a matter of choice and response to the actions of others. A strategic interdependence, a mutual dependence of decision making, has been well coined by the literature of game theory. When forecasting, an investor is forecasting other's forecasts. A prompt behavior of rational individuals under uncertainty is possible through the acquisition of information, especially the readily available costless information rather than costly and scarce information. No reason why the market prices should not become information, especially when it already reveals some of the available information. The market price reflects and conveys other people's information and opinion.(71)

216. Classification: Hard & Soft

Hard information is almost recorded as numbers such as financial statements. It is quantitative, easily collected, and more comparable. It can be entered into a form without significant guidance from an expert like analysts. It is easy to achieve objective measures for the level of accuracy or error. The quality measured by one is identical to that measured by others. The producer or collector can even delegate their duty to others to reduce gathering cost.(72)

Soft information is often communicated in text or narrative formats. It includes opinions, ideas, projections, or plans. One can create a numerical score or index for soft information, which does not make itself hard information. The context and collector of soft information are also inseparable from the information. Therefore, if soft information is separated from the context and collector, then it can be meaningless.(72)

Transforming soft information into a numerical score can be useful, but it does not make it hard information because the context of soft information is a part of soft information. The meaning of hard information should be dependent only upon the information itself.(72)

22. Disclosure And Valuation

221. Introduction

Significance of disclosure

Many theories suggest that voluntary disclosure is enough to provide information for efficient investment decisions while mandatory disclosure is redundant, unnecessary, and problematic. Even though most capital markets adopt mandatory disclosure requirements, voluntary disclosure is still of essential importance in the capital markets in the respect that all information is not subject to mandatory disclosure regulation, and voluntary compliance is a key to successful regulation.

Definition of disclosure

Voluntary disclosure refers to the provision of information by managers in excess of mandatory requirements. Moreover, it can include any disclosure that is not required but recommended by an authoritative organization.[9] Meek, Roberts, and Gray (1995) define voluntary disclosures as *"disclosures in excess of requirements which represent free choices on the part of company management to provide accounting and other information deemed relevant to the decision needs of users..."* (73) FASB (2012) describes the voluntary disclosure as *"disclosure that is not explicitly required by GAAP or an SEC rule."* (74)

Terminologies in this book

Large numbers of papers provide diverse explanations on the inputs and outputs of a firm's disclosure and the subsequent responses of stakeholders. Hence, it is unavoidable that disagreements arise among researchers over a different use of terminology. For the sake of this book, I would like to limit terminologies as below.

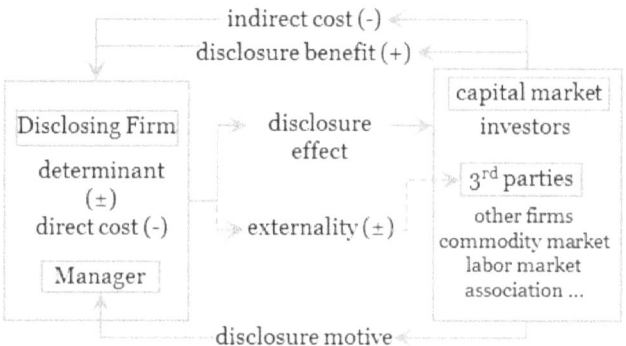

Figure 17 Terminology and Flow of disclosure

a. Disclosure benefit: A positive consequence of disclosure which benefits the disclosing firm, not the manager (e.g., reduction in the cost of capital).

b. Disclosure cost: Direct cost occurs in preparing and distributing disclosure. Indirect cost occurs from the disclosed information. Any harmful impact to the firm value can be classified as indirect cost (e.g., proprietary cost).

c. Disclosure motives: Firm-level or market-level factors that trigger the managers' incentives to make voluntary disclosure. Separating the managers' subjective motives from objective determinants and the opportunism from optimization helps researchers understand agency issues (e.g., stock compensation hypothesis).

d. Disclosure determinant: An objective factor that may promote or deter disclosure. Some determinants may persuade managers indirectly through disclosure benefit or disclosure cost while others directly impact disclosure decisions. Some factors are firm-level factors (e.g., firm size) while others are market-level factors (e.g., shareholder's response).

e. Disclosure effect: A consequence of disclosure, positive or negative, that influences investor, disclosing firm, and third parties. Disclosure effect on the disclosing firm should be disclosure benefit or indirect cost. Disclosure effect on the disclosing firm's manager should be disclosure motives. Disclosure effect on the third parties should be the externalities.

f. Externality: A specific type of disclosure effect that impacts third party other than the disclosing firm. The disclosing firm does not consider the externality when making optimal disclosure decisions.

222. Investor's Investment Decision

2221. Inter-dependency

Both asset prices and manager's decisions are simultaneously affected in such a way that greater disclosure moves the economy from one efficient market equilibrium to another. Managers maximize the firm value that is determined by investors who infer information from managers whose decision is to maximize firm value. Thus, the manager's decisions and investor's assessments are mutually dependent.(75)

2222. Valuation

Income and risk

There are two principal ingredients in valuing an asset: income and risk. It is more persuasive when the impact of disclosure is directly explained by a valuation model. The relationship between disclosure and the components of the valuation model will be a major concern. In economics, investment means a purchase of assets to create "uncertain" future returns at the sacrifice of current consumption. The future return consists of capital gain and investment income, such as dividends and interest that are fluctuating. Thus, it is inevitable for investors to have the uncertainty of outcome and, as a result, how to define the risk of investment affects the valuation.

The concept of uncertainty or risk was mentioned by Knight (1921) and Keynes (1936). According to Knight (1921), "risk" means that the possible outcomes and the probabilities of each outcome are known but not known with certainty. On the contrary, under 'uncertainty,' neither all possible outcomes nor the probabilities of each outcome are known.(76) Keynes (1936) defines "risk" as the possibility of the actual outcome to be different from the expected outcome.(77) In relation to the definition of Keynes (1936), a concept and measurement of risk and expected return should be dependent on the investment environments (i.e., number of assets, degree of efficiency, investment objectives, and approaches). In a single stock context, the risk may be defined as the difference between the expected future cash flow and the outcome of an individual stock. In a multi-stock context, the risk may be defined as a difference between expected return (e.g., the return of market portfolio) and individual outcome.

Counter-measures & Investment Approaches

A rational investor will seek countermeasures to protect herself from investment risk. Counter-measures include information search, risk compensation, diversification, hedge transaction, risk-sharing contract, etc. Those can be classified into two approaches; active vs. passive. The advantages of one approach are the disadvantages of the other. It is essential to study the impact of disclosure on the key component of the valuation model (e.g., cost of capital) that works as a standard of investors' valuation.

a. Active approach with risk compensation: Under the inefficient market, active investors try to find undervalued stocks to gain excess return by evaluating individual risk components (i.e., liquidity risk, firm-specific risk). They seek additional information to reduce risk and ask compensation for information costs and risks assumed.

b. Passive approach with diversification: Under the efficient market with perfect information, investors become passive price-takers who seek diversification to obtain an optimal portfolio and minimize diversification risk. Rational investors require compensation for un-diversifiable risks only. Not excess return but a reward for systematic risk (i.e., systematic return) is pursued.

2223. Income Approach

Valuation model

In general income approaches, the value of a firm depends on the assumption of income and discount rate. Investors can use a proxy for income such as dividends, free-cash-flow, and economic-value-added.

$$\text{Value} = \sum [\text{Income} / (1 + \text{Discount rate})]^t$$

Risk compensation

The income approach is an approach to calculate the firm value that is based on the expected income and the degree of risk associated with investments. In a single-asset investment context, the risk can be defined as a difference between the expected future cash flow and the outcome of an individual stock.

Rational investors require compensation for the time value of delayed consumption and the value of enduring risk. Thus, investment decision becomes a decision making about the compensation for time and risk. The sum of both compensations should be reflected into the valuation model. The risk premium can be added to the risk-free rate to arrive at an adequate discount rate.

$$r = \text{risk free rate} + \text{risk premium}$$

The required rate of return (RRR), perceived risk of investment, reflects the amount of compensation associated with a stock investment. The RRR comprises of the risk-free rate (i.e., the compensation for delayed consumption) and the risk premium (i.e., the compensation for various types of risks assumed by the investor). The risk-free rate is, without a doubt, irrelevant to the firm's disclosure.

Components of risk premium

In the income approach, researchers do not share the common view on which factors should consist of risk factors and risk premiums. Risk factors to build up depends on the preferences of an individual investor. The required rate of return under the income model can be estimated by the rates of return already earned or anticipated, and the estimate should come from investments or assets of comparable risk.

For example, the 'Build-Up Model' is a method of summing risks associated with an investment. Ibbotson & Sinquefield (1976) provides a model that uses both historical data and current inputs to estimate the cost of equity capital, which comprise of the risk-free rate and the additional risk premiums of an equity investment. An investor adjusts the risk premium based on the characteristics of an asset.(78)

$$r_e = r_f + rp_{equity} + rp_{firm\_size} + rp_{industry} + rp_{firm\text{-}specific}$$

r_f: risk-free rate.

rp_{equity}: risk premium of large-cap stocks.

$rp_{firm\text{-}size}$: risk premium of small cap stocks. [10]

$rp_{industry}$, $rp_{firm\text{-}specific}$: industry sector risk premium and firm specific risk premium. (e.g., liquidity risk, size risk, operating risk, and financial risk)[11]

Impacts of disclosure

If disclosure contains any information that may impact the components of the income model, then disclosure can have effects on the discount rate. Investors may consider disclosure an influential input of the valuation model by affecting various valuation components such as expected cash flow, growth rate, the required rate of return, or firm-specific risk premium.

Limits of income approach

The income approach provides a practical model but not a theoretical one. We cannot identify or quantify risk factors to arrive at the appropriate risk premium from each risk factor. Besides, we cannot analyze the multi-asset equilibrium.

2224. Portfolio approach; CAPM

22241. CAPM

Assumptions

The capital asset pricing model (CAPM) assumes a perfect market in which 1) asset prices are exogenously given, and, thus, investors are price takers who have homogeneous expectations about risk and expected return, 2) investors diversify assets without transaction costs, 3) all information is available to all investors. The CAPM is to explain a required rate of return of an asset when investors pursue a well-diversified portfolio in a single-period. The CAPM determines a market equilibrium in a multi-asset and multi-player market while the income approach considers a single investor's decision on a single asset.

Model

Under the CAPM, the rate of return is determined only by the beta. In equilibrium, the reward-to-risk ratio of an individual stock is equal to the reward-to-risk ratio of the market portfolio.

$$[E(R_i) - R_f] / \beta_i = E(R_m) - R_f$$
$$R_e = R_f + \beta (R_m - R_f)$$

Risk

The modern portfolio theory defines "risk" as volatility, and investors are assumed to be risk-averse. The total risk of an asset consists of the systematic risk (aka, un-diversifiable risk) and the unsystematic risk (aka, idiosyncratic risk, firm-specific risk, or diversifiable risk). Unsystematic risk can be diversified away when investor includes many assets in his portfolio. Investors should not take on any diversifiable risk since only non-diversifiable risks are compensated by the market. Efficient portfolios do not have unsystematic risk.

Under the CAPM, the beta means the sensitivity of the expected excess return of the individual asset to the expected excess return of the market portfolio, implying the systematic risk of an asset. As a result, the beta is the single most defining factor of the required rate of return.

$$\beta_i = Cov(R_i, R_m) / Var(R_m) = \rho_{i,m} \, \sigma_i / \sigma_m$$
$$E(R_i) = R_f + \beta_i [E(R_m) - R_f]$$

Impacts of Disclosure

Disclosure is treated as a firm-specific and diversifiable factor in the traditional single period CAPM that is based on perfect information. Thus, there is no doubt that the CAPM does not provide any role for disclosure; rather disclosure itself enables a capital market to satisfy the assumptions of the CAPM.

Limits of the CAPM

The CAPM approach is widely used as it is evidenced by Graham and Harvey (2001) that 73.5% of respondents "always or almost always use the CAPM" as a method of estimating the cost of equity capital.(79) However, the CAPM is a seemingly general model but just a specific one that explains only extraordinary cases far different from the real world.

The assumptions of CAPM is unrealistic. All investors are neither rational, well-diversified, nor risk-averse. What seems to be perceived as a risk by investors is not the variance of returns with symmetric distribution rather the probability of losing money under asymmetric distribution. Besides, a real world is not without transaction costs nor information asymmetry, and investors have chances to respond in a multi-period. As a result, more disclosure can lead to an optimal portfolio and thus affect stock prices when partial information is prevalent or firm-specific risks that are not sufficiently diversified away exist in the real world.

Evidence suggests the CAPM is limited. While CAPM claims that stock return is explained by the single factor (i.e., beta), several pieces of the literature suggest contradicting empirical results that it is multidimensional. For instance, a simple relation between beta and stock return disappears, but other variables (i.e., market equity and book-to-market equity) can explain the average stock returns.(80-82) Barry (1980) cautioned that the thin markets with illiquidity could cause a higher required rate of return than suggested by the CAPM.(83) The CAPM cannot explain why large institutional investors with diversified portfolios pay attention to the firm's earnings forecast. The active portfolio management might pursue an additional increase in value or reduction in risk by searching for more information.

22242. Alternative models

Introduction

Some researchers provide alternative models to allow some flexibility to the traditional CAPM by increasing the width and length of "The bed of Procrustes."

CAPM assumption	Real world	Alternative models
Diversifiability	Non-diversifiability	Modified CAPM
Risk-averse	Downside risk averse	Downside Risk Build-up
Single Period	Multi Period	Inter-temporal CAPM

Single Factor	Multi Factor	APT, Conditional CAPM
Homogeneous	Heterogeneous	-

Modified CAPM

The modified CAPM is designed to calculate the cost of equity capital for a privately-held company where the well-diversification assumption is unrealistic. By modifying CAPM, investors who price firm-specific risks can include relevant firm-specific risk factors into the cost of equity capital.(84) Under the modified CAPM model, investors may include disclosure related risks as a form of firm-specific risks.

$$E(R_i) = R_f + \beta * RP_m + RP_s + RP_u$$

where, RP_m : equity risk premium,

RP_s : firm size risk premium,

RP_u : firm-specific risk premium

Downside risk buildup method

In the real world, investors are risk-averse in that they try to avoid loss (i.e., downside risk) but would not mind higher return (i.e., upside risk). The upside risk is welcomed but not necessarily undesirable. Neither the variance (i.e., a measure of risk) nor the assumption of symmetric risk based on portfolio theory accords with investors' general perception of risk. The risk should measure the likelihood of returns lower than the expected return.

Along with the dawn of the mean-variance theory developed by Markowitz, Roy (1952) already developed the concept of downside risk. Roy (1952) states that *"This paper considers the implications of minimizing the upper bound of the chance of a dread event …"* Markowitz (1991) also states that *"semi-variance is the more plausible measure of risk."*(85, 86)

The downside risk approach is more plausible and "consistent with investors' perception of risk." It uses semi-variance focusing on returns below a 'cut-off point' or 'benchmark rate' under the assumption of non-normal and non-symmetrical distribution. The semi-variance is defined as the deviation from the mean or target value. It is calculated below the cut-off points. Downside risk can be measured relative to any benchmark return, such as mean return or target return, and especially the semi-variance can be the appropriate measure. *"Variance of return alone is not a satisfactory measure of investment risk."* The measure of risk is to consider the likelihood and consequences of an adverse outcome and to measure both the probabilities (i.e., variance) and the severity (i.e., skewness) of adverse outcomes.(84) However, the downside risk model provides no room to explain the relation between disclosure and downside risk. The classic semi-variance formula is as below;

$$\text{Semivariance} = 1/T \sum [\min((R_t - B), 0)]^2$$

where, B denotes a benchmark rate of return

Recent empirical studies are supporting the downside beta. The standard beta could differ significantly from the downside beta, especially in emerging markets where stock returns show a higher skewness.(87, 88) Stocks with higher downside beta have higher average returns, which means that investors demand higher returns for downside risk.(89) Investors incorporate the downside beta in the cost of equity capital, and it is higher than the standard beta.(84)

Conditional CAPM

The traditional single period CAPM assumes unconditional beliefs, and thus all the factors (i.e., mean, variance, covariance, risk premium, and beta) are assumed to be a constant, not a variable. As a result, investors cannot condition their beliefs. However, empirical results show that investor's beliefs are varying over time, and the performance of the traditional CAPM is only poor. The Conditional CAPM, allowing the beta to vary over time, suggest that the beta of an asset may vary with external factors. In the conditional CAPM, disclosure may be considered as one of the conditional factors, or it can change the factors.

Intertemporal CAPM (ICAPM)

Under the intertemporal CAPM with constant beliefs, inter-temporal portfolio rebalancing can affect the market equilibrium prices. However, hence there is no possibility that the firm's disclosure may trigger portfolio rebalancing, the disclosure will not impact the required rate of return under the ICAPM.

Arbitrage pricing theory

Ross (1976) proposed the arbitrage pricing theory (APT) under the assumption that some macroeconomic factors may affect asset returns. Neither assumptions about the distribution of asset return nor the efficiency of a portfolio are required.(90)

$$E(r_j) = r_f + b_{j1} RP_1 + b_{j2} RP_2 + ... + b_{jn} RP_n$$

Where, RP_k is the risk premium of the factor, r_f is the risk-free rate.

Individual asset returns are influenced by unanticipated systematic events or changes (i.e., inflation, industrial production). Unanticipated changes are rewarded as a systematic factor and thereby influence returns.(91, 92) The generality of APT is a strength, but what is its strength is also its weakness. The APT model leaves no room to explain the impact of disclosure on stock price.

223. Manager's disclosure decision

Firm value maximization

From the perspective of economics, it is pertinent to assume that the ultimate purpose of disclosure is to maximize firm value. Managers will voluntarily disclose information only when disclosure benefits justify disclosure costs. Thus, the importance of understanding the manager's objective cannot be stressed enough, and the firm value maximization deserves a starting line of researches on disclosure decisions.

Benefits & costs
A great many of literature illustrate disclosure benefits such as lowered cost of capital and increased liquidity. Jenkins Committee (1994, Exhibit 1) summarized the main benefits and costs of informative disclosure.(93) Especially lowering the cost of capital is an essential object of managers who pursue firm value maximization.[12]

Firm's choices
A listed firm will commit to providing voluntary disclosure when disclosure benefits outweigh disclosure costs. Proprietary cost is also assumed to coerce managers into poor disclosure. Especially proprietary information sensitive to the success of business gives the firm a certain level of competitive advantages. Hence firms do not hesitate to apply numerous measures to reduce the potential risk of proprietary information. If the proprietary costs outweigh disclosure benefits, the firm might provide a lower quality or less informative disclosure that can impair the firm value predictability.

Nevertheless, it is not so simple to develop a one-sided argument. Some firms might make a proactive response with better disclosure while others passive response with a poor disclosure. Either choice will be made at the manager's discretion considering benefits and costs. Firm's choices can be classified into four schematic patterns; voluntary full disclosure, voluntary partial disclosure, withholding, and other-than-disclosure mechanism. In the firm's perspective, the efficient amount of disclosure is neither "no disclosure" nor "full disclosure" because of the characteristics of proprietary information.(18)

a. Voluntary full disclosure
In general, firms have an inclination to hide information since the disclosure generates disclosure cost and potential disadvantage. However, firms might prefer sunlight policy in case that disclosure benefits exceed disclosure costs. Some examples suggest the possibility of voluntary disclosure. For example, when independent verification for proprietary information is impossible, unavailable, or too costly, the firm would like to voluntarily disclose to convince investors for the high demand or quality of its product, thereby increasing its value (i.e., disclosure benefit). Even without third-party verification, the proprietary cost can supply credibility to the unaudited proprietary information. (94) Firms listed in foreign exchange voluntarily provide additional information about cashflow and segment. Peer pressures in international capital markets can induce voluntary disclosure.(95)

b. Voluntary partial disclosure

From the point of view information users, the Blackwell theorem (1951) suggests that finer information is of higher quality.(96) It can be supposed that detailed information more increases the degree of precision and better mitigates information asymmetry. By the way, finer information does not always mean better information in firms' angle. Due to the non-exclusiveness attribute of information, competitors are simultaneously open to the same finer information that leads to higher proprietary costs. When firms face two opposite concerns (i.e., an increase in proprietary costs from full disclosure versus a loss in disclosure benefit from non-disclosure), they might be obliged to provide information but in more aggregated or less fine form. Such a strategic choice will carry much conviction when the disclosure benefits of finer information are expected to be slightly lower than disclosure costs. Some examples of 'aggregation' strategy include segment aggregation. If firms have lower the proprietary cost (e.g., similar performance across segments), then they tend to disaggregate. (97) Firms have incentives to avoid competitors' scrutiny and conceal the performance differences by aggregating losing segments with profiting segments.(98, 99)

c. Non-disclosure: withholding

A firm can deliberately withhold information from release to protect its competitive advantage in the product market, although such a non-disclosure would increase the cost of capital. The lack of transparency can provide firms with a shield against the exposure of weakness in a competitive position. Some show shreds of evidence withholding information. For example, nearly 40% of IPO firms redact information from SEC filings to shield proprietary information from potential rivals.(100) About 42% of public firms fail to report R&D information, non-reporting R&D firms file 14 times more patents than firms that report zero R&D. Managers do not seem to omit R&D information accidentally but attempt to deliberately omit the information since competitors can have access to it.(101)

d. Complete avoidance: other-than-disclosure mechanism

In an extremely exceptional circumstance, some firms may have no choice but to find the other-than-disclosure mechanisms (e.g., voluntary delisting) to escape from grave disclosure costs that are persistently far exceeding disclosure benefits. For example, according to Tang (2009), *"firms with potentially high potential proprietary costs are more likely to choose private placements instead of public offerings."* An industry or a firm with a higher proprietary cost that is proxied by the product market competitiveness is more likely to choose private placements. An increase in product market competition is also associated with an increase in the proportion of private placements. (102)

Manager's utility maximization model

Manager's various disclosure choices can explain how they can react, but those cannot explain in a theoretical manner how they make disclosure decision. Meanwhile, Guttentag (2004) develops a synthetic model with the concept of utility and the theory of optimization in which managers disclose two types of information; agency information and accuracy information. Manager's disclosure decision in shareholder's shoes (i.e., accuracy information) and in his own shoes (i.e., agency information) are integrated into one model.(103)

Mahoney (1995) defines "accuracy information" as "*any information that would affect the stock price*" and "agency information" as "*detailed information about management's compensation and significant transactions between managers and the company.*"(104) Generally speaking, disclosure will serve both purposes concurrently. Accuracy information will principally enhance stock price accuracy, whereas agency information will reduce agency costs mainly.

According to the assumptions of Guttentag (2004), the manager's compensation is equal to the salary plus the expropriatable funds (β+γ/g), the firm value is linear with the manager's effort (L), and the factor "ε" represents the extent to which the manager's effort increases the firm value. Then, subtracting the manager's total compensation (β+γ/g) and the cost of implementing disclosure policy (C_a+C_g) from the manager's contribution to firm value (L·ε) results in the final firm value (v). The manager's optimal effort to maximize the utility is L*= δ·θ·ε, which depends on the desire to earn compensation (δ), the stake ownership (θ), and the influence of efforts (ε).

$$v = L·ε - (β+γ/g) - (C_a+C_g)$$

Guttentag (2004) subtracts the manager's total compensation and the cost of implementing disclosure policy from the manager's contribution to firm value results in the final firm value. As a result, the manager's effort to maximize the utility is optimized, depending on the desire to earn compensation, the stake ownership, and the influence of efforts.(103)

Based on the results of mathematical optimization process, Guttentag (2004) suggests that the shareholder's optimal voluntary disclosure policy of accuracy information (V*(a, ~)) increases with three factors; a higher probability of liquidity shock (τ), manager's effort factor (ε), and the agency cost reduction effect of accuracy information (k). The optimal disclosure policy of agency information (V*(~, g)) depends on the amount of funds the manager can expropriate (γ). (103)

$$V^*(a,g) = \left\{ \sqrt{\frac{\tau \cdot (\delta \cdot \theta \cdot \epsilon^2 - \beta - 2 \cdot \sqrt{\gamma})}{(1-k)}}, \sqrt{\gamma} \right\}$$

23. Disclosure Benefit

231. Introduction

Disclosure is to pump information through markets, as the heart is to pump blood through blood vessels for a healthier body. The ultimate purpose of disclosure is to mitigate information asymmetry and maximize firm value. Disclosure benefit is of considerable importance. Managers will particularly provide more disclosure when they anticipate increased benefits. Whereas disclosure also carries costs, it is unavoidable to be selective. Managers' disclosure decisions should be optimized to achieve the maximized firm value. Moreover, to get answers to many questions on firms' dynamic disclosure decisions, numerous researchers have been extensively attracted to the benefit and cost of disclosure. Disclosure can create various capital market benefits such as reduced cost of capital, increased liquidity, and expanded investor base. [13]

232. Cost Of Capital

2321. Definition

Many studies, such as the Jenkins Committee (1994), state that an essential benefit of greater disclosure is a lower cost of capital.(93) In finance theory, the cost of capital is treated as more important and essential than the cash flow or growth rate, and hence it receives most of the attention from researches who seek to prove firm's disclosure benefit. The cost of capital depends on the risk of an individual investment project, which can be estimated from the expected rate of return on investments with equivalent risk. It can be described as the risk-free rate plus risk premium.

The cost of capital can be viewed and defined from multiple perspectives with different angles but should be the same number. On the manager's financing side, the cost of capital is the "economic cost" to attract investors for capital formation. On the manager's investment side, the cost of capital is the hurdle rate and the opportunity cost that a firm requires for real investment. A rational manager aiming to add economic value will invest only in a more profitable project of which expected returns exceed the cost of capital. On the investor' side, it is the hurdle rate of return that an investor requires for the investment. To add economic value, investors should invest only in assets of which expected returns exceed the required rate of return.

The cost of capital is used to discount the expected cash flows to get a firm value. In equilibrium, the cost of capital should represent investors' expectations, and thus the cost of capital on financing side should be equivalent to the required rate of return of investors. The cost of capital is the price of capital in terms of the expected rate of return that is determined in capital markets. As a result, it strikes a balance between capital supply and capital demand. Thus, the estimates of the cost of capital should come from the markets.

In the traditional income model, the cost of capital can be described as the risk-adjusted discount rate that investors apply to the expected future cash flows to reach the stock price, but the estimation depends thoroughly on individual choice. The cost of capital is frequently estimated by using CAPM that is market-oriented. Notably, the beta (β) is the most relevant factor among components of the cost of capital; risk-free rate, risk premium, and beta. According to the CAPM, the cost of equity is the risk-free rate and the premium for firm's non-diversifiable risk (i.e., the product of the firm's beta and market excess return.)

$$R_e = R_f + \beta (R_m - R_f)$$

2322. Impact streams

According to Botosan (1997, 2006), literature that has been introduced to explain the relation between disclosure and the cost of capital can be classified into two streams: direct vs. indirect link. An indirect link is to analyze the association between disclosure and the cost of capital based on market liquidity or adverse selection. Disclosure reduces information asymmetry and enhances market liquidity, thereby reduces the cost of capital. A direct link is to research without reference to market liquidity or adverse selection. Investor base effect and estimation risk provide a direct link between disclosure and the cost of capital.(105, 106)

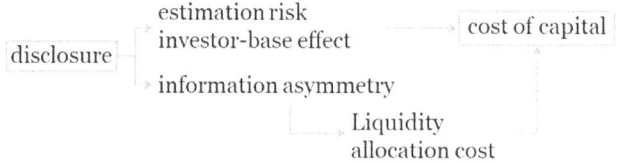

Figure 18 Impact flow to the Cost of capital

2323. Empirical evidence

Introduction

A considerable body of researches provides an association between disclosure and the cost of capital, but consensus has not been reached. Some researchers have examined the impact of disclosure not directly on the cost of capital but indirectly on the proxy variables that are assumed to have a positive relationship with the cost of capital because appropriate estimates are difficult to obtain.(105) Empirical researches tend to rely on various contexts (e.g., firm size, firm type, intermediary, and disclosure type) and methods (e.g., statistical methods and proxies). Therefore, empirical results should be carefully interpreted because the impact on the cost of capital might be triggered not directly by disclosure but by disclosing firm's other characteristics that also explain the price impacts.(107)

Survey result

The survey of Graham, Harvey, and Rajgopal (2005, Table 11) reveals that the cost of capital reduction effect by voluntary disclosure was agreed or strongly agreed by 39% of respondent CFO, while it was disagreed or strongly disagreed by 22%.(108)

Supporting evidence

A growing stream of evidence supports a negative association between disclosure level and the cost of capital. They use segment disclosure, ratings, or rankings. Firms disclosing segment information have a lower cost of capital.(57) The increases in disclosure ratings are accompanied by increases in firms' stock returns.(109) A negative relation was evidenced between the cost of capital and the analyst ranking of annual reports. (110) Firms with more voluntary earnings forecasts or press releases experience less underpricing before IPO.(111, 112) Information (i.e., probability of information-based trading) does affect asset prices.(113) Firms with information asymmetry have incentives to provide voluntary disclosure to reduce the cost of external financing.(114) The seller in an auction can raise the highest expected selling price either by establishing pre-commitment of releasing full information to the bidder or by adopting a policy of expert quality appraisals of the reputable auction house.(115)

Refuting evidence

On the contrary, another stream of evidence indicates that disclosure might increase the cost of capital. Mixed evidence is suggested for the relations between the cost of capital and three types of disclosure: a negative relation for the analyst rankings of annual report; a positive relation for the level of quarterly report; no relation for the level of investor relations activities.(110) Greater disclosure is associated with a lower cost of capital for firms with low analyst following; however, no evidence for firms with high analyst following. (105) Information asymmetry can be diversified away in large economies. As a result, the disclosure should have no impact on the cost of capital. Hughes (2007) argue that, in a large economy, *"idiosyncratic risk is fully diversifiable and affects risk premiums only as a source of noise," "greater information asymmetry leads to higher factor risk premiums and thus higher cost of capital,"* but firm betas are not affected; controlling for betas, information asymmetries do not affect the cost of capital.(116)

Cost of debt

Not so many studies pay attention to the association between disclosure and the cost of debt. Some suggests that careful consideration should be given to the difficulty in controlling the effects of specific provisions in the debt issuance contract. Firms with higher disclosure rating (i.e., AIMR score) have a lower cost of debt, which implies that a timely disclosure reduces the cost of debt.(117) The relationship between financial information, bond rating, and bond yield is multi-faceted. Financial information affects bond ratings that also directly affect bond yields.(118) Investors in the U.S. market demand significant premiums on international bonds issued by non-U.S. firms with low disclosure.(119) Countries experience a significant decline in borrowing costs (i.e., 11% reduction in credit spreads) when they choose to provide macroeconomic information in a more accurate and frequent manner by adopting IMF instituted reforms. (120)

2324. Capital market transaction hypothesis

Concept

With the difficulties of estimating the proper cost of capital, some researchers pursue an alternative approach with firms' reporting practices upon raising capital, which is called a capital market transaction hypothesis. The benefit of the capital market transactions can be another image of disclosure benefit that implies the reduced cost of capital. A capital market transaction hypothesis examines the links between disclosure and firms' incentives to access the capital market. A firm's cost of capital includes a premium for uncertainty about the accuracy of available information. As the signaling theory implies, voluntary disclosure of firm that is seeking external capital is likely to reduce the cost of capital, especially when there is severe competition for capital.(57)

Supporting evidence

Several pieces of literature provide evidence that firms tend to voluntarily disclose more information when they plan to raise new capital. For example, firms improve disclosure (i.e., annual report) to raise a low-cost external capital (i.e., Eurobond market) because managers think disclosure helps firms achieve a successful capital raise.(121) Analysts' disclosure rating is higher for firms issuing securities, and there is a significant increase in the disclosure particularly before equity offering.(122)

Refuting evidence

Many pieces of literature provide negative evidence on the capital market transaction hypothesis. The external capital needs do not encourage firms to disclose more. However, some suggests that researchers should consider securities regulation that might prohibit making disclosure (e.g., forward-looking statements) prior to equity offerings.(123)

2325. Real investment: long-run effect

Under the short-term environment where the level of real investment is assumed to be constant, better disclosure reduces investors' uncertainty about the firm's profitability and persuades investors to pay a higher price, and, as a result, monotonically reduce the cost of capital. In the long-term, however, where the level of real investment is adjustable by disclosure, Gao (2010) suggests that disclosure may differently change the cost of capital under specific conditions. As far as disclosure resolves the uncertainty of profitability in the short-term, managers may consider upward adjustment of investment level in the long-term. As a result, the cost of capital may increase with disclosure if and only if it is sufficiently easy to adjust investment level and the existing investment is highly profitable.(124)[14]

For example, with the given initial investment level (Figure 19, I_0), more disclosure reduces the cost of capital ($C_{00} > C_{01}$, from a to b). If managers who learned the fact that the uncertainty of future profitability was resolved by disclosure, slightly adjust investment to a new level (I_1), then the investor's uncertainty increases and the cost of capital may increase up to the higher level (C_1, to c) but still lower than the initial level (C_{00}). If investment is significantly adjusted (I_2), then the investor's uncertainty will significantly increase and, as a result, the cost of capital may increase to the level (C_2, to d) higher than the initial one (C_{00}). To maintain the cost of capital to a certain level, firms need to provide more information to resolve the uncertainty that was created by the additional real investment.

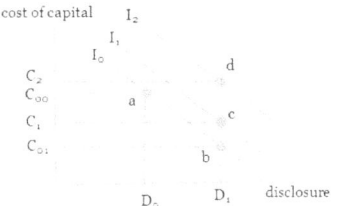

Figure 19 Long-term effect of disclosure

233. Liquidity

2331. Definition

As a general term, liquidity (aka, marketability) can be defined as the ability of quick conversion of an asset into the most liquid asset (i.e., cash). In the capital markets, market liquidity can be defined as the degree of a market to facilitate asset transactions as quickly as possible without affecting its bid price or offer price. Consequently, to judge the liquidity of a stock, we must define the bid-ask spread. While being considered as an insignificant cost factor for less frequent traders, the spread can be a severe cost factor for frequent traders. When an asset is traded with a great deal of leverage, just a penny of spread is nothing but a negligible cost in the light of the percentage over total trading volume but becomes a sizable cost in the light of the percentage over the trader's total equity. Literature provides an indirect link between disclosure and the cost of capital by using the concept of market liquidity. Botosan (1997) explains that greater disclosure enhances stock market liquidity, which reduces the cost of equity capital either through increased stock purchase demand or reduced transaction costs.(105)

2332. Stock purchase demand

Diamond (1985) suggests that the information-search-cost savings effect is produced by the firm's voluntary disclosure that preempts investor's private information search behaviors and reduces information cost and thereby induce the increased-demand.(50) If investors are well-informed, then they may recognize the market price as a fair one, which increases market participation and liquidity. The stock purchase demand will rise because the more precisely informed investors would place large orders, which increase the stock price, and thereby reduce the cost of capital.

2333. Transaction costs

Botosan (1997, 2006) explains that the level of investors' attention is low for stocks with high transaction costs, which leads to a higher cost of capital. Many of studies explain higher transaction costs with information asymmetry and market illiquidity.(105)

a. Liquidity shock: Liquidity shock of a large trade can increase transaction costs. However, greater disclosure reduces the amount of information revealed by a large trade, thus reduces negative stock price shock and improves stock liquidity.(125)

b. Protection/Compensation: Uninformed investors may employ price protection mechanism by requiring compensation which is incorporated in transaction costs. However, they require less compensation when they are provided with greater information. As far as information is more impounded into stock price, the uninformed investors will more rely on the stock price which reveals information. Such a price revelation effect will amplify the reduction in compensation required by the uninformed investors. With disclosure, firms can reduce the adverse selection component of the bid-ask spread and the cost of capital. (13, 14, 125, 126)

2334. Measurement

A transaction cost comprises of brokerage fee and bid-ask spread. Amihud & Mendelson (1986) suggest that liquidity or illiquidity can be measured by the cost of an immediate transaction, i.e., bid-ask spread, which is the sum of a premium for immediate buying and a concession required for immediate sale.(127) The bid-ask spread is a generally accepted measure of liquidity, which is a hidden cost that can erode investor's profits. If the spread is zero, then it is a frictionless asset. The quoted spread refers to the cost of buy and sell trades at the quoted prices.

$$Percentage\ spread = \frac{(ask\ price - bid\ price)}{ask\ price} \times 100$$

$$Qouted\ midpoint\ spread = \frac{(ask\ price - bid\ price)}{(ask\ price + bid\ price)/2} \times 100$$

Components

Bid-ask spread is suggested to arise from three sources; order processing cost, inventory holding cost, and adverse selection cost. It is essential to understand the sources of spread to establish adequate counter-measures of liquidity risk. For example, an informational policy should be taken when bid-ask spread mainly arises from adverse selection problem rather than order processing cost or inventory holding cost. In such a case, by providing high-quality information through voluntary disclosure, firms can improve liquidity. Order processing cost is the cost to fulfill investors' orders immediately.(126, 128) Inventory holding cost is the cost of the market maker in holding inventory to cope with the uncertainty in the arrival of order flow. (129, 130) The order processing cost and the inventory holding cost are fleeting and do not make time-series effects on a stock price because those are not related to the underlying firm value. As Bagehot (1971) explains, market prices do not rely on transaction costs rather on the information. (12) An uninformed trader wants to be compensated for the adverse selection cost that depends on the size of informed traders who have superior information.(13, 14, 131)

Limits as a proxy for information asymmetry

Bid-ask spread is often used to proxy for information asymmetry. According to Botosan (2006), however, using the spread as a proxy can be problematic because it includes other components (i.e., inventory holding cost, order processing costs) irrelevant to information asymmetry. Nevertheless, most studies use the total spread because separating each component is difficult.(106) Furthermore, empirical studies on the spread are conflicting. For example, a study showed that the quoted spread may be decomposed into the following three components; adverse information costs 43%, inventory holding costs 10%, order processing costs 47%.(16) On the contrary, others suggest that order processing cost is the predominant component, whereas adverse selection cost is a smaller proportion (i.e., 8~13%).(132)

2335. Empirical evidence

Survey result

The survey of Graham, Harvey, and Rajgopal (2005, Table 11, Fig. 10) supports voluntary disclosures as a motivator of liquidity improvement. The liquidity benefit of disclosure was agreed or strongly agreed by 44% of respondent CFO, while it was disagreed or strongly disagreed by 17%.(108)

Empirical evidence

Several pieces of literature provide empirical evidence supporting the positive role of disclosure in increasing liquidity (i.e., bid-ask spreads). To examine the relation between disclosure and liquidity, employed are the proxies for "liquidity" such as relative spreads[15], share turnover,[16] and standard deviation of returns, while employed are the proxies for "disclosure" such as disclosure ranking, disclosure score, earning forecast, and reporting standards. Bid-ask spread is inversely related to disclosure score.(133)[17] The increases in analysts' disclosure ratings are accompanied by the increases in liquidity.(109)[18] Firms with higher disclosure scores have lower effective bid-ask spreads.(134)[19] German firms adopting a high-quality reporting regime by switching to international standards exhibit lower bid-ask spread and higher trading volume.(135) Issuing a forecast is effective in improving liquidity.(136)[20]

2336. Spread and cost of capital

Amihud & Mendelson (1986) provides a positive and concave relation between market return and bid-ask spread. Trading at the ask-price and bid-price will incur a loss that equals to a bid-ask spread. A risk-averse investor will require a higher expected return for stocks with a higher spread. Thus, the cost of capital is greater with stocks of wider bid-ask spread. In equilibrium, market return is an increasing function of spread. A transaction cost is amortized over holding periods, and thus stocks with higher spreads are mainly held by long-term investors (i.e., clientele effect). Due to the "clientele effect", a return-spread relation is concave, which means that returns on higher-spread stocks are "less spread-sensitive." The longer the period, the smaller the incremental compensation.(127)

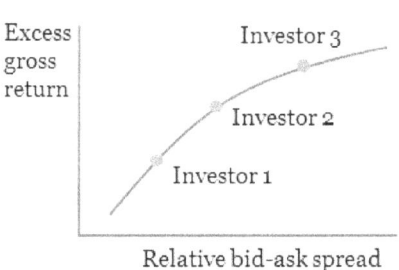

Figure 20 Spread and Return

Source) This graph is modified from Amihud & Mendelson (1986, p.230)

234. Investor Base Effect

Investor's recognition hypothesis

Merton (1987) examined firm's behavior and role in determining the size of the investor base and consequential effect on the cost of capital. Some investors are unaware of certain groups of stocks due to information costs, gathering cost, and set-up costs. Investors pay a significant fixed set-up cost to process information and then become aware of the firm. Due to the fixed cost nature, investors who are not aware of a firm will not become stockholders of the firm. All investors cannot be aware of thousands of stock symbols. A subset of stocks is excluded from the portfolio, which leads to inadequate diversification. As a result, investors will take on nonsystematic risk and, thereby, a firm's required rate of return will depend on the size of the investor base. Meanwhile, voluntary disclosure or mass media coverage can reach a great number of the general public who are not currently shareholders and persuade them to follow the firm. *"The relative size of the firm's investor base will reduce the firm's cost of capital and increase the market value of the firm."* The investor base effect that relies on the information cost is different from the compensation arguments that mainly rely on investor's compensation for illiquidity. Under the compensation rationale, disclosure is assumed to impact an investor's attitude toward information risk while it reduces information cost under the investor base rationale.(48) Arbel, Carvell, and Strebel (1983) suggested that, due to the omnipresent information cost, "neglected stocks" are frequently observed. A neglected stock means a stock with which just a small number of investors are familiar.(47) The information cost rationale of Merton (1987) can be an extension of the neglected stock rationale.

For investors to follow a stock, the expected benefits of investors' following should exceed the expected costs that generally include fixed cost. Investors would not follow the stock when it is below the break-even point. They could not recognize a certain firm because they are limited in recognition. The real market is not without the recognition cost due to incomplete information. Thus, a firm's voluntary disclosure works as an informational subsidy provided by a firm to reduce investor's recognition cost. Firm's voluntary disclosure would reduce investor's recognition set-up cost (Figure 21).

The breakeven point of recognition is not attainable if the limit of recognition is lower than the BEP (Figure 22, BEP_1 under FC_1 and TC_1). As a result, they cannot follow the firm. However, if the fixed recognition cost is reduced owing to voluntary disclosure, then it lowers breakeven point (Figure 22, $BEP_1 \rightarrow BEP_2$), and the limit of recognition far exceeds the breakeven point. As a result, they can follow the firm (Figure 22).

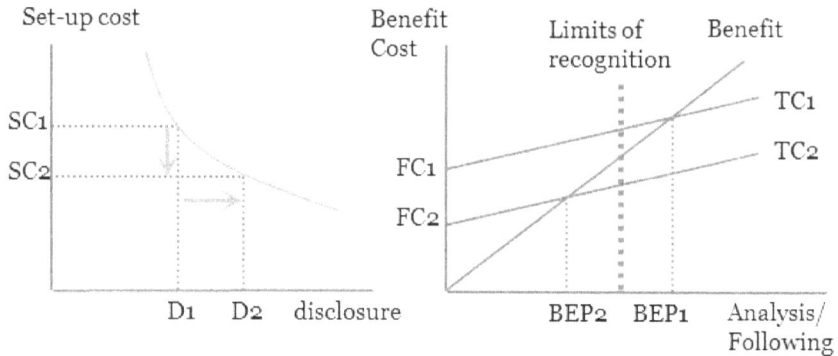

Figure 21 Disclosure and set-up cost   Figure 22 Break-even of recognition

Determinants

Merton (1987) suggested that the investor base effect of disclosure will be greatest for hermitlike firms such as small firms, lesser-known firms, firms producing non-household goods, and firms highly dependent on exporting.(48) Investors with more information will have greater prior precision about familiar stocks and, as a result, require less risk premium for familiar assets like local stocks.(137, 138) The life cycle of a firm also influence the cost of capital. Firms with long operating history will have lower the cost of capital.(139)

Firm's choice to increase investor base

Merton (1987) examine firm's role in determining the size of investor base. An increase in the investor base will reduce the cost of capital. Thus, the managers will spend resources to increase investor base and maximize firm value by inducing the public who are not currently shareholders. Such measures include disclosure, investor relation, and mass media. This rationale provides a persuasive justification for massive investment in investor relation behaviors, reiteratively announcements, and mass media exposure that are designed to make the firm more eligible investment. Managers may experience a considerable increase in investor base when a mass media covers the positive story about a firm. If the prior release had not captured widespread attention from investors, the redundant release could increase the investor base that might raise the stock price.(48)

Negotiated underwriting

Merton (1987) provides a framework for evaluating the benefits and costs of a firm's policy in the viewpoint of the investor base effect. For example, negotiated underwriting is more likely to increase investor base than rights offering or stock dividend/split. If the management put focus on easily and quickly raising new capital, he may use rights offering only to its current shareholders at a subscription price below market price, but "*such a rights offering is no more likely to increase the size of the firm's investor base than the payment of a stock dividend or a stock split."* On the contrary, management can both raise new capital and expand the firm's investor base at the cost of underwriting fees with the help of the underwriter's reputation. Depending on the manager's objectives, *"the terms of the deal can be chosen so as to maximize the number of new shareholders"* or the ratio of long-term investor. *"The underwriting costs can be treated as expenditures for expanding the investor base."*(48)

235. Risk Premium

Fama model

Fama & French (1992) argues *"the efficiency of the market portfolio implies that ... expected returns on securities are a positive linear function"* of their market beta and, thus, information is irrelevant to the expected return. Thus, there is no role of information in their model.(80)

Modified CAPM

Literature have suggested that disclosure reduces the information-related risk premium and, thereby, the cost of capital. Investors can add firm-specific risk premium or disclosure-related risk premium into the income model or the modified CAPM. For example, Easley & O'hara (2004) developed a modified CAPM, an asymmetric information asset-pricing model which provides a linkage between information structure and the cost of capital. Disclosure substitutes public information for private information, and finally lowers the risk premium and the cost of capital. An individual firm's idiosyncratic information influences its risk premium. Uninformed investor demands a higher return under greater private information context while informed investors can incorporate new information into their portfolio. Thus, the uninformed investors require compensation for bearing information risk.(139)[21]

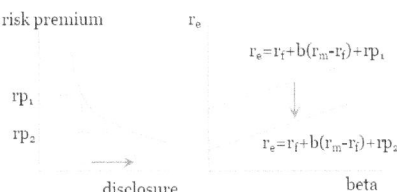

Figure 23 Disclosure, Risk premium and Cost of capital

$$r_e = r_f + \beta(r_m - r_f) + rp_i$$

where, rp_i is the risk premium for idiosyscratic risk ($rp_i > 0$).

"In a rational expectations equilibrium, uninformed traders make correct inferences about this private information from prices."(139) However, uninformed traders cannot perfectly infer information from price, and, conse-

quently, they recognize the stock as riskier one. Thus, the stock with more private information will have a larger expected excess return. Easley & O'hara (2004) seems to be similar to the IPO underpricing model of Rock (1986). The informed (i.e., insiders) assume larger amounts of underpriced stocks, while the uninformed assume most of the overpriced stocks. In equilibrium, the uninformed *"demand a higher expected return to compensate."* The influence of private information will extend across all the outcomes of portfolios, and, consequently, asset returns will reflect a risk that is not completely diversifiable. As more traders are informed by disclosure, so more information is revealed into the stock price. The price revelation of information makes the stock less risky, which reduces risk premium and also the cost of capital.(139, 140)

Litigation risk premium

Litigation risk premium can be an excellent example of how investors incorporate risk into risk premiums. The current legal structure provides managers with the incentive of voluntary disclosure as a means of prohibiting sudden jump in the cost of capital caused by litigation costs. For example, U.S. SEC Rule 10b-5, catch-all provision under §10(b) of the Securities Exchange Act of 1934, prohibits "omission," which may result in fraud or deceit.[22] Managers increase disclosure in pursuit of preventing potential litigation that might arise from non-disclosure.[23] Managers generally exert themselves to maximize firm value by minimizing potential litigation and, thus, they try to reduce the cost of capital by providing voluntary disclosure. The traditional CAPM may explain that the litigation risk premium will also be diversified away. However, it might not be fully diversified away but affect the outcomes of portfolios when the damage from potential litigation is so vast as to be priced by many investors.

Agency cost risk premium

Managers who are not maximizing the firm value but his private value may misappropriate the firm's asset. Investors, however, have no idea whether managers are firm-value maximizing. Thus, investors require the risk premium for firms with low transparency under the assumption that less transparent firms have a higher possibility of misappropriation. Facing the agency cost risk premium, managers who are not seeking private value may provide voluntary disclosure to reduce such a risk premium. In this regard, Lambert, Leuz, and Verrecchia (2007) demonstrated that disclosure influences the cost of capital indirectly by affecting the magnitude of agency costs.(141) Agency cost risk premium might not be also fully diversified away but severely affect the outcomes of portfolios when the damage from potential misappropriation is so vast as to be priced by many investors.

236. Beta

2361. Beta and valuation

Beta, a measure of portfolio risk, is calculated as the covariance between the return of individual stock and the return of the market portfolio, divided by the variance of the return of the market portfolio.

$$\beta = Cov(R_i, R_m) / \sigma^2(R_m)$$

The return of an individual stock is determined by the economy-wide factors (aka, systematic factor) and the idiosyncratic or firm-specific factors. Systematic risk is an aggregate risk or un-diversifiable risk that is vulnerable to economy-wide events that affects aggregate outcomes. Systematic risk that cannot be eliminated through diversification plays an important role in portfolio investment. According to the CAPM, beta is an essential concept in evaluating systematic risk because it indicates the degree of correlation between an asset's expected return and market returns. An equilibrium price of an asset is tied to systematic risk.

2362. Estimation of beta

Market-based beta

Market beta is totally based on the returns in the capital market rather than the earnings in financial statements. The "expected beta" estimated by using regression analysis and past stock returns has problems in that it reflects a firm's business structure and leverage over the past regression period rather than the current or future structure. Thus, market-based beta can be meaningful only under the condition that a firm's business structure and leverage is stable during the analysis period.

Accounting beta

A market-based beta measures the co-movement of an individual firm's return with the market return. By the way, an accounting beta can be defined as the co-variability between the earnings of a firm with that of the market portfolio. In the case of a non-market situation where employing regression analysis is impossible, we need to estimate an accounting beta. Some argue that estimating an accounting beta using earnings or revenues is less noisy than using market prices. The accounting beta depends on three fundamental factors; the nature of business, operating leverage, and financial leverage. The higher the leverage, the higher the beta.(142)

a. Nature of business: Firms with different natures behave differently. Some move more with the cycle while others against the economy. Cyclical firms, firms selling luxury goods, or fast-growing firms tend to have a higher beta.

b. Operating leverage: The existence of fixed costs causes the degree of operating leverage (i.e., the change in earnings due to the change in revenue). The higher the fixed cost, the higher the operating leverage. Firms with high infrastructure needs, smaller firms, or young firms tend to have a higher beta.

c. Financial leverage: The degree of financial leverage (i.e., the change in profit due to the change in earnings) is caused by the existence of debts and fixed interest payments. Highly levered firms tend to have a higher beta.

Association between betas

Bowman (1979) provided a theoretical indication that a market-based beta is highly correlated with an accounting beta, but systematic risk is theoretically proven to be unrelated to other financial variables (e.g., earnings variability, dividends, firm size, or growth rate).(142) Accounting beta is a sensitivity index between earnings of a firm and aggregate market, which is significantly correlated with market beta. A firm with more sensitive earnings is likely to have a higher market beta. Thus, voluntary disclosure of information regarding the determinants of accounting beta can have impacts on the accounting beta, the market-based beta, and thereby the cost of capital.

$$\beta_i^A = \frac{cov(X_i, X_m)}{\sigma^2(X_m)}, \beta_i = \frac{S_m}{S_i} \beta_i^A$$

Where:

X_i = accounting earnings of individual firm
X_m = accounting earnings of market portfolio
S_i = market value of individual security
S_m = market value of market portfolio
β_i = Market-based beta
β_i^A = Accounting beta

2363. Impacts on beta or variance

Assessed covariance

Lambert, Leuz, and Verrecchia (2007) provides a direct link between information and the cost of capital without reference to market liquidity. Information can influence a firm's cost of capital by affecting investor's "assessed covariance" of future cash flows between the disclosing firm and other firms, which is not diversified away in a large economy with a great many firms. Higher quality information reduces the assessed distribution of future cash flow and thereby reduces the cost of capital. (141)

Independency

The CAPM beta is appropriate only when firms are independent of each other, and all investors are homogenous. However, Jorgensen & Kirschenheiter (2003) support the non-trivial association between voluntary disclosures and beta, which suggests that the beta of a firm is affected by other firms' disclosure policies. Other firm's selective non-disclosure makes the beta of a firm drift away from the traditional CAPM beta, while it's full disclosure guides to the CAPM beta.(143)

237. Estimation Risk

Concepts

Many have suggested that theoretical studies paid little interest in the estimation of the parameter (e.g., return) but instead assumed that those are precisely known, while some pieces of empirical literature have just used historical estimates as if they were true parameters since those are unobservable. However, such approaches are not without controversy. A stream of researches suggests that greater disclosure can directly affect the components of the cost of capital (e.g., beta, covariance, and risk premium) by reducing investor's non-diversifiable estimation risk. In the real world, investors face an additional element of risk, "estimation risk." Estimation risk refers to the uncertainty of parameter that should be estimated based on available information. Investors will be quite confident of their estimation for firms with ample information about the parameter while skeptical for firms with little information.(105, 144, 145) The parameters are not known with certainty but must be estimated from both objective and subjective information(146). Estimates are sensitive to the choice of the market index, return interval, and estimation period.(106) Investors bear information risks in forecasting the future payoffs from their investment.(144)

Estimation risk & valuation

If a model incorporates disclosure-related risk as a priced factor, it can clearly explain the association between disclosure and the cost of capital. The usefulness of CAPM in analyzing the association between disclosure and the cost of capital is limited since the factors of CAPM are limited to beta, risk-free rate, and market risk premium. As the CAPM lacks of any explicit disclosure-related priced factors, researchers have no choice but to relate disclosure to the cost of capital through other factors such as estimation risk.(106) As the CAPM treats the estimated parameters to be true, so estimation risk is not incorporated in the model.

Impacts of estimation risk on portfolio

On the contrary, the estimation risk model explicitly incorporates investors' uncertainty into equilibrium pricing. Due to the estimation risk, the systematic risk of a portfolio may be affected, and the seemingly efficient portfolio may not be as efficient as intended. Estimation risk can affect market equilibrium in a way that stocks with little information have higher systematic risk.(144) Estimation risk affects equilibrium, returns, and betas. Low information stocks tend to have higher beta under the estimation risk. (147, 148) Stocks with little information are perceived as risky due to estimation risk, and risk for firms with low information should decline as information increases.(149) The estimation risk influences the optimal portfolio choice under uncertainty. "*Traditional analysis neglects estimation* risk by treating the estimated parameters as if they were the true parameters ... However, as a result of estimation risk, the optimal portfolio choice differs from that obtained by traditional analysis."(145) The composition of the portfolio is identical to the traditional CAPM, but the optimal portfolio choice differs from the traditional CAPM due to the estimation risk.(145, 150, 151)

Impact of disclosure on estimation risk

Investors are willing to pay more for the certainty but ask more for the uncertainty. As far as disclosure reduces the estimation risk and the variability of the stock price, managers will increase voluntary disclosure lest they should increase the cost of capital. Investors tend to require compensation for the estimation risk caused by low disclosure. If it is not fully diversified away, the estimation risk will directly affect the beta. Thus, the reduction in estimation risk by more disclosure will lead to a decrease in the cost of capital. (145, 147, 152, 153)

The estimation risk might be incorporated into a factor model (i.e., CAPM or APT) through the risk premium (e.g., rp_er$_i$) or beta adjustment factor (e.g., 1+er$_i$).

$$r_e = r_f + \beta(r_m - r_f) + rp\_er_i$$

$$r_e = r_f + \beta(1 + er_i)(r_m - r_f)$$

where;

er= estimation risk,

rp_er = estimation risk premium,

er$_2$ < er$_1$, E(er$_i$)>0, E(rp_er$_i$)>0, rp_er$_i$>0, er$_i$>0

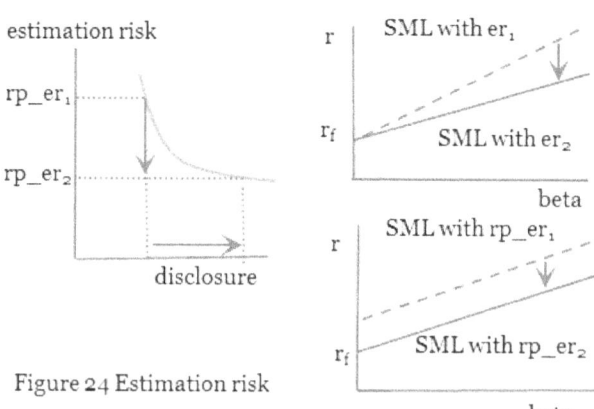

Figure 24 Estimation risk

Non-diversifiability test

If the estimation risk is diversifiable, it will not be priced. Some argue that the estimation risk is largely irrelevant since it is diversifiable. Estimation risk is argued to be idiosyncratic and diversifiable in a large economy.

(154) On the contrary, it should be priced when it survives the non-diversifiability test. Others argue that estimation risk influences the perceived distribution, and it has a systematic component that should be priced. Many researchers conducted studies regarding the non-diversifiable effects of estimation risk. However, the consensus is not yet reached. Investors are found to demand a premium or compensation for bearing the non-diversifiable estimation risk.(48) Prices tend to be higher for stocks with high information because estimation risk cannot be diversified away.(153) The optimal use of sample data generally reduces the estimation risk, but which is unlikely to be eliminated entirely. The estimation risk has a non-diversifiable component to the extent that low information stocks are a non-trivial part of the portfolio. (155)

238. Real Economy

Introduction

To highlight the importance of inter-dependencies between firms' disclosure and the real economy (e.g., real investment) is to treat the real economy as endogenous variables.(156) Some studies show that disclosure has an impact not only upon asset prices but also upon the firm's real decision (i.e., investment, production, and misappropriation). Capital market plays a much bigger role both in the capital resource allocation and in the real economy decisions. The real economy effect may be viewed as the ultimate disclosure benefit or the half-way that finally reduces the cost of capital. The impact paths of disclosure to the real economy include real investment, variance of cash flow, amount of cash flow, competition, reputation, and allocation.

Real investment

Some studies showed that disclosure has an impact on firms' efficiency and investment decision. Managers' investment decision that is not observed by the market will induce the underinvestment problem. On the contrary, disclosure increases price efficiency that leads to a more efficient investment decision.(157) Without hedge disclosure requirements, information about trade motivation (i.e., hedge, speculation) will be blended and cause price inefficiency, distorting the production choices. Thereby industry output is lower than the first-best.(158) Disclosure has an impact not only upon the behavior of equilibrium asset prices but also upon the firm's production-investment decisions.(75) Disclosure is negatively associated with both underinvestment and overinvestment, and the relation between disclosure and efficiency is stronger for firms with poor disclosure environments.(159) Improvements in disclosure quality decrease the cost of capital and lead managers to make more aggressive investment decisions.(141)

Distribution of cash flow

Disclosure quality can affect the distribution of the firm's cash flow. As disclosure quality improves, the mean and variance of the firm's cash flow may increase, but *"...the variance of the firm's cash flow ... increases if and only if the adjustment cost of new investment is sufficiently low..."* (124) Some directly assumed how disclosure quality changes the characteristics of the distribution of the firm's cash flow.(160, 161)

Amount of cashflow; misappropriation

While the decrease in agency cost risk premium comes from the changes in investor's perception, the real economy effect comes from the changes in cashflow that can be generated by the reduction of misappropriation. Disclosure can influence the cost of capital indirectly through the misappropriation. *"If better information reduces the amount of firm cash flows that managers appropriate for themselves, the improvements in disclosure not only increase price, but in general also reduce firms' cost of capital ..."* (141)

Industry competition

Some studies examined the deterring-the-competitor model that explains managers' incentives to exercise disclosure discretion in pursuit of deterring entry or competition in product markets.(46) In the long-run, deterred competition may also reduce the cost of capital. Managers face the trade-off in disclosure policy that is arising both from financial market and product market. They have incentives to provide good news to stockholders and bad news to competitors.(162) However, a piece of evidence argues that the earnings-related bad news is unlikely to be driven by the incentives of deterring entry or competition.(46)

Reputation

Owing to disclosure, a firm's reputation can be enhanced both in financial market and product market. In the long-run, enhanced reputation in product market can also positively influence the cost of capital. The survey of Graham, Harvey, and Rajgopal (2005) show that 92.1% of managers agree or strongly agree with the idea that voluntary disclosure *"promotes a reputation for transparent/accurate reporting."*(108) People tend to form reputation about the firms' positions based on the disclosed information, specifically accounting information indicating performance.(163) Firms with a better annual report score are more likely to be rated among the top 50 national companies in terms of corporate reputation.(164) Firms with higher reputation scores enjoy a lower cost of capital.(165)

Efficient allocation

The efficiency of capital allocation is positively correlated with the amount of firm-specific information. Countries with stock markets that impound more firm-specific information into stock prices (aka. less stock price synchronicity) exhibit a better allocation of capital. More informative prices help investors and managers distinguish between good and bad investments. (166)

239. Non-Diversifiability

2391. Diversifiability arguments

Large economy

It would be of no use to specify the determinants or paths of disclosure benefits when those are fully diversified away in a portfolio. It is argued that *"estimation risk is fully diversifiable in large economies."*(149) Information asymmetry can be diversified away in large economies, and, as a result, the disclosure should have no impact on the cost of capital. In a large economy, the idiosyncratic risk is eliminated through diversification and *"affects risk premiums only as a source of noise"*; *"greater information asymmetry about systematic factors leads to higher factor risk premiums and thus higher costs of capital,"* but firm betas are not affected; *"there is no cross-sectional effect of information asymmetries on cost of capital."*(116)

Practicality of the CAPM

There are quite a number of rationales arguing that firm-specific factors such as disclosure are well diversified and, thus, disclosure cannot affect the stock price. These are generally based on the CAPM that assumes the risk-averse and homogeneous investor, the diversifiable residual distribution, and the non-existence of transaction cost. Such strict assumptions of the CAPM could serve as a starting line of theoretical analysis on the determinants of the portfolio. However, when it is viewed by real world, those assumptions and conclusions are so unrealistic. Assumptions of the CAPM that influence the non-diversifiability include below.

Assumption of CAPM		Real world	Model
Market side	Transaction cost	Non-zero cost	-
	Distribution	Non-diversifiability	Non-zero error term
Investor side	Risk-averse	Risk-taking	Downside risk build-up
	Homogeneous	Heterogeneous	-

Trends in firm-specific risk

Bloomfield, Leftwich, and Long (1977) suggested a conventional rule of thumb that a portfolio of 20 stocks attains large diversification benefit. (167) However, Campbell, Lettau, Malkiel, and Xu (2001) reported a substantial increase in firm-level volatility compared to market volatility over the period from 1962 to 1997. Not only aggregate market return but also idiosyncratic firm-level shocks are also important components of individual stock returns. Accordingly, the number of stocks needed to achieve a given level of diversification has increased. For example, a portfolio of 20 stocks was required before 1986, but a portfolio of 50 stocks was required after 1986 to reduce 5% of excess standard deviation. The adequacy of diversification depends on the level of idiosyncratic volatility, which is increasing. (168)

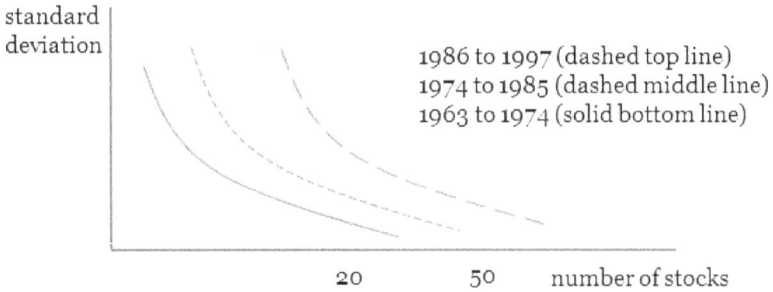

Figure 25 Standard deviation

Source) This graph is summarized from Figure 6 in Campbell, Lettau, Malkiel, and Xu (2001)

2392. Market-side non-diversifiability

Transaction cost

Under the idealized conditions of CAPM, the equilibrium prices of risk assets are determined simply by expected return, variance, and covariance. In the real world, however, if investors face serious transaction costs in forming and managing a portfolio, then they cannot sufficiently increase the number of stocks in their portfolio, and thereby the residual variance might be larger and will not be fully diversified away. A residual variance should not be treated as a noise term when it is larger.[24] For example, the limitations of diversification to reduce risks are already indicated by Lintner (1965), providing useful empirical evidence that a residual variance is larger than zero. According to the evidence of Lintner (1965), the average residual variance was over 8% that is twice the average risk-free return over the same period. Over 85% of large mutual funds had conditional standard errors of estimate (i.e., residual risk) greater than the risk-free return (i.e., 4%). Stock prices are perfectly unique when the residual variances of each stock are not zero. The ex-ante unsystematic uncertainties are found to be essential determinants of the relative value of different stocks.(169)

$$\sigma^2(\epsilon_i) = \frac{\left(\sum \epsilon_i^2\right)}{N-2} = 0, where\ N\ is\ large\ enough.$$

$$\sigma^2(\epsilon_i) = \frac{\left(\sum \epsilon_i^2\right)}{n-2} > 0, where\ n\ is\ not\ large\ enough.$$

Distribution

Some studies suggested that disclosure affects the distribution and, thus, the cost of capital. The primary rationale includes synchronicity, non-diversifiable covariance, industry level externality, and skewed distribution.

Synchronicity; R^2

According to Jin & Myers (2006), strong positive relationships exists between the measure of stock market synchronicity (R^2) and the measure of transparency or opaqueness. *"The pattern of R^2 could reflect higher macroeconomic risk or lack of diversification."* The level of transparency changes the distribution patterns of firm-specific risk between insiders and outsiders. Stocks with poor disclosure tend to move together, increase exposure to market risk, and thereby reduce the advantages of diversification.(170)

Non-diversifiable covariance

To prove the non-diversifiability of covariance, Lambert, Leuz, and Verrecchia (2007) classified two components of covariance (i.e., firm's own variance, covariance with other firms) and suggested that the covariance with other firms is not fully diversified away. As the number of firms increases, the variance converges not to zero but to the average covariance with other firms. They explained the effects of the quality of accounting information on the cost of capital in both ways: direct and indirect effect. *"The direct effect occurs because higher quality disclosures affect the firm's assessed covariances with other firms' cash flows, which is non-diversifiable. The indirect effect occurs because higher quality disclosures affect a firm's real decisions, which likely changes the firm's ratio of the expected future cash flows to the covariance of these cash flows with the sum of all the cash flows in the market."*(141)[25]

$$Cov\left(V_j, \sum_{k=1}^{J} V_k\right) = Cov(V_j, V_j) + Cov\left(V_j, \sum_{k \neq j} V_k\right)$$

$$Variance\left(\frac{1}{J}\sum_j R_j\right) = \frac{1}{J} AverageVar(R_j) + \frac{J-1}{J} AverageCov(R_j, R_k)$$

Industry-level externality

In estimating a firm's future cash flow or growth rates, investors use industry average data that is affected by externalities in the industry. Such externalities exist almost in all industries, and thereby a certain firm-specific risk (i.e., disclosure-related risk) may serve as if it were systemic risk that cannot be fully diversified away to a certain degree. Rather than diversification, disclosure may intensify the covariance through the externality. For example, some economic factors can affect the leading firm's decision that is seemingly idiosyncratic but actually systematic. As a result, a similar disclosure pattern can be observed in the industry, which leads to non-diversifiable risk. There are many reasons why such a systemic pattern is established in an industry: industry leader following, workforce exchange, the existence of industry association, and industry regulation.

Skewed distribution

It is inferred that the distribution of disclosure event and its impact on the return is not fully diversifiable when the disclosure event shows non-normal distribution. It is evidenced that stock returns and residuals are either non-normal and non-symmetrical.(171, 172) For example, firm size is not normally distributed but very skewed.(48) The disclosure quality may also be skewed as it tends to depend on firm size due to the fixed component of direct disclosure cost. Thus, the distribution of disclosure and its impact on the stock return will not be fully diversifiable.

2393. Investor-side non-diversifiability

In the real world, disclosure can be diversified away and affect the cost of capital only partially due to the investors' specific natures such as heterogeneousness, risk-taking investor, and limits of portfolio selection.

Heterogeneous Investor

In the traditional CAPM, investors are assumed to have perfect information and homogeneous expectations about the risk and expected return, which is far from real-world conditions. On the contrary, real world investors have heterogeneous expectations, and their ability of disclosure analysis is not evenly distributed. Experts are well positioned at the top, while lay investors at the bottom. As a result, disclosure may affect the cost of capital.

Risk-taking investor

In the real world, a large portion of risk-taking investors seeks to maximize excess return by searching superior information. They would become a price maker in a market by employing a non-diversified but focused investment strategy, thereby require a risk premium for an idiosyncratic event. In markets dominated by risk-taking investors, disclosure may affect the cost of capital. It is not difficult to find evidence showing that investors tend to have less than 20 stocks in their portfolios, which may lead to non-diversifiability.

Limits of portfolio selection

For better diversification performance, a rational investor includes stocks that satisfy the assumptions of the CAPM. It is so rational to assume that investors would not mindlessly constitute a portfolio but carefully employ several layers of filtering processes on which stocks are in full accordance with the assumptions of the CAPM. Such a filtering process serves as a self-protection mechanism against poor diversification risk. If a certain stock is far from the essential assumptions of the CAPM, especially due to the lack of information, and might cause a diversification risk, then it can be excluded from the candidate stock list for the portfolio. This rationale leads to the idea that some of the portfolio investors may also require a premium for diversification risk or exclude from the portfolio when they noticed that the stock or firm is not in accordance with the assumptions of the CAPM. The firm's enhanced disclosure policy can satisfy the assumptions of the CAPM, persuade investors to include the stock into their portfolio, and thereby reduce the cost of capital. Such a portfolio selection behavior may result in the non-diversifiability of the influences of disclosure.

24. Disclosure Cost

241. Significance

According to the studies on disclosure, full disclosure is assumed to be obtained in the absence of disclosure cost; however, disclosure costs may be substantial in the real world. Unfortunately, no uncontentious evidence exists about the magnitude of disclosure cost because it is not easy to measure. Disclosure cost is less highlighted than its importance because researchers tend to make it a rule to assume disclosure cost to be an exogenous variable in economic analysis. Some reasons below may justify why they assume the cost-free disclosure: It is difficult to explain or measure disclosure cost; Some component of disclosure cost is becoming less significant because communication costs are likely to become smaller owing to new technology; Disclosure cost can be severe when firms are required to disclose only for investors, but they should produce similar information for other internal or external purposes also.(57, 173)

However, disclosure cost deserves more highlights since high disclosure cost might coerce managers into poor disclosure. Even though managers have already identified investors' needs for information, the information may not be disclosed automatically. Disclosure cost has a highly significant meaning since managers should make decisions whether to disclose or withhold considering disclosure costs. This is why other researchers pay attention to disclosure cost. If disclosure cost increases, then firms will obviously make less desirable disclosure. Managers would fail to disclose material information, and, as a natural consequence, the optimal level of disclosure may not be obtained. Since capital market regulation has two pillars of regulation, disclosure regulation and insider regulation, managers cannot evade disclosure cost whichever choice they make between "disclose or abstain."

242. Direct Cost Vs. Indirect Cost

2421. Classification

One may think of disclosure cost just as the cost of preparation and dissemination, but it should be defined so broadly to capture various strategic reactions of managers and information users. In this sense, disclosure cost can be classified into direct costs and indirect costs. Direct cost is an explicit cost that is generated in the courses of preparation, certification, and dissemination of information, whereas indirect cost is an implicit cost where no actual payments are made. Direct cost will not vary whichever response was made by information users, whereas indirect cost depends on information users' response. Thus, indirect cost should be taken into serious account along with direct cost. Disclosure cost generally becomes the main constraints of voluntary disclosure, and the magnitude of constraining power depends on the characteristics of disclosure cost. Major contentious issues of direct cost include the economy of scale, whereas the strategic responses of managers and information users will be the crux of the indirect cost issue.

2422. Direct cost

Definition

Direct cost includes any costs in the process of preparation (e.g., employee, office, printing), certification (e.g., auditing, legal expenses), and dissemination of information, regardless of how information users react. It is relatively easier to observe and quantify direct cost since it is an explicit cost in that actual payments are made. Merton (1987) assumes that direct information cost can be classified into two parts: the cost of gathering and processing data, the cost of transmitting information to investors. A firm's cost of gathering and processing data would be small since the firm is a prime source of information, but the cost of transmitting information can be considerable.(48)

Direct cost by phase

A subset of disclosure cost in each phase of disclosure process can have different impacts on disclosure quality or quantity. A considerable preparation cost and a lack of human resources in preparation may reduce the quality or quantity of disclosure. Certification cost affects the credibility of disclosure, and the amount of certification cost depends on the current level of the firm's credibility. Dissemination cost affects the accessibility of information users, and the degree of equality among investors will affect information asymmetry among investors.

Opportunity cost

Though forming a small portion over total disclosure cost, direct cost could be a substantial constraint of disclosure when the manager considers opportunity cost such as managerial time. For example, Leuz (2015) suggests that paying such a great deal of attention to disclosure may divert managers' attention from maximizing shareholder value.(174)

Determinants of direct cost

Many studies suggest that such factors as listing period, frequency of disclosure, nature of information (e.g., segment information), and firm size are major determining factors of the direct cost of a disclosing firm.

a. History: Firms with longer exchange-listing status are more familiar with the information user's needs, and whose direct cost is sustained lower.(175) The disclosure cost of production and dissemination tend to be higher when firms are not accustomed to preparing disclosure.(175, 176)

b. Segment information: Regarding the direct cost of segment information, there are numbers of issues, such as defining the scope of segments and allocating overhead costs among segments. These issues may become trickier when disclosed segments do not match with the firm's internal organization. As a result, segment information might be far costlier.(175)

c. Firm size issue: A fixed disclosure cost rationale provides a significant implication in relation to firm size. To produce and disseminate information, a firm should bear the fixed cost that induces the economies of scale. The greater the quantity of information disclosed, the lower the per-unit direct cost. Direct cost is relatively lower for larger firms because of a large fixed component, meaning that a large firm would have a smaller direct cost per firm size than a smaller firm. Besides, dissemination cost may be relatively lower for large firms because news media and analysts are more likely to pay attention to large firms. A large firm that has an advantage in per-unit-cost over a small firm would increase its disclosure, even though the total cost is increasing with firm size. A fixed disclosure cost rationale implies that direct cost can be severe constraints for small firms. [26]

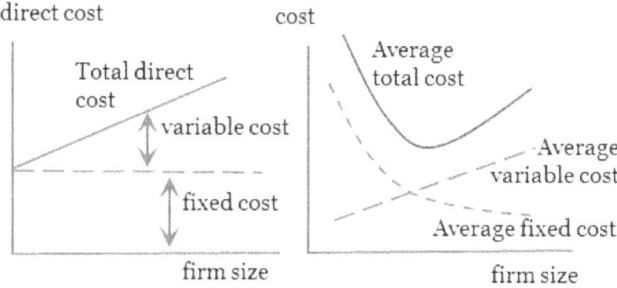

Figure 26 Disclosure cost

Some empirical evidence examined the economies of scale. Larger firms (i.e., market value) provide more and better disclosure.(122) The dissemination cost of a small firm can be even higher than that of a large firm in absolute terms since the news media and analysts are more likely to cover only large firms.(174) The survey of Coates (2007) indicates that audit cost (i.e., certification cost) increases with firm size, but the audit cost per firm size of a larger firm is less than that of smaller firms. Larger firms pay less per unit firm size.(177)

Empirical evidence

Some studies focus on the direct cost of context-specific disclosure items, but studies on comprehensive disclosure documents do not exist. U.S. SEC (2002) estimates direct cost in pursuance of the amendment proposal for the Form 8-K disclosure requirements. SEC estimated that, as a result of the proposed amendment, the total annual dollar cost of complying with

Item 10 Form 8-K increases about 300% from $23 million to $70 million, including outside counsel costs.(178) A survey of Coates (2007, 2014) shows that direct cost of the SOX Act was the substantial amount, and it has fallen by between 15% and 40% according to the post-SOX deregulation. (177)

2423. Indirect cost

Concept

Information users such as investors, employees, competitors, news media, and regulators can freely use the publicly disclosed information. Thus, the disclosing firm should bear additional implicit cost that may occur from the strategic responses of numerous information users. Indirect cost can be defined as an implicit cost that includes various types of losses, burdens, and negative impacts that may occur to the disclosing firm by the strategic responses of information users. A firm's disclosure may be a boomerang that comes back to the disclosing firm. The indirect cost of disclosure can be viewed as a rent that is extracted by outside information user groups. Proprietary cost is a rent extracted by competitors, and other indirect costs are by politicians and labor unions.

Characteristics

One may assume that the disclosed information does not affect the disclosing firm. However, depending on the characteristics of information and the responses of information users, the disclosed information may cause the disclosing firm to bear unexpected costs, and consequently firms may be incentivized to abstain from disclosure or make inadequate disclosure. An incisive comparison between the natures of direct cost and indirect cost will lead us to a better understanding. Indirect cost differs from direct cost in that a) it originates from the information user's response, and b) it does not connote fixed cost. As a result, the characteristics of indirect cost cannot be uniquely explained because those depend on the characteristics of information but also on the dynamic responses of information users, and there is no leeway to apply the concept of economies of scale to indirect cost.

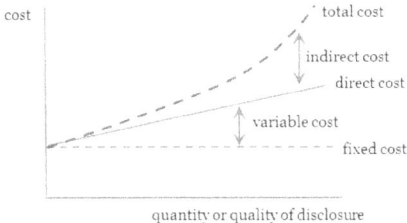

Figure 2 - Disclosure cost structure

Classification

The characteristics of information are influential factors in determining the magnitude of indirect cost. However, it is not easy to identify the characteristics of each pieces of information. Meanwhile, the severity of indirect cost is mainly determined by the information users' responses. Thus, it is better to classify indirect cost by the information user groups (e.g., competitors, employees, regulators, and politicians) in that each group has different incentives and responses that influence the magnitude of indirect costs.

Firms will respond more quickly to competitors than other users when the disclosed information may harm their competitive advantage that can continuously affect future earnings power and future valuation. In contrast, when it comes to the specific indirect cost (i.e., non-proprietary cost) other than proprietary cost, the firm may accept it as a given cost or just a non-recurrent cost because it is irrelevant to its competitive advantage.

To put it briefly, it is meaningful to classify the indirect cost into proprietary cost and non-proprietary cost. Such a classification connotes the characteristics of information and the response of information user groups altogether.

Product market: Proprietary cost

Non-product market: Litigation cost, Political cost

Patterns

In general, disclosure leads to a sharply increasing indirect cost (Figure 28 left graph). However, indirect cost varies with the firm's characteristics, the attributes of information, and the strategic responses of information users. Thus, we cannot figure out the complete nature of indirect cost by relying on a monolithic approach. For example, the manager will strategically increase voluntary disclosure when it is expected to reduce indirect cost such as litigation cost (Figure 28 right graph). The most important criterion of disclosure decision regarding indirect cost should be whether firms have something to lose from disclosure. Nothing to lose, nothing to fear. One who has nothing to fear dares to tell the truth.

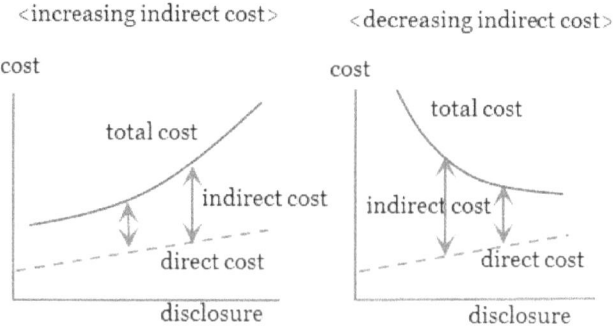

Figure 28 Indirect cost

Survey result

In general, indirect cost is deemed to be more important than direct cost. The survey of Graham, Harvey, and Rajgopal (2005, Table 12) supports the importance of indirect cost, especially proprietary cost. About 58.8% of respondents answered "agree" or "strongly agree" for the question "avoid giving away 'company secrets' or otherwise harming our competitive position". (108)

Limitations of empirical researches

Admitting that disclosure connotes significant side effects, it is not easy to provide empirical evidence on the magnitude of indirect cost. One may say that there are little rooms left for managers to make strategic behaviors against the direct cost since they have no choice but to take the direct cost as given. On the other hand, indirect cost is treated with special attention since it leaves much room for managers to behave with various strategies.

In spites of pernicious effect, it is impracticable to accurately measure the indirect cost. Many studies highlight the specific topics of indirect cost (e.g., segment information, litigation cost), and a more comprehensive study will be essential in coming up with a better understanding of indirect cost. However, considering the dynamic characteristics of indirect cost, it is not as easy as a piece of pie. As Coates (2014) mentioned, the tasks of estimating the indirect cost are more difficult than the tasks of estimating the direct cost, and until now, it is far beyond to achieve much precision in estimating indirect cost. (179)

243. Product Market Indirect Cost: Proprietary Cost

2431. Proprietary information

Lexical meaning

Lexical meaning of "proprietary" refers to *"one that possesses, owns, or holds exclusive right to something," "something that is used, produced, or marketed under exclusive legal right of the inventor or maker."* [27] There is a point to be considered: All information is proprietary to some degree.

Conventional usage

Proprietary information is widely used in various forms in the capital market. It may include such information as secret formulas, production processes, technical methods, business strategy, marketing plans, and customer lists. Generally illustrated examples include below.

    a. Financial: segment information, costs of goods sold.

    b. Production: new product, output level, vendor, and resources.

    c. Marketing: market demand, market share, and customer lists.

    d. R&D: technical specifications, research plans.

Legal concepts: United States

The US disclosure rules do not describe the concept of proprietary information, but the confidential treatment provision describes "any information" or "business confidentiality" as a requirement of the confidential treatment request.[28] Chapter 435 (Confidential treatment) covers more in detail.

"Rule 24b-2 Nondisclosure of information ...
(a) Any person filing any registration statement, ... or other document ... may make written objection to the public disclosure of any information ...."

"Rule 83 Confidential treatment procedures ...
... (c) ... (1) Any person who ... submits any information ... may request that the Commission afford confidential treatment ... to such information for reasons of personal privacy or business confidentiality ... "

Legal concepts: EU regulation

To protect the issuer's legitimate interests without harming investor's protection, Article 17(4) of Market Abuse Regulation (MAR) sets out the criteria of delaying disclosure: legitimate interests, confidentiality, and non-misleading. Besides, Paragraph 50 of MAR preamble illustrates a non-exhaustive list of circumstances that may relate to the issuer's legitimate interests; *"(a) ongoing negotiations ... where the outcome ... would be likely to be affected by public disclosure ... ; (b) decisions taken or contracts ... which need the approval of another body ... in order to become effective ... provided that public disclosure of the information ... would jeopardize the correct assessment of the information by the public."* The salient point of the MAR is that it does not limit the delaying disclosure procedure only to the competitive disadvantage (i.e., legitimate interests and confidentiality) but extend to the non-misleading effects.

Though it is unrelated to corporate disclosure, the "Capital Requirements Regulation based on EU Regulation No. 575/2013"(CRR) that is prudential requirements for credit institutions and investment firms seems to define the proprietary information, focusing on the competitive position. According to the CRR, *"information shall be regarded as proprietary to an institution if disclosing it publicly would undermine its competitive position. It may include information on products or systems which, if shared with competitors, would render an institution's investments therein less valuable."*(180)

Regulators do not pay careful attention to the technical definition of the proprietary information, because firms should show evidence why their information should be protected. A basic concept to introduce the exceptional procedure is enough. Both firms and regulators are more interested in the potential impacts of public disclosure.

Academic concepts

The definition of proprietary information may differ from researchers to researchers according to the purpose and scope of analysis.

a. Broad definition

There have been many studies to analyze disclosure cost by using the concept of proprietary information. For example, Verrecchia (1983, p.181) mentioned proprietary information as the information that is proprietary in nature and potentially damaging. *"...Typically, one thinks of the disclosure-related cost as solely the cost of preparing and disseminating information for traders' inspection. I prefer to regard this cost more broadly so as to also include the cost associated with disclosing information which may be proprietary in nature, and therefore potentially damaging..."*(51) Dye (1985) defined proprietary information in a broad sense as *"any information whose disclosure potentially alters a firm's future earnings."*(181) Scott (1994) explained that pension plan information is proprietary with respect to labor unions.(182) The main purpose of those studies is not to define the concept of proprietary information but to examine the overall impacts of "disclosure-related cost" or "indirect costs."

However, once we define proprietary cost in a broad sense regardless of product market or competitive advantage, it includes all types of indirect costs, such as political costs and litigation cost. A broad definition provides the advantage of covering all disclosure cost except for direct costs but might attenuate the importance of product-market competitor's unique responses.

b. Narrow definition

On the contrary, it seems natural to define the proprietary cost using the concept of proprietary information. This information-based approach is conceptually attainable in defining proprietary cost. Regulator that seeks the balance between firms and investors tends to use the narrow approach because a policy to overextend the concept of proprietary information or proprietary cost may result in excessive non-disclosure. Besides, proprietary information is commonly interpreted by market participants to mean the information in which firms have a legitimate interest, and disclosure thereof may cause potential loss of comparative advantages in product market.

However, proprietary information may include any information from the commonly used "knowledge" or "data" to the "trade secret" that is protected by law. As a result, it is not easy to tell which information is proprietary, and furthermore information that was classified as proprietary may not generate any proprietary cost. The information may be proprietary to a firm but non-proprietary to other firms.

2432. Proprietary cost

Concept: narrow definition

As the concept of indirect cost was already introduced in Chapter 2423 to comprehensively include the disclosure-related costs, proprietary cost can be defined in a narrow way to signify the specific type of indirect cost that is associated with the disclosure of proprietary information, and thereby damaging the competitive advantage of the disclosing firm. Some may put emphasis on the proprietary nature of information while others on the dynamic impacts.

Proprietary cost includes any type of a potential cost, burden, damage, or harm to the disclosing firm. Damodaran (2006) mentioned that the proprietary cost is not just a perception or emotional burden but a real cost that reduces the firm's economic value. *"For some firms, at least, there are real costs to disclosing more information to financial markets. Competitors may use the information to fine-tune their strategies ..., especially when the firm is in financial trouble."*(107)

Competitive advantage and its loss

Industry competition is the core of successful management. A competitive advantage is an attribute that allows a firm to outperform its competitors, which generates greater economic value. Porter (1985) outlined the two basic types of competitive advantage: low cost and product differentiation.(183) A competitive advantage is attributed to a variety of factors, including easy access to low-cost resources, skilled labor, brand, and entry barrier.

Competitive advantage provides an edge over the rivals in the marketplace, while its disclosure places the disclosing firm at the risk of losing such advantages. Loss of information control would mean a loss of advantage and value. Furthermore, due to the non-excludability of information, managers cannot prevent competitors from using the released or leaked information. Non-excludability refers to a specific nature of information. It is a non-excludable asset or resource when the owner cannot prevent others from using it. Once information is released, it is impossible or extremely costly to prevent others from using it.

Disclosure of proprietary information can reduce the competitors' information search cost to find out the weak point of the disclosing firm. Besides, it provides competitors with the opportunities to find the strong point and exploit the competitive advantages of the disclosing firm. Such losses of competitive advantage include a variety of harm to business: leakage of technology, loss of market leadership, and human resource outflow. For example, if the firm is perceived by stakeholders to be no longer an industry leader, it is more expensive for the firm to retain its customers and employees.(184) The firm has to invest more to attract them or lose competitive advantage. A firm might experience troubles caused by the disclosure of bad news, which could lead to the ship-abandonment by employees or fund providers.(107)[29]

Proprietary cost hypothesis

Proprietary cost has been commented as the important element of disclosure cost by researchers who are in opposition to mandated disclosure. For example, the proprietary cost hypothesis of Verrecchia (1983) described that *"the incentive to disclose information is a decreasing function of the potential proprietary costs attached to a disclosure"* because the release of proprietary information results in higher disclosure cost. In the absence of proprietary cost, manager will provide full disclosure. However, managers will disclose information only when disclosure benefit exceeds a certain threshold level of disclosure cost under the assumption that uninformed investors cannot infer bad news from nondisclosure.(51)

Segment information and cash flow information

Leuz (2003) found that cash flow information is primarily governed by capital-market benefits, while segment information is associated with proprietary cost. Both concepts such as dis-aggregation and alternativeness answer to the question why segment information is more proprietary in nature. First, segment information is more sensitive and proprietary in nature because it reveals disaggregated information about each line of business, while the cash flow statement is aggregated at the firm level. Second, the benefits or costs of specific disclosure depend on the availability of alternative information. The proprietary costs of cash flow disclosure might be lower than segment disclosure because competitors can utilize the alternative information (e.g., income statement) as a proxy of cash flow statement. (95)

Product information and customer information

Disclosure of product information or customer information can entice competitors to develop an imitation product or take the best customers, which increases proprietary cost. As a result, managers are likely to disclose information irrelevant to products or customers. Empirical studies suggest that less product-related information is revealed in the prospectus by biotech firms that face higher proprietary cost.(185) Proprietary cost is associated with less frequent disclosures of nonfinancial information (i.e., product development).(186) Firms choose to withhold information of either very high or low aggregate demand for a product.(187)[30] Firms with larger expenditures on R&D, advertising, and intangible assets have a greater propensity to hide information about major customers.(188)[31]

2433. Determinants of proprietary cost

There are particularly influencing determinants of proprietary cost. A variety of literature introduces many variables as proxies for proprietary cost, which can be classified into three dimensions; information-, firm-, and industry-level factors.

1) **Information-level determinants**

The magnitude of proprietary cost can be associated with the nature and level of proprietary information that is disclosed. Studies highlight the favorability of information, level of detail.

Favorability

Regarding disclosure decisions, managers have a variety of incentives to affect competitors in the product market. They face trade-offs between shareholders and competitors; providing good news to investors for capital market benefits but bad news to competitors for product-market benefits. According to empirical studies, managers may voluntarily disclose bad news to deter the entrance of potential competitors into the product market.(189) In the threat of competitor entry, the voluntary forecasting is decreasing for good news, whereas increasing for bad news.(190)

Detailedness and fineness

In an aggregated reporting, information is combined so that less detailed strategies are exposed to competitors. High level of detailedness contributes to the completeness or quality of information that enables a holistic understanding. The more disaggregated the segment information, the more useful it is to competitors, resulting in the higher proprietary cost. It is evidenced that firms are more likely to voluntarily provide segment information when it is highly aggregated or lower in detailedness. (95, 97, 191)

2) Firm-level determinants

Proprietary cost can be affected by the nature of information provider. Studies on firm-level determinants highlight on profitability, growth rate, and firm size.

Profitability, growth rate

Disclosing proprietary information may reveal the existence of profiting and growing business opportunities to competitors. Profitability or growth rate can be meaningful proprietary information especially when a firm is on the verge of initial disclosure because it might be a result of entry barriers or lower competition that are significant industry-level determinants of proprietary cost.

Proprietary cost is likely to increase as the profitability of disclosing firm increases, and, as a result, voluntary disclosure is expected to be negatively related to the firm's profitability and growth rate. Some pieces of evidence support the proprietary cost hypothesis. Firms are more likely to voluntarily provide segment information when they are less profitable (i.e., return on asset).(95) Firms with higher abnormal profitability disclose the aggregated information.(98)

However, the association between voluntary disclosure and profitability/growth rate is complex. On the other hand, it is expected that the higher the profitability, the more the firm is incentivized to disclose information to increase the capital market benefit. Some studies provide conflicting evidence to the proprietary cost hypothesis and support the capital market benefit hypothesis. For example, firms are more likely to redact current disclosure when they are suffering loss.(192)[32]

According to Prencipe (2002), there is no clear evidence concerning the relationship between segment disclosure and profitability/growth rate. Regarding the influences of profitability or growth rate, a counterbalancing effect exists between the positive impact of disclosure benefit and the negative impact of proprietary cost. Such a trade-off may have led to a less significant empirical association between profitability/growth rate and segment information.(175)

Firm size

Large firms generally have a stronger position in the product market, which leads to a high entry barrier. As a result, they are less vulnerable to competition, and the proprietary cost might be relatively lower. The extent of segment disclosure is evidenced to have significant relation with firm size.(193, 194) Attention should be paid to the fact that large firms naturally have something to disaggregate, while small firms have nothing but the aggregated information.

3) Industry-level determinants

Competitive forces

Since proprietary cost is mainly related to the product market competition, the impact of competition deserves the main highlights. Competitive forces refer to the factors that threaten the profitability and prevent growth of a firm in an industry. If the competitive forces are intense, no firm earns attractive returns on investment. If the competitive forces are benign, firms are profitable.(195) As a result, the competitive advantage or competitive forces hold an important position in identifying the determinants of proprietary cost.

Competition in an industry goes beyond the rivals among existing competitors to include other competitive forces as well. Such competitive forces affect rivalry, affect the nature of interactions, and form the structure of an industry. Porter (1979) illustrates five forces framework as a tool for analyzing competition or rivalry of a business: a) rivals among existing competitors, b) the threat of new entrants, c) the threat of substitutes, d) bargaining power of customers, e) bargaining power of suppliers. These forces determine the competitive intensity and the attractiveness of a business in terms of its profitability.(195)

Entry competition: threat and barrier

Proprietary information appears to be either conspicuously sensitive for firms facing potential "threat" of entry, while it is less sensitive for firms with a strong "entry barrier." So far as the public release of proprietary information increases the likelihood of new entrants that can harm the disclosing firm's competitive advantage, managers will be reluctant to make better disclosure.

Some pieces of evidence of the new entry competition support the proprietary cost hypothesis. In the threat of entry, forecasts are decreasing for good news firms, whereas increasing for bad news firms.(190) If the capital intensity is relatively high (i.e., low threats and high barriers), then the level of predictability of cash flows is higher, and firms are more likely to provide segment information.(95, 196)[33]

Post-entry competition

The amount of proprietary cost may depend on the magnitude of competition among "incumbent firms" already competing in the product market. The number of competitors, the industry growth rates, and the distribution of firm size and market power can be used as proxies of post-entry competition.

Some pieces of evidence support the proprietary cost hypothesis of post-entry competition. *"Managers ... are more likely to withhold information about sales and costs if they perceive that current or potential competition is strong."*(197) In an industry with high market share concentrations, firms are more likely to redact(192)[34], less likely to be reported as industry segments (198), issue less specific forecasts (199), and thus are negatively associated with cash flow predictability.(196)[35]

The relation between competition and disclosure depends on competition type. According to Shin (2002), firms facing "capacity competition" are in need of capital and provide more disclosure to lower the cost of capital, whereas firms facing "price competition" reduces disclosure due to high proprietary cost and less acute capital need.(200)

Considerations

Most competitive forces seem to be meaningful determinants of proprietary cost. However, the impact of industry competition forces depends on many factors; market structure, competition type (product vs. price), perceived degree of deter-the-entry effect, and favorability of the disclosed information (good vs. bad).[36]

2434. Responses

1) Firms

Full disclosure

The disclosure benefit originating from the product market, if there is any, can persuade managers to provide proprietary information voluntarily. It is evidenced that there exists the product-market-level disclosure benefit. For example, incumbent firms may disclose proprietary information to deter the product-market competition (e.g., entry, investment). For example, Kirby (1988) suggested that firms in an oligopolistic industry might share information about market demand to prevent overproduction. An efficient equilibrium and increased consumer surplus can be obtained by information sharing through a trade association.(201) Other example of the capital-market-level disclosure benefit include the market credibility. Gigler (1994) showed that, when independent verification for proprietary information is impossible, unavailable, or too costly, the firm would like to voluntarily disclose to convince investors for the high demand or quality of its product, thereby increasing its value (i.e., proprietary benefit). Even without third-party verification for the unaudited proprietary information, the existence of significant proprietary cost itself can generate meaningful credibility.(94)[37]

Non-disclosure; withholding

There are many shreds of empirical evidence that examine other negative effects of proprietary costs on voluntary disclosure decisions. If a firm discloses information on high demand, the competitor will take advantage of the firm's disclosure by increasing production. So the firm will choose to withhold or hide information on market demand to prevent competitive disadvantage.(187)

Some studies of non-disclosure use such proxies as redaction and missing information. Nearly 40% of IPO firms redact information from SEC filings to shield proprietary information from potential rivals.(100) Firms missing R&D information have 14 times more patent applications than firms reporting zero R&D. Managers do not seem to omit R&D information accidentally but attempt to deliberately omit the information since competitors can have access to it.(101) About 86% of industrial firms responded to the draft of SFAS 131 on segment disclosures with the opposition on the grounds that it can put them at a competitive disadvantage. (202) A trade association is associated with disclosure patterns. When the level of competition in the product market is above a certain threshold level, firms will choose to initiate a trade association to withhold information from competitors.(187)

Complete avoidance

When the withholding or non-disclosure is not attainable to reduce proprietary cost, firms may find a way to escape from proprietary cost by using private placement. Tang (2009) present that firms with higher proprietary cost are more likely to choose private placements instead of public offerings. An industry or a firm with a higher proprietary cost that is proxied by product-market competitiveness are *"more likely to choose private placements"* and *"firms operating in multiple lines of business and more profitable firms are more likely to choose private placements."*(102) Firms may completely escape from the market by using voluntary delisting

Partial disclosure

In the real world, neither non-disclosure nor full-disclosure prevails. In general, managers tend to disclose proprietary information not in every meticulous detail but a summary. Thus, neither investors will discount the price, nor competitors will learn by watching. Braendle & Noll (2005) showed that the efficient amount of disclosure is neither "no disclosure" nor "full disclosure." The characteristics of proprietary information do not lead to non-disclosure; instead, voluntary disclosure would do better than mandatory disclosure. (18) Some pieces of empirical evidence analyze aggregation and missing information. If firms have lower proprietary cost (e.g., similar performance across segments), then they tend to disaggregate to conceal the performance differences from competitors.(97) Firms have incentives to avoid the competitor's scrutiny by aggregating the losing segments with profiting segments.(98, 99)

2) **Investors**

Against the firm's non-disclosure of proprietary information, investors would potentially respond with information search or underpricing mechanism. When a firm's disclosure of proprietary information is sub-optimal, private information acquisition would be an alternative approach, as suggested by Diamond (1985).(50) Investors may respond with an underpricing strategy. Redacting firms experience greater underpricing due to investors' discount for greater uncertainty. (100)

3) **Regulators**

In the investor's angle, a full disclosure policy for proprietary information would greatly reduce the investors' aggregate expenditure on information acquisition. However, in the firm's angle, disclosure of proprietary information can be the sub-optimal choice because firm's competitive position may be seriously hurt.(50) A regulatory policy for the withholding of proprietary information is often adopted by many countries to achieve a fair balance between investor's need for more information and a firm's need for reduced proprietary cost.

SEC rule is a great example of such a disclosure exemption policy. Under SEC Rule, any firm filing reports may make an objection to its public disclosure and request confidential treatment for competitively sensitive information contained in material agreements. The firm can request redaction for specific content such as competitively sensitive terms, specifications, or deadlines. If it is determined by the SEC that the objection of disclosure should be sustained, then the confidential portion which the firm desires to keep undisclosed will not be made available to the public, but a notation will be made at the appropriate place in the material filed.[38] According to Boone, Floros, Johnson (2016), firms that redacted are evidenced to exhibit superior financial performance post IPO, and their level of private information seems to abate by the fourth year.(100)

"Principles for Ongoing Disclosure and Material Development Reporting by Listed Entities" of IOSCO (2002) describes the principles of disclosure delay policy as below. Companies' application for confidential treatment should be granted by the competent authority.(203) Both Chapter 435 and Chapter 4442 cover country-specific regulations more in detail.

> "…, disclosure may be subject to delay, to be granted in some jurisdictions by the competent authority, if: (a) the information is confidential under legislation; (b) the information concerns an incomplete proposal or nego-

tiations, or the disclosure ... is such as to prejudice the legitimate interests ...."

2435. Segment information

No one would deny that segment information is the most typical example of proprietary information. Regulators generally require firms to include information about operating segments in financial statements. Segment information disclosure is intended to provide information to investors regarding the financial performances and the positions of outstanding operating units. Firms should report segment information, including the factors used to identify reportable segments, the types of products and services, revenues, material expense items, and profits-and-losses, but it depends on country-specific accounting requirements.

Line-of-business disclosure

In 1947, the SEC adopted requirements to disclose the relative importance of important lines of business. In 1951, the SEC required disclosure of the relative importance of a segment that contributed 15% or more. In 1969, the SEC required segment reporting for each line of business that contributed 10% or more. (204)

SFAS No.14 vs. SFAS No.131

In 1976, he Financial Accounting Standards Board (FASB) issued the Statement of Financial Accounting Standards (SFAS) No. 14 (Financial Reporting for Segments of a Business Enterprise) to meet investor's needs for segment information. The SFAS No. 14 segment disclosures convey incremental information over the previously reported SEC line-of-business information that is relevant.(205)

However, under SFAS No. 14, firms followed the "Industry Approach" where segments corresponded to SIC industry groups and identified the firm's segment on its discretion.[39] Hence, many large and complex firms aggregated segments to avoid a competitive disadvantage.

On the contrary, under SFAS No. 131 (Disclosures about Segments of an Enterprise and Related Information) issued in 1997, firms followed the "Management Approach" where firms have to establish segments that correspond to how the businesses are organized.(206) The SFAS 131 increased the number of reported segments and provided more disaggregated information.(207) *"Over two-thirds of the sample firms have redefined their primary operating segments upon adopting SFAS No. 131. There has also been an increase in the number of firms providing segment disclosures ..."*(208)

Impacts of rigorous segment disclosure

If the highly segmented information is mandated, the proprietary cost is expected to increase sharply, while disclosure benefit increases slowly. Thus, firms have no choice but to bear a serious amount of negative net disclosure benefit (Figure 29).

According to such rigorous disclosure regulation on segment information, investors are provided with more segment information, and their welfare will be better off (Figure 30 situation A).

However, if investors are less interested in the mandated segment information or experience complexity, they may be diverted to other types of information (e.g., Y). As a result, additional regulation might create a severe proprietary cost to the disclosing firm with just a limited increase in social welfare. Investors might not use the additional segment information (Figure 30 situation B).

If the additional segment disclosure is of little use to investors in forecasting earnings, then it more helps the competitors of product market by revealing the firm's proprietary information. Investor's welfare might increase a bit, but it comes at a significant price to the disclosing firm; proprietary cost.

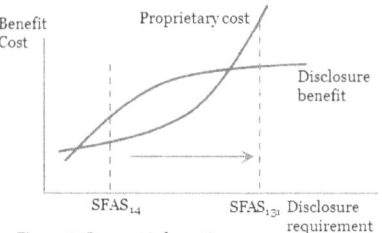

Figure 29 Segment information -1

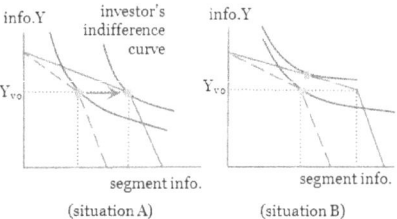

Figure 30 Segment information -2

Usefulness to investors

Some studies focus on the usefulness to investors and the predictive accuracy of earnings forecast by analyzing disaggregated industry information and find that segment disclosure improves the predictive accuracy. Predictions based on the disaggregated segment-level data are found to be more accurate than predictions based on the consolidated firm-level data. The accuracy of prediction might be further increased by segment information. (209) The SEC product-line disclosure was evidenced to provide significantly more accurate estimates of future firm-level earnings.(210) A regulatory switch to SFAS 131 was evidenced to have achieved goals to increase the number of disclosed segments by eliminating much of the managers' discretion in segmentation. A significant improvement in forecast accuracy was also evidenced.(207) On the contrary, others found that additional segment requirements improve only marginally. For example, geographic segment data enhances the predictive ability for annual income and sales data, but its usefulness is reduced because detailed geographic segments are frequently not reported.(211)

244. Non-Product Market Indirect Costs

Proprietary cost provides the main explanation for many characteristics of indirect cost. Besides, it may create lasting influences on the value of the disclosing firm because the competitor's strategic response may harm the longstanding competitive advantage of the disclosing firm. However, it should be noted that proprietary cost does not cover the indirect cost entirely. Thus, a specific type of indirect cost other than proprietary cost deserves a considerable attention.

Political cost and litigation cost are the most frequently mentioned indirect cost other than proprietary cost. These two types of indirect cost deserve special attentions due to their distinctive natures. These tend to be huge in amounts of cash flow when it is realized even though these are one-time cost and irrelevant to the product market competition. Litigation cost differs from political cost in that disclosure-related litigation cost is regardless of political group, while political cost is regardless of a lawsuit.

2441. Litigation cost

24411. Legal environments

Lexical meaning

Litigation is time and effort-consuming and generally involves many expenses. In general, "litigation cost" refers to the amount of expense spent on a lawsuit, including costs related to preparation as well as costs spent during the trial. Litigation cost includes attorney fee and filing fee. The most common litigation cost is attorney fees that is paid for the lawyer. It is sure that various other costs can arise regarding a lawsuit, including money, time, and efforts that could have been used for other profitable area (i.e., opportunity cost). As a result, managers should consider potential litigation cost.

Litigation cost in disclosure research

Litigation cost hypothesis argues that managers are likely to deter disclosure due to litigation cost. However, the world of disclosure research seems not to clearly classify specific types of litigation cost. To gain a better understanding, we should understand the intrinsic nature of securities regulation; the dual pillar structure.

Dual pillar natures of securities law

A better understanding of the basic nature of securities law is a prerequisite to analyze the litigation cost. Due to the special nature of securities law, litigation cost can be given much weight among various types of disclosure cost. SEC Rule 10b-5, catch-all provision under §10(b) of the Securities Exchange Act of 1934, prohibits not only the "untrue statement" of material fact but also "omission" resulting in fraud or deceit.[40] Rule 10b-5 requires managers to correct and update inaccurate, incomplete, or misleading statements. As a result, a previously released disclosure creates a legal liability to correct and update, which can affect a firm's litigation risk.

Also, non-disclosure for the misleading prior information may be construed as a failure that triggers litigation. Besides, the dual pillar structure is represented by the "disclose of abstain" rule. As a result, if managers are involved in stock trading without prior disclosure, then they could face a litigation from "neither disclosure and nor abstain."

In conclusion, disclosure-related litigation cost can be classified into the "litigation cost from disclosure" and the "litigation cost of non-disclosure." Disclosure-related litigation cost should refer to the litigation cost that the shareholders or regulators might raise by using firms' disclosed information or by using the fact of non-disclosure.

Litigation cost from disclosure

The litigation cost from disclosure means the indirect cost from disclosure that is triggered by the disclosed information. It covers any damage or liability that might occur from a potential lawsuit. Therefore, litigation cost from disclosure refers to the potential indirect cost that firms face when the shareholders or regulators might raise a lawsuit by using firms' disclosed information.

The dual pillars of securities law inevitably lead firms to the trade-off structures between trigger risk and non-disclosure risk. The plaintiff would initiate litigation based on the clues gathered from the disclosed information. They identify defendants and find conclusive fraud evidence of a misstatement or omission of a material fact. This drives firms to a litigation trigger risk, which increases indirect cost of disclosure. The plaintiff must show evidence on injury in connection with the purchase or sale of a security. A previous disclosure tends to provide a hint of misstatement, delay, or forecast error. As a result, increased disclosure would generate more litigation. It is evidenced that most Rule 10b-5 cases are brought as a result of allegedly omitted or misleading information with a sharp decline of the stock price.(212).

Litigation cost of non-disclosure

On the contrary, when firms disclose more actively, the probability of litigation alleging insider trading, failure to abstain from trading, or omission of material information would be reduced. As a result, increased disclosure would reduce the litigation risk of non-disclosure. The litigation cost of non-disclosure means the cost of non-compliance with mandatory disclosure requirements, irrelevant form indirect cost. "Litigation cost as indirect cost" is litigation cost from disclosure that occurs from the compliance of disclosure regulation, while "litigation cost of non-disclosure" is litigation cost from non-disclosure that occurs from the non- or poor-compliance of disclosure regulation.

Dual pillar and firms' trade-off

Due to the dual pillars of securities regulation, firms face a trade-off between the dual pillars of risks: trigger risk and non-disclosure risk. Both probabilities are independent but tend to move in the opposite direction, which makes managers complicated. An increased disclosure can increase

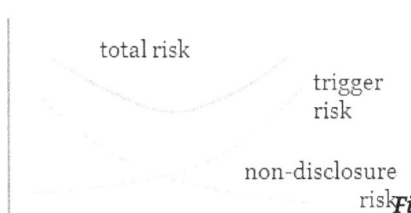

Figure 31 Non-disclosure risk

the probability of trigger risk but decrease the probability of non-disclosure risk. When it comes to optimization between both risk exposures, ceteris paribus, the solution is to minimize the total risk for a given disclosure benefit.

Firm's decision under the dual pillar

Under the voluntary disclosure context free from insider trading regulation, managers will make optimal disclosure decisions only to maximize the net benefits of disclosure, without considering non-disclosure cost. However, mandatory disclosure under the dual pillar regulation gives birth to non-disclosure cost. Considering the magnitude of non-disclosure cost and benefit, managers should compare the net benefits of disclosure and that of non-disclosure. Rational managers would disclose so long as the net benefit of disclosure exceeds that of non-disclosure (case 1~2), unless the net benefit of disclosure is worse than that of non-disclosure (case 3). As a result, firms would disclose even though the net benefit is minus only to evade the severe non-disclosure cost.

Table 1 Disclosure decision

Cases	Net benefit of each option		Decision
	Disclosure	Non-disclosure	
Case 1	100	70	
Case 2	100	-10	Disclosure
Case 3	-30	-50	
Case 4	-50	-10	Non-disclosure

Investor's litigation decision

It is essential to understand how investors make litigation decision, especially the conditions for initiating litigation. When does it pay to file a lawsuit for a victim? A lawsuit is worth for the plaintiff to initiate only if the expected value exceeds the expected cost. The plaintiff aims to maximize the payoff that equals the expected judgment amount net of the expected litigation cost.

$$\text{Plaintiff's Payoff} = P_p * J - C_p$$

- Probability (P_p): The plaintiff's probability of winning the suit.
- Judgment amount (J): The amount that the defendant is

expected to pay the plaintiff when judgment is entered for the plaintiff.
- Cost (C_p): The plaintiff's legal cost.

Class action

Though both of insider regulation and disclosure regulation are important dual pillars of capital market regulation, securities lawsuits are mainly driven by poor disclosure. Plaintiff, without much hardship, might allege poor disclosure based on the firm's preceding disclosure and manager's duty to update. Disclosed information might increase the plaintiff's probability of winning the suit while reducing the plaintiff's litigation cost. This may supply a cogent reason for the outnumbering disclosure lawsuits. Stanford Securities Class Action Clearinghouse(SCAC 2014) shows that most of class action allegations repeatedly fall under the category of the disclosure.(213)

Table 2) 2014 Allegations Box Score
(2010-2014, Percentage of total filings)

Allegations	'10	'11	'12	'13	'14
Misrepresentations in financial documents	93	94	95	97	94
False forward-looking statements	45	56	62	54	47
insider trading	16	12	17	17	16
GAAP violations	26	37	23	24	36
Announced restatement	7	11	11	11	17
Internal control weaknesses	23	24	20	20	24
Announced internal control weaknesses	3	6	8	8	10

Note) The percentages do not add to 100 percent because complaints may include multiple allegations.

Source) Figure 6, Stanford Securities Class Action Clearinghouse, Securities Class Action Filings 2014 Year in Review(213)

The total "Disclosure Dollar Loss (DDL)" in US market recorded $57 billion in 2014. (213)[41] Such a huge amount of capitalization losses from litigation is enough to leave hot issues behind since disclosure-related allegation occupies a leading place in the above allegation box score. A strong suggestion can be made that performing a rigorous and regular legal risk analysis provide firms with an excellent disclosure strategy. (213)

24412. Firm's optimization decision

Firm's exposure

Exposures of trigger risk and non-disclosure risk depend respectively on the probability of litigation (P_t, P_n), the amount of judgment (J_t, J_n), and the cost (C_t, C_n). Firstly, the firm must estimate the probability of trigger risk (P_t), add the plaintiff's costs (C_t) to the expected judgment amount (J_t), and multiply the trigger exposure (J_t+C_t) by the probability. Secondly, the firm must estimate the probability of non-disclosure risk (P_n), add the plaintiff's costs (C_n) to the expected judgment amount (J_n), and multiply the non-disclosure exposure (J_n+C_n) by the probability. To reach the total exposure, sum both exposures.

$$\text{Total exposure} = P_t * (J_t + C_t) + P_n * (J_n + C_n)$$

- Probability: The probability of initiating litigation driven by trigger risk (P_t), the probability by non-disclosure risk (P_n).
- Judgment amount: The amount that the defendant is expected to pay the plaintiff when judgment is entered for the plaintiff by trigger risk (J_t), the amount driven by non-disclosure risk (J_n).
- Cost: The plaintiff's legal cost by trigger risk (C_t), by nondisclosure risk (C_n).

Impacts of cost structures

Managers facing only direct cost will make disclosure decisions on D_1 (Figure 32). When managers consider indirect cost such as litigation cost, disclosure level will be reduced to D_2 (Figure 33). When managers consider non-disclosure cost, disclosure level will increase to D_3 pressured by the non-disclosure cost (Figure 34).

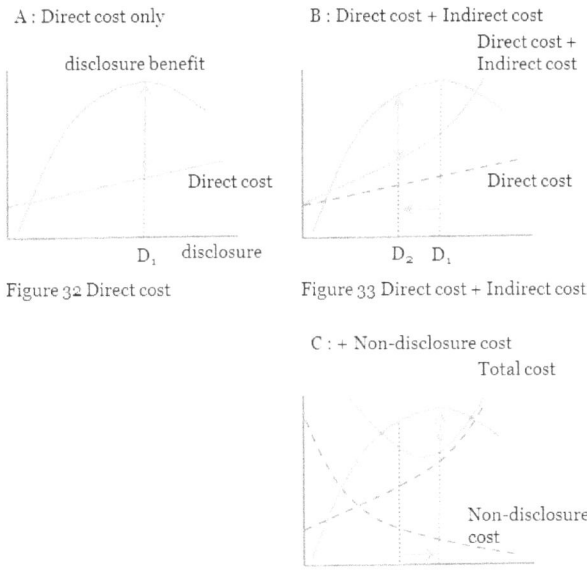

Figure 32 Direct cost

Figure 33 Direct cost + Indirect cost

Figure 34 Nondisclosure cost

Firm's diversified choices: optimal level

The magnitude of each risk and its subsequent cost depends on the firm's attributes and attitudes toward both risks. Thus, if firms' attributes are asymmetric, they may react in an extremely different way: quality- or poor-disclosure. More disclosure may increase the probability of trigger risk, while it may decrease the probability of non-disclosure risk. Manager who are averse of trigger risk will perceive trigger risk as serious (Figure 35), and thus the optimal disclosure level will be lower than that of the non-disclosure risk aversive firm. Manager who were previously sanctioned will become more attentive of non-disclosure risk, perceive non-disclosure risk as severe one, and will prefer more disclosure to reduce total risk (Figure 36).

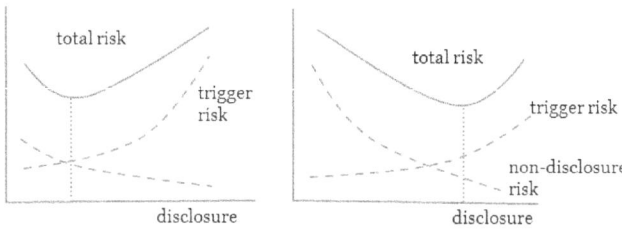

Figure 35 Trigger risk aversive firm   Figure 36 Non-disclosure risk aversive firm

Impacts of changes in legal environments

Once the shareholder activism that is focusing on fault-finding from disclosure is on the rise, the probability of initiating litigation increases. An increased trigger risk may lift the total exposure upward and deter voluntary disclosure (Figure 37). However, if shareholder activist pays more attention to firms with non-disclosure, then the non-disclosure risk increases, and managers will increase disclosure level to optimize, ceteris paribus (Figure 38). If regulators adopt stricter insider trading regulation, then the non-disclosure risk increases due to the increase in the probability of initiating litigation and the expected judgment amount, and managers will provide more disclosure to minimize the total exposure at a given level of disclosure benefit (Figure 38).

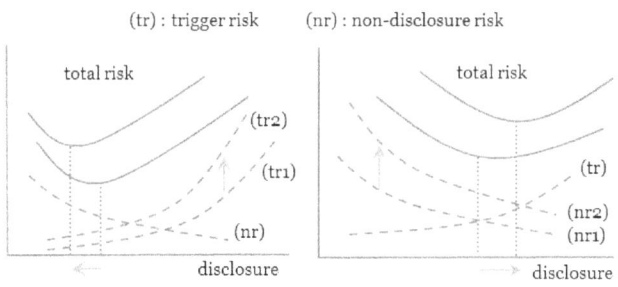

Figure 37 Increase in trigger risk   Figure 38 Increase in non-disclosure risk

3. Preemption

Benefits of preemptive disclosure

Public disclosure of material information limits the managers' information advantage. However, managers are precluded from trading with material non-public information by the "disclose or abstain" rule, so they appear to provide public disclosure in advance of personal trading.(214) Preemptive disclosure means disclosure released by managers to preempt the probability of litigation that might occur from non-disclosure. For example, announcements of earnings shock increase the likelihood of litigation. Thus, managers have incentives to preempt earnings shock by early disclosure. Preemptive disclosure provides firms with some benefits in many aspects. For example, "voluntary" disclosure before the deadline makes the plaintiff's argument less convincing, which reduces the plaintiff's probability of winning a lawsuit. "Early" disclosure supports the disclosing firm in the arguments for timely disclosure, reduces the period of non-disclosure, the number of plaintiffs, the possible damage, which reduces the probability and judgment amount.(46)

Preemption timing and non-disclosure risk

Investors are assumed to raise a lawsuit when non-disclosure risk is above a certain level. If non-disclosure risk is below the "litigation threshold level," then the firm is very unlikely to be in litigation. If a firm's non-disclosure risk is very low regardless of disclosure timing (L), then it would not make preemptive disclosure. If a firm's non-disclosure risk is sharply increasing with disclosure delay (S), then it is likely to employ a preemption strategy to reduce non-disclosure risk.

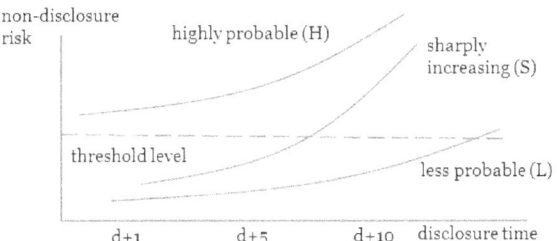

Figure 39 Preemption timing

Timing vs. quality

There are two contradicting arguments with the empirical evidence between disclosure and litigation cost: deterrent vs. stimulator. The potential litigation against firms based on inadequate disclosure can change the firms' attitude of voluntary disclosure.(57) Managers, to avoid the risk of non-disclosure or delayed disclosure, may mindlessly jump to hasty disclosure as soon as they are informed.

However, not only disclosure timing but also disclosure quality affects the plaintiff's probability of winning a lawsuit and the judgment amount. Too early disclosure may incur another type of litigation risk driven by low-quality disclosure. Early but hasty disclosure can increase the litigation cost of disclosure. The best disclosure policy is not just more or early disclosure but the optimal disclosure in time, volume, and quality. Rational managers who face the trade-off between timing risk (i.e., delayed disclosure) and quality risk (i.e., inaccurate disclosure) should minimize the total risk of preemption, ceteris paribus.

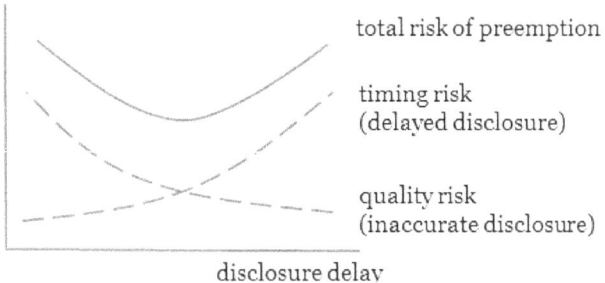

Figure 40 Timing risk vs Quality risk

Evidence of trigger effect

In a survey, about 46.4% of the respondents agree or strongly agree with the litigation cost hypothesis that the reduced voluntary disclosure helps firms to avoid possible lawsuits that might occur if future results do not match forward-looking disclosure.(108) Given that there are various benefits of earnings forecasts, all bidders do not release forecasts. There is substantial post-merger litigation cost in merger forecasting. A quantitative forecast increases the likelihood of litigation by 13% compared to a qualitative forecast.(215) Firms at risk of litigation provide more cautionary language (e.g., boilerplate warnings) in MD&A to reduce the expected litigation cost.(216) Early disclosure does not appear to be a litigation deterrent but a trigger. About 62% of the litigation samples were based on an earnings forecast or a preemptive earnings disclosure.(212) The litigation process discourages firms from disclosures for fear that they may be held accountable. Firms facing litigation risk do not seem to improve disclosure but reduce the disclosure level.(217) According to Butler (2006), *"An important aspect of SOX's indirect costs is the Act's impact on litigation. SOX gives litigators the benefit of 20/20 hindsight to identify minor or technical reporting mistakes as the basis for lawsuits ... Litigation on this scale should not be confused with shareholder protection. SOX has created a ticking litigation time bomb."*(218) The more rigorous the regulation, the serious the unintended side-effect from the indirect cost such as the litigation cost from disclosure. More litigation should not be confused with better protection.

Evidence of preemption effect

There is a survey that about 76.8% of the respondents reveal bad news faster to reduce legal risk.(108) Managers have incentives to preempt the large negative earnings surprises more frequently than favorable earnings to reduce the potential litigation cost from disclosure. Early voluntary disclosure makes it more difficult for the plaintiff to argue delayed poor disclosure, also reduces the period of nondisclosure and the plaintiffs' damages.(46) Turnaround firms in industries of high litigation risk are more likely to provide positive earnings forecasts than firms in industries of low risk.(219) A significant increase in the frequency of forecasts issued following the safe harbor provision of the PSLRA of 1995. The disclosure is increasing in firms' ex-ante litigation risk.(220) Firms with higher litigation risk are more likely to disclose, and early disclosing firms can lower litigation risk.(221) Managers have the incentive to revise existing forecasts downward more often than upward. This asymmetric revision pattern is consistent with the legal liability argument or litigation cost hypothesis.(46)

According to Waymire (1985), *"...firms which issue earnings forecasts more frequently ...are characterized by less volatile earnings processes relative to firms which issue such projections on an infrequent basis ..."* The less-volatile earning patterns reduce the potential forecast error and the probability of raising a lawsuit and thus put managers at ease. Besides, *"volatility should be a more important consideration for good news management forecasts relative to bad news projections,"* because forecast error of good news is likely to trigger more litigation risk than that of bad news. As a result, managers recognize that forecast accuracy of good news is more important than that of bad news due to the asymmetric legal liability.(222)

24414. Determinants of litigation cost

Any factor that might influence investor's litigation initiation can be a probable determinant of the litigation cost from disclosure. Those come from intrinsic attributes of firm or industry, information, and litigation structure.

Litigation structure

There are several attributes of litigation that can affect litigation costs probability, damage, and filing cost. The probability of winning the suit which is inherently uncertain. Litigation structure is related with the other determinants of the litigation cost from disclosure or non-disclosure.

First, if managers make voluntary disclosure prior to the mandated deadline, the plaintiffs' argument against managers loses its ground. Early disclosure lowers the probability of a lawsuit by weakening investors' claim that the managers made untimely disclosure and also reduces the probability of a large stock price drops that can trigger class action lawsuits.(212)

Second, the greater the damages, the more valuable the lawsuit. Higher volatility of price or earnings may increase the probability of winning a lawsuit and the potential damage and judgment amount. Any factors can be influential determinants when it affects the expected judgment amount.

The potential damage and judgement amount are directly related with the period of nondisclosure. By the way, voluntary disclosure might reduce investor's damage because it reduces the exposure time period to the misleading prices. As a result, the incentives of plaintiff to bring a lawsuit will be reduced.

Third, a severe increase in filing cost will reduce the probability of raising a lawsuit.

Firm

Some natures of firms such as firm size, profitability, earnings volatility, governance, and prior litigation experience affect litigation cost.

a. Firm size: Disclosure scores are higher for larger firms because the direct cost of disclosure per unit firm size is decreasing. Besides, large firms (i.e., market capitalization) with deeper pockets have the incentive to disclose more to deter litigation because large firms are more exposed to litigation risk than small ones.(223) Large firms have deep pockets that can be extracted by the plaintiffs, but it is not easy to win a lawsuit against such large firms. As a result, a large-scale litigation does not occur frequently, but once it becomes sensational

b. Profitability: Loss firms are more likely to minimize litigation risk by legally withholding proprietary information through the SEC redaction procedure that is unlikely to trigger litigation.(192) The higher the volatility of earnings, the higher the earnings forecast error, and the higher the probability of sudden price drop, which is likely to trigger litigation. "Managers of firms with more volatile earnings are reluctant to disclose their forecasts due to increased exposure." Firms that issue earnings forecasts more frequently are characterized by less volatile earnings.(222) Firms with larger earnings surprise disclose more quantitative and earnings-related the disclosure.(223)

c. Governance: Investors may have pre-conception that firms with weak internal control and corporate governance are poor in disclosure. They might be more apt to initiate litigation against such poor governance firms expecting higher probability of settlement. Low governance firms can be the prey of a strong investor group.

d. Prior experience: Regulators intend to enhance transparency by way of lawsuit, but it is evidenced that firms reduce the level of information after they are sued. Sued managers may have learned that disclosure potentially provides a reason for a subsequent litigation or give the litigants another hint. Examination of the behavioral changes of sued firms suggests that the litigation process discourages firms from disclosure after being sued for which they may be held accountable again.(217)

Industry

The risk characteristics of an industry or business model can have an impact on the magnitude of litigation risk. For example, firms in a high technology industry are positively associated with warning disclosure such as earnings surprise. High tech firms are exposed to lawsuits because they show large price fluctuations resulting in potential losses to investors. They disclose more or better to fend off the litigation risk.(223) Firms in a high litigation industry are more likely to disclose forward-looking information than firms in industries with low litigation threats.(219) Litigation cost is a major concern for young firms, listed on small exchanges.(108)[42]

Information

A stock price movement depends on the attributes of information. Thus, the magnitude and direction of litigation cost are related to the attributes of information such as uncertainty, completeness, and favorability.

a. Uncertainty (forecast): Information with higher uncertainty is more associated with lower accuracy. Investors may easily find fault with uncertain information, which can increase the probability of lawsuits. For example, investors may raise a lawsuit when the earnings result is found out to be lower than forecast. This can potentially reduce managers' incentives to provide forward-looking disclosures.

b. Completeness: Investors cannot evaluate their stocks based on partially disclosed information. Thus, partial information could be worse than no information because separated non-holistic information may be distorted and, as a result, drive litigation. It seems intuitively obvious to say that litigation risk increases with unexpected earnings disappointment.

c. Favorability: Due to the characteristics of bad news that enables investors to prove their damage easily, legal actions can be easily taken against firms that provided bad news. Thus, managers have stronger incentives to preempt (i.e., more, earlier) bad news disclosure to minimize the total litigation costs. Loss firms are more likely to disclose bad news to reduce litigation costs.(224) If there is no affirmative duty to disclose, managers will withhold the unfavorable information as much as possible. However, firms in a highly litigious environment voluntarily disclose regardless of the favorability of information. For example, if legal environment is highly litigious due to the affirmative duty to disclose, managers will release either good news or bad news. The good news disclosure is even expected to be more precise than the unfavorable one.(225)[43]

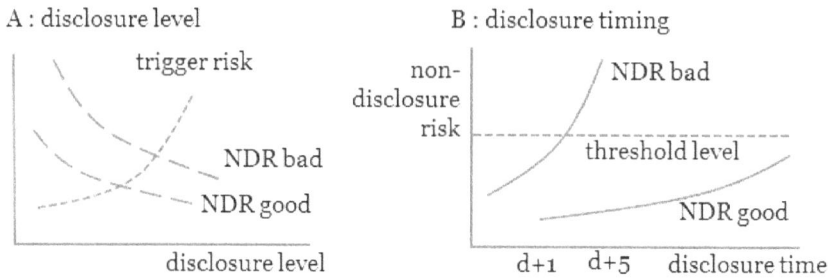

Figure 41 Disclosure level vs Disclosure timing

2442. Political cost

1) Political cost hypothesis

Political cost

Political cost of disclosure refers to a type of indirect cost of disclosure triggered by the behavior of political group or regulators, and thereby damaging the disclosing firm.

Political cost hypothesis

Political group has an incentive to introduce new regulation or change current regulation to make a particular thing should or should not happen in an industry. Besides, political group, such as labor union, has the power to affect the firm's decision for public welfare. Disclosure can provide some reasons for the politician to intrude on the disclosing firm, which may generate political cost. Consequently, managers would prefer to withhold information or limit the quality or quantity of information that can be used by political group against the disclosing firm.(226)

Sources

Political cost can be classified according to the source of reaction into two ways; internal vs. public. Political cost can be generated by the behaviors of internal people or organizations (e.g., employees, labor unions). It can also be generated by the behaviors of external organizations or institutions (i.e., regulators, politicians, and associations).

Firm's choices

The more visible the firm, the higher the political cost. More politically visible firms can employ various forms of devices; passive or active. Passive devices include withholding disclosure and cliched disclosure to avoid the attention of politicians. Active devices include proactive voluntarily disclose to preempt the political costs.

2) Determinants of political cost

Politicians prefer to target firms with conspicuous features such as large size, high profits, intensive labor, high press coverage, or monopolized product market because they have prominent features and can bear the political cost. The magnitudes and patterns of political cost may differ from country to country since political cost reflects the culture and customs of a country. Some shreds of evidence exist for the determinants of political cost; firm size, profitability, industry, nature of the information.[44]

Large firms with high profitability are more likely to reduce voluntary disclosure to avoid political attacks, and they are more likely to use accounting choices to reduce reported profits than small firms.(227) On the contrary, large firms are politically sensitive and have incentives to disclose more to alleviate political criticism or governmental intervention.(228) The larger the company, *"the more nonfinancial information is voluntarily revealed."* (73)

According to Meek, Roberts and Gary (1995), there is an industry effect in the oil, chemicals, and mining group. Such an industry group may be more politically sensitive. *"Political costs are also likely to vary across nations, given that they reflect cultural and social norms."* For nonfinancial information, an industry effect is more pronounced. Political cost varies across the type of information as well as society or market. Social differences in cultural and social norms determines political cost, which encourage the variations in voluntary disclosures of nonfinancial and social items.(73)[45]

3) Political group

Internal: Labor unions

Political cost can be imposed by labor unions. For example, pension plan information is considered political in nature due to the conflict of interests between managers and labor unions. It is not surprising that the response of labor union can be included in political cost.

However, the political cost of labor unions should be disentangled from the other sources of political cost since there are differences in the characteristics of information. Besides, labor unions are not entirely outsider. Other political costs may arise from any information, but political cost of labor unions mainly arise from the profitability information. Labor unions devote their time and efforts to improve their bargaining power in an attempt to extract a larger portion of the rent from the firm.

Facing an increased probability of rent extraction by labor unions, firm's manager may choose to withhold pension information. The magnitude of such a political cost depends on the degree of the conflicts of interest between manager and labor unions.

For the improved decision of relevant information users, FASB statement No. 158 requires firms to recognize the funded status. The disclosure on a defined benefit pension fund reveals information about the current status and the ability of pension fund to generate future cash flows. Information users in the capital market are avid for more information about pension plans to make an accurate forecast, while labor unions seek the information of the overfunded or underfunded status of a defined benefit plan. When it comes to the pension information disclosure, managers faces the trade-off between the increased benefits in the capital market and the political cost in the labor market.[46]

Some suggest empirical evidence in support of the political cost hypothesis. Labor unions basically seek rent extraction, and thus managers facing frequent strikes of labor unions would refrain from the disclosure of pension information. The strike incidences that represent the magnitude of political cost in the labor market are negatively associated with the firms' voluntary disclosure of defined benefit pension plan.(182) Managers voluntarily disclose pension liability information in annual reports. (229)

Politician

Politicians may seek to put political pressures on specific firms to redistribute resources ostensibly for the protection of public interest. Firms may employ many devices such as lobbying, social media, accounting choices (i.e., profit reduction), disclosure (i.e., full- or non-disclosure). By avoiding the attention of political society, managers can reduce the likelihood of adverse political actions. If disclosure seems to generate a greater political intervention, then firms with huge profits may be reluctant to disclose voluntarily.

Tax authority

Political cost can be persuasive in explaining various tax-related accounting methods. The higher the profits, the larger the political cost (i.e., tax). For example, tax authorities may use geographic segment disclosures in examining tax evasion, and, as a result, the geographic segment disclosures create political cost to the disclosing firm.(95, 230)

Regulator or opinion leaders

Firms might prefer non-disclosure of information that regulators might use against them. Such a political cost can be created by the regulator, association, trade unions, and media.(231)

25. Determinants of disclosure

Various types of determinants that affect disclosure cost are already summarized in the previous Chapter. In this Chapter, the conceptual background and the empirical results on the determinants of disclosure are summarized by and large.

251. Backgrounds

Determinism

Determinism is the philosophical idea that event or output is determined by initial condition or input, regardless of human's free will. Mechanical models are mostly deterministic. A purely deterministic system refers to a system in which no randomness is involved in producing output. A specific determinant will always produce the same output. For example, large firms (determinant or input) will always provide full voluntary disclosure (output). A deterministic approach mainly highlights the importance of the determinant that is affecting market. They often use such terms as guide, motivator, or constraint. Determinism includes a variety of branches, such as causal determinism and predeterminism.

a. Causal determinism is the idea that output comes from antecedent input with the law of nature, which is known as a cause-and-effect. Output is bound by causality in a way that it is completely determined by input. There is an unbroken chain of causes-and-effect, and nothing is un-caused or self-caused. [47]

b. Predeterminism is the idea that output is determined in advance, and a cause-and-effect chain has been pre-established, and thus human actions cannot interfere with outcomes. It can be termed as a pre-established causal determinism. [48]

Indeterminism

On the contrary, indeterminism is the idea that event or output is not caused by deterministically but more related to the combination of human's free will. Some event happens without any precedent cause, so it is not easy to predict future outcome. Outcome is probabilistic, and no event is certain. A model that is not deterministic but involves randomness can be called stochastic.

Once researchers are fixated on a deterministic approach, they may lose the managers' strategic behaviors that are based on free will. On the contrary, researchers who are fixated on manager's deliberation or free might not obtain a meaningful conclusion. In a broad sense, one may try to study the manager's behaviors that are based on his free will with causal deterministic analysis. This approach may provide some meaningful implications when the manager's behaviors are stylized. The more the manager's free will is stylized, the regulator can develop regulatory mechanisms (e.g., incentive-compatible mechanism) to enhance transparency.

Research history

Buzby (1975) mentioned Cerf (1961) as the first to deal empirically with some of the factors that might influence the adequacy of disclosure.(232) Cerf (1961) found that disclosure quality tends to improve with better exchange (i.e., NYSE), firm size (i.e., assets, stockholders), profitability (i.e., the ratio of net income to net worth).(233) Followed by Cerf (1961), many empirical studies have explained the relation between firm-specific determinants and the extent of a voluntary disclosure.

252. Classification

1) Approaches

Literature points out some characteristics of determinants that influence voluntary disclosure, which ranges from firm-specific characteristics to managers' incentives. The primary purpose of many researches is to show the existence of statistical association between specific variables and disclosure. Such being the case, an approach to disentangle and classify might provide additional understanding.(108, 234)

First, we may classify determinants into supply-side and demand-side. A supply-side determinant relies on the nature of information providers (i.e., firm, manager), which includes firm-level characteristics, managerial motives, and opportunism. A demand-side determinant relies on the nature of information users, which includes disclosure pressure and disciplining force that make firms meet with information demands. As the capital market develops, demand-side is getting more important.

Second, we may classify determinants into a unidirectional determinant and a bidirectional determinant. A unidirectional determinant is a constant that affects the extent of voluntary disclosure, but the same is not true in reverse. However, a bidirectional determinant is a variable that affects the extent of voluntary disclosure, and the same is true in reverse. It is very useful for understanding the interaction between both variables.

Third, we may classify determinants into a motivator and constraints. A motivator of voluntary disclosure includes disclosure benefits or incentives such as capital markets transactions, corporate control contests, stock compensation, and management talent signaling. A demotivator or constraints that limit managers from voluntary disclosure include proprietary cost, agency cost, and political cost.

Table 3) Classification of Disclosure Determinants

		Factors	Direction
Information provider	Firm	firm size, income variability, financial structure, competition	unidirectional
	Manager	stock option, family ownership	unidirectional /bidirectional
Information user		institution ownership, foreign ownership, analyst coverage, investor base, share concentration	bidirectional
Environments		litigation law, enforcement	unidirectional

2) Unidirectional determinants

If a firm's attribute is constant, fixed, or independent from output, then it affects other dependent variables such as the extent of disclosure, but the same is not true in reverse, at least in the short run.[49] Such firm's attributes can be called "unidirectional or asymmetrical." The relationship between firm's constant attributes (e.g., firm size) and the quality of voluntary disclosure is a unidirectional relation. Firm size can be a variable that can be changed in the long run but is a constant in the short run.

Some of firm-specific attributes such as firm size, listing status, and industry type can be classified as unidirectional determinants, and thus "pre-determinism approach" may be considered in explaining the relationship between the firm's attributes and disclosure. For regulators or exchanges, it is well worth trying to use unidirectional determinants as the reference of disclosure policy under the condition that these are stable and influential in the long run.

3) Bidirectional determinants

When both variables affect each other, these are bidirectional or symmetrical. The firm's intrinsic attribute can be a bidirectional determinant when it affects the market and is also influenced by the market responses in the short run, which means that a bidirectional determinant and voluntary disclosure are mutually influencing.

There is no room for "predeterminism" for bidirectional determinants. For example, an enhanced disclosure quality leads to an increased foreign institutional shareholder ratio, which can also increase disclosure pressure and thereby enhance disclosure quality again. In general, a firm's attribute that is in relation to information users tends to be bidirectional. As the significance of investor's dynamic and strategic response increases, growing attention is being paid to bidirectional determinants of the disclosure.

253. Determinants of disclosure

As Meek, Roberts, and Gray (1995) illustrate, firm-specific characteristics such as firm size, country or region, listing status, industry are the most attention receiving determinants of voluntary disclosure.(73)

1) **Environment**

Listing status, listing period

The capital market transaction hypothesis provides theoretical explanations for the role of listing status or listing period in disclosure decision.

a. Multiple listing: Companies listed in global exchanges disclose more information to comply with foreign regulations and obtain funds on favorable terms.(235)

b. Listing status: The level/quality of disclosure is related to listing status.(233,236,237)

c. Listing age: The shorter the listing period, firms are more likely to provide voluntary disclosure. [50] On the contrary, some evidence strongly suggests that the extent of voluntary disclosure is not affected by listing-status.(232,233)

Multi-nationality

Internationally-diversified firms are equipped with various types of information to meet with the requirements of each jurisdiction and tend to disclose more information than domestic firms.(228)

Auditor

The relation between auditor and firms' disclosure is multi-dimensional. A transparent firm may choose to be a client of high-quality auditors to signal their quality, and a firm audited by a credible auditor is pressured to provide more information.

a. Audit firm size: A big audit firm that cares about its reputations are more likely to persuade firms to disclose more and better.(238) Firms audited by large accounting firms are more likely to provide non-mandatory information.(239) However, no significant association was also found between disclosure and the size of audit firm.(237)

b. Type: Empirical evidence between the type of audit firm and disclosure are mixed. A significant positive relationship is evidenced (240), while the type of auditor is evidenced to be non-significant explanatory variables. (241,242)

Analysts following

A positive association is evidenced between the level of disclosure and the number of analysts following.(122) The association between disclosure and analyst following is bidirectional.

a. Disclosure benefit: More and better disclosure can attract analysts and increase analysts following.

b. Determinant: Larger analyst following may put pressures on managers to increase disclosure.

Disclosure precedent

Once specific information is disclosed to the public, information users as a free rider would expect the disclosing firm to maintain the disclosure policy consistently, and an abrupt turn-back from the precedent disclosure policy may give rise to a potential litigation. Thus, managers feel pressure on maintaining the same disclosure patterns. As a result, such a disclosure precedent works as the constraining determinant or the cost of voluntary disclosure.(234) Managers are evidenced to try to avoid setting a disclosure precedent for fear that they might not be able to maintain it in the future. As 69.6% of 401 financial executives avoid or strongly avoid *"setting a disclosure precedent that may be difficult to continue"*, setting a precedent is surveyed to be the most common constraint of disclosure (108)

2) **Financial status**

Firm size

Many studies find that there is a significant relationship between resource availability, such as firm size, and the extent of voluntary disclosure.

First, several explanations relate to using the concept of disclosure benefits.

a. Capital market transaction: Large firms that are relatively more aware of the importance of investor confidence tend to rely more extensively on external financing and commit to more disclosure.(232)

b. Liquidity benefits: Large firms are more concerned about liquidity benefits, and they will voluntarily disclose more information. (125)

c. Cost of capital: For smaller firms, investors will choose smaller positions. The cost of capital for smaller firms will not be affected by large traders, so they disclose less information.(125)

Second, several explanations relate by using the concept of disclosure cost.

a. Direct cost: Larger firms have relatively lower average costs of information production and dissemination due to the fixed component of direct cost; thus, they tend to disclosure more. (73, 232) [51]

b. Proprietary cost: Large firms have lower proprietary costs and less likely to withhold segment information. (175, 232) [52]

c. Political/legal cost: Larger firms are more closely monitored by information users incurring higher political costs, and, as a result, they are more incentivized to disclose better to lessen undesired political or legal pressures.(232)

d. Takeover: Small firms coupled with managerial entrenchment tend to make earnings forecasts less frequently in a hostile bid because they do not expect earnings forecast as a defense mechanism.(243)

In general, the positive impacts of firm size on voluntary disclosure are evidenced. However, the researcher may encounter unexpected results suggesting that the firm size effect is not significant. One persuasive explanation; most stock exchanges accept large firms to protect investors by adopting higher listing requirements (e.g., asset size, profit size), as a result, the size of overall sample firms exceeds a certain level, and thus researcher may encounter unexpected results suggesting that firm size effect is neither significant nor clear. (125, 175)

Implications of studies may be different according to what type of disclosure they analyzed.

a. Annual report: Firm size may be the key explanatory character that is positively associated with the disclosure score of an annual report. A positive association between firm size and the transparency rankings of Standard & Poor's based on the annual report, which suggests that small firms provide less disclosure.(244)

b. Pre-disclosure: Larger firm investors are provided with more private "pre-disclosure" information because a large firm attracts more attention from the market than a small firm. (245)[53] The higher frequency disclosure group in the journal appears to be composed of larger firms (journal). (222)

c. Forecast: Forecast accuracy of a financial analyst is positively associated with firm size.(246)

Financial leverage: debt-to-asset ratio

Studies tend to relate financial leverage to disclosure through the capital market transaction benefit and the agency cost rationale. Leveraged firms will voluntarily disclose more information in order to increase the benefit of capital market transaction (e.g., external financing at lower costs) or to reduce monitoring costs.(228, 237, 247) The ratio of debt to total equity is determined to be statistically significant in explaining the extent of financial disclosure.(248)

Performance: profitability and earning volatility

A theoretical explanation for positive relationships between the voluntary disclosure and performance includes disclosure benefit, the managers' personal motive. Firms disclose positive information (e.g., high performance) and withhold negative ones to maximize disclosure benefit (e.g., investors' confidence).(51) Other highly profitable firms may disclose more information only to increase the managers' compensation.(236) The relation between firms' performance and disclosure is mixed as it is expected to be very dynamic in its nature.

a. Positive: Bad news is more voluntarily disclosed in order to prevent legal actions or to notify about earnings disappointments. Larger disappointments were preceded more often by a more quantitative warning.(46, 223) In addition, firms that issue management forecasts more frequently tend to be characterized by low earnings volatility.(222, 249, 250)

b. Negative: Disclosure indexes vary negatively with profits.(238, 251).

c. Insignificant: Some find an insignificant association between profitability and voluntary disclosure.(228, 252)

3) Ownership, governance

Ownership; concentration

For firms with diffused ownership, the conflicts of interest between manages and shareholders increases, resulting in higher monitoring cost. Thus, information demand and disclosure pressure will be greater. Firms with more dispersed shareholdings prefer public disclosure, while managers of a firm with large block shareholdings are likely to provide private information to large shareholders. Thus, the extent of the disclosure will be greater for firms with diffuse ownership, and accordingly a negative association is evidenced between disclosure quality and ownership concentration in the U.S. market. (243, 247, 253-257)[54]

Ownership; number of shareholders

Agency theory also predicts that managers will respond to the information demand of shareholders, and, as a result, the extent of disclosure level will be positively related to the number of shareholders. The number of shareholders is evidenced to be positively associated with the disclosure index scores of annual reports.(233, 248) It is plausible that shareholder activists are watching firms with a large number of shareholders, which may lead to more disclosure. Shareholder activists might be more monitoring larger firms to be a high-profile campaign.

Ownership; family ownership

Insiders or family owners have relatively free access to private information but less incentive to respond to minor shareholders' information demand. Firms controlled by the family are likely to provide less information. Thus, "*the percentage of family members on the board is negatively related to the extent of voluntary disclosure.*"(258-260)

Ownership; managerial ownership

Lower managerial ownership increases the likelihood of hostile takeover bids. Thus, if managers do not have sufficient ownership to resist the bid, then she tends to rely on alternative defense mechanisms such as forecast disclosure. (243)

Institutional ownership

"*Institutions with a large number of portfolio stocks prefer higher quality disclosure as a way to offset monitoring costs*," and, as a result, the extent of voluntary disclosure and ownership ratio of the institutional investor will be positively associated.(125, 261)

Foreign ownership

Foreign investors who are geographically separated from managers tend to demand more information, and, as a result, foreign ownership is positively associated with the extent of voluntary disclosure.(262) The effect of foreign ownership pressure is expected to be greater in developing countries.

Corporate governance

The structure of corporate governance is essential in reducing the possibility of low-quality disclosure. A variety of studies include board, audit committee, and non-executive director. When the roles of the CEO and the board chair are combined, the quality of disclosure (i.e., share options disclosure) needs to be monitored.(263) The existence of an audit committee is positively related to the extent of voluntary disclosure.(258) The ratio of independent non-executive directors to the total number of directors is positively associated with the comprehensiveness of financial disclosures.(264)

4) Industry

Industry type

The industry type or sector may have an impact on the extent of voluntary disclosure because proprietary cost or political cost vary across industry type. Firms in the industrial or commercial sectors are more likely to provide voluntary disclosure.(73, 239, 265) Firms operating in a more regulated industry are likely to experience more political cost and thereby have less incentive to disclose.

Industry practice

Some of the non-firm specific determinants include such as industry practice, regulatory environment. Firms can be influenced by rules and social practices, such as disclosure practice of an industry or association. Thus, researches are approaching with social and cultural determinism that is the theory that social and cultural interactions determine individual behaviors.

For example, timeliness of annual earnings announcements (e.g., reporting lag) appears to be more associated with industrywide disclosure patterns and traditions than firms' individual attributes.(266) Disclosure quality in the same industry is not easily observable, but industrywide disclosure practice is observable. Such a nature makes firms a follower of industry disclosure practice. For example, a misreporting could increase with product market competition. Firms can be enticed to manage their earnings to catch up with product market competition, especially when they face with fraudulent disclosure of industry-leading competitors (e.g., inflating performance).(267, 268)

Product market competition

Product market competition impacts disclosure. Perfect competition leads all firms to have homogeneous information that may result in a voluntary disclosure. In a competitive market, firms can make a rational conjecture about the competitors' financial conditions. The associations between competition and disclosure are frequently explained by the rationales of proprietary cost and agency cost.

a. Proprietary cost: Proprietary cost depends on product market competition and impacts the extent of voluntary disclosure.(189, 198, 269)

b. Agency cost: Product market competition works as an efficient 'disciplinary and monitoring mechanism' by deterring managers from less credible disclosure (i.e., misreporting).(268) It aligns managers' incentives with shareholders' interests and reduces the agency cost and the private benefits of control.(270, 271) Due to such an alignment, there is a positive relationship between product market competition and voluntary disclosure.

254. Limitations & considerations

Proxy of disclosure

Empirical evidence on the determinants of disclosure depends on the proxy of disclosure. A determinant can be associated positively with some types of disclosure while negatively with other because the firm's incentive depends on the characteristics of information. A cost structure of forecast information is far different from that of descriptive information. Thus, researchers should pay attention to the attributes of the disclosed information. For example, empirical evidence researched with the proxy of annual reports can be inconsistent with the evidence with the proxy of forward-looking information.

Impact pathway

Although a factor is evidenced to have a significant statistical relation with disclosure, the impact pathway should also be evidenced. Especially, if a determinant is expected to impact disclosure behavior through both disclosure benefit and disclosure cost, then the impact pathway will provide more implication than empirical relation itself. Without a proper understanding of its pathway, a firm's or regulator's policy to enhance disclosure quality might bring about the unexpected side effects.

Dynamic natures

The impact of a bidirectional determinant is inherently dynamic. Manager's decision is strategic, while investor's responses are not homogeneous. Empirical research is very limited in analyzing such dynamic interactions.

Correlation

Most of the determinant analysis rely on correlation analysis but interpret as if there exists a cause-and-effect relation. It is not sure whether the bidirectional factor affects disclosure quality or the converse is true.

Endogenous relationship & manager's motives

A determinant of disclosure can affect disclosure decisions in combination with the manager's personal motives. A disclosure will generally reduce information asymmetry. However, the current level of transparency can also affect the manager's disclosure decision. For example, managers facing severe information asymmetry may provide voluntary information to enhance current disclosure quality proactively. On the contrary, managers can reduce disclosure when they are contaminated by opportunistic motives. A complex endogenous relation between disclosure and information asymmetry should be considered in interpreting empirical evidence.

Sources of complexity

If we find out what affects disclosure, then we can learn how to enhance transparency by improving the determinants of disclosure. However, firms' disclosure policy is not solely affected by a single factor. It is the manager who makes disclosure decision, but they are influenced by several factors; environmental factors (e.g., economic, legal, political), firm's attributes (e.g., size, structure), and managers' private motives (e.g., bonus, stock option). To top that off, some factors work as catalysts or motivators of disclosure, while others as deterrents or constraints. Thus, research on the determinants of disclosure is not simple, even though it might first appear straightforward.

Context-specific nature

Furthermore, determinants are context-dependent from country to country, from market to market. For example, industry (i.e., agricultural sector) is significantly associated with voluntary disclosure in Kenyan capital market, while the agricultural sector is not mentioned to be a significant factor at all in developed markets.(272)

26. Disclosure effect

There is no consensus for the concept of the "disclosure effect." It depends on the purpose of individual study, and terminologies are different by researchers. For the specific purpose of this book, the "disclosure effect" is defined as realized consequences of disclosure that influences investors and third parties (e.g., competitors, regulators, commodity markets, and labor markets) whether intended or unintended, positive or negative. Any consequences that are already mentioned, such as disclosure benefits, disclosure costs, and disclosure motives are excluded from disclosure effect.

261. Effects on investors

Subsidy effects

Investors can derive significant benefits from the subsidy of firms' disclosure. They can save the information search cost and thereby search for more information about the firm or other firms, which can increase investor's welfare (i.e., utility) and overall liquidity (e.g., trading volume, investor base). A reduced information search cost results in an increased investment yield.

Reduction of duplicative investment

If firms do not publicly release information, individual investors will devote themselves to a private information search. As a result, they can be individually better off by the private information search but collectively worse off because they are making a duplicative investment. Diamond (1985) develops a model to explain firm's voluntary disclosure that provides benefit to all investors by creating an information cost savings effect and reducing the duplicative investment of private information search. Through this information cost savings effect, disclosure leads to increased liquidity. (50)

Firm's cost advantage in information production

It is reasonable to assume that firm has a cost advantage over investors in information search. Since the firm's information production cost is assumed to be less than the aggregated costs of all investors, firm's disclosure policy can significantly reduce the aggregate cost of information acquisition and make all investors better off. Investors generally attach the information search cost to the bid or ask price, resulting in the wider bid-ask spread. In a market of full disclosure, the bid-ask spread can be reduced by the imputation of information cost from individual investors to the disclosing firm, and investors would trade more because the breakeven point can be lowered by reduced information cost. (50)

262. Effects on third parties

2621. Externality

Background

Henry Sidgwick (1838~1900) is credited with initiating the term "spillover costs and benefits (externalities)," and Arthur C. Pigou (1877~1959) is credited with formalizing the academic concept of externality. Pigou illustrated the concept of the externality by using the example of railway sparks that could ignite and destroy the surrounding forest.(273, 274) While the case of "railroad and forest" is a negative externality, the frequently illustrated case of "beekeeper and flower house" is a positive externality. The externality of disclosure in the capital markets can be viewed as a similar case of a positive externality.

Informational externalities

Historically, the concept of externality was coined to capture the effects occurred to other parties that are located near. In the capital markets, the disclosure of a firm conveys informative "implications" to its peer firms and related firms, and a firm's decision sometimes happens to affect other firms' decisions when they are related or similar.

In the accounting and finance literature, terms such as "information transfer effect," "information spillover effect," or "contagion effect" refer to the association between the disclosure of "a firm" and the stock price movements of "other non-disclosing firms" that might or might not share common attributes.

Regardless of whatever name is given, such an informational externality in the capital market context is about how investors of other firms respond to the disclosure of a firm. Consequently, in defining the externality of disclosure, it could be useful to capture all types of effects that are generated to other firms by the disclosure of a firm.[55]

Economic implications

The externality of disclosure is generated when a firm's disclosure guides investors to reassess other firms that have the similarity, relatedness, or rivalry with the disclosing firm. Such externalities generated by disclosure potentially help investors in reducing the information asymmetry of other firms.

Due to the disclosure of X, investors can reduce the cost of analysis for firm X and instead reallocate their resources to search for more information about Y, which increases investor's welfare; it may be called the "budget reallocation effect." Investors save the information search cost for information X due to the disclosure of firm X and obtains more information Y from the voluntary information search (i.e., resource reallocation) (Figure 42, A→B).

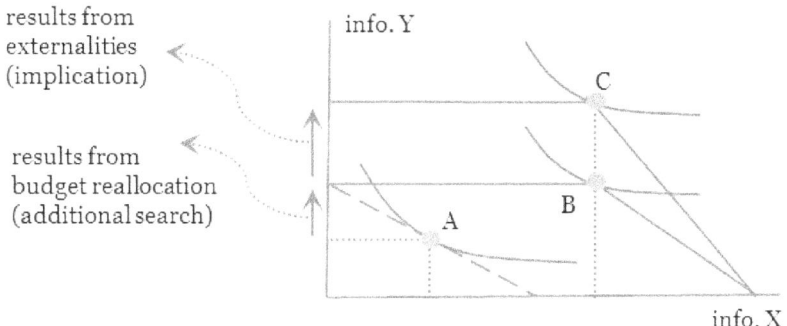

Figure 42 Budget reallocation vs. Externality

What happens if we consider the externality? Investors who obtained the disclosure of X will recognize the similarity to or relatedness with other firms. They can make expectations on the degree of externalities because the disclosure of firm X provides useful informational implications about the inside information of non-disclosing firm Y. Such an informational implication to other firms generates an "income effect," which enlarges the budget line and thus subsidizes investors (Figure 42, B→C). Without additional search for information Y, investors obtain meaningful implications for Y from the disclosure of firm X. Disclosure of a firm X provides investors not with information for Y but with quasi-disclosure (i.e., implication).

2622. Sources of externality

Sources of externalities

If a beekeeper is kept in a greenhouse isolated from a flower house, then there is no room for externality. Disclosure of a firm isolated from other firms cannot affect the stock price of other firms. A firm generally discloses its information not to affect the stock price of other firms but to reveal its true value. As a result, the stock prices of non-disclosing firms are generally expected to be independent of the disclosing firm's disclosure. In an autarky economy in which a firm is completely isolated from others, the stock price of non-disclosing firm is independent from a firm's disclosure.

In the real world, however, any firm is rarely an absolute autarky firm. As a result, a firm's disclosure may affect the stock price of other firms, and such externalities are not uniform but various in patterns, reflecting firm-specific or information-specific natures. Besides, firms that are competing in an industry have the similarity of nature, affected by others, which makes it very complicated to analyze the sources and impacts of externalities.

A real-world economy is differentiated from an autarky economy in the aspect of the "relation." If a "firm-level" attribute such as "relation" creates a "subsistent and objective" cause-and-effect relationship, one event of a firm (i.e., cause) can "actually" affect another event of other firms (i.e., effect) that have been previously independent in an autarky economy.

By the way, some firms may act as if it is an autarky firm in the real economy. Such a firm may have no "objective" relation with other firms and is quite seemingly isolated from others, and, as a natural result, the stock price of the firm would be independent of other firms' disclosure. However, any firm is rarely an absolute autarky firm, even though it is seemingly isolated from the disclosing firm. Besides, even among autarky firms that have no actual relationship with each other, investors may find the "similarity" from firms' attributes and recognize an association that is not subsistent but perceptional or subjective. Due to such a market- or investor-level mechanism of "investor's perception," even the disclosure of a seeming autarky firm can be recognized as if it affects the stock price of other similar firms.

To sum up, a firm-level mechanism (i.e., relation) and a market-level mechanism (i.e., investors' perception of similarity) can be attributed as sources of the externality of disclosure. A firm-level "relation" generates an "objective and subsistent" cause-and-effect relationship, while investors' perceptions a "subjective and seeming" cause-and-effect relationship. Investors' perception can never change a firm's intrinsic nature but often create a perceptional and seeming cause-and-effect relationship in the capital markets.

In general, the degree to which a disclosing firm is identified by other firms seems to determine the type or degree of externalities. For example, Jorion and Zhang (2010) suggested that the externality arises the firm-specific nature of firms (i.e., relation, similarity) and the investor's perception. (275) The relatedness leads to the causality effect regardless of the heterogeneous nature, while the similarity leads to the similarity effect.

Table 4) Sources of Externality

Sources		Similarity		
		Homogenous (Similar)		Heterogenous (different)
		Same industry	Other industry	
Relation	Related	Causality	Causality	Causality
	Non-related	Similarity Competition	Similarity	Systematic

Relation: causality effect

Some firms have an objective and direct relationships with other firms. Firms often establish such strategical relations to achieve their purposes of firm value maximization. What represents such a strong relatedness includes financial relations (e.g., shareholder, loan), operational relations (e.g., customer, trade), strategic relations (e.g., coalition, alliance), or geographical proximity (e.g., high-tech industry complex).

A counterparty risk can arise among firms when they have direct or indirect, commercial or financial relations that generate a cause-and-effect relationship in many areas. As a result, disclosure of a firm that is "related" with other firms can naturally reveal direct implicative information about other firms. Especially large firms tend to have more diverse relations. For example, the financial distress of a firm can affect other firms that are closely tied.(276, 277)

The direction of the causal effect is often in the same direction but basically depends on the nature of the relation. The fact that the real-economy relation creates substantial effects on the counterparty, regardless of whether investors perceive or not, deserves particular emphasis. For example, a credit risk or default disclosure can cause financial distress on other firms that are in close business ties, regardless of whether investors perceive the business relation or the default news.

The impact is reported to be stronger if high-type firms (e.g., large firms) signal bad news because large firms imply more diverse relationships with multiple counterparties and more trusted. (275, 278) Firms that are more related (e.g., subsidiary, or same auditor) would have a more pronounced externality. The more related to those of the restating firm, the more pronounced the externality.(279, 280)

Similarity: similarity effect

Without any relation between firms, the stock price of other non-disclosing firms is independent of the disclosure of a firm, and an independent variable cannot affect other independent variables. In the capital markets, however, human's perception can create an effect as if there were a specific relation between independent variables.

Typically, investors alter their opinion, attitudes, and decisions in response to what they perceive. Disclosure of a firm of which attributes are "similar" to other firms can provide implications of other non-disclosing firms. Such a similarity effect may be defined to include such cases as the intrinsic nature of business is in higher resemblance to each other even without any significant real-economy relation. As a result, the similarity effect makes the other non-disclosing firms' stock price move together with the disclosing firm's stock price.

Disclosure of a firm with similar firm-specific natures might potentially imply other non-disclosing firms' inside information. Investors perceive the existence of the similarity in firms' natures and also calculate the probability of a similar event that might happen to other non-disclosing firms. If a firm is more similar to other firms, then it may be inferred that other non-disclosing firms' stock price might react in the same manner with the disclosing firm's stock price. The more the similarity, the stronger the inference of a similar event.

The externality generated from the similarity effect is purely an informational effect that comes from the investors' perception and predictive responses in the capital market. The causality effect comes mainly from the existence of relation, while the similarity effect comes purely from the investor's perception about the similarity of firm-specific natures. The perceptional externalities driven by the similarity effect have been ever-present in the capital markets.

Researchers have attempted to find out the existence and determinants of the externalities in the capital markets by analyzing the association between the disclosure of a firm-specific event and the stock price movements of other firms. Studies include material disclosure events such as bankruptcy(281), debt rating(275), M&A and seasoned equity issue(282), restatement(279), earnings announcement(279), forecast(279, 283), dividend(279, 284, 285), earnings performance(286). More similar firms in the cash flow, product line, or disclosure quality would have a more pronounced externality. The more similar the competitor's characteristics to the restating firm, the more pronounced the externality (i.e., contagion effect).(279, 280) Evidence shows that a firm's accounting restatements adversely (i.e., same direction) affect non-restating firms in the same industry.(286) Investors may require an additional risk premium for other non-disclosing firms in the same industry when a firm's bad news signifies industry-wide shock.(275)

Competition effect

The competition effect can arise from a firm's disclosure due to the product market competition. A firm's disclosure of an event that may weaken the competitive advantage of the disclosing firm can increase the competitors' stock price. The direction of the competition effect occurred to competitors is opposite to that of the disclosing firm. For example, a firm's disclosure of epoch-making innovation negatively affects the stock price of other competing firms that are not ready for such technology, and bankruptcy of a firm leads to an increase in the stock price of other competing firms that are robust in finance. One man's mistake is another man's opportunity, and one man's opportunity is another man's problem. For example, competitors can benefit from the reduction of production capacity of the disclosing firm and attract customers of the bad news disclosing firm. (281, 287)

Systematic effect

Systematic effect refers to an effect that spreads over the market or industry affecting the entire group. Systematic effect of disclosure may be defined as the stock price movement of other non-disclosing firms that vary coherently from a firm's disclosure and therefore produce systematic responses, which finally result in the systematic errors of stock returns that cannot be reduced to zero by averaging. Systematic effect may occur when a firm discloses an economy-wide common factor, regardless of the similarity or relatedness. For example, if a large firm discloses material information that signals a future economy-wide recession, then all stock prices can vary coherently with the stock price of the disclosing firm.

Comparison: competition effect vs. proprietary cost

The proprietary cost of disclosure means the indirect disclosure cost that occurs "to the disclosing firm" by the firm's disclosure of information that is proprietary in nature. In contrast, the competition effect is the disclosure effect, especially externality, that is generated by a firm's disclosure "to investors" about other non-disclosing competitors. However, the proprietary cost and the competition effect are not completely different but the two sides of the same coin.

Attention should be paid to the origin of both concepts: the competition effect is coined mainly to explain the externality by comparing with the similarity effect, while the proprietary cost is used to explain the principle of the manager's disclosure decision. Consequently, what is significantly different from the competition effect is that the proprietary cost provides the rationale of "confidential treatment."[56]

2623. Determinants of externality

Causality/Similarity

The degree of externality depends on what determines the investor's perceptions. It depends on the degree of causality/similarity and the nature of firms.

a. Similarity or causality: The degree of the similarity or causality between a disclosing firm and peer firms will determine the degree of investor's perception and externality. If firms are more similar or strongly related, then a firm's disclosure can generate more externalities. For example, investors impose a larger penalty on peer firms when the peers and the restating firm use the same external auditor (i.e., similarity). (286)

b. Conspicuousness: The degree of disclosing firm's conspicuous nature (i.e., leveraged, large size) may be an influential determinant since disclosure of a more conspicuous firm can be easily perceived by investors. The conspicuous disclosure of a firm or the disclosure of a conspicuous firm can persuade investors to alter the investment decisions on other firms. (279) Evidence reports that a sudden change in the spread of a defaulted large firm can generate greater change in the perception of risk in the bonds of other firms, regardless of the causal effect relationships.(288) Bad news (e.g., rating downgrade) of a high-type firm (e.g., higher-rated, investment grade) are more likely to create the contagion effect. (275)

c. Sensitivity: The degree of the sensitivity of peer firm's nature can determine the degree of externality. If peer firms have more susceptible characteristics (i.e., poor governance, low disclosure quality), then there might be more pronounced externalities. For example, firms with high leverage will have more pronounced externalities than low leveraged firms. The greater the leverage, the more sensitive the equity value is to accounting restatement.(279) Evidence shows that peer firms with lower accounting quality (e.g., high accruals) experience a more stock price decline than those with higher disclosure quality. Investors seem to presume peer firms with higher accruals are more similar to the restated firm or more likely to restate.(286)

Competition effect: Competition of industry, competitiveness

The determinants of the competitive effect are various. The degree of the competition effect depends on the degree of competition, the nature of a disclosing firm and peer firms.

a. Competition: If firms are more competing in the industry, then the competition effect is greater. For example, Goldman, Peyer, and Stefanescu (2009) found that the competition effect is strong in the concentrated industry, which tends to have a greater competition effect because firms in such an industry have more to lose. (281, 287) Chen, Ho, and Shih (2007) concludes that "rivals' share prices are more adversely affected when ... the industry is less competitive ..." (289)

b. Deep/easy pocket: If the disclosing firm leaves more, then the competition effect is greater. For example, Goldman, Peyer, and Stefanescu (2009) found that the competitive effect is particularly stronger with large firms. Customers of a large fraud firm might move to rival firms, leaving more that can be picked up by rivals.(281, 287) By the way, if the disclosing firm leaves something to be picked up easily by others, then the competition effect is greater. For example, Jorion and Zhang (2010) found that industry rivals are more likely to benefit from the bad news (e.g., rating downgrade) of a low-type firm (e.g., speculative-grade), implying that the competition effect is greater for the bad news of low-type firms. The severity of financial distress of a firm is positively associated with the extent of benefits to industry rivals.(275, 290)

c. Ability to prey: If rival firms of a disclosing firm are more likely to pick up from the disclosing firm, then the competition effect is greater. For example, Goldman, Peyer, and Stefanescu (2009) found that rival firms with better governance experience a higher return (i.e., competition effect). However, rival firms with greater information asymmetry experience a serious externality in the same direction (i.e., spillover effect) by a firm's fraud announcements, implying that investors seem to conjecture the possibility of fraud based on the degree of information asymmetry of other non-disclosing firms.(281, 287)

Nature of information

The degree and direction of externalities depend on the attributes of the disclosed information: good news vs. bad news, proprietary information vs. non-proprietary information, financial statements vs. narrative statements, or economy-wide impacts (e.g., bankruptcy) vs. firm-specific impacts (e.g., restatement). If investors perceive that the disclosure of a firm involves an economy-wide common factor (e.g., signs of recession), then the firm's disclosure may trigger the economy-wide externalities that affect all firms, regardless of the similarity or relatedness, which may be named as the "systematic effect."

2624. Net effect

Most firms are operating in an industry and thus share the similarity among firms to a certain degree. However, even though firms in the same industry are basically similar, individual firms can have apparently different natures. Besides, a disclosing firm's mistake is competitors' opportunity, which generates the competition effect. Consequently, disclosure can have countervailing effects; similarity effect and competition effect. The competition effect is unique in the sense that its direction is opposite to the similarity effect. In general, bad news of a disclosing firm tends to yield a negative abnormal return, but it is not clear how bad news impacts the stock prices of other competitors. Both effects should be discussed in a balanced way to properly measure the overall impacts. When the similarity effect dominates the competition effect, the stock price of the rival firms will show the same pattern with that of the disclosing firm. But, when the competitive effect dominates the similarity effect, it will show the opposite pattern.(279, 281, 291)

In conclusion, the net effect of externality depends on the relative magnitude of each effect. The similarity effect dominates the competition effect when the other firms are apparently similar in natures from the disclosing firm. For example, if other firms are recognized to be apparently similar to the disclosing firm regarding the technological advances, then the similarity effect may dominate the competition effect even though the disclosing firm disclosed technological advances very enthusiastically. In contrast, if the degree of the similarity quite scant, and the similarity among firms is originated only from the fact that they are in the same industry, then the competition effect of the disclosing firm that is disclosing epoch-making innovation will dominate the similarity effect. However, it is very tough to separate one effect from another in the empirical studies.

The original level of bond rating influences the net effect of bond rating downgrade. The similarity effect dominates when firms with an investment-grade rating experience a rating downgrade, while the competition effect dominated for firms with a speculative-grade.(275)

Investors of firms with an investment-grade rating might respond sensitively to a bond rating downgrade of other similar firms because they pay careful attention to the downgrade news that affects their investment returns. In contrast, investors of firms with a speculative-grade might have nothing to fear about additional downgrades and thus do not pay attention to a downgrade of other similar firms. However, a speculative-grade investor who is risk-taking might respond to competitors' downgrade news when the rating downgrade of competing firm with a speculative-grade seems to enhance the competitive advantage in the industry. In the U.S., the similarity effect is evidenced to dominate for Chapter 11 bankruptcy announcements (i.e., reorganization), while the competition effect dominate for Chapter 7 bankruptcy (i.e., liquidation).(281, 292) A firm that discloses the liquidation quits its business, and as a result competitors may benefit more, which results in the greater competition effect.[57]

Some evidence are suggested for bad news such as bankruptcy announcements or earnings restatements. Regarding bankruptcy announcements, a net contagion effect is evidenced that *"the competitive effect is dominant in industries where leverage and the degree of competition ... are low."*(281) Regarding earnings restatements, it is reported that there is a significant similarity effect but no competitive effect. Earnings restatement neither have a long-run impact on the investor confidence of rival firms nor significantly change the cost of equity Of rival firms. Thus, the similarity effect can only be attributed to changes in the perceived short-run risk of rival firms.(279)

27. Opportunistic disclosure

271. Discretion & opportunism

2711. Neoclassical approach: discretion

Unavoidable needs of discretion

Disclosure discretion is often defined as the ability of managers to decide whether to disclose and how to disclose. Firms make a voluntary disclosure to provide the benefits of reducing both information asymmetry and agency conflicts between principals and agents. Managers are expected to make strategic disclosure decisions based on their experiences, which can contribute to the firm value maximization. In order to achieve those ends, managers inevitably exercise disclosure discretion up to a certain extent. Altogether, the existence of disclosure costs that are various and dynamic gives a lucid explanation for why managers should exercise their discretion in disclosure decisions.

Discretion is inescapable

From time to time, there are cases where disclosure discretion weakens disclosure regulation or shareholder's requirements. Besides, where rigorous regulation is in place but without any explicit guidelines on what and how to disclose, managers will disclose something but exercise discretion over the quality of disclosure.(293) As a result, we need to pay attention to the possibility of the abuse of discretion. We should not rule out the necessity and significance of managers' disclosure discretion, even in the mandatory disclosure context. Any law cannot be written without allowing discretion. Instead, regulators should serve the capital markets to guide the managers to exercise their disclosure discretion in accordance with the interests of firms and investors.

Optimum level of discretion

It is an essential issue for information users, whether and why managers disclose or withhold. Naturally, a better understanding of the principles of how managers make a discretionary decision will lead investors to interpret the disclosed information properly and guide regulators to more effective regulation.

Managers take into account both potential benefits and costs that are associated with discretionary disclosure. Be careful that managers are assumed to exercise disclosure discretion for firms and act in the best interests of the firm under the neoclassical theory that assumes dedicated and non-opportunistic managers who act in good faith and in the best interests of the firm. They should not involve self-interest because they have the duty of loyalty, pursuing firm value maximization and thus exercising the optimal level of non-opportunistic discretion only to maximize firm's net benefits of disclosure.(294)

As a result, the interests of manager and investors are aligned. Managers who pursue the maximum level of discretion will choose to exercise their discretion at the highest level of the benefit of discretion (Figure 43, A). However, manager's discretion is not boundless but restricted by the cost of discretion perceived by managers. As a result, managers who pursues the optimum level of discretion will exercise their disclosure discretion to maximize the net benefit of discretion at level B. For example, managers exercise discretion to limit disclosures at the aggregate level so as to more effectively guide investor attention to summarized financial data.(295)

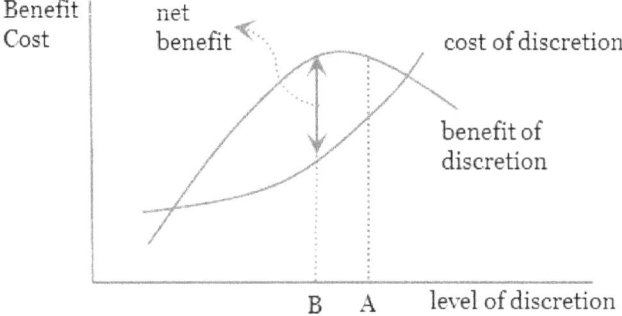

Figure 43 Optimal level of discretion

2712. New institutional approach: opportunism

Principal-agent relation

Discretionary disclosure decision rationale based on the firm's optimization principle under neoclassical theory is not be telling all the truth of disclosure practices. "*The truth is rarely pure and never simple.*"[58] We should pay careful attention to the possibility of managers' opportunistic disclosure decisions. The neoclassical theory overlooks the role of "institutions."

On the contrary, the "new institutional economics" attempts to explain the behavior of institutions that were beyond the scope of neoclassical economics. Transaction cost, such as agent cost, is a typical example of a fundamental concept in the new institutional economics. When it comes to the transaction cost, optimization is not attainable by market mechanisms. As a result, information-related institutions, such as disclosure regulation and insider trading regulation, emerged to be a new institution to complement the market mechanism. New institutional economics focus on the adverse impacts of many factors that were assumed to be exogenous in neoclassical economics. Among many issues are asymmetric information, agent-principal problem, agent's opportunism, and monitoring costs. For example, they assume that managers (i.e., agents) can be self-serving and opportunistic in their disclosure decisions.

Manager's opportunistic/private optimization

Managers exercise their discretion sometimes to maximize firm value and at other times to maximize their private value. Both freshwater and saltwater are not meant to flow from the same spring, but it happens in the human world. Therefore, it would be more persuasive to assume that managers optimize their disclosure decision by comprehensively considering all the benefits and costs, including their private motives. In the real world, the interests of managers and investors are not aligned, and the guideline of the business judgment rule is easily breached because the agent is separated from the principal. As a result, the neoclassical theory is limited and cannot fully explain various mismatches of the voluntary disclosure motives between firms and managers. The mismatch of disclosure motives inevitably leads to that of the final consequences of disclosure decisions.

In the new institutional view, managers are not assumed to make disclosure decisions on the shareholders' side. In particular, it is probable for managers of firms with severe agency costs to have private disclosure motives that are misaligned from the shareholders' interests at any time. By the way, managers' disclosure incentives can arise from a variety of sources. These incentives include option exercises, insider selling, upcoming equity issues, managers' career concerns, personal litigation risk, receiving option grants with a lower exercise price, and avoiding negative earnings surprises.

The optimal level of opportunistic disclosure discretion is determined by the managers' attitude toward the opportunistic benefits and costs of disclosure discretion. Some opportunistic managers may choose to exercise their e discretion only to maximize their private benefits of disclosure, regardless of the cost of discretion (level A). However, the manager's opportunistic discretion is not boundless but restricted by the private cost of discretion perceived by managers. Thus, opportunistic managers who are rational may refrain from exercising the highest level of discretion but choose the optimal level of opportunism at the level that maximizes their private "net benefit" of discretion (level B).

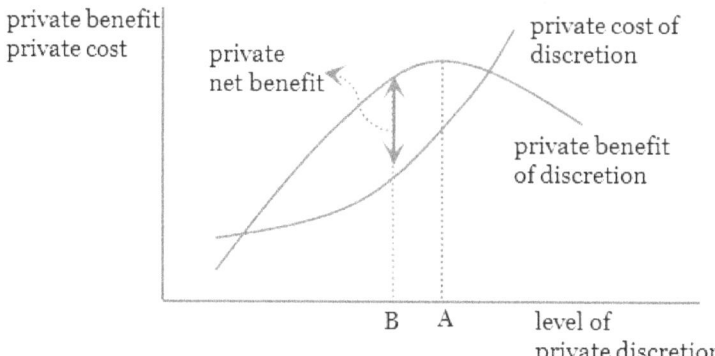
Figure 44 Optimal level of private discretion

2713. Opportunistic disclosure policy

Ritualism vs. opportunism

Gibbins, Richardson, and Waterhouse (1990) identifies two dimensions of managers' disclosure positions; "ritualism and opportunism." The difference lies in whether the manager plays an active or passive role in the disclosure decision. "Ritualism" refers to the propensity of following predefined norms to which the managers are asked to adhere. Ritualistic behavior is passive, repetitive, and standardized.[59] "Opportunism" is the propensity of managers to seek private benefits or a firm's specific advantages by actively managing the disclosure process.(296) However, adhering to the current ritualist procedure might also be opportunistic in some specific environments.

Informational vs. opportunistic

Managers' contradicting purposes of discretionary accruals may include informational vs. opportunistic purposes. First, with discretionary accruals, managers appear to improve information contents by providing private information to the market. Managers' discretion improves investor's ability to predict the profitability and firm value.(297) Second, managers are incentivized to select discretionary accruals for opportunistic private benefits (i.e., bonus awards, stock option). For example, they choose income-decreasing accruals when bonus plans are upper binding.(298)

272. Private motives of disclosure

1) Classification

It is the managers who makes disclosure decisions, but the benefits and costs of disclosure are eventually attributed to shareholders. Since the managers' private incentives under the principal-agent conflicts can give rise to a severe consequence to shareholders, it is useful to classify disclosure motives into "optimization" and "opportunism." "Optimization" refers to a decision that managers, as a faithful fiduciary agent, make disclosure decisions considering the firm's benefits and costs of disclosure. In contrast, "opportunism" refers to the motives that managers make disclosure decisions only by considering private benefits and costs of disclosure, regardless of the firms' benefits or costs.

Table 5) Optimization vs. Opportunism

Optimization	benefits	Capital market transaction hypothesis (upcoming issues, increased liquidity, reduced cost of capital) Deterring competitor, Reducing agency cost Litigation cost hypothesis (deterring)
	costs	Proprietary cost hypothesis Political cost hypothesis Litigation cost hypothesis (trigger risk)
Opportunism /Private motives	benefits	Corporate control contest Management talent signaling/reputation Management entrenchment Reduction of private litigation cost
	costs	Private opportunity cost (loss of information advantage) Private indirect costs

2) Private benefits of disclosure

Corporate control contests

When hostile bidders typically try to attack the poorly performing target firms, target managers try to defend with whatever tactics, such as voluntary disclosure of earnings forecast. Voluntary disclosure may successfully result in the failure of bids.

For example, it is evidenced that, in the contested takeover bid, firms tend to disclose additional information, such as profit forecast voluntarily. (299) Brennan (1999) finds that managers of target firms are more likely to make earnings forecasts as an effective weapon to defend the takeover. In the contested bids, target firms may disclose earnings forecasts as a defense tactic that can be taken without shareholder approval. Managers can be motivated to provide earnings forecast as a catalyst to boost the offer in the shareholders' interests seeking the best price since earnings forecast is useful to signal that the true value is higher than the bid price and that the target firm's manager is to resist the bid strongly.

However, no significant association was found between earnings forecasts and the success of bids where "success" is defined as the increase in the offer price.(243) In a survey, profit forecasts are the most common defense so far as the 45% of targets provided profit forecasts after bid attack. However, no significant associations are found between profit forecasts by targets and the success of the bid. Some explanations are suggested that profit forecasts might not provide meaningful information, or investors were skeptical.(243, 300)

Management talent signaling/reputation

The management talent signaling hypothesis describes that managers are more likely to disclose good news voluntarily in order to increase firm value, distinguish themselves from their colleagues or competitors, and reduce the risk of being replaced. An entrenched manager may try to inform the market actively only for personal reputation, even though the leakage of the critical proprietary information to competitors can harm the firm's value seriously. A talented manager whose objective is to maximize firm value will be motivated to make earnings forecasts voluntarily in advance of actual earnings announcements. It is assumed that investors assess the managers' ability more favorably when the managers anticipate the firm's future earnings accurately. In other words, the market value of a firm depends on the investors' perception of the management ability to forecast future earnings.(301)

The accuracy of the earnings forecast is associated with higher compensation and career prospects. Managers with the ability to forecast accurately deserve higher rewards because such ability signals the managerial talent and higher firm value. It is evidenced that superior forecasters are reaping the rewards, such as higher salary, equity pay, and career advancement in the subsequent year.(302)

Managers have to bear the reputational costs if they fail to make high-quality disclosure. Information users dislike low-quality disclosure, such as adverse earnings surprises or delayed bad news. If managers fail to disclose bad news in a timely manner, then information users impose reputational costs on less candid managers and decide not to follow the stocks, resulting in the lower stock price and liquidity. Thus, managers may have reputational incentives to make preemptive disclosure even for the negative news. (46)

Management entrenchment

During an economy-wide depression, not poor performance but poor disclosure could be blamed by shareholders. Managers might disclose information over legal requirements in order to keep investors well informed of poor performance, as a result, retain corporate control and position.(57) Poor performance frequently provides the justification for CEO turnover and increases the probability of hostile takeovers. However, if the stock return reflects the information on managers' efficiency, then the probability of management turnover can be reduced. As a result, managers may try to lower the risk of job loss by explaining away the poor performance with the voluntary disclosure.(303, 304) Since earnings forecast is handy to signal that the target firm's managers are competent, managers can be motivated to provide the earnings forecast as an entrenchment tool to retain their jobs.

(243)
Reduction of private litigation risk: Private preemption effect
"Stockholders may sue when there are large stock price declines on earnings announcement days since stockholders can allege that managers failed to disclose adverse earnings news promptly. Managers can be held personally liable in such suits, ..."(46) Thus, Managers refrain from trading prior to management earnings forecasts but trade more after forecasts, which means that managers do not exploit private information but rather bond themselves due to the potential legal liability (i.e., private litigation cost of non-disclosure). (214)

3) Private cost of disclosure

Private opportunity cost: loss of information advantage
Information is a valuable asset, and thus there can be severe conflicts of interests between information producers and users. "Information advantage" (i.e., information rent) means a status of having superior information than others, which may contribute to a superior performance. An increased disclosure reduces the information advantage and, as a result, the expected trading profits of insiders. As managers increases the amount of disclosure, the degree of manager's informational advantage necessarily decreases. In contrast, a poor disclosure keeps the market from the effective monitoring but maintains managers' information advantage. Thus, managers have private incentives to avoid the public disclosure.

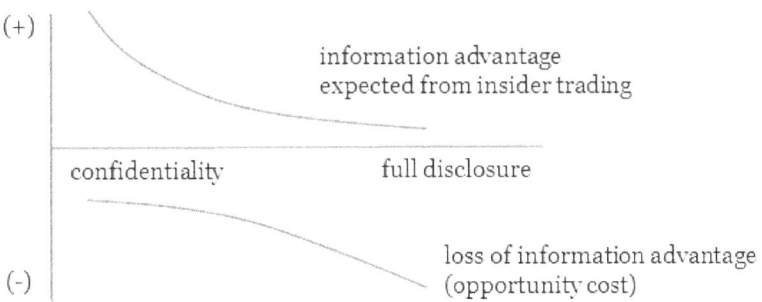

Figure 45 Information advantage and its loss

Private indirect costs
A public release of monopolized inside information can generate indirect cost to both firms and managers. Thus, neoclassical concepts on indirect costs such as proprietary cost, political cost, and litigation cost that occur to the disclosing firm may also be applicable to the disclosing managers in the form of private indirect costs.

a. Private litigation cost: Investors or regulators may find manager's mistakes by using firms' disclosed information and file a lawsuit demanding that the CEO should pay huge amounts of money in damages.

b. Private political cost: Obtaining disclosed information, politician or industrial unionism may place some social stigma on managers for damaging the working conditions and environments, thereby deterring the manager's advancement or job search.

c. Private proprietary cost: All managers who are competing in the job market can take a hint about the management knowhow from the disclosure of competing firms. The managers' skill or knowhow in the job market may be likened to the firm's competitive advantage in the product market. [60]

273. Empirical evidence

Non-existence of disclosure policy

Even though the idea of full disclosure is persuasive, many empirical results have suggested that managers exercise disclosure discretion. According to Bamber & Cheon (1998), a majority of managers (i.e., 76% of respondents) answered to have no particular disclosure policy for the earnings forecast, which signifies that most firms have no formal policies for voluntary disclosure for earnings forecast but rely on the manager's discretion.(199)

Various patterns of discretion

Given that it is difficult for researchers to observe managers' private information directly, empirical studies on managers' disclosure discretion are very limited, but many have tried to assess whether managers exercise discretion in various contexts.

a. Timing: Managers make strategic timing decisions to maximize private wealth by selling more stocks after good news but buying more after bad news disclosure.(214) They tend to report good news during the market trading but release bad news after the market trading.(305) Bad news tends to be delayed, but the reporting lag appears to be more related to the industry patterns than to the firm's attributes. (266)

b. Ex-post verifiability: Managers have the incentive to exercise discretion (i.e., optimistic bias) in using the soft-talk forecast, which can reduce the level of ex-post verifiability. They have the incentive to be optimistic in providing the soft-talk cash flow forecasts.(306)[61] They choose to provide the lowest possible benchmark in evaluating current earnings to highlight the most favorable change in earnings.(307)

c. Missing: Accounting standards provide guidelines on R&D expenditure, but there are rooms behind for managerial discretion. Managers can deliberately attempt not to separate R&D from other expenses. Missing R&D information is not just an accidental outcome but a deliberate choice.(101) They exercise discretion in filing patents because a highly significant technical knowledge can be exposed to the competitors.(308)

Characteristics of information

The nature of information differently affects the disclosure benefits and costs, the motives of discretion, and thus the patterns of discretion.

a. Favorability: Managers show asymmetric patterns in exercising discretion. They are likely to release positive earnings forecasts more often than bad news. Some explains such asymmetric patterns of motives with option exercises, insider selling, and managers' career concerns. (37, 45, 304, 309, 310) Good news disclosures tend to be quantitative estimates (i.e., point, range), while bad news tend to be qualitative to preempt large negative earnings surprise. However, managers have a strong incentive to report bad news early to reduce the litigation cost of delay.(46) Managers are motivated to disclose bad news to receive stock options at a lower exercise price.(311) They provide qualitative disclosures with similar frequency, regardless of the favorability of forecasts. But, they are more likely to supplement good news forecasts with verifiable forward-looking statements to increase credibility.(62)

b. Earnings management: Earnings management can be viewed as a managers' discretionary choice. However, evidence is mixed. (298)

c. Segment disclosure: Regarding segment information, evidence is consistent with the proprietary cost hypothesis. However, researchers also point out that agency costs are also important; managerial agency costs could also explain the discretion in segment disclosure.(99, 312, 313)

274. Consequences of opportunistic discretion

Graphical implication

Managers' discretion based on the opportunistic purpose is likely to increase market noise, while discretion based on the information signaling purpose might improve the informativeness and credibility. As a result of opportunistic discretion, investors face a welfare reduction, and the disclosing firm can be associated with a variety of costs.

Once the degree of accuracy falls below a certain threshold level driven by opportunistic discretion, the disclosure *"becomes a liability rather than an asset." "It becomes "misinformation," and people will stop using it."*(61)

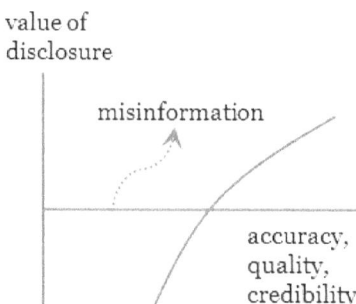
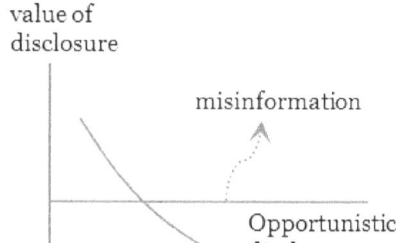

Figure 46 Value of misinformation   Figure 47 Opportunistic disclosure

Source) Figure 46 is modified from NewZealand Government (2018)(61)

If the manager of firm X exercises opportunistic discretion in providing information X, the budget line is expanded, the disclosure will be provided at x_1 and the "nominal equilibrium" is NE (Figure 48). But the "actual equilibrium" will stay at AE if the disclosed information is not well assimilated. Higher level of indifference curve cannot be achieved if the opportunistic disclosure is not well assimilated. As a result, rational investor's "actual" equilibrium is far different from the "nominal" equilibrium. In worst case, opportunistic discretion results in the deterioration of rational investor's welfare (shifting from NE to AE).

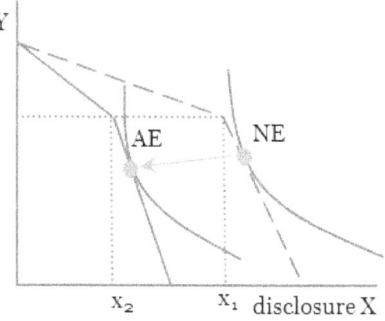

Figure 48 Opportunistic disclosure

Empirical evidence

The rational investor who can discern the managers' disclosure strategies will force them to internalize the information-gap cost that is incurred by misrepresentation. Thus, in equilibrium, managers are likely to report truthfully to avoid the information-gap cost.(314) Consequently, how opportunistic disclosure discretion is interpreted by the market is an important issue. The degree of investors' skeptical response for opportunism determines the magnitude and direction of stock price reaction.

   a. Price: Stock price reacts to the early earnings announcements more prominently than to the late announcements, which implies that information quality decreases with the reporting lag, and investors' skepticism for the manager's discretion is reflected in the price.(266)

   b. Credibility: In a mandatory disclosure context, investors pay less attention to the reporting reputation or incentives of managers. In a voluntary disclosure context, investors pay serious attention to the credibility of disclosure. For example, the disclosed information inconsistent with the managers' incentive of disclosure is considered more credible.(315)

275. Measures against opportunism

1) Regulation on discretion

Pros

Investors are interested in the quality and credibility of voluntarily disclosed information. Thus, the manager, as a faithful and royal agent, should exercise disclosure discretion only to maximize the firm's net benefits of disclosure by eliminating opportunistic and private motives. One may suggest that manager's disclosure discretion should be limited or restricted to prevent the deterioration of investors' welfare. Regulators who believe that managers exercise discretion opportunistically may come up with a way to limit the manager's discretion.(316) For example, regulators or standard setters adopt more detailed reporting forms and guidelines to limit the manager's reporting discretion.

Cons

There can be some rationale on why disclosure discretion should not be regulated. Whether the opportunistic effect is more significant than the information effect is yet evidenced. Adopting regulation on disclosure discretion may create unexpected byproducts such as a complete disclosure avoidance due to a high cost burden. Neither theory nor evidence supports a specific regulation that can generate optimal disclosure decisions. Besides, managers' strategic disclosure does not necessarily mean fraudulent misrepresentation. In a mandatory disclosure context, evidence suggests that the credibility of reporting is unrelated to manager's reporting reputation, and information users accept the news with the higher levels of credibility even though the reported news is consistent to managers' incentive.(315)

2) Contractual mechanisms to reduce opportunism

Stock compensation hypothesis

Managers are motivated by performance-based compensation or remuneration (e.g., stock appreciation rights, stock option grants) to limit the manager's opportunism. A variety of stock-based compensation schemes provide managers with the incentives of voluntary disclosure to correct undervaluation, increase market liquidity, and meet insider trading regulations.

Many empirical studies are consistent with the stock compensation hypothesis. As a tool to face the agency problem, Baiman & Verrecchia (1996) suggested a plausible stock-based compensation and predict a positive relationship between the stock-based compensation and the level of disclosure. (317) Managers are more likely to provide earnings forecasts when they have managerial compensation incentives. Analyst's disclosure rating is positively associated with stock price-based incentives.(219, 318)

Nevertheless, managers with stock-based compensation can still have a stronger incentive to increase disclosure to achieve private wealth maximization. They may actively disclose private information about future firm value when such disclosure is expected to raise stock prices but withhold with obstinacy when they have bad news. Managers can make opportunistic disclosure to maximize stock compensation. For example, they delay good news but accelerate bad news prior to the award periods since the exercise price is set based on the price of the stock option award date. The abnormal returns of firms that award before earnings announcements are significantly higher than those of firms that award after announcements.(311)

Healy (2001) warns that the agency problem that is related to disclosure cannot be automatically solved by mindlessly adopting stock-based compensation. First, stock-based compensation can be an effective contractual mechanism to mitigate disclosure-related agency problems when it is designed in alignment with appropriate disclosure behavior. A poorly designed stock-based compensation can worsen the agency problem. Second, if stock price deviates from a firm's true value, then stock-based compensation is no more efficient remuneration. Managers will disclose private information about future firm value if such disclosure is expected to raise prices or reduce the risk of the wrong valuation.(57)

Manager's voluntary mechanisms: reputation

A good reporting reputation can be an effective remedy when investors are skeptical of the manager's discretion. For example, if the classification of hybrid securities is discretionary and the manager's classification choice is consistent with their incentives, then investors are sensitive to the manager's reporting reputation.(315) Managers who want to be highly esteemed or avoid litigation would commit to establish an efficient internal control system and prohibit himself from opportunism by adopting firms' policies promoting disclosure and restricting insider trading.(319) A strict internal control system, when in place, generally prohibit managers from opportunistic discretion. However, the self-regulation mechanism at the firm level is not entirely effective. Primarily, a firm's policy promoting better compliance should be established in such a way as to protect shareholder's benefits beyond merely avoiding litigation risk of non-disclosure. Additionally, firms are best advised to avoid adopting the boiler-plate internal control system.

3) **Insider trading regulation**

Disclosure regulation mainly aims to reduce the opportunism of information provision but induce proper disclosure. However, the information is the asset of a firm that might generate severe disclosure costs. As a result, firms should be allowed to exercise disclosure discretion. By the way, the managers' information advantages can be realized by way of insider trading but disclosure regulation about information provision is not enough to reduce the opportunism of insider trading. Thus, securities laws usually adopt insider trading regulations that are based on the philosophy of "disclose of abstain" rule.

28. Disclosure credibility

281. Concept

The primary objective of disclosure is to mitigate information asymmetry by providing material information that is useful for investment decision. The degree to which voluntary disclosure mitigates information asymmetry depends on the degree of credibility. Only credible disclosure can be recognized as a meaningful signal by rational investors. Consequently, researchers have paid much attention to the credibility issues of disclosure. Especially with the increasing attention to the manager's self-serving behaviors, the credibility issue is becoming more important.

However, it is not easy to differentiate credibility from reliability or quality since they have similar meanings to a certain extent. Some may use those concepts interchangeably. According to the lexical definition, "credibility" refers to *"the quality or power of inspiring belief."*[62] As a colloquial term, credibility frequently refers to the degree of power of inspiring belief by the trustworthiness of signal and signaler.

The Statement of Financial Accounting Concepts (SFAC) No. 8 of FASB in September 2010 made it clear that credibility also implies "trustworthiness of management."(320)[63] Considering the opinion of FASB, the colloquial expressions, and the manager's increasing self-serving behaviors, it is recommendable to define credibility as to include the credibility of both individual signal and signaler. Thus, "disclosure credibility" may be defined to signify the power of disclosure or the disclosing firm to inspire information users' belief.[64]

282. Dimensions of credibility

1) Scopes of credibility

The literature on "communication" conceptualizes and measures the credibility of communication by using source credibility, message credibility, and media credibility since the credibility of communication is influenced by its source, message, and media.(321, 322) As disclosure is a type of communication, researches about the credibility of voluntary or mandatory disclosure can also be classified in a similar way. The effectiveness of disclosure is largely determined by the credibility of signaling source (i.e., firm, manager), message (i.e., signal, contents), and media (i.e., channel).

2) Source credibility

The information source, such as disclosing firms and managers, can be used as a predictor of disclosure credibility besides the message and media. Due to the source dependent attributes of information, disclosure source significantly affects the degree of credibility or trustworthiness of disclosure. *"Likewise, every good tree bears good fruit, but a bad tree bears bad fruit."*[65]

Disclosing firm

Firms' attributes are expected to reveal different levels of credibility since the managers' disclosure incentive depends on attributes such as financial distress, earning patterns, and market venue.

a. Financial distress: Managers of stressed firms make optimistic disclosure, and information users discount such optimistic disclosure.(323) Koch (2002) found that the degree of optimistic forecasts is positively associated with the degree of financial distress; however, forecasts of distressed firms tend to be viewed as less credible than forecasts of normal firms.(324)[66]

b. Earnings: Management earnings forecasts of firms with the long patterns of increasing EPS are credible. Investors recognize the disclosure of such firms as more accurate and credible because such firms have more to lose from inaccurate forecasts (e.g., losing reputation). The positive association between EPS growth patterns and credibility is more pronounced for small firms than large firms.(325)[67]

c. Market venue: The market venue can play an important role in credibility. Since OTC investors have fewer information sources, the price reaction to the earnings announcement of OTC firms is more significant than that of NYSE-listed firms.(245, 326)

Disclosing manager: opportunism

Managers are entitled to exercise discretion in disclosure decisions to create greater disclosure benefits, which may harm the source credibility. Altogether, managers face tradeoff relations between the desirable disclosure for investors and the opportunistic self-serving disclosure. As Jennings (1987) explained that the private motives of disclosure determines the credibility of earnings forecasts, and the incentive problems are linked to the source credibility.(327)

Disclosing managers: ability

If managers are free from the opportunistic incentives to bias forecasts, then disclosure credibility mainly depends on the managers' ability to forecast earnings. Jennings (1987) explained that the credibility of earnings forecasts is also dependent on the managers' ability to predict future earnings accurately. The accuracy of prior forecast forms the managers' personal reputation and source credibility.(327) Williams (1996) found that the accuracy of the prior management earnings forecast serves as a useful indicator of the believability for the current management forecast. Investors are likely to recognize subsequent forecasts as being more credible because the managers who disclosed accurately in the prior forecast and established a forecasting reputation are considered to have more ability in the forecast. (328)

3) **Media credibility**

Along with the advent of the Internet, the cases that journalists are convicted of violating the law of insider trading draw researchers' attention to media credibility. The credibility of disclosure depends on the characteristics of medium through which information is disseminated. To study the media credibility, researchers can make a comprehensive survey to rate the investors' subjective opinion on the credibility or trustworthiness of individual media.

283. Measures of credibility

Credibility can be measured by using specific proxies that represent each dimension of credibility. In contrast, the ultimate measure of credibility based on investor's perception and response could also be persuasive because the credibility is a multi-dimensional concept that should be comprehensively measured. Comprehensive approaches to measure the credibility may include; investor's market reaction approach or analyst's response approach.

Investor's market reaction approach

Jennings (1987) suggested that information users' attitudes and responses toward disclosure are determined by the degree of credibility. Their responses toward disclosure, such as the change in belief/portfolio and the price movements, are likely to be more pronounced for more credible disclosure.(327)

Empirical literature that is assessing the credibility of voluntary disclosure assumes that investors recognize disclosure (e.g., forecast) as more credible when those are more associated with market reaction, such as abnormal returns. They are using the market returns as the proxy of disclosure credibility. Market reaction to earnings forecast is larger for more credible forecasts. More credible disclosures have more information contents and, in result, generate stronger stock price reaction.(40, 43, 44, 325, 329, 330)

When disclosed information is perceived to be less credible, investors are more likely to respond with delayed underreaction to protect themselves. When disclosed information is perceived to be highly credible, investors are more likely to respond with a strong reaction. Investors underreact to earnings announcement in the short term, and market drifts to correct in the longer term. Thus, the degree of credibility determines the degree of market under-reaction.(330)

Market reaction approach in determining the level of credibility assumes that investors are perfectly rational. However, market reaction cannot be a complete proxy of credibility because investors suffer from limited rationality. Furthermore, an investor's perception of the disclosure credibility of each firm would not be determined only by the disclosed numbers. They may pay more attention to the unmeasurable and qualitative characteristics of disclosure.

Analyst's response approach

It is rational to assume that managers' forecasts would be more accurate than information user's forecasts (e.g., analyst). Thus, a rational analyst would pay more attention to credible sources and messages. It can be assumed that the credible managers' forecast will subsequently generate analysts' forecast revision. It is evidenced that financial analysts revise their forecasts in response to management forecasts to reduce forecast error. (324, 327, 328, 331) Analyst agreement means the extent to which analysts agree with management forecast. When the consensus of analysts' forecast is close to the management forecast, such forecast is highly credible. As a result, the degree of analysts' agreement with management forecast is a good proxy of the degree of management forecast credibility.

284. Message credibility: disclosure quality

Another line of research moves focal points on the credibility of delivered messages. Studies on the message credibility can be explored by focusing on quality, such as comprehensiveness, accuracy, and discrepancy. Disclosure quality can be viewed as a study on the message credibility.

Information quality

In business, the quality of product or service generally means a status of being suitable for its intended use while satisfying consumer's expectations. In society at large, the concept of "quality" has many variances depending on the arena it is used; however, a significant commonality exists everywhere. The common element of quality is that it refers to the degree to which the users' expectations are met. Quality is inherently a perceptual, conditional, and subjective concept. As information is perceived by humans, so the information quality varies among individual users. Considering the definition of "data quality," "information quality" may be defined as *"the fitness for use by information users,"* or the degree to which information meets the needs of its users.(332)

In contrast, when information quality is used by information producers, they might measure information quality with the degree to which the information meets the producer's needs. Regulators may measure information quality with the degree of how much it is reliable, maintainable, or sustainable. In practice, information quality is rarely measured; instead, they tend to rely on a subjective and rough guess or anecdotal evidence.

In the same manner with commodities, the more the better rule applies to information to a certain extent. The higher the information quality is, the more useful and valuable it is. As information quality increases, the value of information increases but at a diminishing rate. However, inaccurate information is poisonous to information users in terms of wrong decision and inefficiency. Once the information quality falls below a certain level, *"it becomes a liability rather than an asset."* At that level, *"it becomes "misinformation," and people will stop using it."* (61)

Attributes of high-quality information

A considerable number of researches on information quality involve the identification, classification of the desirable attributes of information, showing a huge diversity. Andrus (1971) suggested the utility approach to determine the information quality by discussing four types of utilities. (333)[68] Want and Strong (1996, figure 2) proposed the hierarchical framework of elements used in assessing data quality.(332)[69]

Necessity and limitation of empirical definition

It is very challenging to measure information quality directly due to the nature of information. To top it off, researchers and investors, as an outsider, cannot discern whether the disclosed information is true or not. Therefore, most literature on disclosure relies on a variety of proxies to measure disclosure quality.(334) Operational definitions and empirical measurements of disclosure quality can more or less deviate from the true or theoretical concepts of disclosure quality, which leads to lower the performance of research.

Disclosure satisfaction

Disclosure satisfaction can be defined as the status of investors' satisfaction with the output of disclosure. We cannot directly measure the utility of disclosure in investment decisions but may use the disclosure satisfaction as a substitute to measure the utility of disclosure.(333, 335) For example, CFAI (2018) surveyed the level of satisfaction and general perceptions about segment disclosures. Most of the respondents answered that they are not satisfied since *"segment disclosures are not always presented clearly and ... made comparative analysis more difficult."*(336) The limit of disclosure satisfaction is quite clear: Investors may be satisfied with poor disclosure only because they have outperformed.

285. Measurements of disclosure quality

A great many of studies have attempted to measure disclosure quality, which can be classified by the types of proxy, natures of information, and methodologies.

2851. Classification by the proxy type

It is very simple to classify researches by using the proxy type; direct vs. indirect. Some use the direct approach that uses the proxies of disclosure based on the original disclosure, such as annual reports. Others use the indirect approach that uses the proxies without recourse to the original disclosure.(334)

Indirect approach: disclosure environments-based proxies

The indirect approach does not directly depend on disclosure, but they infer disclosure quality by using proxies that are closely related to disclosure quality.

Direct approach: disclosure-based proxies

Beattie, McInnes, and Fearnley (2004, Figure 1) classified the narrative disclosure in the annual report into the subjective and semi-objective contents.(337) Researchers can study disclosure by analyzing the content of disclosure or constructing the disclosure index based on the content of disclosure.

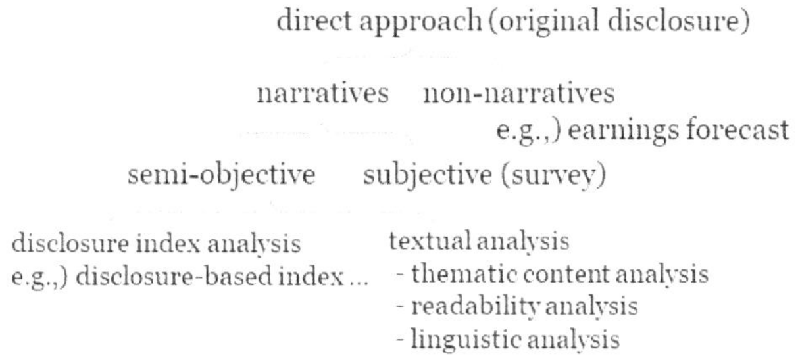

```
                    direct approach (original disclosure)

                  narratives    non-narratives
                                       e.g.,) earnings forecast
        semi-objective    subjective (survey)

   disclosure index analysis    textual analysis
   e.g.,) disclosure-based index ...   - thematic content analysis
                                       - readability analysis
                                       - linguistic analysis

        Figure 49 Direct approaches
```

Source) Figure 49 is modified from Beattie, McInnes, and Fearnley (2004, Figure 1)(337)

2852. Classification by information

Financial information

The financial statement is the most typical hard information that is almost recorded as numbers. It is quantitative, easily collected, and more comparable. It is relatively easier to measure the disclosure quality of financial information. The accounting-based approach will try to measure the magnitude of accruals as a proxy for earnings quality. However, accruals can be created not only by earnings manipulation but also by normal accounting; thus, it is not easy to discern which one is the main cause. Some construct an index with the number of missing or non-missing financial items based on the Blackwell theorem (1951), suggesting that finer information is of higher quality.(96)

Management earnings forecast

Manager's earnings forecasts have different characteristics from other disclosure since it includes forecasts, not facts. Nonetheless, it has been widely used as the measure of disclosure quality since it can be easily verified by calculating forecast accuracy or error. One may argue that forecast accuracy is only the measure of manager's forecast ability, not the measure of disclosure quality. However, an opportunistic manager has the incentive to provide intentionally exaggerated forecasts, which can be interpreted as low-quality disclosure. A high-quality forecast is defined as a forecast with high accuracy and lower distribution.(338-340)

$$\text{Forecast accuracy} = \frac{|(\text{Forecast EPS} - \text{Realized EPS})|}{\text{Price}}$$

$$\text{Forecast dispersion} = \frac{\text{Standard deviation of forecasted EPS}}{\text{Price}}$$

Narrative non-financial information

Non-financial information is often communicated in text or narrative formats. It includes not only facts but also projections and plans. The measurements of disclosure quality for narrative non-financial information can be classified as subjective and semi-objective approaches. The subjective approach includes a disclosure survey. Semi-objective approaches using the disclosure index prevails.

2853. Narratives: subjective approach

The subjective approach can be made by a disclosure survey that examines information users' subjective perceptions and opinions on firms' disclosure. Researchers examine the information user's perception of disclosure quality. This approach is labor-saving even for a sizable number of firms compared to other approaches. For example, the Financial Analysts Federation (FAF) disclosure score is a well-known example of a disclosure survey that provides a comprehensive measure of the extent of disclosure (i.e., periodic report, press releases that are difficult to quantify). The score reflects the perception of financial analysts for firm's disclosure.(338) The Credit Lyonnais Securities Asia (CLSA) examine the analysts' perceptions of corporate governance, transparency, and emerging markets disclosure. (341) ADR-issued firms from emerging markets have incentives to increase the level of voluntary disclosures.(342)

According to Beattie, McInnes, and Fearnley (2004), however, the quality of survey heavily depends on the survey design and the accuracy of respondents' answer. The neutrality and objectivity of respondents are questionable.(337) A disclosure survey is limited because it depends on the subjective opinions of respondents; the researcher cannot understand how the quality is evaluated, and the content of disclosure is not the object of study. Furthermore, respondents might possibly have assigned high scores not for firms with proper disclosure but for firms that are expected outperform.(343)

2854. Narratives: semi-objective approach

Overview

As Beattie, McInnes, and Fearnley (2004) explains, there can be no purely objective approaches to measure disclosure quality; as a result, semi-objective approach is most popular. It includes disclosure index analysis and textual analysis. A great many of empirical research try to measure disclosure quality with many variations of the operational concepts for disclosure quality.(337)

Disclosure index analysis

Disclosure index is invented to measure the extent of disclosure that can cover the extensive lists of disclosed items, including annual reports, interim reports, and conferences. Cerf (1961) is mentioned to be the first to use the concept of disclosure index. (232, 233) Disclosure index analysis is persuasive in showing multifaceted characteristics with a compact format. Many researchers choose to construct their indices that are assumed to be a good proxy of disclosure quality and satisfy their research needs. Disclosure items included in the disclosure index can be weighted or not. (337) (334)

Disclosure quality, in nature, cannot be precisely measured. Under the assumption that disclosure "quality" is positively and strongly associated with disclosure "quantity," many adopt disclosure quantity as a proxy of disclosure quality. Disclosure amount is a primitive measure of disclosure quality. For example, Cerf (1961) used four variables (i.e., method of trading shares, asset size, stock ownership, and profitability) to find positive correlations with disclosure amount. Disclosure quantity includes the amount (e.g., length, bytes) and frequency.(344) Some construct a measure of disaggregation and use it as a proxy of disclosure quality. They capture the degree of disaggregation by counting the number of non-missing financial items reported in firms' annual reports.(345)

Disclosure index analysis is widely used but limited because a simple index is not enough to represent the substance and complexity of disclosure quality that is multidimensional. Altogether, sometimes other researchers cannot follow and reproduce the self-constructed index developed by a researcher. Besides, we should remember that any measure of quantity cannot wholly substitute disclosure quality. Judging from the frequently raised issues of information overload, a positive and strong association between quantity and quality might not always appear to be the case.

Textual analysis

Textual analyses, such as thematic content analysis, readability analysis, and linguistic analysis, are designed to measure the quality of narrative disclosure.

a. Thematic content analysis

The purpose of thematic analysis is to *"extract and analyze themes inherent within the message to identify trends, attitudes ..."*(334)

b. Readability analysis

Readability analysis is to analyze the readability of disclosed information. It tests the degree of the difficulty of disclosed narratives. Readability can be defined as the level of ease with which information user can understand disclosed information. They paid attention to readability analysis after the plain English disclosure regulation of U.S. SEC.

There are some empirical results using the Gunning Fog index.[70] Analysis for the cautionary language suggests that firms at greater risk of litigation provide more readable and less boilerplate disclosure.(216) The negative relationship is evidenced between the readability of annual reports and financial performance (e.g., level of earnings). Managers have an incentive to provide more complex and less readable disclosure to obfuscate bad performance.(346)

However, there are many arguments. the Gunning Fog index is designed to measure the readability of general sentences, so it is not pertinent to technical sentences such as firms' disclosure. It just measures the degree of length of sentence and complexity of words but not the degree of information users' understandability.(337) Simply using the Fog Index is not enough to measure overall understandability. Complex words can be easy to understand. A short word can be difficult to understand when it is not an everyday word. The index is becoming popular in measuring disclosure readability, however, Loughran (2014) questioned how the simple measure of average words and percent can be good at measuring capital market readability, rather found that *"a simple count of the number of words in a 10-K is a better proxy for readability."*(347)

c. Linguistic Analysis

Some use software program for linguistic analysis. It counts the number of words of disclosure under each category; positive or negative emotion, unique or repetitive, strong and weak, predictive and vague, future and past-related, overstatement and understatement. Firms disclosing with more informative words (e.g., numbers, past and future related words, and factual content) are less likely to be sued.(348) Media pessimism predicts downward pressures on market price and trading volume.(349)

5. Indirect approach: disclosure environments-based proxies

Various proxies

The indirect approach does not directly depend on disclosure. They infer disclosure quality by using market-based proxies that are assumed to be closely related to disclosure quality. Such proxies cover the issuance in the foreign market, and the attributes of analysts' forecasts (e.g., following, dispersion, and forecast revisions). Examples of researches using indirect approach include trading venue (350, 351), analysts following (122), forecasts (338, 352), special events (135, 353).[71]

Market-based disclosure index

It would not be easy to achieve the consistency in analyses with a self-constructed disclosure-based index. A market-based measure, however, can provide consistent analyses across various types of disclosure, regardless of the formats or characteristics of the disclosed information, because they construct a market-based measure with various factors other than disclosure, such as firm's characteristics and investor's response.[72]

There can be a specific context where market-based measures are more meaningful than disclosure-based measures. Rogers (2008) argued that market-based measures (e.g., changes in liquidity) can be a better proxy of disclosure quality when the market response indicates more properly the true value of the disclosing firm than the properties of disclosure. It is paradoxical but meaningful that a direct approach can be insufficient to determine the usefulness of disclosure, rather an indirect approach with market-based measures can be of better service.(293) A market-based measure includes the bid-ask spread and the changes in liquidity. However, special attention should be paid because the market-based measure can more distort the results because it is not easy to control all the variables.(293, 337)

Regulatory compliance score

A meaningful association was evidenced between the MD&A compliance scores as assessed by SEC and the analyst forecast error and dispersion. According to Barron, Kile, and O'Keefe (1999), "*High MD&A ratings are associated with less error and less dispersion in analyst's earnings forecasts,*" and "*MD&A information has a substantial effect on earnings forecasts.*" (339) Clarkson, Kao, and Richardson (1999) showed evidence that the MD&A quality scores vary directly with upcoming performance, signifying that regulators who pursue the efficient resource allocation in the process of disclosure monitoring have incentives to target the financially distressed firms.(354)

286. Disclosure Quality Management

2861. Firm's disclosure quality management

While the firm's disclosure quality management is a relatively unfamiliar concept and less researched area, the idea is not entirely new. Many approaches of quality management in other area may provide significant implications for firms that pursue a higher quality of disclosure.

If a firm can improve the effectiveness of disclosure through better disclosure quality management processes, the firm is reducing the cost of capital by eliminating investors' uncertainty. An adequate disclosure quality management will reduce the probability of unintended low-quality disclosure and thus the potential litigation risk that can harm firm's brand. So far as disclosure is a fundamental value relevant factor, firms have no reason to hesitate to establish adequate quality measurement.

A great many of literature has focused on the determinants and consequences of disclosure quality, and many firms are seeking better quality management. Managers whose incentives are aligned with investors' may attempt to improve disclosure quality by adopting more effective quality management techniques. An effectively managed quality control process should increase the credibility and investors' understanding. However, it is not easy to establish an adequate quality control process. Besides, there exists no consensus on how to manage the disclosure quality efficiently.

First of all, firms have to establish their standards of disclosure quality management on what is the goal of disclosure, how to implement quality control, and internal standards of procedures. Managers who controls the disclosure quality should confirm that the procedures and standards of the firm's disclosure are consistent with the goals of the firm, investors, and regulators. The objectives of a firm's disclosure quality management should be in compliance with regulations and the firm value maximization.(61)

2862. PDCA Cycle vs. transformation

The PDCA cycle,[73] aka the Deming cycle, is an iterative four-step management method used in business for quality control. The PDCA cycle will be repeatedly implemented until the problem is solved. The iterative PDCA cycle can be well fit for the mass production function on a practical level. Considering the natures of information and disclosure, the quality management approach used in the mass production fields should not be directly or mindlessly adopted, but many aspects should be refined and filtered to fit for disclosure quality management.

By the way, "transformation approach" should be also considered. A more optimized approach led by the firm's leadership with profound knowledge and experience would help firms to "transform" the current disclosure process and improve the fundamental outcomes in disclosure quality. Disclosure quality management is the responsibility of all members of a firm, but top management has more leverage toward the fundamental improvement of disclosure quality. A jumbo roll of pumpkin is better than hundreds of rolls of sesame. Manager's role is significant in enhancing disclosure quality to such an extent as to the manager's reputation of good disclosure matters in job market. As Juran (1964) identified, the human is an essential factor in quality management. The education and training of managers can be the key solution because human relation and employee's resistance to change is often illustrated as the root cause of quality issues. (355)

2863. Policy & guidelines

It is not a regulator but a firm that can identify the potential risks of non-compliance to disclosure requirements. Many regulators and exchanges provide disclosure guidelines, but they pay attention not to supporting firms with disclosure quality management tools but to guiding or directing the sufficient compliance and overall disclosure quality that is required. Some guidelines for successful IR activities are provided, which might suggest meaningful implications for better disclosure quality management. Such guidelines can be used by firms as part of improving disclosure quality management. Firm-level guidelines, codes, or principles of disclosure should be established that describe the components needed for ensuring high-quality disclosure. For example, it is recommendable to describe the role of disclosure officers. Disclosure plans and processes should be checked, tracked by experts, and monitored by the board with appropriate feedback. Disclosure officers should establish an appropriate reporting calendar and identify a firm's possible risks, maintain disclosure-related crisis management and communication plans, review the investor's information needs regularly, and assess how the firm's disclosure could improve. Firms need to develop disclosure policy to enhance the quality by studying many guidelines, such as the investor relation guidelines and the information management guidelines of other organizations. These would help firms to establish better disclosure quality management mechanism.(356)

2861. Disclosure audit

In order to achieve a higher level of quality and enhance current disclosure practices, firms might adopt the procedure of disclosure audit as a tool of disclosure quality management. However, there appears to be no research in this area. Thus, useful concepts and methodologies can be borrowed from the researches of "information audit." Disclosure audits can be viewed and implemented in relation to the internal PDCA cycle or external accounting audit. Botha and Boon (2003) defined that *"an information audit entails the systematic examination of the information resources, information use, information flows and the management of these in an organization. It involves the identification of users' information needs and how effectively (or not) these are being met."*(357)

In 1980, the researches of information audit took a narrow approach by focusing on the identification of formal information sources. After 1990, they started to pay more attention to organizational analysis.(358) Among various methodologies, nothing might directly match disclosure audit, but the benefits of information-related audits, such as communication audit and information audit, might be similar to the outcomes of disclosure audit. Consequently, the benefits of disclosure audit can be similarly inferred from the information audit of Botha and Boon (2003) and the communication audit of Downs (1988).(357, 359)

 a. Validity benefit: If it is properly performed, disclosure audit will contribute to the information production that is valid and accurate.

 b. Diagnostic benefit: It will diagnose and identify any compliance gaps.

 c. Feedback benefit: It provides managers with feedback benefit, and thus managers can learn whether specific disclosure generates the desired outcomes. It includes evaluation and correction effect.

 d. Information benefit: Disclosure audit will draw the firm's attention to the value, process, and improvement of disclosure practices.

e. Training benefit: It will provide firm's staff with pragmatic training opportunities guiding them to have a better picture of their role.

2862. Regulator's role

A lack of proper disclosure regulation and guidelines may lead to poor disclosure. Thus, regulators need to establish proper reporting requirements and guidelines. Regulator's high-quality standards would lead to a higher quality of disclosure that is credible. Regulators or standard setters may be recommended to provide any guidelines that can be used by firms as a part of the internal education and communication process for improving disclosure quality management.

3. DISCLOSURE REGULATION

31. Introduction

32. United States: Traditional state regulation

33. United States: Modern federal regulation

34. EU: Fragmentation vs. Harmonization

35. ASIA

36. International disclosure standards

37. Quality of disclosure regulation

38. Socially optimal disclosure regulation

31. Introduction

311. Goals Of Securities Regulation

The "Objectives and Principles of Securities Regulation" is a main standard of International Organization of Securities Commissions (IOSCO) that was adopted in September 1998. *"The IOSCO Principles are based on three basic objectives: the protection of investors; ensuring that markets are fair, efficient, and transparent; the reduction of systemic risk."*(360)

    a. Investors protection: "Investors should be protected from misleading, manipulative or fraudulent practices." Investors are particularly vulnerable to misconduct by firms, but individual investors' ability to take action may be limited. Thus, investors should have access to a mechanism such as courts or dispute resolution. "Where a breach of law does occur, investors should be protected through the strong enforcement of the law." Especially, "full disclosure of information material to investors' decisions is the most important means for ensuring investor protection … Accounting and auditing standards should be of a high and internationally acceptable." (360)

    b. Fair, efficient, and transparent markets: These objectives are closely linked to investor protection. Securities regulation should detect improper and unfair practices and aim to ensure investors to have fair access to information. Securities regulation should "promote market practices that ensure fair treatment of orders and a price formation process that is reliable …" The dissemination of relevant information should be timely and reflected in the price. Securities regulation should promote market efficiency and ensure the highest levels of transparency. (360)

    c. Reduction of systemic risk: The objectives of securities regulation to reduce systemic risk is closely linked to investor protection. Securities regulation should not suppress appropriate or rational risk-taking but promote and effective risk management.

    Hicks (1992) explained that how regulatory issues are resolved will depend on the normative goals; efficiency and investors protection. An efficient market relies on competition, while investor protection relies on regulatory restraints. It is difficult and challenging to harmonize those inherently bipolar normative goals.(361)

312. Approaches To Securities Regulation

1) Deductive vs inductive

    There are two ways to make scientific researches; deductive and inductive reasoning. These can be applied in the area of setting the principles, standards, and requirements of disclosure.

Deductive approach

In setting the standards with a deductive approach, regulators or standard setters start with specifying the objectives, clarify the definitions and assumptions, and develop a logical structure in order to reach the objectives. The process moves from the general to the specific (i.e., top-down). Regulators develop an assumption based on the existing theories. In a deductive approach, the conclusion is either valid or invalid; there is no degree of validity.(362-364) A deductive approach provides more logical and consistent disclosure frameworks.

However, regulators clinging to logical consistency might mandate disclosure for the information that is less occurring or far from investor's information needs. Thus, regulators should collect abundant observations to confirm or refuse the hypothesis that the new disclosure requirement would sufficiently contribute to the objectives.

Inductive approach

The inductive approach starts from "observations" (i.e., data, event) without any theory and derives a generalized "conclusion" (i.e., principle, standard). A tentative general principle or standard is inferred by observing specific cases by using qualitative methods. The researcher should gather observations without any biases, prejudice, or impartial attitudes. The inductive approach uses observations to develop general principles; from concrete to general (i.e., bottom-up). Principles are generalized based upon limited observations. It is assumed that, from specific observations, patterns can be found and developed into abstracts and general rules. The inductive approach does not require any model as a pre-requisite.(362, 365-368)

For example, regulators might list the major events they have observed. They might try to identify and classify observed events by the degree of stock price sensitiveness. Once it occurs to them that the market has a substantial tendency to react to a specific event, then regulators may establish disclosure requirements upon the assumption that the historical data of the specific events suggest a certain trend useful in valuation and investment decision. An inductive approach can well reflect the current market demands for information.

However, market reaction and information demand vary from time to time, and, as a result, changing disclosure requirements that is coupled with the changes in market reaction is very costly. The market reaction for disclosure requirements may widely deviate from firm to firm, which makes it less practicable. To make matters worse, it can harm logical consistency among overall disclosure requirements, which might lead to the inconsistency of enforcement and aggravate investor confidence. Thereby, the inductive approach should be based on long-term observations.

Comparison

The inductive approach that may be preferred by the regulators or standard setters who are willing to become firefighter against hot scandals may result in voluminous standards that can be incompatible or inconsistent with each other. The deductive approach that may be chosen by the regulators or standard setters who prefer a more conceptual or comprehensive view might lack the ability to put out a fire in a specific circumstance. With the growing significance of economic thinking, the deductive approach became dominant in financial accounting. With the developments of technology, it is easy to conduct the inductive method. The inductive approach is more applicable to the quantitative research and the rule-based approaches, while the deductive approach is more applicable to the qualitative research and the principle-based approaches. With the recent trends of shifting towards a principle-based approach, the deductive approach would be more popular.(362)

However, both approaches are not meant to be always mutually exclusive but supplementary. Both approaches work together to provide a more comprehensive regulation. The inductive approach may be used as a means of evaluating the usefulness or suitability of the standards that had been established by the deductive approaches.(362, 369) *"During the deductive phase, we reason toward observations; during the inductive phase, we reason from observations. Both deduction and induction offer routes to the construction of social theories, and both logic and observation are essential."*(365)

Ethics

Regulators or standard setters can be limited in their knowledge of the theoretical relations among the variables. Along with limited knowledge, empirical observation depends on the cultural and social context. Thus, a generalization from specific observations may lead to a wrong conclusion.(366) *"Choosing a theoretical orientation for the purpose of encouraging a particular conclusion, for example, would generally be regarded as unethical."* However, when regulators and standard setters *"intend to bring about social change through their work, they usually choose a theoretical orientation appropriate to that intention."*(365)

2) Rules-based vs. Principles-based

Prescription vs. general obligation

The International Ongoing Disclosure Standards (IODS) of IOSCO illustrates two types of implementation approaches; prescription approach and general obligation approach. A prescription approach provides a comprehensive list of disclosure items that are presumed to be material. A general obligation approach is to mandate firms to disclose all material information that may affect investors' investment decision. In the prescription approach, a set of numerous disclosure requirements that are presumptively material is specified in the disclosure rules. For example, the U.S. SEC requires firms to disclose a specific and comprehensive list of presumptively material events. The list of disclosure items has been substantially increased in many countries that had adopted the prescription approach. In the EU, regulators provide firms with a general obligation of materiality (i.e., price sensitiveness or materiality) without specifying an exhaustive list of events that would be presumptively material. However, *"even under the general obligation approach, a body of accounting standards, listing rules, legislation or regulation may prescribe certain types of information, including specific events, which should be disclosed."*(203) This classification is similar to the classification into the principles-based and rules-based approach.

Rules-based approach

A rules-based regulation prescribes a set of specific rules that should be applied for specific situation. Managers should disclose information prescribed in the rules. It takes the form of a prescription approach. The main advantages are the simplicity, transparency, and certainty of disclosure requirements, which limits disclosure cost to a certain degree. Less-trained staff in a firm can comply with requirements. Managers who worry about the litigation risk that may arise from wrong judgment seem to favor the rules-based regulation. It may reduce the possibility of opportunistic behavior, support easier comparison among similar issuers, and provide protection to investors who want to avoid issuers with much of discretionary judgment.

Furthermore, it is relatively easy for regulators to investigate any violation. A specific event is precisely discernible on whether it is subject to disclosure or not. Even though firms might be burdened by voluminous event-specific rules, they can be relieved from the burdens of vulnerable enforcement actions that might be triggered by poor management judgment.

Nosy disclosure requirements of rules-based regulation can prevent managers from making opportunistic disclosure decisions because requirements are definitely mandated. However, regulatory complexity may be inevitable when disclosure requirements increase. Issuers may be restricted from making discretionary disclosure choices, even though they are unique and tend to provide boilerplate responses. A rules-based regulation may be left far behind the rapid market changes such as the financial services innovation or the changes in information demand.

Principles-based approach

A principles-based approach provides a set of principles, objectives, and explanations. Some examples can be provided as guidelines. Not only the rules-based approach but also the principles-based approach starts from a set of rules. The difference is that, in a principles-based approach, managers are guided but not coerced by the rules. Rules are characterized by rules-of-thumb rather than hard-and-fast rules. The managers are free to exercise discretion. For example, the disclosure rule of FSA in the U.K. (i.e., Disclosure and Transparency Rule) does not include detailed disclosure events. The guidance of FSA provides a non-exhaustive list of items that are likely to affect the valuation and investment decision of a reasonable investor.

The advantages of the principles-based regulation are diverse. It enables both regulators and firms to customize unique disclosure requirements for a specific situation, which is not easy under the rule-based regulation. From the perspective of the regulator, the principles-based approach can be a more cost-effective regulation as they provide a general and broad guideline that can be used in a variety of situations. Sometimes the principles-based approach may unavoidably include detailed rules or guidelines, which do not cover every situation and context. Investors can benefit unexpected disclosure of material information to which they had not paid attention.

The principles-based approach is criticized by the nature of uncertainty and inconsistency. It introduces uncertainty into disclosure decisions since managers make decisions depending on specific contexts. Different managers may make different decisions, and even the same manager may make apparently inconsistent decisions under different circumstances.

Managers should be ready to justify their decision. The experts' review before release to minimize litigation risk will increase disclosure costs. Some expenditures on training staff are unavoidable since simple rubber stamping with limited expertise can seriously increase litigation risk. A failure to train new staff might have an immediate impact on the quality of subsequent disclosures.

Under the rules-based regulation, regulators assume the burdens to identify disclosure requirements. Whereas, under the principles-based regulation, the burdens to figure out their obligations are shifted to firms. Firms are the ones who should evaluate the impact of a specific event and make disclosure judgments. Without pertinent guidelines, the principles-based approach can provide inconsistent and less compatible information, reducing the comparability among firms. On the contrary, conservative managers might choose to provide voluminous information only to avoid any potential litigation risks.

Even under the principles-based regulation, regulators need to have some rules to guide firms in the right direction. To effectively comply with the principles-based regulation, firms are recommended to have a higher level of expertise and adequate risk assessment procedures of disclosure decisions. In addition, unless the regulated firm accepts an ambiguity of enforcement, the principles-based regulation would not be well rooted within the markets. Regulators should make efforts to minimize the ambiguity by providing useful guidelines.

Comparison

All regulatory frames are mixtures of rules and principles. A principles-based approach can be said to rely primarily on principles and secondarily on rules when it is necessary. The principles-based regulation contains more principles that are represented in more general and broad terms. Rules are more certain but rigid, which can guide firms to find loopholes. Principles are uncertain but flexible, which can make regulators more arbitrary.

Benefit and cost of PBR

Ford (2009) provides potential benefits and costs of principles-based regulation in the perspectives of issuers and regulators. The benefits and costs of one approach are the flip-side of the other. However, the effects of both approaches should not be oversimplified since *"rules and principles operate along a spectrum"* and *"the rigid dichotomy fails to consider how important application is."*(370)

Table 6) Benefit and cost of PBR

	Cost	Benefit
Issuers	Resource-demanding in interpretation, Uncertainty from contextual judgments, Fewer opportunities for loophole, Smaller issuers forced to develop new compliance	Tailored process to business needs, Permits flexibility & innovation, More compliant behavior, More flexible/Less heavy for small firms
Regulators	More costly to implement, Requiring more skills, Risk of regulatory creep, Voluminous guidance	Less costly to promulgate, Suitable for fast-moving markets, Efficient use of regulatory resources, Flexible guidance, Responsive to scandals
Investors	Lower standards & lax regulation, less transparent & credible	Better regulation/fewer loophole, More transparent & credible

Source) Table 6 is summarized from Ford (2009)(370).

Significance of enforcement

One may argue that adopting a principles-based regulation will guide firms to disclose relevant information effectively, resulting in the mitigation of the disclosure issues. However, Hellman, Carenys, and Moya Gutierrez (2018) found *"no clear pattern of higher compliance"* for IFRS that relies more on principles-based approach. *"More reliance on principles and less reliance on specific requirements is not likely to solve the need for more relevant information and will most likely lead to lower disclosure quality among poor disclosers."* It is unrealistic to assume that firms are not incentivized to make poor disclosure but fully comply with disclosure requirements. Thus, anticipating a firm's action in good faith is very risky, and, as a result, disclosure should be enforceable. The disclosure requirements should be *"enforceable and auditable in order to secure a certain minimum level of disclosure."* Introducing more principles-based disclosure regulation must be accompanied by enforceable mechanisms. Simply turning from rules to principles is not likely to be an automatic solution for the needs of more relevant information but might mislead to lower disclosure quality. Regulators should put more emphasis on how to design disclosure requirements that are more enforceable at a low cost.(371)

313. Standard Features Of Disclosure Regulation

In most countries, an initial disclosure document for the primary market is named as a prospectus and the like. Ongoing disclosure may represent secondary market disclosure. The term used for secondary market disclosure differs from country to country. Such terms as continuous disclosure, ongoing disclosure, timely disclosure, ad-hoc disclosure, and price-sensitive information disclosure are often used. The International Ongoing Disclosure Standards (IODS) of the IOSCO classifies ongoing disclosure by two: disclosure on an immediate basis and disclosure on a periodic basis.(203) Most countries tend to have established similar disclosure frameworks following the U.S. disclosure regulation.

a. Periodic disclosure: Investors need to assess the financial position and prospects of the issuer by using periodic reports such as annual reports and interim reports. It enables investors to better monitor and compare the performance over regular intervals.

b. Non-periodic disclosure: Timely and immediate disclosure of ad-hoc material events and developments is essential for investors.

c. Prospectus: A prospectus is a disclosure document that must clearly describe material information, such as business operations, financial statements. It aims to enable the investor to assess the firm's financial position and future prospects. It should be distributed to potential investors. (372-374)

d. Enforcement: Many regulators conduct disclosure enforcement for the prospectus or periodic reports. Some exchanges also conduct review on non-periodic timely disclosure.

32. United States: Traditional State Regulation

Studying the history of the U.S. disclosure regulation would be meaningful because most countries adopt disclosure regulation that is similar to the U.S. disclosure regulation. Notably, many pieces of research about the blue-sky law in the early capital markets provide fundamental understanding and theoretical explanations, even though the debates are outdated.

Some company laws predated the Securities Act of 1933, and such forerunners took the form of "prospectus disclosure." The Joint Stock Company Act of 1844 in the U.K. required the filing of a "prospectus" with the government before disseminating it to the public. This Act is considered the first modern prospectus requirement by introducing mandatory disclosure in the form of prospectus.(372) In U.S., the Companies Act of 1900 specified the prospectus with more detail and comprehensive disclosure of material facts. In 1903, the state of Connecticut adopted a statute requiring "mining and oil companies" to disclose financial status and business activities to the State. In 1910, the state of Rhode Island adopted a statute that required certain issuers to file the statements of condition with the State.(375)

321. Blue-Sky Law

3211. Introduction

Concept

The blue-sky law is a state regulation in the United States designed to protect the public investors from securities fraud by regulating the offerings and sales of securities. Each state law administered by state regulatory agency requires the registration of securities offerings and sales, but the specific provisions vary among states. State regulatory laws are commonly termed as "blue-sky laws," and speculative securities were colloquially termed as "blue sky" in many sources. Especially, Joseph N. Dolley, the bank commissioner of the State of Kansas who pushed for the passage of the first blue-sky laws, has been given credit for naming the blue-sky Law. (376)[78] Using the term "blue sky," the Justice Joseph McKenna also expressed his opinion in the case of U.S. Supreme Court that addressed the constitutionality of state securities laws and upheld states' regulatory power on securities offering.[79]

Initiated by Kansas

Motivated by investors' complaints about financial fraud, many states passed blue sky laws to prevent issuers from selling worthless securities to lay investors. In April 1910, the state of Kansas announced to create a new state agency to protect Kansas from worthless stock sales by the swindlers.

In 1911, the first blue sky law was adopted in Kansas.

National and global diffusion

The Kansas law generated great attention among other states and became a benchmark model. All states except Nevada adopted blue sky laws prior to the enactment of the federal securities laws in 1933.(377, 378) The law quickly expanded to Canada and Australia. In 1917, the Supreme Court upheld the constitutionality of blue sky laws when firms are involved in interstate securities selling.(379)

3212. General Features

Typical functions

Blue sky law aims at preventing fraud, and a number of measures were invented. While some states adopted common patterns, others refuse to adopt certain features, and, as a result, it may dramatically differ from the typical functions.(380) Each state law can be classified into three typical functions: registration or exemption, merit review, anti-fraud provision. (381) State administrators required an issuer either to register securities or to qualify for an exemption from registration. Under the merit review, they imposed certain standards (aka. merit standards) as a prerequisite to selling securities. The Kansas-style statute gave administrators more leeway to approve or reject an offering based on merit standards.[80]

State registration

State registration procedures have been administered by a state's securities commission or an administrator. It begins by filing a registration statement and submitting disclosure documents prior to issuing securities. The registration statement may or may not be reviewed depending on the regulation or guideline. Merit states will review and comment. If the security offering was verified legitimacy and approved by the regulator, the firm can sell securities to the public within the approved state.(380, 381)

State exemptions

To avoid regulatory duplication, some issuers that are already governed by other statutes are exempt from registration requirements of Kansas blue sky law, such as bank, trust companies, mortgage companies, and nonprofit corporations. The coverage of the blue-sky law is generally restricted to speculative securities. Such a state exemption policy became the cornerstone of federal exemption policy.

Merit review

The blue-sky law provided the state commissioner with broad discretionary power to approve or reject offerings to prevent fraud. An offering could be rejected if the offerings are judged to be unfair, unjust, inequitable, or if the business did not promise a fair return.[81]

Anti-fraud provisions

Blue-sky laws included antifraud provisions against any fraudulent behavior or failure to disclose. However, the specific requirements that form a fraud claim depend on individual statutes and the remedies available to investors against fraud differ from state to state. Some states rejected merit review but gave the administrator the authority to block a fraudulent offering. Offering cannot proceed without pre-clearance, which is determined based on more objective fraud criteria. Financial centers (e.g., New York, New Jersey) adopted the most lenient patterns that do not require any pre-clearance of offerings but prohibit ex post fraud.(378)

3213. Theoretical backgrounds

1) Overview

Regulatory theories that are typically applied in the law and economics literature can be applied to explain the theoretical backgrounds of the blue-sky law. The public interest approach explains economic regulation as a normative judgment that the regulation is an efficacious solution to an externality. Blue-sky law is explained as a reaction to an increasing securities fraud in the early twentieth century. In contrast, private interest theory focuses on the economic interest of a specific group (e.g., associations, labor unions). Local small banks advocated the blue-sky laws to reduce competition for funds. The political theory focuses on the broad-based coalitions with a similar ideology that can influence regulatory policy and allow collective action to influence regulation.(378)

2) Public interest theory

Securities fraud hypothesis

A traditional view of regulation is the "public interest approach" that explains regulation as a solution to market failure caused by externalities. The public interest approach explains that efficient regulation creates net social wealth. To achieve such purposes, fraud prohibitions should be efficient, reducing the contract cost. And the regulator should engage in ex-ante screening with enough professional staffs at a lower cost than the issuer could voluntarily develop its own reputation mechanism.(378)

Seligman (1983) explained that there was a "fraud wave," a dramatic increase of dishonest issuers in the early twentieth century.(382) The blue-sky law can be understood as a reaction to serious market failure or abuses in securities markets. A variety of market abuse prevalent in the early twentieth century that necessitated governmental intervention includes such as non-disclosure, expropriation, and fraudulent sales.(378) Issuers failed to inform investors adequately of the risk of the securities being offered. The blue-sky laws were mainly passed to prevent the expropriation by managers and the rampant sale of fraudulent securities to unsophisticated investors. In addition to the securities fraud rationale, there can be other possible rationale explains such as market pressure, internal control, and regulation costs.(383, 384)[82]

Opponents

Under the public interest argument, the last adopter with larger financial markets should have been the first to adopt blue sky law because of greater economies of scale in fraud detection.(378) According to Mahoney (2003), however, the evidence of rampant fraud is extremely thin. Even though the merit state rejected a substantial percentage of offerings, such evidence of rejection rates provides no basis for inferring fraud when the administrators are less competent, or their motivation was other than preventing fraud. According to the public interest theory, the most eager state might be the state of which social cost of securities fraud is higher and expected to adopt earlier for a larger net benefit from regulation. However, the net benefit of regulation could have been larger for the last adopter. The first adopters are farming states like Kansas, Arizona, Louisiana, and Vermont, while the last adopters are larger financial markets like New York, Pennsylvania, and Connecticut. Thus, *"it is not plausible that the social cost of securities fraud was higher in the first adopters than the last adopters."*(385)

3) Private interest theory

Introduction

Private interest theory is sometimes known as a public choice theory. Economic regulation can be explained as an outcome of a political process of interest groups to transfer the wealth from others. In the late nineteenth century, many economic changes created a nationwide market in the U.S., and larger companies and organizations struggled to reduce the competition with the help of captured government.(378, 386) Interest groups influenced the legislation favorably, and the private interest mainly came from the financial market competition and product market competition.(384)

Financial market competition

In the early twentieth century, financial market competitions for funds can be explained in two ways; a) industry competition in the same state between banking and securities, b) inter-state competition between farming states and urban states.(386) First, regarding industry competition, the blue sky laws were promoted by the private interests of small banks to reduce competition with the securities industry for funds since mandatory registration would increase security issuance cost and, as a result, investors crowd out into the banking deposit. Second, regarding inter-state competition, a large percentage of money was being taken by the promoter of urban states. The purpose of the law was to keep credit from being taken out of state and to patronize the local industry.

Some interest groups were in favor of the blue sky law (e.g., smaller banks, farmers, and small businesses), while others are opponents (e.g., securities industry, big issuer, bigger bank).(386) Facing a serious threat from securities firms, small banks supported the law as a means of lowering the competition and seem to have lobbied successfully for the enactment of the laws.(378) Nonbank business (e.g., farmers, small business) also supported the law to stifle competition from out-of-state borrowers. It is so natural that Kansas, a farming state, was the first to adopt the law, and many farming states adopted strict statutes.(386)

The bigger banks in urban areas were threatened not by competition but by regulatory intervention such as the blue-sky law. Many indications imply that banks were an active opponent to the blue sky laws.(378) Big issuers (e.g., manufacture, railroads, and public utilities) who would raise a significant amount of money by issuing securities were in opposition of the law.(386) The Investment Bankers Association (IBA) had been continuously active in the state legislatures to obtain reasonable and broad exemptions, and, as a result, many states added exemptions to the blue-sky statutes. (386).

Product market competition

The free market system has been held back by the political influences which primarily came from the incumbents in product markets who had established a dominant position. Especially, the financial market is sensitive to political winds, and incumbents would prefer to stay in power. Incumbents wishing to reduce potential competition in the product market by raising the costs of external financing could exert a strong influence on the adoption of investor protection laws or the deterrence free financial market law.(387) Hypothetically, the blue-sky laws might have been passed in response to the lobby of incumbent firms, as they would find it easier to grow in size and profits due to the improved monopoly power in product markets.

Evidence is mixed. Incumbent mining firms show negative evidence, while large manufacturing firms show positive evidence. *"Political lobbying by incumbent mining firms did not play a significant role in promoting the passage of blue-sky laws."* Instead, *"the laws appear to have a positive effect on the quantities of ores sold and an insignificant or negative impact on the prices of mineral ores; product markets appear to become more competitive after the investor protection laws are passed."*(384) Some proposed that the adoption of investor protection laws could result from the influence of incumbent firms who wish to reduce the entry of competitors.(387) However, other opposed that regulators who adopted the blue-sky law do not seem to be captured by incumbent firms because the passage of the blue sky laws resulted in more competitive product markets by increasing the quantities of goods sold. (384)

Evidence

Mahoney (2003) provided the Canada case as an example that explains the limits of private interest theory. The blue-sky law quickly spread to Canada shortly after Kansas. However, unlike the United States, Canada had a highly concentrated banking system without a powerful interest group (e.g., small banks). Hence, the blue-sky law should not have been enacted in Canada because Canada was without powerful driving forces behind the law.(378) Macey & Miller (1991) also found no evidence to support capture theory.(386)

4) Political theory

Mahoney (2003) introduced another theory that ideology is the principal driving force behind the regulation; agrarian group and progressive movement. The blue-sky laws were adopted by the lobby of the coalition group to curtail the power of financiers not for private purposes but an ideological purpose.(378) In the early twentieth century, progressivism that was concerned with economic injustice was rising in the United States. Before 1933, securities offering was subject to minimal regulation, and fraudulent public offerings were common since investors had no reliable resource to determine whether the offered stock was valuable. The blue-sky law was the result of progressivism to protect the money of Kansas residents (i.e., farmer, investor) and solve the prevalent injustice in Kansas.(372)

5) Summary

According to the researches on the adoption timing, types of laws, and effects on the profitability of banks show mixed results. A single theory cannot explain all the story behind the adoption of the blue-sky law. It was partly determined by the prominence of small banks supporting the private interest theory and partly by the strength of broad-based coalitions supporting the political theory. (378)

322. Merit Regulation

3221. Concept

Definition

Many definitions of merit regulation include such terms as "substantive standards," "discretionary power," "allow or deny," "fair," or "risk." Many state laws require that the offering meet certain "standards of fairness," referred to as "merit regulation."(388) Merit regulation gives the administrator to *"issue a stop order denying the effectiveness of any registration statement if he finds that the offering is being made on terms that are unfair, unjust, or inequitable."*[83] Merit regulation is a regulatory system that authorizes regulators to deny registration of a securities offering unless the substantive terms of the offering ensure a fair relation and provide public investors with a reasonable relation of risk to return.(380)

Purpose

The average investors are relatively unsophisticated, risk-averse, inattentive to disclosure, and uninformed by the issuer. Merit regulation is a device which attempts to "lessen the investment risks" for investors in newly promoted firms.(389) It is primarily designed to protect investors from exploitation by establishing a minimum level of fair treatment and fraud prevention.(380, 381) It is to ensure fair offering price for the public investors who are less attentive to mandated disclosure. Owing to the offering price adjustment by merit regulator, investors are more likely to pay for the true value. It is to reduce the degree of risk created by investment opportunities. It is to promote a more prophylactic effect of dissuading the swindlers from entering markets of which antifraud provisions are not effectively protecting investors. Ultimately, it is to facilitate capital formation by bolstering greater investor confidence with the help of minimum quality criteria.

3222. Merits of merit regulation

Market Failure

The supporters of merit review conclude that lower standards of regulation that are without merit regulation would result in excessive compensation, increased unfair overpricing, and poor disclosure. Such market abuse will be exacerbated at times of high speculation, and the market does not work well enough to ensure the minimum level of investor protection. Hence, at least to respond with such types of issues, administrative intervention in a format of merit regulation is necessary, and the minimum standards of merit review are the effective restraints on a variety of market abuse.

Comparative strength of merit review

Merit review can cover a broader range of review than SEC disclosure review since state merit authority is empowered with full discretion. The SEC does not make disclosure review for all the offerings. A properly conducted merit review is more likely to find the problems than the SEC review since merit authority can scrutinize all the facts and issues.(380)

Insufficiency of alternative mechanisms

Sargent (1986) suggested some essential arguments in support of the merit regulation and the insufficiencies of other alternative mechanisms. Many prospectuses are neither effectively reviewed by the SEC nor read by the investors. Disclosure documents are either incomprehensible or ineffective on the investment decision. Hence, SEC disclosure is useful but should not be the sole source of protection. Both private incentives and market forces are insufficient to ensure fair treatment and appropriate pricing since public investors are unable to affect the overall terms of the offering. Private remedy such as litigation that is driven by the investors provides insufficient protection against fraud because it is just an expensive doctor after death without any preventive effect.(380) Investors might try to rely on the underwriter for fair treatment and investor protection. However, the underwriters can provide just a minimum level of due diligence because they are worried about losing a business opportunity.(388)

3223. Main features

In reviewing a registration statement, merit states determine whether "issuing merit review comment" or "denying." Merit regulation gives the administrator a right to issue a stop order denying the effectiveness of any registration statement if he finds that the offering is being made on terms that are unfair, unjust, or inequitable.

Merit safe harbor provisions provide an exemption from merit review for the offerings that meet the safe harbor conditions. Merit safe harbor offerings will be excused from the compliance with merit standards and regarded fair, just, and equitable. A merit safe harbor is an exemption from merit review, not registration. When state registration requirements are adopted for the merit review, offerings exempted from state registration are also exempted from state merit review.(380) The California Corporations Code set out the merit review safe harbor that was adopted in 1968 is the oldest and most limited.(380)[84]

Regarding merit standards, common examples of merit review provisions that include the following:

Cheap stock provision is to limit sales of stock to insiders at a significantly low price near the offering. Option and warrant provisions are to limit issuing such securities to a certain percentage of the outstanding stock at the public offering. Unequal voting rights provision is to limit allowing such rights. Specifying offering price provision is to limit prices in relation to book value or price/earnings multiples.(390)

323. Benefits & Costs

3231. Benefits

Regarding the state's responsibility to protect unsophisticated investors, the main issue should be whether the benefits of state regulation outweigh the costs of state regulation, especially merit regulation. Many analyses of the benefits and costs of state regulation have been made, but they are non-quantifiable and lack in part because the comprehensive study is very difficult. Some advocated the idea of retaining the state regulation based on empirical evidence and abundant experiences in the enforcement area, even though there are flaws in the state securities regulatory system.(388)

Effective filtering

Proponents of state merit regulation claimed its effectiveness. They argue there are replete cases where state securities regulation is beneficial in maintaining soundness or fairness of market by avoiding fraud issuers. The merit review can be an effective fraud filter.(381)

Out-performance of registered stocks

"Companies that were granted registration under the state's merit standards outperformed companies denied registration by the commissioner."(381) Even though flawed, the state blue sky laws are well-designed to prevent serious and widespread securities frauds. About 75 percent of companies applied for permission to do business were mining, oil, gas, and fraudulent stocks in which there could be no possible return. About half of the remaining 25 percent were also highly speculative.(391) [85]

Positive impacts on firm's policy

The evidence is *"strongly supportive of theories which predict that investor protection laws have a significant impact on corporate investment and financing policy,"* and *"firms respond to the blue sky laws by paying out greater dividends, raising equity, and increasing firm size."*(384) Investor protections by regulation leads to increased outside equity issuance because investors become more willing to participate.(392) Owing to better protection, investors can exercise more pressure on managers to increase dividends by decreasing expropriation.(393) The regulation led to increased firm size (e.g., total asset, physical capital) and allowed firms to access positive NPV projects better. The law causes firms to improve operating performance (e.g., return on assets).(394) The state regulation contributes to the prevention of securities fraud.(382, 383, 395) Some argue that the blue sky laws had an impact on the firm's policy through the channel of reduced expropriation risk, while others argue that it was through the reduced adverse selection. (384)

Ripple Effect of industry standard

Due to the merit regulation, many issuers have voluntarily complied with the state regulation only to preventively avoid any substantial problems caused by non-compliance. As a result, state regulations such as merit standards became industry standards.(388)

Empirical study: Wisconsin study

A study of merit regulation in Wisconsin compared the performance of registered securities with that of denied securities using three indices: performance-price, book value, and dividend distribution. It concluded that denied securities performed on average less than granted securities.(396) However, the blue-sky law could have created serious indirect costs such as anti-competitive effects through the reduction in the number of companies. Analysis that does not cover the costs to society may yield useless information but fails to support the efficacy of merit regulation.(397) The case where skepticism is more appropriate signifies that it is the right time to promote the role of merit regulation. In addition, it is such a meaningful argument that merit regulation is appropriate for first-time issuers. Merit regulation can play a useful role in protecting investors in a market where market forces and disclosure regulations do not suffice enough level of investor protection.(380)

3232. Costs

Compliance cost

The cost of compliance with the blue-sky law can be classified into the disclosure review cost and the merit review cost. The disclosure review cost includes filing fees and attorney fees, of which main component of the merit review cost might be attorney fee that is mostly variant depending on the issuer's circumstances. In case the issuer has to negotiate with merit administrator to clear the review process, such cost may be severe. The large portion of compliance cost is fixed, and, as a result, smaller issuers would have difficulties in complying with state merit regulation.(380)

Delay cost

The direct compliance cost is likely to be fixed to a certain amount. The indirect compliance cost with the blue-sky law includes the delay cost. The impact of delay can take many forms. Sometimes merit review may create a postponement of a national offering or withdrawal.(380) The issuer might have to delay an investment project or bear some negative consequences, such as damages on brand or losses of market potential.

Investment impediment cost

There can be more significant but less quantifiable cost; investment impediment cost. Many suggested that the two-tier system between state and federal only inhibits capital formation.(388, 397) From the early stage, it was strongly suggested that the blue-sky law might result in severe and unexpected economic consequences with respect to entrepreneurial problems (e.g., financing a new business).(397) State merit regulation has been argued to be an obstacle in facilitating capital formation and establishing a national market system. (398) Venture capitalists play both functions; providing capital and pursuing profits. They require substantial incentives to bear information costs and investment risks. As a result, there has been a tension between merit review and the incentive to bear the cost. Besides, merit regulation contributes to fostering new ventures. For example, states with strong merit regulations have fostered startup companies. We should not make the one-sided conclusion that state regulation has generated a high social cost by interfering with investment activity as far as there is no absolute empirical evidence on the effect of merit regulation on venture capitalist's incentives.(380)

Conflict cost and competitiveness encroachment cost

A variety of variations between state and federal regulations may generate costs in excess of benefits. For example, the lack of uniformity can generate conflict costs. The state regulation generates the inter-state complexity cost and the costs of conflict from state-federal and state-to-state relations. Dual regulation may weaken the competitiveness of the capital market, but the development of a uniform national regulation is expected to enhance the competitive power in global markets by reducing competitiveness encroachment cost.(398)

324. Critics

The blue-sky law consists of antifraud regulation and registration regulation that includes filing (i.e., disclosure review) and merit review. Most studies focus on the merit review. Some have strongly defended merit regulation highlighting the success of merit standards. Debates on the efficacy of blue sky law has been continued from the very inception of the law.(381)

Paternalistic interference

Although merit regulation is, to some degree, justified by its benefit to enhance investor confidence, it has been criticized as a paternalistic interference which directly pursues price regulation and, as a result, inhibits capital formation.(398)

Philosophically unsound base

Some argue that the level of disclosure should be decided by the market, not by the government, because market pressures would force the firms to provide sufficient information to the public at a lower cost.(399) The federal disclosure requirements are so sufficient that there is no need for state regulators to impose additional disclosure requirements. Even assuming the necessity of mandated disclosure, federal regulation is so enough that additional state requirements are unnecessary.(381)

Firm's regulatory avoidance

The possibility of issuers' regulatory avoidance was suggested. For example, some firms in a merit state may choose to relocate the business center to other non-merit states only to avoid compliance costs (e.g., registration costs, fraud liability).(384)

Limited benefits

Opponents argued that the benefits of merit regulation would be limited. Merit regulation cannot substitute for private antifraud remedies and federal enforcement powers. Start-up companies can have difficulty in complying with merit standards, and, as a result, merit regulation expels riskier companies from merit states, which may benefit some risk-averse investors in that state. On the contrary, it is of no benefit for the risk-taking investors.(380) Investors are protected not by the merit regulations but by the disclosure and antifraud provisions. One could argue that *"the only effect of merit regulation is to protect investors from their stupidity and greed. Society should not be asked to pay much for this."* (381)

Challenges on constitutional grounds

From the beginning, the blue-sky law was challenged on its constitutional grounds. However, in 1917, the U.S. Supreme Court upheld the state blue sky law of Ohio, South Dakota, and Michigan. After that affirmative case, the blue-sky law gained more popularity, and every state had adopted the law by 1931. The case also influenced the 1933 Act to include Section 18 not to preempt state blue-sky law by describing that *"Nothing in this Subchapter shall affect the jurisdiction of the securities commission ... of any*

State."(398)

Case: Apple Computer

In 1980, an Apple Computer faced denial from strong merit states. The Wall Street Journal reported that *"In any case, Massachusetts investors will be excluded from any market play in the stock. ... state regulators said the offering is too risky and barred sale of the shares ... The decision affects individual investors, but doesn't extend to financial institutions, which are presumed to be sophisticated. ..., the Apple stock fall short of several provisions ... that don't have solid earnings foundations. ... the offering is not being made in at least six states with strong securities laws. ..."*(400)[86] In 2018, the CNBC reports that *"A $1,000 investment in Apple on the day of its initial offering, or IPO on December 12, 1980, would be worth around $430,000 today, according to CNBC calculations. That includes price appreciation and dividends."*[87]

325. Challenges & Measures

3251. State-federal conflicts

Dual regulation

The dual regulation system between state and federal agency was adopted by the 1933 Act and has not been changed after the 1933 Act.[88] State regulators pursue investor protection at a local level, while federal regulators focus on fraudulent activities at a national level. The federal laws deferred to the state laws by giving a wide berth to "merit review approach" and by confirming the "state control of securities."(391) Some argued that the "federal-state-SRO" system of securities regulation does not have an efficient allocation of responsibilities and priorities, which involves considerable duplication and conflicting philosophies.(398)

Regulatory duplication cost

Federal and state regulators are increasing coordination to minimize the duplication cost. Nevertheless, as far as the state regulation resembles the federal rules, it is redundant and superfluous. Thus, regulatory duplication is inevitably confusing and costly. For example, the antifraud provision of the Uniform Securities Act (USA) is substantially overlapped with the rule 10b-5 under the 1934 Act.[89]

State-federal regulation gap

The federal law requires the full and timely disclosure of material information, while state laws require the issuer to file information for the administrator to decide whether the offering meets fairness standards. Blue sky laws require that securities either be registered with the state administration or be exempt from the registration requirements, which is basically the same rule as the 1933 Act. However, the exemptions from state registration differ somewhat from federal exemptions.

The dual regulation has been criticized. States could define the state provisions differently from the federal provisions. Such variations in definitions would substantially increase the regulatory complexity, and this can provide the basis in favor of federal pre-emption. For example, if states define "materiality" more broadly than the federal courts, issuers would evaluate the materiality standard in multiple jurisdictions, which would raise the cost. With the pernicious effects of inconsistent definitions, there has been scant reason for the states to enact separate securities laws.(381)

State-federal conflicts

Because listing requirements of stock exchange protects investors over and above the federal securities laws, most states have an exemption provision for exchange listed securities (aka. blue chip exemption). On the contrary, increasing competition among stock exchanges might undermine the higher listing standards of stock exchanges. If this is the case, merit states might take a different approach to blue chip exemptions, which can seriously increase state-federal conflicts.(398)

Dis-advantage of state regulation

Many pointed out disadvantages of state regulation. For example, there was no meaningful benefit from state regulation to society, while federal disclosure requirements were sufficient. The blue-sky laws merely increased conflicts but created no additional investor protection. The social costs of blue-sky law were not insubstantial. States spent a lot regarding blue sky laws that also generated a high direct cost to issuers. Administrative resources were spent each year on a state regulation that generated no significant investor protection but bureaucratic entrenchment.(381)

3252. State's response: strengthening vs elimination

Some states resisted challenges to merit authority and expanded its scope. The State of New Jersey and the State of Maine state adopted legislation expanding the basis for merit authority.(380) In 1980s, several states have considered the modification, restriction, or elimination of merit regulation.(388) Some states eliminated merit restraints and shifted to disclosure system. In 1983, the State of Illinois eliminated the merit authority. The State of Louisiana and the State of Wisconsin reduced the merit authority. The State of Michigan and others developed novel techniques of investor protection. They adopted an expert system to get an appraisal of motor company.(380)

3253. Measures for uniform regulation

As the federal-state conflict is a deep-rooted issue, it should not be dealt with single measures. The concept of standardization arose from the beginning stage of blue-sky law. For example, Brach (1918) suggested an idea that the only way to prevent the sale of worthless stock would be a strict Federal Blue Sky Law, which would provide greater protection.(401)

There have been a number of uniformity initiatives by many organizations such as SEC, NASAA, SRO, and each State. A uniform regulation can be achieved either by standardization, cooperation, or federal preemption. State regulation is perceived to be in the public interest to some degree as to achieving market fairness. However, there have been ongoing debates about the value of state merit regulation that it should be generally preempted by the uniform federal standards of the SEC or SROs. State requirements can be standardized for simplification, but the standardization cannot mitigate all the fundamental federal-state conflicts.(398)

3254. Standardization policy

Uniform securities act (USA)

The National Conference of Commissioners on Uniform State Laws (NC-CUSL) developed uniform securities acts in 1930, 1956, 1985 and 2002.[90] The Uniform Securities Act ("USA") was an attempt to provide a model that can standardize and integrate state securities regulations for uniformity and consistency. It is a standardized legal framework for states to adopt in their own securities legislation. It sets a standard for registration requirement, denial, suspension, and revocation of registration (Sec.306), federal covered securities (Sec. 307), and exemptions (Sec. 402). It was aimed to reduce regulatory complexity cost by mitigating the state-to-state conflicts.

RUSA of 1985

The Revised Uniform Securities Act of 1985 ("RUSA") included an exemption from securities registration for NASDAQ NMS securities. It was evaluated to solve some problems of exemption policy but was not widely adopted in many states.(400) RUSA does not attempt to eliminate the merit provisions of the USA, but it has attempted to restrict the merit authority to a certain degree.(380)

USA of 2002

The USA of 2002 is aimed to increase the coordination in federal-state regulation and provide the uniformity in state regulation but has been adopted only by 12 states. Regarding uniform exemptions, state securities laws provide an exemption that is similar to the federal securities act for certain securities or transactions.[91] Regarding the regulation method, the USA describes three types of registration: notification, coordination, and qualification.[92]

Uniform limited offering exemption

The Small Business Investment Incentive Act of 1980 amended Section 19(c) of the 1933 Act for the SEC to cooperate with states (i.e., NASAA) to establish a uniform exemption for small issuers. In 1982, the SEC adopted Regulation D to encourage the capital formation of small businesses at the federal level. In 1983, NASAA adopted the Uniform Limited Offering Exemption ("ULOE") containing major elements of Regulation D to provide a uniform exemption for offerings at the state level. Approximately 30 states have adopted ULOE with some modifications.

Model accredited investor exemption of NASAA

Most states have a limited offering exemption based on the number of purchasers, the dollar amount of offering, or the concept of "accredited investors." In April 1997, NASAA adopted a "model accredited investor exemption" to facilitate uniformity and coordination between federal and state exemptions. Any offer or sale of a security by an issuer in a transaction that meets the requirements of the NASAA exemption is exempted from the state law requiring registration and filing when the guideline is accepted by the state. Sales of securities shall be made only to accredited investors defined in Regulation D.[93]

SCOR statement of policy of NASAA

The Small Company Offering Registrations ("SCOR") program allows an exemption for small companies from federal registration pursuant to Rule 504 of Regulation D under the 1933 Act. Considering the circumstances that individual states were operating state-level SCOR programs, NASAA adopted in 1996 and amended in 2019 the "Small Company Offering Registrations (SCOR) Statement of Policy" that provides the uniform treatment of SCOR. This Statement of Policy sets out policies about issuer eligibility[94], financial statement disclosure[95], bad actor disqualification[96], and review standards.[97] Securities laws of most states are patterned after the USA of 1956. Nevertheless, many jurisdictions have adopted the USA with significant variations of its own in the language or interpretations of the statutes and regulations, the degree of merit review.(380)

3255. Federal preemption

1) NSMIA

Concept

The National Securities Markets Improvement Act (NSMIA) of 1996 amended Section 18 (Exemption from State Regulation of Securities Offerings) of the 1933 Act which re-aligned the relationship between federal and state regulators. The NSMIA was enacted in response to the failure of uniform state regulation for national securities offerings. The NSMIA was the first attempt to make federal preemption of the state securities laws. It was to promote efficiency and capital formation by uniformly regulating national securities offerings. It preempts the state-level registration of "covered securities" and transfers enforcement authority from the states to the federal government. Thus, offerings of "covered securities" are subject to federal regulation, while offerings of securities that are not "covered securities" are subject to the dual system.[98]

Scope of preemption

As a result of the NSMIA, the state regulators may no longer require any registration for covered securities. The scope of a "covered security" is defined in Section 18(b) of the 1933 Act, considering the trading venue, product type, and investor.[99]

Preservation of state authority

Section 18(c) of the 1933 Act preserves state authority with respect to anti-fraud[100], notice filings[101], fee collection[102], and enforcement of the requirements[103] for covered securities.

Report on the NSMIA uniformity

Section 102(b) of NSMIA requires the SEC to conduct a study on the extent to which the uniformity of state regulation has been achieved for securities that are not "covered securities." According to the Report on the NSMIA Uniformity (1997), NASAA and individual state regulators are found to have made significant progress toward enhancing uniformity in regulating offerings of both "covered securities" and "non-covered securities." The main results of the survey include: significant efforts were made by the states; a state compliance cost decreased; state regulators played an important role in the regulation of securities offerings; and state regulatory system coordinated with each other. The report also includes survey responses. Respondents indicated that there is still more to reduce disparity for the offerings of securities that are not "covered securities." For example, the disparity includes the differences in merit review standards and the length of comment periods.(390)

2) **SLUSA**

PSLRA to avoid frivolous class action

The class action was anticipated to be an effective mechanism to protect investors but began to make an unintended turn toward targeting deep-pocket defendants. As a result, frivolous or nuisance suits were harshly criticized for injuring the economy. Adopted in 1995, the Private Securities Litigation Reform Act (PSLRA) intended to impose new restrictions for securities class actions by heightening the standard of pleading to reduce frivolous litigation.

Suits arbitrage: substitution effect

Originally, plaintiffs may choose to file the class action lawsuits in state court or federal court. After the enactment of PLSRA, plaintiffs avoided filing class action in federal courts. Instead, they preferred filing in state courts where many of the provisions of PLSRA do not apply. Contrary to the naive assumptions that plaintiffs would stick to the federal court, many plaintiffs avoided federal court seeking refuge from the heightened requirements of PSLRA, hence, the PSLRA created an unintended shift from federal court to state courts. As a consequence, the concerns for non-uniform judgments were crystallized into a reality. The "substitution effect" of the PSLRA was evidenced. The PSLRA appears to have had little effect on the aggregate number of companies sued, but has created a "substitution effect," moving from federal court into state court.(402)

Measures against avoidance: suit preemption

In 1998, the Securities Litigation Uniform Standards Act of 1998 (SLUSA) was adopted to prohibit plaintiffs from avoiding federal PSLRA. SLUSA is a federal legislative act that amended the 1933 Act and the 1934 Act to preempt certain class actions for state securities fraud claims. Such lawsuits cannot be filed in state court. It is to preempt state class action and implement a uniform law of securities fraud. Section 16 of the SLUSA describes class action limitations in two ways; non-maintenance and removal.[104]

3256. Coordination

Federal-state coordination

The USA of 1956 provides three types of methods for registering securities offerings with the states; Registration by Notification[105], Registration by Coordination, Registration by Qualification. According to Section 303 of the USA of 1956, any security for which a registration statement has been filed under the federal 1933 Act may be Registered by Coordination. A registration statement becomes effective at the moment the federal registration statement becomes effective if all the conditions are satisfied (e.g., no stop order is in effect). The Registration by Coordination is meant to streamline the content of the registration statement and the procedure, but not the substantive standards. According to the Section 304 of the USA of 1956, any securities may be registered by qualification.

A registration statement under the Registration by Qualification shall contain required information specified in Section 305(c).[106] The Registration by Qualification becomes effective when the Administrator so orders.

State-state coordination

The Coordinated Equity Review (CER) program is designed to expedite the registration process and save resources, such as expenditure and time, by streamlining the processes for a multi-state registration. Under the supports of the NASAA, states have created *"coordinated review protocols for equity, small company and franchise offerings; direct participation program securities; and for certain offerings of securities pursuant to Regulation A..."*[107] This program targets small offerings (e.g., 5 or 20 million USD) that are registered in the SEC and traded on the regional exchanges or OTC markets.[108]

CER program consists of program administrator, lead state, and non-lead states. Once the lead state clears the application, all participating states agree to clear it as well.(390)[109]

33. United States: Modern Federal Regulation

331. Registration Statement

Federal approach

Before the 1933 Act and the 1934 Act, there was no federal securities regulation in the United States. In response to the widely adopted blue-sky law, securities interest groups had begun to initiate the idea of federal securities regulation between 1913 and 1917. The Investment Bankers Association (IBA) had drafted a "model securities act" and then attempted to convince states that the federal approach would sufficiently protect investors. The 1933 Act was designed to regulate interstate sales of securities at the federal level, and the 1934 Act to regulate sales of securities in the secondary market. (379, 403)

Public offering

The 1933 Act sets out rules for public offerings in interstate. A company must file with the SEC a registration statement before a public offering is made. It is unlawful to make a public offering in interstate unless registration statement and prospectus are filed for full disclosure of all material facts regarding the investment and financial status. The filing does not imply that the SEC has approved the accurateness of disclosures. Instead, it means that the filer is subject to the enforcement and may be liable for damages to purchasers of the securities. There are private offerings and public offerings.[110] A public offering means an issue of securities for sale to the public and is governed by securities law.

However, there is no direct definition of "public offering" found in the 1933 Act. Public offering that means regulated transaction is defined not directly but indirectly by using the concept of complementary set. To be more specific, a registration statement must be filed prior to any offering, except for securities offerings exempt under the provisions of Section 3 or 4 of the Securities Act. Such a complementary approach signifies that the 1933 Act was intended to provide all-inclusive regulation except for the specified exemptions under SEC Rules. The universal set of "offering" is defined in Section 2(a)(3) of the 1933 Act.[111] Offering shall include every attempt or offer to dispose of, or solicitation of an offer to buy, a security or interest in a security, for value. Section 5(a) set out that it shall be unlawful for any person to make use of any means of communication to sell or offer to buy security unless a registration statement is in effect.[112]

By the way, Section 3(b) set out that the SEC may add any class of securities to the securities exempted if it finds that the enforcement is not necessary for the public interest and the protection of investors by reason of the limited character of the "public offering."[113] Section 4(a)(2) set out the provisions that Section 5 (Prohibitions ...) shall not apply to the transactions not involving any "public offering."[114]

Case: SEC v. Ralston Purina

SEC v. Ralston Purina (346 U.S. 119 (1953)) is a landmark case in the public offering and exemption of the registration statement. The test represented in the Ralston Purina case has been widely used in determining whether an offer qualifies the exemption. The Supreme Court decided whether Ralston Purina's offering of treasure stock to its "key employees" is within this exemption. At first, Ralston Purina gave the following as explanation about what it means by the key employees; *"those who were officers, ... , or other employees whom the Company considered eligible for future promotion to a position of greater responsibility ... – one who was ambitious and likely to develop and grow with the Company's business ..."*[115]

The Supreme Court acknowledged that *"Among those responding to these offers were employees with the duties of artist, ... , and veterinarian. ...,"*[116] but decided that *"These employees were not shown to have had access to the kind of information which registration under the Act would disclose ... The natural way to interpret the private offering exemption is in light of the statutory purpose. ... An offering to those who are shown to be able to fend for themselves is a transaction not involving any public offering. ... some employee offerings may come within 4(1), e.g., one ... who ... have access to the same kind of information that the Act would make available in the form of a registration statement. Absent such a showing of special circumstances, employees are just as much members of the investing public ... ."*[117]

In 1960s, *"the transactions by an issuer not involving any public offering, the so-called private offering exemption"* had been increasing. In 1962, the SEC have made it clear that *"Whether a transaction is one not involving any public offering is essentially a question of fact and necessitates a consideration of all surrounding circumstances, including such factors as the relationship between the offerees and the issuer, the nature, scope, size, type and manner of the offering,"* and, according to the decision of the Supreme Court, *"the exemption must be interpreted in the light of the statutory purpose to protect investors by promoting full disclosure of information."* As the Court declared *"the number of offers is no conclusive as to the availability of the exemption"* and, as a result, the SEC is prevented from using some kind of numerical test in deciding when to investigate exemption claims.[118]

Prospectus

In the US, a registration statement is a document that a company must file with the SEC to initiate IPO under the 1933 Act. It consists of two parts: "prospectus" and "additional information." Part I is the prospectus that is a disclosure document to be delivered to offerees, while Part II contains additional information that should be filed with the SEC but does not have to be delivered to offerees. The prospectus that is required to be filed with the SEC as part of a registration statement is a disclosure document that provides investors with information, such as the business, financial statements, officers, and directors, including compensation. The issuer may not use the prospectus to proceed sales until the registration statement becomes effective by the SEC.

Preliminary prospectus

A preliminary prospectus (aka. red herring) refers to a draft registration statement that a company files before proceeding of a public offering.[119] The issuer should not accept an offer before the registration become effective. It is to solicit expressions of interest in the public offering by providing investors with material information. It can be released before an official offer becomes effective. It offers a price range and issue size and is often accompanied by a roadshow to build interests in the public offering. A road show serves as an educational or informational mechanism for the potential investors who are not familiar with the offering firm.

Confidential draft registration statement

In the US, the number of listed companies has drastically fallen during the 1990s and 2010s. The number of effective IPOs has also fallen from 624 in 1996 to 35 in 2008.[120] The Jumpstart Our Business Startups Act (JOBS Act) was enacted in April 2012 with a goal to establish an IPO On-ramp which reduces the disclosure burden and improve access to capital markets for smaller companies, amended Section 6(e) of the 1933 Act.

It sets out that any Emerging Growth Companies (EGC) may confidentially submit to the SEC a draft registration statement only for the confidential and nonpublic review. The SEC shall not be compelled to disclose any information provided or obtained.[121] Such registration statements are in a draft form for the staff only to review not to disclose. EGCs may withdraw the draft registration statement and terminate all the process without any public disclosure, which removes any potential disincentives. EGCs that are testing-the-water can immediately proceed with a private placement when the market is in an adverse condition.

In a market where valuation or market demand is uncertain, and the timing of IPO also depends on regulator's approval. Combining test-the-water and confidential submission process will provide flexibility, issuers can get useful feedback from markets while maintaining confidentiality. Section 5(d) of the 1933 Act sets out an Emerging Growth Companies (EGC) to engage in communications with the Qualified Institutional Buyers (QIB) to find out whether investors might be interested. As Section 5(d) excludes test-the-water communications from the definition of "offer," such communications will not be jumping the gun so long as they are compliant with Section 5(d).[122]

Expansion of confidential submission process

In 2017, the SEC announced that the staff would accept voluntary draft registration statement submission from "all companies" for nonpublic review to expand the benefits of the JOBS Act that was previously available only to the EGCs. This movement is to provide a more flexible initiative to bolster capital formation with a tool that does not require legislation. After going through the test, in 2019, the SEC adopted new Rule 163B that provide flexibility by enabling "all issuers" to engage in test-the-water communications.

Evaluation of JOBS Act

During the six years of enactment, the number of IPO has increased by nearly 25%, and more than 80% of all IPO have been by EGC. The disclosure patterns of EGCs have changed. The percentage of EGC filers disclosing financial statements of short term (e.g., two years) has been steadily increasing from 26% to nearly 75%.[123] Most EGCs have reduced executive compensation disclosures.[124] To sum-up, EGCs have strongly supported the JOBS Act, and these trends are expected to continue, but disclosure amounts have reduced.

332. Periodic Report

Annual/Quarterly report

An issuer with securities that are registered under Section 12 of the 1933 Act is subject to the periodic reporting requirements of Section 13 and 15 of the 1933 Act on an ongoing basis.[125] The purpose of periodic reporting is to keep shareholders informed on a regular basis. A periodic report includes annual reports, quarterly reports, current reports, and proxy statements.[126] Periodic reporting is the main part of the disclosure requirements imposed by statute. Issuers should provide substantial disclosures on an annual and quarterly basis.[127] The deadlines for Form 10-K and Form 10-Q depend on whether the public company is a large accelerated filer, an accelerated filer, or a non-accelerated filer, that is classified and defined by Rule 12b-2 of the 1933 Act.

Table 7) Annual/Quarterly reports

Filer Status	Public floating	Periodic Report Filing Deadline		
		10-K	10-Q	20-F
Large Accelerated Filer	$700 mil. ~	60days	40days	
Accelerated Filer	$75 ~ $700 mil.	75days	40days	4 months
Non-Accelerated Filer & Smaller Reporting Companies	~ $75 mil.	90days	45days	

Regulation S-K

In 1977, the SEC adopted Regulation S-K to streamline the disclosure documents and to assure uniform information. Regulation S-K is a regulation under the 1933 Act that describes reporting requirements for public companies. It applies to the Form S-1 registration statement, ongoing disclosure requirements, such as Form 10-K, Form 8-K, and tender offer. From 1977 to 1982, the SEC made changes to Regulation S-K to integrate the disclosure requirements to simplify reporting.[129] In 1982, Regulation S-K facilitated an integrated disclosure system of the registration statement disclosure requirements and the periodic reporting disclosure rules. The SEC issued a report to modernize and simplify disclosure requirements and reduce compliance costs for EGCs as required by Section 108 of the JOBS Act.[130] Recently, the SEC proposed rule amendments to modernize some descriptions in Regulation S-K to improve disclosure for investors and simplify the issuer's compliance.[131]

Proxy statement

A proxy statement is to solicit votes in shareholder's meetings. All issuers with registered securities are subject to the proxy statement disclosure in Section 14 of the 1933 Act.[132] The proxy statement must be filed with the SEC in advance of solicitation. Issuers must disclose material facts concerning the relevant voting issues.[133]

Measure: current report 8-K

An issuer with securities registered under Section 12 is subject to the current reporting requirements of Section 13 or 15(d) of the 1933 Act. Current reports on Form 8-K are required to report a broad range of certain material events often within four business days after the occurrence of the event.[134] The instruction of Form 8-K describe the events to file a current report.[135] The SEC amended the current report in 2004 to amplify disclosure requirements to executive compensation. Issuers should be aware of the regulations of stock exchanges that requires an advance notice of material information including the items of Form 8-K.[136] By filling an informational gap of periodic report, current report plays a significant role in the periodic disclosure regulation, which is aimed to provide investors with a continuous disclosure.

333. Deregistration: Going Private Vs. Going Dark

Going private vs. going dark

A "going private transactions" generally involves cash-out "transactions" in exchange for the firm's existing public share so that the shareholder base is reduced and the issuer becomes eligible to delist and deregister its shares. Transactions can take various forms, such as a merger, tender offer, or reverse split.[137] The SEC requires extensive disclosure for going private under Rule 13e-3.[138]

In general, a "going dark" refers to the voluntarily delisting from a national securities exchange and the deregistration under the 1933 Act without transactions or changes in investor base only by filing a SEC form. In practice, going dark issuers rarely have sufficient assets to make a liquidity event (e.g., tender offer).[139] Going dark may significantly increase confidentiality and guide issuers to focus on the business while reducing managerial diversion and public scrutiny. However, they should bear the cost of reduced public exposure. Not only registration but also deregistration is governed by disclosure regulation.

Deregistration of domestic issuers

a. Deregistration under Section 12(b)

Going dark procedure depends on the relevant reporting regulations. According to Section 12(b), a security may be registered on a national securities exchange by the issuer filing an application with the exchange. Listed issuers may voluntarily delist and deregister securities under Section 12(b) of the 1933 Act by filing a Form 25 with the SEC. Once submitted, most SEC reporting obligations are suspended (Rule 12d2-2).[140]

b. Deregistration under Section 12(g)

According to Section 12(g)(1) of the 1934 Act, every issuer that is engaged in interstate commerce shall register the security by filing with the Commission a registration statement within 120 days after the fiscal year-end on which the issuer has total assets exceeding $10 million and a class of equity security held by either 2,000 persons or 500 non-accredited investors. Even though it is delisted, the issuer with more than 500 holders of record and total assets exceeding $10 million may be required to continue reporting obligations pursuant to Section 12(g) of the 1934 Act. To avoid such obligation, the issuer can deregister and suspend reporting obligations when the issuer has shareholders of less than 300 or a total asset of less than $10 million (Rule 12g-4(a) and 12h-3). Section 15(d) reporting obligations will not be terminated but only be "suspended," once the issuer file a Form 15 certifying the deregistration requirements. If the number of shareholders increases to more than 300, then the issuer's obligation to the SEC's disclosure requirement will be reinstated for the protection of investors.

c. Deregistration of foreign issuers

In 2007, the SEC adopted amendments to the rules that govern when a foreign private issuer may terminate the registration under section 12(g) of the 1934 Act.[141] Due to the limited benefits of registration and the significant disclosure costs, many foreign firms decide to be deregistered. They must file a Form 15F certifying that they meet the requirements set out in Rule 12h-6(a) and make a public notice to warn investors of "termination."

Listed companies also need to be delisted before the Form 15F application. Rule 12h-6(a)(4) describes quantitative requirements of termination to file Form 15F (e.g., 5% trading volume, 300 shareholders).[142]

Economic justification of deregistration requirements

The 1934 Act and SEC Rules allow deregistration for issuers that have less than 300 shareholders or less than $10 million in total assets. The 1934 Act seems to perceive that the social cost from deregistration might exceed the social cost of deregistration when issuers exceed the deregistration requirements.

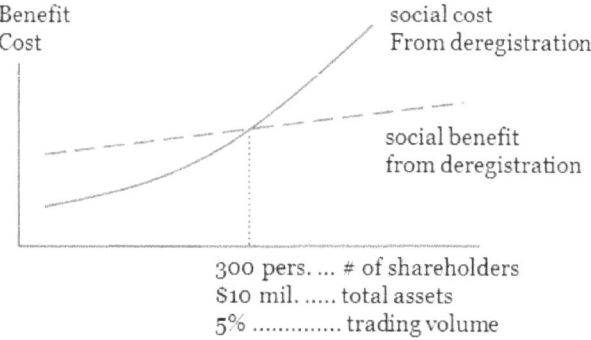

Figure 50 Deregistration

The public interest theory argues that not only disclosure regulation but also deregistration policy is necessary to cure market failure and protect investors. As a result the rationale of disclosure regulation can be applied to the rationale of deregistration policy to minimize social welfare costs. The factors that should be used in deregistration policy is similar to the factors that is used to impose disclose requirements.

The social benefit from disclosure regulation or the social harm from deregistration may be greater for firms with greater shareholder liquidity needs or firms with larger sizes. As the social welfare of disclosure regulation increase with the investor's liquidity needs, so the social harm of deregistration also increases with the higher liquidity (e.g., over 5% trading volume). Besides, the reduction of social welfare from deregistration would be positively associated with firm size (or value). As a result, it might be socially beneficial to prohibit deregistration for larger firms, which is consistent with the current SEC policy.

Agency cost: conflicts of interest

Agency costs should also be included in the public interest model because severe conflicts of interest may exist among shareholders with respect to the going dark decision. Controlling shareholders can be welcoming the going dark as they are less interested in public trading than nonaffiliated shareholders. In respect to such potential conflicts of interest, "...

it may be nevertheless desirable to have a special committee of independent disinterested directors consider the decision to go dark. The special committee should be able to retain and consult with its own legal and financial advisors in accordance with procedures and practices ... ."[143] To minimize conflicts of interest that might exist, regulators will make an effort to require various deregistration requirements and procedures that may reduce conflicts of interest. The SEC requires extensive filings for some going private deregistration. If there are severe potential agency costs, then the social cost from deregistration may arise.

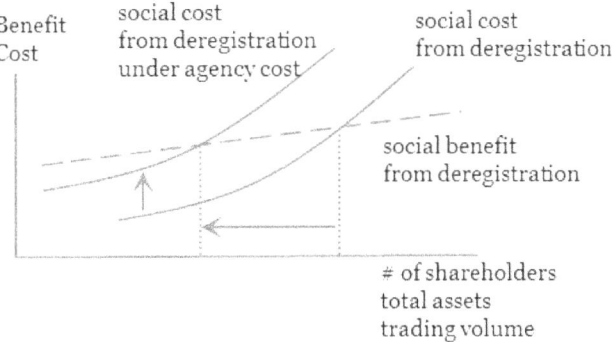

Figure 51 Deregistration under agency cost

Evaluation of deregistration

A sharply increasing going dark in the mid-2000s has been largely attributable to the SOX. Many firms go dark due to both internal reasons (e.g., poor prospects, distress, private benefits) and external reasons (e.g., increased compliance costs) and finally experience large negative abnormal returns. Controlling shareholders of firms with weak governance, are found to take the opportunity of going dark to protect their private control benefits and reduce outside public scrutiny.(404)

Notwithstanding the merits of going private or going dark, issuers need to consider some potential reasons against such a decision. From the past, markets have put some stigma on "going dark" issuers. Equity-based incentives will not be meaningful to attract employees of ability, and financial flexibility will be limited. It is commented that *"In many instances, after a thorough review, the board of directors may conclude that going over to the "dark side" is not such an unpleasant option after all."*[144] Many issuers going dark for legitimate business purposes do not experience litigation.[145]

334. Confidential Treatment

Confidential treatment request

The SEC Rules allow filing firms to request confidential treatment when firms submit letter using two separate versions; the redacted version excluding confidential information and the confidential version including confidential information. The SEC releases only the redacted version after some questions. Firms must provide an appropriate basis for the confidential treatment request.(405) Confidential treatment request can be made pursuant to some rules.[146] In addition, the SEC Rule 83 provides a procedure by which issuer may request withholding under the Freedom of Information Act (FOIA).[147] A confidential treatment order is only in effect for a designated period of time. Sometimes issuers may by requested to provide evidence on why public disclosure would generate competitive harm. Certain type of information will not be appropriate for CTR such as the identity of a 10% customer. In 2019, the SEC adopted new rules and procedures for exhibits containing immaterial, competitively harmful information. This new rule *"permit registrants to file redacted material contracts without applying for confidential treatment of the redacted information (i) is not material and (ii) would be competitively harmful if publicly disclosed."*[148]

Comparison with draft submission

There are many differences between the confidential draft registration submission and the confidential treatment request. The former is to facilitate capital formation for EGCs during IPO stage, while the latter is to protect competitive advantage and reduce proprietary cost. The CTR will not be approved for the paragraphs of contents but on a phrase-by-phrase basis; i.e., name of contracting party, terms of agreement, and detailed technology.[149]

Table 8) Confidentiality

	Confidential Draft Registration Submission	Confidential Treatment Request
Purpose	Support capital formation	Proprietary cost
Firm	EGCs	All issuers
Stage	IPO	IPO + Others
Range	All or part	Word-by-word

Trade-off

The SEC is required to balance conflicting purposes; the public interest of protecting firm's proprietary information and the public interest of promoting transparency for investors. The SEC applies greater scrutiny to firms with low disclosure quality. The CTR review of SEC is to reduce the risk of oversight, and thus SEC allocates resource based on firm's disclosure quality.

CTR scrutiny

In principal, firms are expected to request CTR for proprietary information. However, firms may opportunistically request CTR only to avoid disclosure of material information. Therefore, the SEC should play an important role and be entitled to scrutiny, approve, or deny the CTR. For instance, the SEC may make decision based on the quality of prior disclosure, or it may apply greater scrutiny for firms with low disclosure quality.

34. European Union: Fragmentation Vs. Harmonization

341. Background

1) History

Veil (2017, p.21) describes that *"… it becomes apparent that all steps in EU legislation were preceded by impressive reports written by independent experts: The Segré Report in 1966, the Lamfalussy Report from 2000, and the de Larosière Report in 2009 significantly influenced European legislation on capital markets law."*(406)[150] Chapter 11 of the Segré Report covers the operation of the European securities market regarding information for the public as below.(407)[151]

2) Legislative background

General principles of European Union law

Background knowledge about the general principles of EU law is essential to understand the EU securities law. The general principles of EU law determine the lawfulness of the EU legislatives. The accepted principles include fundamental rights, legal certainty, equality, subsidiarity, and proportionality. The principle of subsidiarity is in relation to whether the Union may exercise its power, while the principle of proportionality is on how it should design. The sources of general principles include the principles of law common to all legal systems, international law, and the national legal system of EU member states. Subsidiarity and proportionality deserve the main attention.[152]

a. Subsidiarity: Article 5(3) of the Treaty on European Union states that "Under the principle of subsidiarity, in areas which do not fall within its exclusive competence, the Union shall act only if and in so far as the objectives of the proposed action cannot be sufficiently achieved by the Member States, …, but can rather, …, be better achieved at Union level." The principle of subsidiary aims to guarantee the independence of member states. Under the principle of subsidiarity, the involvement of the Union is justified when members are unable to achieve the objectives satisfactorily. The central authority may not take any action unless it is more effective than the actions taken at lower authority. [153]

b. Proportionality: The principle of proportionality is recognized in Article 5(4) of the Treaty on the European Union, stating that "Under the principle of proportionality, the content and form of Union action shall not exceed what is necessary to achieve the objectives of the Treaties." Thus, whether the Directive is lawful depends on whether it was appropriate and necessary to achieve the objectives. The least onerous alternative must be chosen among several appropriate measures. [154]

Legislative instruments: primary vs secondary

EU legislation is divided into "primary legislation" and "secondary legislation." A treaty, aka primary legislation, is the basis and starting point of all EU law. It is the rule to regulate the EU institutions and the relationship between the EU and member countries, which is ratified by their parliaments after all the EU countries agree with it.[155] Secondary legislation is derived from the principles and objectives of treaties.

Five forms of secondary legislations

Article 288 of the Treaty on the Functioning of the European Union (TFEU) defines five forms of secondary legislation; regulation, directive, decision, recommendation, and opinion.[156]

A "regulation" shall have a general application. It is a more direct and inflexible legislation and shall be binding in its entirety and directly applicable in all Member States. Undergoing ratification of the EU Parliament, the regulation comes into effect. Prospectus Regulation (i.e., Regulation (EU) 2017-1129) is a good example of the EU Regulation.

A "directive" shall be binding but shall leave to the national authorities the choices of forms and methods. It sets out a goal for all EU countries to achieve. However, Member States have more leeway in the implementation of directives into national law. It is justified by the rationale that a directive complies with the principle of "subsidiarity." As different Member States have different legal environments (i.e., tradition and procedure), each Member State should have leeway to choose its own statutory wording. Transparency Directive is a good example of the EU Directive.

A "decision" shall be binding in its entirety. A decision specifies those to whom it is addressed and shall be binding only those.

A "recommendation" does not impose any legal obligation but allows EU institutions to suggest a line of action.

An "opinion" is a non-binding instrument for EU institutions to make a statement. For example, the committees can make opinions from their specific viewpoint when laws are being made. "Recommendation" and "opinions" shall have no binding force.

Legislative instruments: legislative act and non-legislative act

Secondary legislation is classified into "legislative act" and "non-legislative act." Article 289(3) of the TFEU defines legislative acts as *"Legal acts adopted by legislative procedure shall constitute legislative acts."* Other forms of legal acts are non-legislative. Non-legislative acts can be generally adopted by the European Commission according to specific rules regardless of the legislative procedures. The legislative act must be adopted in prior and delegate to the Commission the power to adopt the non-legislative act.[157]

a. Delegated act: Article 290 of the TFEU set out "1. A legislative act may delegate to the Commission the power to adopt non-legislative acts of general application to supplement or amend certain non-essential elements of the legislative act. The objectives, content ... shall be explicitly defined .... The essential elements ... shall not be subject of a delegation of power. 2. Legislative acts shall explicitly lay down the conditions to which the delegation is subject ... 3. The adjective 'delegated' shall be inserted in the title of delegated acts." [158] As the legislative acts are binding, so delegated acts are legally binding.

b. Implementing Act: Primarily, Member States shall adopt all measures of national law necessary to implement legally binding EU acts. However, in case that EU acts require uniform implementation, the Commission or the Council may be empowered to adopt implementing acts according to Article 291 of TFEU. [159]

Legislative hierarchy and process

The Lamfalussy architecture is the specific approach to the regulatory development process in the financial service industry used by the EU, which was adopted in the securities sector in order to make regulatory process quicker and more effective. After the financial crisis, the EU reformed Level 3 for better supervision by establishing the independent authority (i.e., ESMA) that replaced the level 3 committee.[160] The Lamfalussy architecture is composed of four levels by clearly defining legislative roles and responsibilities among various levels of institutions.(406)[161] European Parliament has the power to approve EU legislation, the Commission drafts proposal and prepares "Impact assessments," and the Parliament and the Council can propose amendments.[162]

Case: Failure to transpose directives

In the case of Francovich v Italy (1991), the European Court of Justice (ECJ) ruled that *"1. The provisions of Council Directive ... must be interpreted as meaning that the persons concerned cannot enforce those rights against the State ... where no implementing measures are adopted ... 2. A member State is required to make good loss and damage caused to individuals by failure to transpose Directive ...."*[163] ECJ established a decision that Member States could be liable to compensate losses or damages of individuals who suffered by the Member State's failure to transpose an EU directive into national law. This is also known as the "principle of state liability."

Harmonization: minimum vs. maximum

Minimum harmonization refers to a minimum requirement that EU national legislation must meet. Minimum harmonization approach is mainly used in EU regulation because it enables easier agreement among the Member States. The national law of the EU member states may exceed the terms of the EU legislation. On the contrary, maximum harmonization is expected to prohibit unnecessary regulatory competition when it is transposed into national law. The burden of stringent EU legislation has risen the request for deregulation, but maximum harmonization is not common in EU legislation.

3412. Capital market legislations

Regulation

In the capital market context, the regulation includes Prospectus Regulation, Market Abuse Regulation. The objective of Prospectus Regulation (Regulation (EU) No 2017/1129) is to harmonize prospectus requirements when firms are offering securities to the public. Prospectus Regulation replaces the previous Prospectus Directive. The objective of Market Abuse Regulation (MAR, Regulation (EU) No 596/2014) is to enhance market integrity and investor protection by preventing market abuse. It replaces the previous Market Abuse Directive.

Directives

Corporate disclosure aiming better investor protection is covered by a number of Directives in many areas; prospectus, periodic & ongoing disclosure, accounting standard, audit, takeover, and governance.

a. Market in Financial Instruments Directive (MiFID I) is to increase competition and investor protection by providing harmonized regulation for investment industry in the EU.

b. MiFID II is to establish a new regulatory framework and improve investor protection in various markets.

c. Prospective Directive is to ensure the disclosure of prospectus when securities are offered to the public or admitted to trading.

d. Transparency Directive is to ensure the transparency of corporate information by way of disclosure.

e. Accounting Directive is to harmonize the financial information provided by issuers in order to ensure a high degree of transparency, comparability of financial statements.

f. Audit Directive is to set out conditions for the registration of statutory audits, the rules on objectivity and frameworks for public oversight.

g. Takeover Bid Directive is to protect the interests of the securities of companies governed by the law of a Member States when the companies are the subjects of a takeover bid.

Guidelines

The European Supervisory and Markets Authority (ESMA) is entitled to issue guidelines and recommendations addressed to competent authorities or financial market participants, which is to achieve regulatory convergence among EU.[164] Under the Transparency Directive, Guidelines on Alternative Performance Measures and Guidelines on the enforcement of financial information are issued. Under the Market Abuse Regulation, three guidelines are issued.[165] "Guidelines on risk factors under the Prospectus Regulation" to support Article 16(4) of Prospectus Regulation is under construction.

APMs guideline
"ESMA Guideline on Alternative Performance Measures" are addressed to regulated market issuers to publish the Alternative Performance Measures (APMs) in a useful and consistent manner. APMs usually appear in the financial statements or the ad-hoc disclosures that are required by Article 17 of the MAR. Examples include operating earnings and EBITDA. ESMA's approach to APMs is to *"ensure consistent, efficient and effective supervisory practices and a uniform and consistent application"* of disclosure requirements.(408)[166]

342. Prospectus

1) Overview

Concept
As prospectus is an essential disclosure prior to the public offer of securities, it is vital in protecting investors. Besides, prospectus harmonization aims to establish a cross-border passport mechanism that enables the effective functioning and growth of the EU market. If issuers face different rules among states, then prospectus approved in one state could be disapproved in other states. Divergent approaches among EU states will inevitably result in market fragmentation.

To ensure the well-functioning market, the EU established a uniform prospectus disclosure framework. Harmonized disclosure framework can ensure uniformity of disclosure, which mitigates differences among states and removes obstacles of smooth functioning markets.[167] Once prospectus is approved by the supervisor of the home Member State, the issuer can raise capital across all EU markets. Single passport rights in the financial industry began to be applied in the late 1980s, which essentially means that a European entity that has been approved by its domestic authority has the right to finance or provide services in the other Member States.

A prospectus is a filing that *"...shall contain the necessary information which is material to an investor for making an informed assessment of: (a) the assets and liabilities, profits and losses, financial position, and prospects of the issuer ...; (b) the rights attaching to the securities; and (c) the reasons for the issuance and its impact on the issuer."* Information that shall be described in a prospectus may vary depending on *"(a) the nature of the issuer; (b) the type of securities; (c) the circumstances of the issuer; ..."*[168] The EU Directive on the prospectus (Directive 2003/71/EC) mandated issuers that are offering securities to the public to disclose the prospectus. Securities shall only be offered to the public only after the publication of a prospectus that is in accordance with Prospectus Regulation.[169]

Revamping the prospectus

Prospective Directive was amended several times until the EU Prospectus Regulation took effect on 21 July 2019. In 2015, by revamping the prospectus regime, the "Action Plan on Building a Capital Markets Union" was suggested to lower barriers of capital markets and provide markets with more diverse opportunities for investment. The regulation is aimed to make it easier and cheaper for SMEs to access capital markets, to provide simple and flexible procedures, especially for secondary issuances and frequent issuers which are already well-known, and to introduce an investor-friendly disclosure framework. The new prospectus regime is in pursuit of the balance between reducing issuer's burdens and protecting investors by ensuring that the firm's life-cycles are fully covered from the start-ups to the frequent issuers. Specific requirements and procedures are applied for each stage of funding escalator. For example, startups raising small amounts of capital will be exempt from the requirements of prospectus disclosure. A tailored disclosure requirement will help SMEs to utilize capital markets without disclosing a full prospectus. Frequent issuers that are already known to markets can benefit from a fast-track procedure when they choose a "Universal Registration Document (URD)" that reduces redundant information.(409)

Repealing the Prospectus Directive and the prior Prospectus Regulation (809/2004), the new Prospectus Regulation (Regulation (EU) 2017/1129) came into force in July 2017. The new regulation aims to facilitate capital raising and ensure the harmonization of format, content, and process across EU members.

Validity of prospectus

Prospectus and universal registration document shall be valid for 12 months after the approval.[170] Once approved by the home Member State, the prospectus shall be valid in any number of host Member States, provided that ESMA and the competent authority of each host Member State are notified. In addition, competent authorities of host Member States shall not undertake any approval or administrative procedures relating to prospectuses and supplements.[171] However, the disclosure requirements of Prospectus Regulation do not prevent a Member State from imposing other particular requirements (e.g., corporate governance). Such requirements should not restrict the content and the dissemination of a prospectus approved by a competent authority.[172]

2) **Components**

Universal registration document

A registration document, a securities note, and a summary shall constitute a prospectus once individually approved by the competent authority. A registration document describes details of the issuer, business, financial status, board of directors, shareholding structure, risk factors, material properties, and any other material information. A securities note describes the shares offered and the terms and conditions.

By the way, frequent issuers can make use of the Universal Registration Document (URD). Once issuers are approved by the authority to obtain the status of the frequent issuer, they would benefit from a fast-track approval process. The authority must make a decision on a draft prospectus within five working days that is half of the usual ten working days.[173] If frequent issuers are allowed to draw up prospectus as separate documents, they can reduce the cost of compliance and swiftly react to market windows. If an issuer meets with the criteria and submits the URD for approval to the competent authority, the issuers are deemed to be a frequent issuer.[174] An issuer that has received approval for a URD for two consecutive years are considered "well-known" and, as a result, all subsequent URD can be filed without prior approval. Instead, the competent authority may conduct disclosure review on an ex-post basis where it is deemed to be necessary.[175] As the main part of the prospectus has already been approved, the frequent issuers who have drawn up a URD should benefit the fast-track approval process to facilitate cost-effective access to the capital markets.[176]

Prospectus: risk factors

Disclosing risk factors in a prospectus is aimed to ensure that investors make a fully informed assessment of a firm's risk factors. Therefore, risk factors to be disclosed should be "material and specific" to the issuer and corroborated by the content of prospectus. Disclosure of "general" risk factors only serves as a disclaimer that could obscure specific risk factors and prevent investors from better understanding. For example, once environmental, social, and governance (ESG) information constitutes specific and material risks for the issuer, it should be disclosed. The issuer should selectively limit the number of risk factors, adequately present and include the risks in the summary. The most material risk should be presented first.[177] Article 16 (Risk factors) of the Prospectus Regulation details on how to draw up prospectus regarding risk factors.[178] Nowadays, regulators tend to focus on the risk factors particularly.

Prospectus: summary

The summary of prospectus consists of four sections: introduction, key information on the issuer, the securities, and the offer. Too overly proscriptive disclosure of the content of the summary often results in the disclosure of immaterial information. However, the new regulation requires that the summary should be short (i.e., no longer than seven sides of A4 paper), simple, and easy for investors to understand better. Issuers should use clear, non-technical language to improve readability. The number of most salient risk factors presented in summary is limited up to 15.[179] Besides, *"No civil liability should be attached to any person solely on the basis of the summary, ... unless it is misleading, inaccurate or inconsistent ... The summary should contain a clear warning to that effect."*[180] To facilitate cross-border offers, not the entire prospectus but only the summary should be available in the language accepted by the competent authority.[181]

3) Special treatments

Exemptions

The Prospectus Regulation *"lays down requirements for the drawing up, approval, and distribution of the prospectus to be published when securities are offered to the public or admitted to trading on a regulated market situated or operating within a Member State."*[182]

However, it is likely to be disproportionate to mandate the standard prospectus disclosure for small offers, which explains why exemptions for small offers are set out. For example, prospectus disclosure requirement shall not apply to an offer of securities to the public with a total consideration in the European Union of less than EUR 1,000,000 over 12 months. The obligation to publish a prospectus shall not apply to an offer of securities addressed solely to qualified investors or fewer than 150 persons, an offer of a total consideration of at least EUR 100,000 per investor, shares issued in substitution for already issued shares, and securities offered to arm's length parties (e.g., takeover, merger, division, and dividend).[183]

Considering the variance of market size across the EU, Member States are given the option to exempt from the harmonized prospectus. Member States are allowed to decide a prospectus exemption criterion which shall not exceed 8 million Euro in terms of the total consideration of each offer under the condition that the exemption applies only to domestic offers.[184] Member States should not extend the obligation of a prospectus to offers with a total consideration below the threshold. However, Member States may require other disclosure requirements at the national level to the extent that such requirements do not constitute a disproportionate or unnecessary burden.[185]

Simplified prospectus for well-known issuers

Around 70% of EU prospectus are disclosed by firms of which securities are already listed, and, as a result, they are already subject to appropriate ongoing disclosure requirements and Market Abuse Directive (MAD). (409) In order to reduce the compliance cost and avoid duplicative disclosures, a lighter prospectus for secondary issuances was devised through the Directive 2010/73/EU under which a proportionate prospectus was introduced for the offers of new shares by issuers of which shares of the same class are already admitted to trading.[186]

The new simplified prospectus provides a significantly wide range of scope where the issuer can disclose a lighter prospectus that applies to secondary issues. For investor protection, a simplified prospectus should be available only for well-known issuers. Issuers that have listed for at least 18 months on a regulated market or SME growth market can be eligible well-known issuer since they have disclosed annual report at least once.[187] The new simplified prospectus consists of a summary, a specific registration document, and a specific securities note, and requires only one year of historical financial information.[188]

However, the simplifying policy is not without a counterargument. The prospectus is the main source of relevant information. Simplifying or reducing the prospectus requirement may lower the disclosure burden but not necessarily lower overall burdens of the issuer. Instead, many investors are likely to seek additional relevant information and ask questions on what is not presented in the lighter prospectus. As a result, the lighter prospectus might transfer the information channel from official prospectus to private one-on-one questions.(410)[189]

Frequent issuers admitted to trading on regulated markets or multilateral trading facilities can choose an optional fast-track mechanism that is subject to the "universal registration document." Issuers can draw up a complete registration document annually and thereby benefit from quick approval whenever they submit a prospectus. If the supervisors already scrutinized the universal registration document that is the central part of the prospectus, then they would be able to scrutinize the securities note and summary within five working days. Frequent issuers are admitted to integrate the periodic disclosure obligations under Transparency Directive into the universal registration document, which reduces duplicative requirements and alleviates unnecessary burdens. As a result, investors can focus on a single document that is updated every year.

EU growth prospectus

SMEs have been deterred from public offering by paperwork and compliance costs. European capital markets have aimed to make it easier for SMEs to raise capital. It should become easier for SMEs to fulfill disclosure obligations under the new regulation, and investors should be well-informed.

"Small and medium-sized enterprises (SMEs) represent 99% of all businesses in the EU. The definition of an SME is important for access to finance and EU support programmes targeted specifically at these enterprises."[190] The "small and medium-sized enterprises" or "SMEs" are defined as companies that meet at least two of the following three criteria: 1) an average number of employees of less than 250, 2) a total balance sheet not exceeding 43 million Euro, and 3) an annual net turnover not exceeding 50 million Euro.[191] Included are the companies that have an average market capitalization of less than 200 million Euro.[192]

The proportionate disclosure regime for SMEs may not create as many advantages as expected. Firms that do not want to be perceived as providing a lower quantity or quality of disclosure are likely to prefer the standard disclosure regime. According to the feedback statement on the online public consultation in 2015, a large majority responded that "... *the proportionate disclosure regime for SMEs has not met its original purpose. In practice, issuers who would eligible to it choose to prepare a full-blown prospectus instead. ... the benefits of applying the proportionate disclosure regime are too limited and do not outweigh the disadvantage of being perceived by investors as providing more limited information when compared to large companies.*"(411)

Under the proportionate disclosure regime for information X (X_{SME} vs X_{Large}), the welfare level of SME investors will be lower than that of investors who trade large firms (Figure 52 left graph) due to the lower disclosure regime. In addition, however small the SME may be, the disclosure requirements of SMEs should exceed the minimum level that is required to protect investors. Thus, proportionate disclosure requirements may result in a trivial reduction of disclosure cost for SMEs. The cost reduction effect (ΔCost) could be trivial, but the benefit reduction effect (ΔBenefit) could be severe from the proportionate disclosure regime. As a result, the net benefit of SME might be far smaller than that of larger firms (Figure 52 right graph, $NB_S << NB_L$).

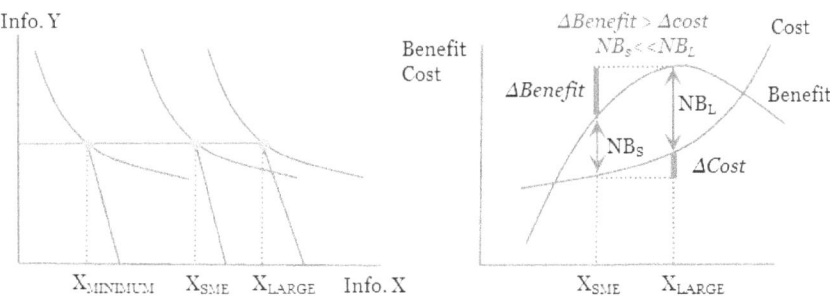

Figure 52 Firm size-Budget line / Benefit-Cost

SMEs are usually likely to raise relatively smaller amounts of capital, but their compliance cost to draw up a standard prospectus would not be proportionately reduced, which might deter the access to the capital markets. On the contrary, investors require sufficient information especially for SMEs with a shorter track record because they might carry more specific risks. In order to encourage financing by SMEs, regulators should give balanced consideration between SMEs and investors. The success of SME venues depends on the balance. It is appropriate to establish a proportionate disclosure regime for growth markets, but it is more important to strike a fair balance between low-cost market access and high-quality investor protection.[193] For example, regulators should consider conflicting objectives. Material and relevant information should be mandated, while proportionality between firm size and fundraising needs are ensured within the limited level of compliance cost.[194] If introducing a firm-size-based two-tier disclosure regime might seriously harm investors' confidence, then it should be reconsidered.[195]

Issuers offering securities to the public with a total consideration in the Union not exceeding a certain threshold (e.g., EUR 20,000,000) would benefit from easier access to financing at proportionately lower costs. Certain eligible issuers may choose to draw up an EU Growth prospectus with lighter disclosure requirements and a standard format that is intended to be more attractive to issuers, provided that they have no securities traded. Eligible issuers include a) SMEs, b) issuers whose securities are traded on an "SME growth market" with an average market capitalization less than 500 euro million, and c) issuers with a total consideration less than 20 Euro million and employees less than 499.[196] Requirements of the simplified prospectus and the EU Growth Prospectus seems to be lower than the disclosure requirements under the United States' Rule 144A.(412)[197]

4) Issuer friendly disclosure

Tri-partite prospectus

"The issuer ... may draw up the prospectus as a single document or as separate documents. ... a prospectus composed of separate documents shall divide the required information into a registration document, a securities note, and a summary."[198] In case a prospectus is drawn up as separate documents, aka tripartite prospectus, separate documents can be approved separately. Issuers may prepare the registration document in advance and then complete securities note and summary later. The tripartite prospectus provides issuers with flexibility so that issuers can raise capital with a great sense of timing when market conditions are favorable. (409)

Omission

In order to avoid a detrimental effect on the disclosing issuer, the omission of sensitive information should be allowed by the competent authority. According to Article 18, the competent authority of the home Member State may authorize the omission of specific information from the prospectus, where a) disclosure would be contrary to the public interest, b) disclosure would be seriously detrimental to the issuer, provided that the omission would not be likely to mislead the public, and c) such information is of minor importance and would not influence the assessment. The competent authority shall submit an omission report to ESMA every year.[199]

Incorporation by reference

In case that documents have been published electronically, issuers can incorporate documents by reference that is known as "incorporation by reference." Incorporation by reference should facilitate drawing up a prospectus at a lower cost. Issuer should be careful with information that is no longer relevant due to material change. Any regulated information should be eligible for the incorporation by reference in a prospectus.[200] However, *"the summary shall not contain cross-references to other parts of the prospectus* or incorporate information by reference."[201] *"Information may be incorporated by reference in a prospectus where it has been previously or simultaneously published electronically,"* where it is contained in other disclosures such as regulated information, annual and interim financial information, audit reports and financial statements, management reports, and corporate governance statements.[202] The documents may be published and distributed separately provided that those documents are made available to the public.[203]

5) User-friendly disclosure

Content and format of prospectus

ESMA published consultation papers containing draft technical advices on a) the format and content of the prospectus(413), b) the scrutiny and approval of the prospectus(414), and c) the content and format of the EU Growth prospectus(415). Commission Delegated Regulations are issued as regards a) the format, content, scrutiny and approval of the prospectus (416) and b) the regulatory technical standards on key financial information in the summary of a prospectus (417).[204]

Supplement and amend disclosure

It shall be presented in a supplement without undue delay when every significant new factor or material mistake in a prospectus may arises between the approval of the prospectus and the closing of the offer period. Such a supplement shall be approved in a maximum of five working days. The summary shall also be supplemented. Investors who have already agreed to purchase shares shall have the right to withdraw their acceptances. Financial intermediary or issuer shall inform investors of the possibility of a supplement, and they shall assist them in exercising their right to withdraw acceptances in such case.[205] As long as the universal registration document has not become a constituent part of an approved prospectus, it should be amended either voluntarily or by request of the competent authority. When the competent authority identifies a material omission, mistake, or inaccuracy, the issuer should amend the universal registration document without undue delay.[206]

6) Prospectus scrutiny

Purpose

Prospectus Regulation is also aimed to eliminate different approaches by competent authorities in the scrutiny and approval process through the harmonization of the rules and criteria for the scrutiny and approval process. It is important to enable the scrutiny policy (e.g., criteria, process) to converge to the required level of completeness, consistency, and comprehensibility. Guidance on the approval of a prospectus should be publicly available, and ESMA should foster supervisory convergence.[207]

General procedures

A prospectus shall not be published unless the relevant competent authority has approved it. The competent authority shall notify the issuer of its decision regarding the approval of the prospectus within 10 working days of the submission of the draft prospectus. The time limit shall be extended to 20 working days where the offer involves securities issued by a first-time issuer. The competent authority shall notify ESMA of the approval of the prospectus as soon as possible. Where the competent authority finds that the draft prospectus does not meet the standards, it shall promptly inform the issuer of and clearly specify the changes or supplementary information that are needed. Where the issuer is unable or unwilling to make the necessary changes or to provide the supplementary information requested, the competent authority shall be entitled to refuse the approval of the prospectus and terminate the review process.[208]

URD review

The competent authority may at any time review the content of any universal registration document which has been filed without prior approval. The competent authority has 10 days to scrutinize after the issuer has submitted a draft prospectus. The review process shall consist in scrutinizing the completeness, consistency, and comprehensibility of the information. Where the competent authority finds that the Universal Registration Document (URD) does not meet the standards or that amendments or supplements are needed, it shall notify it to the issuer.[209] However, they do not check whether the information is correct and truthful but oversees the general compliance with the Prospectus Regulation.(409)

Guidelines

The European Commission adopted the "Commission Delegated Regulation (EU) 2019-980 as regards the format, content, scrutiny, and approval of the prospectus" to specify the criteria for the scrutiny and review of the universal registration document and the procedures of the approval and filing.[210] According to Article 16 of the Prospectus Regulation, ESMA prepared the guideline in order to encourage better disclosure of risk factors by assisting competent authorities with the review process of the specificity and materiality of risk factors.[211]

343. Transparency Directive

3431. Transparency directive of 2004

Background

To achieve transparency, issuers should ensure appropriate disclosure, and certain shareholders should also inform issuers of the changes in major holdings so that issuers can keep the public informed. On the contrary, a higher level of investor protection could hinder new issuer's market entrance to the regulated markets. Thus, the Member States other than the home Member State should no longer restrict market entrance by imposing more stringent disclosure requirements.[212] As a result, the harmonization of transparency rules among the EU became a vital mission. A convergence of financial reporting standards is already established for international accounting standards.[213] Transparency Directive (TD) builds on this Regulation with regard to periodic reporting. Under the TD, issuers are applied by the rules of the home state, regardless of member states in which the issuer's securities are listed. It aims to improve the harmonization of transparency of issuers whose securities are admitted to trading on the regulated markets of the EU by establishing minimum requirements of information disclosure.

Transparency directive of 2004

Transparency Directive (Directive 2004/109/EC) requires securities issuers in the regulated markets to ensure appropriate transparency through the disclosure of regulated information. TD includes the duty of periodic disclosure and ongoing disclosure, including the ad-hoc notification, that should be imposed by supervisory authorities. The Directive mandates firms to disclose periodic reports, such as annual financial reports and half-yearly financial reports. Firms have to disclose annual reports not later than four months after the end of the fiscal years, including audited financial statements, and management reports. In case half-yearly report is audited, it has to be disclosed as well.[214] Compatibility is attained when investors can be sure that the information will be disclosed within a regular time period. An annual financial report should ensure information over the years to support investors to compare annual financial performance. TD introduces half-yearly financial reports for issuers to allow investors to make a more informed assessment.[215] Investors also require more frequent disclosure of interim information. The additional requirement should be introduced to disclose an interim (e.g., quarterly) management statements. Issuers who already disclose quarterly financial reports should not need to publish interim management statements.[216]

However, it should be noted that the TD allows member states to adopt more stringent requirements. For example, each country might adopt additional requirements, including quarterly reports, at a country level. In addition, issuers may provide more information on a voluntary basis as long as it does not mislead. The European Securities and Markets Authority (ESMA) plays a supervisor role by promoting common practices. ESMA aims to ensure that supervisory authorities converge along the approaches established by ESMA.(418)

Regulated market

A regulated market means a multilateral market system operated and/or managed by a market operator (e.g., stock exchange), which brings together or facilitates the multiple third-party trading interests in a way that results in a contract. The financial instruments should be admitted to trading under its rules. The market operator should be supervised (authorization, requirements, admission to trading, suspension, and monitoring) in accordance with the provisions of Title III of MiFID.[217]

Regulated information

Regulated information means all information the issuer is required to disclose under TD, Article 6 of MAD, or the laws, regulations, or administrative provisions of a Member State adopted under Article 3(1) of Transparency Directive.[218] TD regulates periodic information such as annual financial reports, half-yearly financial reports, and interim management statements and ongoing information.

Dissemination

Easy access to the regulated information should be ensured. The central transparency gateway will guide investors to better access and analysis. "*The home Member State shall ensure that the issuer ... discloses regulated information in a manner ensuring fast access ... on a non-discriminatory basis and makes it available to the officially appointed mechanism ....*"[219] In addition, "*The issuer ... may not charge investors any specific cost for providing the information.*"[220]

3432. TD Amendment of 2013

Impact assessment on transparency directive of 2004

Commissioned by the European Commission, MAZARS (2009) provides a comprehensive survey result on the Transparency Directive (TD) of 2004. Below are the summary.(419)

a. Usefulness: A majority of stakeholders consider TD to be useful and appropriate in achieving the objectives of transparency.

b. Impacts on listing: Economic impacts on the listing is not conclusive. "Overall, the Directive is perceived as a regulatory measure that did create neither obstacle nor incentives to listings on regulated market." [221]

c. Uneven transposition: Some EU members adopted more stringent requirements, which resulted in the uneven transposition of TD.

d. Compliance: Stakeholders perceive that issuers generally comply with obligations. The smaller issuers tend to experience larger difficulties with the deadlines. [222]

e. Compliance cost: The compliance cost does not appear to be high. 49% of stakeholders do not consider that the compliance is onerous. [223]

f. Impact on investor: Insufficient harmonization increased substantial costs for cross-border investors. Some investors view that more harmonized Directive could have reduced costs.

Key issues

According to MAZARS (2009), the fundamental principles of TD on the usefulness of disclosed information and the degree of obligations are not questioned by market stakeholders.(419) However, some questions are raised regarding firm size, quarterly report, and notification of major holdings. European Commission (2010) also provided reviews on TD of 2004 describing the emerging main issues especially as to minimum harmonization.(420) Finally, these efforts led to the Transparency Directive Amendment of 2013.

a. Firm size: Proportionality issue

Demarigny (2010) explained that Transparency Directive has set disclosure requirements irrespective of firm size, and, as a result, generating too high barriers for SMEs in terms of compliance costs. The liquidity has extremely concentrated on major issuers, which supports the necessity of proportionate regulation for SMEs.(421)[224] Whether the two-tiered transparency rules should be adapted to increase the attractiveness of regulated markets for SMEs became a hot issue that is recurrent in the global market. There could be many opponents who argue that a tiered regime for SMEs is not necessary, the current requirements are not too demanding, and SMEs should not be admitted as a listed company if they cannot meet the requirements. Thus, tiered measures should be carefully devised to avoid undermining investor protection.

b. Quarterly report: Short-termism issue

The usefulness of the quarterly financial reports was another emerging issue on whether it contributes to short-termism. The short-term vision of both issuers and investors has been pointed out as playing some role in the financial crisis. For example, investors with short term vision might put pressure on management by using short-term mechanisms (e.g., compensation) to take large bets on risky choices in meeting quarterly targets.(419) UK House of Commons (2009) found that *"bonus-driven remuneration structures encouraged reckless and excessive risk-taking and that the design of bonus schemes was not aligned with the interests of shareholders and the long-term sustainability ..."* and proposed a number of reforms including enhanced disclosure requirements on remuneration structures.(422) The disclosure of quarterly financial reports might serve as a contributor to short-termism, and therefore removing the requirement to publish quarterly financial information from Transparency Directive would seemingly alleviate the short-term pressure on issuers. However, a majority of market participants already perceive the disclosure of quarterly financial information is valuable. Thus, many large issuers would continue to disclose quarterly financial information, and even the obligation is removed. Only some of SMEs might benefit from the removal of quarterly disclosure. (422)

c. Notification of major holdings of voting rights

The notification obligations of major holdings have a dual objective: market efficiency and corporate governance. The notification regime provides the market with information about significant transactions, contributing to informed decisions while preventing market abuse. On the other hand, issuers and investors can identify the changes of major shareholders for corporate governance purposes. The uneven transposition of the disclosure requirements about major holdings can result in difficulties for investors, which is considered to be the most problematic issue. Due to the divergences in definitions, scope, exemptions, and thresholds, the notification obligation of major holdings was calculated in a different manner across the EU. As a result, the minimum harmonization regime is questioned on whether it is an appropriate tool to achieve a harmonization of transparency in the EU. The stakeholders surveyed are largely in favor of single EU rules for the notification of major holdings. In addition to the uneven transposition, the existing thresholds are pointed to be too high to capture relevant changes in major holdings, but stakeholders' views are *"mixed on the need to lower the initial disclosure threshold."*(419)[225]

TD amendment of 2013

The Transparency Directive of 2004 was amended in 2013 by the Transparency Directive Amending Directive (Directive 2013/50/EU). The main purpose of the amendment is to reduce the disclosure burden of SMEs by removing the disclosure requirements to publish interim (i.e., quarterly) financial reports.[226] The European Commission identified areas to improve and simplify with the aim of making more attractive markets. The administrative burden should be reduced for SMEs in order to improve their access to capital. Disclosure of interim management statements and quarterly financial reports appear to be the most important burden for SMEs, which boosts short-termism.[227] According to the amended Article 3, the Member States may require issuers to add additional (e.g., quarterly) periodic disclosure requirements, on the condition that it does not constitute a disproportionate burden, in particular for the SMEs, and the content is proportionate to the factors of investment decisions. The Member States shall assess both whether it may lead to issuers' short-termism and whether they may impact negatively on the SMEs.

344. Market Abuse Regulation

3441. Insider trading and legitimate trading

Concepts

Market Abuse Directive (MAD) was designed to achieve a single EU market by integrating the EU financial markets. To a certain degree, however, MAD has failed in achieving the goal as the Member States had been implemented national laws in various ways. Market Abuse Regulation (MAR) on insider dealing, unlawful disclosure, and market manipulation came into effect in July 2016, replacing the Market Abuse Directive (MAD). The scope of financial instruments has been expanded from the financial instruments traded on the regulated market to the financial instruments traded on a multilateral trading facility (MTF) and organized trading facility (OTF).[228]

Public disclosure of inside information

MAR set forth the basic principles of public disclosure of inside information. *"An issuer shall inform the public as soon as possible of inside information which directly concerns that issuer. The issuer shall ensure that the inside information is made public in a manner which enables fast access and complete, correct and timely assessment... The issuer shall not combine the disclosure ... with the marketing of its activities... The issuer shall post and maintain on its website for a period of at least five years, all inside information it is required to disclose publicly."*[229]

Inside information and insider dealing

Issuers are required to publicly disclose the "inside information" as soon as possible. Inside information shall comprise the *"information of a precise nature, which has not been made public, relating, directly or indirectly, to one or more issuers or to one or more financial instruments, and which, if it were made public, would be likely to have a significant effect on the prices of those financial instruments or on the price of relate derivative financial instruments."*[230] In addition, *"... insider dealing arises where a person possesses inside information and uses that information by acquiring or disposing of ... financial instruments to which that information relates. The use of inside information by cancelling or amending an order ... shall also be considered to be insider dealing."*[231]

Unlawful disclosure of inside information

"A person shall not ... unlawfully disclose inside information."[232] *"... unlawful disclosure of inside information arises where a person possesses inside information and discloses that information to any other person, except where the disclosure is made in the normal exercise of an employment, a profession or duties ... ."*[233]

Legitimate behavior of legal person

From the mere fact that a legal person is in possession of inside information, the legal person shall not be deemed to have engaged in insider dealing, where the legal person a) has established adequate internal arrangements that effectively ensure that neither the natural person (e.g., employee) who made investment decision nor another influenced natural person was in possession of the inside information; and b) has not encouraged the natural person who traded the financial instruments.[234]

Market manipulation

MAR set forth the scope of market manipulation in detail. Market manipulation shall comprise such activities as giving false or misleading signals.[235]

3442. Delaying disclosure

Delaying disclosure

The public disclosure of inside information is essential for issuers to avoid insider trading and ensure that investors are not misled. Therefore, issuers should be required to disclose inside information as soon as possible. However, disclosure obligation may prejudice the issuer's legitimate interests under certain circumstances. MAR tightens the ongoing disclosure regulation because MAR extends disclosure obligation to uncertain information relating to future events. To protect the issuer's legitimate interests without harming investor's protection, MAR sets out criteria of delaying disclosure: legitimate interests, non-misleading, and confidentiality.[236]

In addition, MAR preamble illustrates a non-exhaustive list of circumstances that may relate to the issuer's legitimate interests; *"(a) ongoing negotiations ... where the outcome ... would be likely to be affected by public disclosure ... ; (b) decisions taken or contracts ... which need the approval of another body ... in order to become effective ... provided that public disclosure of the information ... would jeopardize the correct assessment of the information by the public."*[237]

Delaying disclosure guidelines

The Committee of European Securities Regulators (CESR) believes that *"as the right to delay the disclosure of inside information is a derogation from the general rule rather than the norm, it would not be appropriate to give a long list of (other) circumstances in which the issuer has the right to delay."*[238] In 2016, ESMA issued the "MAR Guidelines Delay in the disclosure of inside information" only to establish a non-exhaustive list of information to indicate which information is reasonably expected or required to be disclosed. (423)[239]

This guideline includes the situations where immediate disclosure is likely to prejudice the issuers' legitimate interests. Immediate public disclosure would likely jeopardize the outcome of material events, such as contractual negotiation (e.g., mergers, acquisitions, and splits), financial recovery, third-party procedure (e.g., approval by another body of the issuer, intellectual property rights, and plan to trade a major holding in another entity). This guideline also illustrates the situations in which the delay of disclosure is likely to mislead the public. The delay of inside information can mislead the public when it is materially different from the previous public announcement or when the inside information that is intended to be delayed is in contrast with the market's expectations.

Graphical implications

Inside information is the property rights of a firm. Disclosure regulation is forcing firms to publicly disclose and allocate the property rights to investors. Let us assume that manager has two options on disclosure timing: preemption and delay. If manager delays disclosure, the firm's proprietary rights can be more protected, resulting in the decrease of proprietary cost and the decrease of misleading effects on investors. Managers choice of disclosure time will shift the disclosure cost curve and disclosure benefit curve.

a. Delayed disclosure

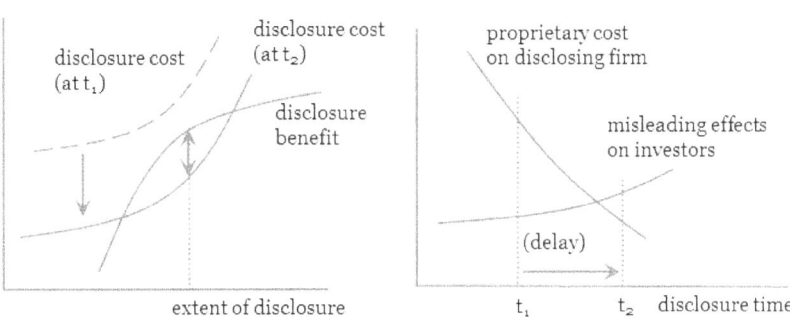

Figure 53 Delayed disclosure

Let us assume the situation where the proprietary cost curve is steep, but the misleading effect curve is flat (Figure 53 right graph). If the misleading effect on investors is flat, then investors are not severely affected by delayed disclosure or preemptive disclosure, and, as a result, the structure of disclosure benefit or disclosure cost will not be changed. However, if proprietary cost sharply decreases with delayed disclosure, then delayed disclosure will shift the disclosure cost curve downward. Firms would not disclose voluntarily early at t_1 because disclosure cost is higher than disclosure benefit at t_1, but make voluntary disclosure delayed at t_2 (Figure 53 left graph).

b. Delayed disclosure

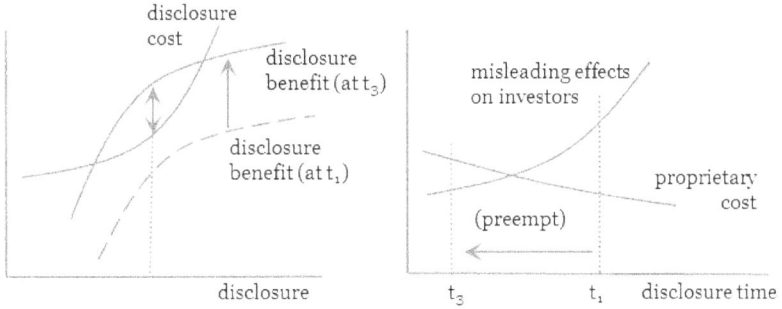

Figure 54 Misleading effects

Let us assume the opposite situation where the proprietary cost curve is flat regardless of the disclosure time, but the misleading effect curve is steep. If the manager considers the delayed disclosure (Figure 54 right graph t_1), then the misleading effect on investors will increase, which makes disclosure benefit lower or disclosure cost higher.

As a result, the manager would not choose to delay disclosure because the net benefit of disclosure is negative at t_1. However, the manager's choice to make preemptive disclosure (i.e., disclosing at t_3) will significantly reduce the misleading effects on investors, which shifts the disclosure benefit curve upward or the disclosure cost curve downward, generating the positive net benefits of disclosure. Under such situation, firms would not delay disclosure at t_1, but voluntarily make preemptive disclosure at t_3.

345. Accounting Directive

In 2013, Accounting Directive (Directive 2013/34/EU) on the annual financial statements and consolidated financial statements was adopted. It amended Directive 2006/43/EC that was adopted as regards the statutory audits of annual accounts and consolidated accounts.[240] Non-financial reporting Directive (2014/95/EU) was adopted to amend the Accounting Directive to introduce non-financial information disclosure requirements. Article 19a and 29a of the Accounting Directive introduced the disclosure requirements of non-financial information.[241] Non-financial information disclosure requirements apply only to large public-interest companies with more than 500 employees. It provides companies with the flexibility to disclose relevant information in a way that is in accordance with their own characteristics and business environments. In 2017, the European Commission issued non-binding guidelines on non-financial reporting.[242]

346. United Kingdom

3461. FCA
Regulatory changes
After a series of financial scandals in the 1990s, including the collapse of Barings Bank, a demand arose to establish the consolidated regulatory structures. The Financial Services Authority (FSA) began to exercise statutory powers by the Financial Services and Markets Act 2000 and undertook the self-regulatory roles of other entities. In 2013, the FSA was separated into the Financial Conduct Authority (FCA) and the Bank of England. The FCA is empowered as the UK Listing Authority (UKLA), financed by the fees of financial industry, and operated independently from the government.[243] The FCA Handbook sets out numerous rules on listing, prospectus, and disclosure. FCA acts as the competent authority for listing, Prospectus Directive, Transparency Directive, and Market Abuse Regulation (MAR). The FCA can also take the responsibility of enforcement by imposing penalties on the breaches of the listing rules and laws.

Listing rule

The "Listing Rule" of the FCA, a UK Listing Authority (UKLA), provides a guide to listing. It recognizes many market classifications; Main market, Premium, Standard, Specialist Fund Segment, and High Growth Segment.[244] The Listing Rule (LR6) includes rules governing disclosure requirements in circulars.[245] According to LR14, a listed issuer must comply with the "Disclosure Guidance and Transparency Rules" (DTR) on an ongoing basis, and non-compliance may result in the listing suspension. The UKLA oversees the issuers' admission processes to a regulated market by assessing the eligibility of listing applicants and reviewing the Prospectus. Listing applicants must apply to the stock exchange to meet the admission requirements and disclosure standards in parallel to the application to the UKLA. They recommend listing applicants to contact the stock exchange as early as possible for assistance with the admission process. Admission becomes effective once issuers are approved by both. The stock exchange and the UKLA jointly announce the final decision.

Disclosure guidance and transparency rules (DTR)

The FCA adopted the Disclosure Guidance and Transparency Rules (DTR) that is mandating ongoing disclosure. Chapters 2~3 of DTR are implemented to comply with the requirements of the Market Abuse Directive (MAD), and Chapters 4~6 are implemented to comply with the requirements of the Transparency Directive. FCA provides the Technical Note as guidance.

Delaying disclosure: MAR 17, DTR 2

Notwithstanding, issuers can delay the disclosure if certain conditions are met. Issuers must notify the FCA after delaying disclosure of insider information, and they do not need to provide a written explanation on the reasons of delaying but should keep appropriate records about relevant conditions for delaying in case the issuers are requested by the FCA. The FCA provides guide and internet form for issuers to notify the FCA with delayed disclosure under DTR 2 and Article 17(4) of the Market Abuse Regulation.[246]

Information distribution

National Storage Mechanism (NSM) is an official and central database storing regulated information as required by the Transparency Directive.[247]

3462. LSE

Continuing disclosure obligations

LSE Group owns the LSE and Borsa Italiana. LSE markets are classified by the Main market (EU regulated market), AIM (exchange regulated market), PSM, SFM. According to the "Admission and Disclosure Standards" (hereafter "Standards"), "...*issuers must be in compliance with: (a) the requirements of any securities regulator by which it is regulated; ... and (c) the provision set out in the Standards, including modification to the application of the Stand-*

ards which has been notified via out website." In addition, *"MAR provides for separate disclosure obligations... The disclosure obligations in MAR relate to the disclosure of insider information and disclosure of transactions by persons discharging managerial responsibilities..."* (Rule 4.1~2).[248] Ongoing obligation for a Main Market includes the requirements of the UKLA and the Standards of LSE.[249]

Warning notice

"Admission and Disclosure Standards" (Standards) set out the warning notice such that *"LSE may issue a warning notice to an issuer for a breach of the rules"* (Rule 5.3), *"A warning notice forms part of an issuer's formal compliance record"* (Rule 5.4).

Suspension

Under the Standards, LSE may suspend trading of securities as it may determine to ensure the orderly operation of its markets. Any request by an issuer to suspend trading must be confirmed by the Exchange in writing (Rule 4.12~14).

347. Germany

BaFin is the federal financial supervisory authority in Germany, which monitors the listed firms' compliance with the securities law and enforces insider trading, market manipulation, and disclosure. Frankfurt Stock Exchange (FSE) operates the EU regulated market, such as Mainboard, General Standard, and Prime Standard. FSE also operates the exchange regulated unofficial market that is aimed to provide SMEs with an easy and cost-effective way of financing. It requires a quarterly financial statement in German and English as a prerequisite of the Prime Standard. The FSE Rule enhances the utilization of periodic reporting obligation. Besides, the listing rules of FSE imposes higher continuous disclosure standards than those in the law (i.e., WpHG). Issuers listed in the FSE Prime Standard must provide ad hoc disclosures in both German and English.

348. Swiss

The Listing Rule of SIX Exchange Regulation set out periodic reporting (annual reporting and interim reporting) and further duties to provide information which includes the obligation to disclose potentially price-sensitive facts, postponement of disclosure, notification of changes in the rights attached to securities, and disclosure of management transactions. "Directive on Ad hoc Publicity" (DAH) of SIX details the information on the issuers' obligation to disclose potentially price-sensitive facts pursuant to the Art 53 of Listing Rule. Especially, Art 6 of DAH describes the "Principle of equal treatment" that *"The public must be notified in order to ensure that all market participants have the same opportunity to become aware of poten-*

tially price-sensitive facts. Selective notification of market participants constitutes a violation of the principle of equal treatment."[250]

The Listing Rule sets out the types of sanctions that may be imposed cumulatively: reprimand, fine, trading suspension, delisting, reallocation to a different regulatory standard, exclusion from further listing, withdrawal of recognition. SIX Exchange Regulation AG publishes legally enforceable sanction notices in anonymized form.[251] In addition, the Sanctions Commission may decide to publish the sanction decisions against participants by name.[252] The frequently enforced type is the non-compliance of the ad-hoc publicity, such as selective notification.[253]

35. Asia

351. Japan

In Japan, statutory disclosure requirements are based on the Financial Instruments and Exchange Act (FIEA), while timely disclosure is operated under the Securities Listing Regulation of the Tokyo Stock Exchange (TSE).[254] Since timely disclosure is vital for a fair price in the capital market, JPX-R, as a self-regulatory organization, establishes enforcement rules for a prompt, accurate, and fair disclosure. JPX-R shall conduct disclosure examination concerning the disclosure timing, inconsistency, and appropriateness.[255] JPX-R examines whether listed firms' timely disclosure is in line with the disclosure rules. It takes account of the following examination points: timing, false statement, lack of information, and misunderstanding.[256] JPX-R can designate an issuer as "Securities on alert" when JPX-R deems that improvement is highly necessary to the internal management system.[257] JPX-R can require an issuer to submit an "Improvement Report" when the issuer has violated the provisions concerning timely disclosure.[258] In case an issuer is in a state where it does not disclose corporate information immediately, JPX-R can designate the issuer as a "Disclosure In Question Security."[259] JPX-R can also make a public announcement and impose penalty for a violation of listing agreement.[260]

352. Singapore

Continuous disclosure

According to the Securities and Futures Act 2002 that describes the statutory support for the continuous disclosure by exchange, a person must not intentionally, recklessly, or negligently fail to notify the exchange of such information on specified events or matters as is required to be disclosed under the listing rules.[261] The SGX Mainboard Rule describes the disclosure requirements of material information. An issuer must announce any information which is necessary to avoid the establishment of a false market or would be likely to affect the price or value of its securities materially.[262]

Examples of events to disclose

SGX provides an illustrative but not exhaustive list of events that are likely to require immediate disclosure: joint venture, merger or acquisition, the acquisition or loss of significant contract, significant litigation, tender offer, and significant dispute.[263]

Disclosure exemption

The SGX Mainboard Rule describes when an issuer may withhold disclosure. An issuer may not disclose when it would be a breach of law to disclose or each of the following conditions applies; a) a reasonable person would not expect the information to be disclosed; b) the information is confidential; and c) one or more of the following: a trade secret, an incomplete proposal or negotiation, insufficiently definite, internal use.[264] Unusual trading activities may suggest that the information is no longer confidential. Therefore, during the disclosure exemption period, the issuer should watch and check trading activities and be ready to make an immediate disclosure if necessary.[265]

Guideline for other public announcements

Mainboard Rule provides a short guideline for the preparation of press releases and other public announcements. It recommends that an announcement should be reviewed by an official who is familiar with the announcing matters, SGX rules, and securities laws. It is desirable to assign, on a continuing basis, public relations staffs who are with experience and have documents reviewed by legal counsel before disclosure. If material information is inadvertently disclosed at the selective meetings with analysts or others, it must be publicly disseminated as promptly as possible.[266]

Public announcements

The Corporate Disclosure Policy describes that the content of a press release or other public announcement is as important as its timing. Each announcement should be factual, clear, and succinct, containing sufficient quantitative information. It should be balanced and fair, avoid over-technical language and promotional jargon, and explain the relevant consequences or effects. It should avoid any statements that might lead to misunderstanding: omission of unfavorable facts, presentation as more probable than is the case, presentation of projections without sufficient factual basis, and negative statements phrased to create a favorable implication.[267]

Disclosure channel

The Mainboard Rule describes that *"An issuer must release all announcements via SGXNET unless specified otherwise."* If an issuer releases material information to the media but did not to the SGXNET, the information might become generally available, but the issuer is in breach of Rule 703 as Rule 702 requires an issuer to release via SGXNET, unless specified otherwise.[268]

Awards

Some exchanges, such as Korea Exchange and SGX, have adopted an award procedure to encourage best disclosure practices. In Singapore, *"the Best Annual Report Award was first introduced in 1974 to encourage listed companies to increase the extent and quality of voluntary disclosure in their annual reports."* The Singapore Corporate Awards (SCA) was launched on

September 2005 to consolidate existing awards. This award is jointly organized by the Singapore Exchange, the Institute of Singapore Chartered Accountants, etc. The objectives of the SCA are to recognize and honor listed companies which effectively implemented and promoted corporate disclosure standards and practices.[269]

353. Australia

Corporations act 2001

Chapter 6CA (Continuous disclosure) of the Corporations Act 2001 sets out details of the continuous disclosure requirements, and Section 674 sets out the continuous disclosure requirement of the listed firm. If the provisions of listing rules require the firm to notify the exchange of information about specified events or matters, the firm must notify the exchange of that information. A person who is involved in the listed firm's contravention is deemed to contravene Subsection 674(2). Failure to comply with Subsection 674(2) may result in an offense and civil penalty. An infringement notice may be issued for an alleged contravention of Subsection 674(2).[270]

General disclosure requirements

The Corporations Act describes the concept of material effect on price or value.[271] Listing Rule describes an immediate disclosure requirement for material information. *"Once an entity is or becomes aware of any information concerning it that a reasonable person would expect to have a material effect on the price or value of the entity's securities, the entity must immediately tell ASX that information."*[272] Listing Rule provides non-exhaustive examples of the "Immediate notice of material information" that could require disclosure: the transaction that will lead to a significant change in the nature or scale of the firm's activities; material mineral or hydro-carbon discovery; a material acquisition or disposal; giving or receiving a notice of intention to make a takeover; and any rating applied by a rating agency to an entity or its securities and any change to such a rating.[273] In addition, Listing rule 3.2~19 provides lists and explanations of the "Notice of specific information" that require disclosure, such as takeover bid, buy-back, capital, options, director's interests, and dividends. "Guidance Note 8 Continuous Disclosing: Listing Rules 3.1~3.1B" provides detailed guidance for better understanding and compliance.

Exception to immediate disclosure

Listing Rule describes exceptions only for the particular information that is confidential, would not be expected to be disclosed, and meets one or more of five specific situations.[274] Listing Rule makes it clear that a confidentiality agreement cannot prevent a firm from complying with disclosure requirements. The mere existence of a confidentiality agreement should not be allowed as a basis of an exception to avoid intentional misuse.[275]

Quarterly disclosure

Most listed firms are not mandated to report quarterly reports. Mining, oil, and gas firms must disclose a quarterly report no later than one month after the end of the quarter.[276] In addition, if the firm was required to comply with the asset test described in listing rule 1.3.2(b) because of the application of the official list, then the firm must complete and disclose quarterly cash flow reports.[277] The listing rule deals with industry-specific additional disclosure standards, such as additional reporting on mining, oil, and gas production and exploration activities.[278]

Infringement notice

Australian Securities and Investment Commission (ASIC) is entitled to issue an infringement notice under Section 12GXA of the Australian Securities Investment Commission Act 2001. If ASIC has reasonable grounds to believe that a person has contravened an infringement notice provision, ASIC may issue an infringement notice to the person. Section 12GXB states that an infringement notice must give details of the alleged contravention, describes the maximum pecuniary penalty that the Court could order the person, and specifies the penalty that is payable in relation to the alleged contravention.

According to the Section 12GXD, if the person is in compliance with an infringement notice (e.g., the person pays the penalty specified in the infringement notice within the infringement notice compliance period), then the person is not regarded as having contravened the infringement notice. No proceedings may be started or continued in relation to the alleged contravention of the infringement notice provision. If the person fails to comply with an infringement notice (e.g., fails to pay the penalty), the infringement notice is not withdrawn, and the person is liable to proceedings under the Subdivision G (Enforcement and remedies).

Compliance with disclosure requirements is critical to the integrity and credibility of the capital market. Listing Rule has been given the statutory force under Section 674 of the Corporations Act. Thus, a breach of Listing Rule 3.1 constitutes a breach of the Corporations Act. A criminal offense can be punishable by a fine of up to $110,000, and a civil penalty provision offense can be punishable by a civil penalty of up to $1,000,000. Alternatively, ASIC can impose administrative action by issuing an infringement notice of up to $100,000.[279]

Voluntary suspension

A trading halt may be necessary when there are indications that the information may have leaked or is likely to cause a significant change in the market price and where the firm is not in a position to give an announcement. A voluntary suspension may be appropriate where: a) the firm has been in a trading halt, but the relevant disclosure issue has not been or will not be resolved within the trading halt period; or b) the firm is in serious financial difficulties, and continued trading is likely to be materially prejudicial for the completion of the transaction that is critical to its continued financial viability. ASX strongly encourages the firm to monitor the market price, news media, and internet.[280]

36. International Disclosure Standards

IOSCO
The disclosure standards of international organizations can be of great help in enhancing the effectiveness of disclosure regulation. For example, the International Organization of Securities Commissions (IOSCO) was organized in 1983 and has been recognized as the key international standard setter of which members regulate more than 95% of the world's securities market.[281] The policy of IOSCO is conducted by eight committees. The Committee 1 (Issuer Accounting, Auditing and Disclosure) is dedicated to improving and enhancing the quality and transparency of the information that investors receive. IOSCO considers *"the accuracy, integrity and comparability of issuer disclosure to be essential for maintaining investor confidence."* IOSCO have issued a lot of disclosure-related principles, standards and reports as below. (424)

- 1998, Objectives and Principles of Securities Regulation.

- 1998, International Disclosure Standards for Cross-Border Offerings and Initial Listings by Foreign Issuers.

- 2001, Adapting IOSCO International Disclosure Standards for Shelf Registration Systems.

- 2002, Principles for Ongoing Disclosure and Material Development Reporting by Listed Entities.

- 2003, General Principles Regarding Disclosure of Management's Discussion and Analysis of Financial Condition and Results of Operations.

- 2007, International Disclosure Standards for Cross-Border Offerings and Initial Listings by Foreign Issuers.

- 2010, Principles for Periodic Disclosure by Listed Entities.

- 2019, Statement on Disclosure of ESG Matters by Issuers.

Objectives and principles of securities regulation
The "Objectives and Principles of Securities Regulation" (Principle) were adopted in 1998 and endorsed by both the G20 and FSB as the relevant standards. The Principles and the "Methodology for Assessing Implementation of the IOSCO Objectives and Principles of Securities Regulation" (Methodology) are standards recognized by the FSB as being key to sound financial systems. These are the basis of evaluation for the Financial Sector Assessment Programs (FSAP) by the IMF and World Bank. Those play an essential role in promoting a sound financial regulation. The IOSCO recommends that local regulators should implement the Principles under the relevant legal framework to achieve the Objectives. The Principles are based upon three

objectives of securities regulation: protecting investors; ensuring that markets are fair, efficient and transparent; reducing systemic risk. The objectives are mutually related. A policy to ensure fair, efficient and transparent markets also provide investor protection and reduction of systemic risk, vice versa. The Principles are grouped into ten categories. (425)

> A - Principles Relating to the Regulator
> B - Principles for Self-Regulation
> C - Principles for the Enforcement of Securities Regulation
> D - Principles for Cooperation in Regulation
> E - Principles for Issuers
> F~J - Principles for Other entities[282]

The first category "A. Principles Relating to the Regulator" states eight recommendations.[283] The second category "B. Principles for Self-Regulation" states one recommendation as below.

> "Where the regulatory system makes use of Self-Regulatory Organizations (SROs) that exercise some direct oversight responsibility for their respective areas of competence, such SROs should be subject to the oversight of the Regulator and should observe standards of fairness and confidentiality when exercising powers and delegated responsibilities."

The third category "C. Principles for the Enforcement of Securities Regulation" states three recommendations as below.

> "The Regulator should have comprehensive inspection, investigation and surveillance powers. The Regulator should have comprehensive enforcement powers. The regulatory system should ensure an effective and credible use of inspection, investigation, surveillance and enforcement powers and implementation of an effective compliance program."

The fourth category "D. Principles for Cooperation in Regulation" states three recommendations as below.

> "The Regulator should have authority to share both public and non-public information with domestic and foreign counterparts. Regulators should establish information sharing mechanisms that set out when and how they will share both public and non-public information with their domestic and foreign counterparts. The regulatory system should allow for assistance to be provided to foreign Regulators who need to make inquiries in the discharge of their functions and exercise of their powers."

The fifth category "E. Principles for Issuers" states three recommendations as below.

> "There should be full, accurate and timely disclosure of financial results, risk and other information which is material to investors' decisions. Holders of securities in a company should be treated in a fair and equit-

able manner. Accounting standards used by issuers to prepare financial statements should be of a high and internationally acceptable quality."

Methodology for assessing

In 2003, IOSCO developed the Methodology[284] for the use of self-assessment for the level to which IOSCO Principles are being implemented. The Methodology sets out the Key Questions relevant to the implementation of the Principles. The assessment is a tool for identifying potential gaps and as a basis for framing priorities for reforms. The assessment process involves a questionnaire for the details of laws and regulatory program so as to meet the objectives of the Principles. The status of implementation can be assessed with five types of Assessment Categories; Fully Implemented, Broadly Implemented, Partly Implemented, Not Implemented, Not Applicable. The Principles has been used by the World Bank/IMF in the Financial Sector Assessment Program (FSAP) that was initiated in 1999 and designed to analyze potential vulnerabilities in the financial sectors.(426)

International equity/debt disclosure standards

In 1998, IOSCO published the "International Disclosure Standards for Cross-Border Offerings and Initial Listings by Foreign Issuers" to make it easier for multinational issuers to make cross-border public offerings for equity securities. It may be named as "IDS Equity."(427) In 2007, IOSCO published the "International Disclosure Principles for Cross-Border Offerings and Listings of Debt Securities by Foreign Issuers" to make it easier for multinational issuers to make cross-border public offerings for debt securities. It may be named as "IDS Debt."(428) Both IDS Equity and IDS Debt set forth nonfinancial statement disclosure standards for offerings and listings. One disclosure document that is compatible with those standards would be accepted in multiple jurisdictions.

International ongoing disclosure standards

Due to the adoption of non-financial statement disclosure standards for equity and debt, one disclosure document could be accepted in multiple jurisdictions and thus cross-border offerings could be facilitated. With the voluminous secondary trading by retail investors who are more in need of information, investor protection by providing high quality information on an ongoing basis became more crucial. In recognition of the importance of reliable, timely and readily accessible ongoing disclosure, in 2002 IOSCO has developed "Principles for Ongoing Disclosure and Material Development Reporting by Listed Entities" that the listed entity should provide material information. The principles are referred to as the "International Ongoing Disclosure Standards" or IODS. IODS is to facilitate the minimum standards for ongoing disclosure for listed entities which does apply in relation to all entities with shares listed in a recognized exchange and individual jurisdictions can require additional requirements. To satisfy timeliness, IODS states that the listed entity shall disclose ongoing information on a timely basis, which could require disclosure on an immediate basis (i.e., as soon as possible or within specified days) and periodic basis (i.e., quarterly, annual). IODS also states that, in some jurisdictions, disclosure may be subject to delay if a) the information is confidential under legislation; b) the information concerns an incomplete proposal or negotiations; the listed entity must maintained the relevant information strictly confidential.(203)

Principles for periodic disclosure

An ad hoc basis ongoing disclosure of material events is not sufficient for investors to make investment decisions. Investors should be supported to use periodic reports such as annual reports and interim reports. Periodic reports enable better monitoring and useful comparison of performance over regular intervals. In 2010, IOSCO published the "Principles for Periodic Disclosure by Listed Entities" which has identified the principles that is essential for periodic reports. Periodic reports should contain relevant information. For example, annual reports should contain audited financial statements and a Management's Discussion and Analysis (MD&A). Periodic reports should not be misleading or should not make omission of any material information. Periodic report should be presented in a clear and concise manner and be consistent with the other already-released information. (429)

IDS for shelf registration

In 2001, IOSCO published a report "Adapting IOSCO International Disclosure Standards for Shelf Registration Systems" which states specific approach of some jurisdictions that IDS Equity could form a fast track for making offering. IOSCO members could expand the use of short form prospectuses or the automatic shelf registration statement that becomes effective immediately upon filing. These approaches provide issuers with the flexibility of raising capital more quickly and reduction in preparation costs.

Principles for MD&A

In 2003, IOSCO published the "General Principles Regarding Disclosure of Management's Discussion and Analysis of Financial Condition and Results of Operations." The Management's Discussion and Analysis (MD&A) enables investors to analyze the firm with the viewpoints of management. The corporate collapses have highlighted the need for improved disclosure for accompanied information by financial statements. It is narrative explanations and often referred to as MD&A. MD&A disclosure provides a context within which the financial results can be interpreted. It enables investors to assess the financial condition, changes, and prospects for the future including information on the potential impact that are reasonably likely to have material effects such as a reduction in product prices, decrease in market demand. Some useful guidance has been suggested for issuers in preparing MD&A disclosure. MD&A disclosure; 1) highlight the most relevant information; 2) be clear, concise and meaningful, and in plain language; 3) enhance the comprehensibility of the issuer's financial statements to investors; 4) be provided at the same time as the presentation of the relevant financial statements. Firms are also advised to take the following precautions when preparing MD&A; 1) avoid the use of boilerplate or stock language; 2) properly craft to address a company's specific situation; 3) provide an objective analysis that could reflect negatively on the firm.(430)

37. Quality Of Disclosure Regulation

Concept

One may need to develop the concept of "regulatory quality" to measure and enhance the effectiveness of current disclosure regulation. "Regulatory quality" can be defined as the appropriateness of regulation to support markets and foster public interests.[285] Regulatory quality is directly related to "regulatory reform" which refers to *"changes that improve regulatory quality to enhance the economic performance, cost-effectiveness, or legal quality of regulations and related government formalities."*[286]

Good regulation

OECD (2005) provides a concept on a good regulation. *"Good regulation should: (i) serve clearly identified policy goals, and be effective in achieving those goals; (ii) have a sound legal and empirical basis; (iii) produce benefits that justify costs, ...' (iv) minimize costs and market distortions; (v) promote innovation through market incentives ...; (vi) be clear, simple, and (viii) be compatible as far as possible with competition, ..."*(431) Regulatory quality should cover all the process of regulatory development, enforcement, and outcomes. Besides, policy for regulatory quality should not be merely in pursuit of maintaining levels of regulatory performance but of achieving continuous improvements over time.

Recommendations on improving the regulatory quality

In many countries, concerns about regulatory quality have emerged, and governments are experiencing similar problems in regulation. The expansion of regulation systems has given rise to concerns about the growing costs of regulation, the openness of regulatory decision processes. In addition, regulatory quality has become more important than ever to international competitiveness.[287] To ensure the quality of regulation, in 1995, the OECD published the "Recommendations of the Council on Improving the Quality of Government Regulation" which recommends that OECD member countries take effective measures such as: *"i) Examining the quality and performance of administrative and political processes ...; ii) Developing ... administrative and management system ...; iii) Integrating decision-making principles for efficient, flexible, and transparent regulation into regulatory processes at all levels of government; iv) Paying particular attention to regulatory quality and transparency ..."*[288] OECD has continuously upgraded the "Recommendations of the Council on Improving the Quality of Government Regulation" in 2005 and 2012.[289]

Below is the summary of "Recommendation of the Council on Regulatory Policy and Governance" of 2012.[290]

"1. ... The policy should have clear objectives and frameworks for imple-

mentation to ensure that, if regulation is used, the economic, social and environmental benefits justify the costs, the distributional effects are considered and the net benefits are maximised.

1.2 ... governments should ... develop programmes to reduce the administrative and compliance costs of regulation ...

1.5 Regulatory policy should include a preference for performance-based regulation, ...

2. Adhere to principles of open government, including transparency and participation ... This includes providing meaningful opportunities (including online) for the public to contribute to the process ... Governments should ensure that regulations are comprehensible and clear ...

2.2 Government should co-operate with stakeholders on reviewing ...

2.4 Make sure that policies and practices for inspections and enforcement ... are designed to maximized the net public benefits ...

2.6 Governments should have a policy ... using plain language. They should also provide clear guidance ...

3. ... actively provide oversight of regulatory policy ... and thereby foster regulatory quality.

4. ... Clearly identify policy goals, and evaluate if regulation is necessary ... Consider means other than regulation ... to identify the best approach.

5. Conduct ... programme reviews ... to ensure that regulations remain up to date, cost justified ...

6. Regularly publish reports on the performance of regulatory policy ...

7. Develop a consistent policy ... in order to provide greater confidence that regulatory decisions are made on an objective, impartial and consistent basis ...

7.3 Independent regulatory agencies should be considered in situations where:

There is a need for the regulatory agency ... to maintain public confidence;

Both the government and private entities are regulated under the same framework...; and

... there is a need to protect the agency's impartiality.

8. ... Ensure that citizens ... have access to these systems of review ... and receive decisions in a timely manner.

9. ... apply risk assessment, risk management ... Regulators should assess how regulations will be given effect and should design responsive implementation and enforcement strategies.

10. ... promote regulatory coherence through co-ordination mechanisms ... Identify cross-cutting regulatory issues at all levels ... to promote coherence

... and avoid duplication or conflict of regulations.
11. Foster the development of regulatory management capacity and performance ...
12. ... give consideration to all relevant international standards and frameworks for co-operation ... "

Principles for regulatory quality

OECD (2005) provides some guiding principles for regulatory quality and performance. The regulator should *"adopt ... broad programme of regulatory reform that establish clear objectives and frameworks for implementation," "assess impacts and review regulations systematically to ensure that they meet their intended objectives efficiently and effectively ... It should consider alternatives to regulation where appropriate and possible, including self-regulation, that give greater scope to citizens and firms ..."* It should *"ensure that regulations ... are transparent and non-discriminatory," "eliminate unnecessary regulatory barriers ... and enhance the consideration and better integration of market openness, thus strengthening economic efficiency and competitiveness,"* and *"support the development and use of internationally harmonized standards as a base of domestic regulations ..."*(431)

Evaluation of regulatory performance

The regulation aims to change behaviors of the regulated in order to make desired outcomes. Regulators need to develop a framework to evaluate the design, implementation, and performance of regulations and policies, i.e., by using indicators to measure relevant outcomes. Regulators should have an established procedure to analyze the expected impacts of new regulation and also evaluate the ex-post impacts. Governments will need indicators to measure relevant outcomes by measuring the contribution of regulatory policy to overall performance. When evaluating the performance of the regulatory policy, evaluators need to pay attention to the substantive outcomes and the relevant procedures.

According to the Coglianese (2012), indicators can be classified into three types: i) net-benefits (benefits minus costs); ii) cost-effectiveness (costs per a given unit/level of impact); iii) impact. In theory, the net-benefits measure will be the best indicator. However, the benefits cannot be easily termed into monetary units, nor the monetary unit of benefit may be different from that of cost. The cost-effectiveness includes similar issues. In so far as the cost of regulation can be assumed to be somewhat constant, an impact-based evaluation might be a feasible measure in practice. For better evaluation, there should be ongoing support for systematic and continuous approaches for regulatory evaluation.(432)[291]

Regulatory quality index

To improve regulatory policies by diagnosing success and failures, OECD developed the Indicators of Regulatory Policy and Governance (iREG) which present up-to-date evidence of the regulatory policy.[292] Regulatory indicators can be used as a stand-alone indicator or as a component of a nation/international level indicator, i.e., WGI. Worldwide Governance Indicators (WGI) project report aggregate governance indicators after 1996 for six dimensions of governance: Regulatory Quality, Rule of Law, Control of Corruption, Government Effectiveness, Political Stability and Absence of Violence, Voice and Accountability.[293] In measuring WGI, Regulatory Quality is designed to capture the perceptions of the government's ability to formulate and implement sound regulations that promote private sector development. The capital market variables that are used to construct Regulatory Quality include such as *"Investment freedom, Financial freedom, Capital markets (foreign and domestic) are easily accessible, Foreign investors are free to acquire control in domestic companies."*[294] The capital market regulator may develop a regulatory quality indicator specialized in the capital market area to analyze the regulatory practices over time, which may provide regulators with broad insights on trends of regulatory reform toward more efficient and cost-effective regulation.

Oversight body

Regulatory oversight body that oversights regulator's regulatory quality has been a key component of regulatory reform to enhance regulatory quality. Some countries have integrated oversight bodies into the administration body, while others may separate it. A well-organized and monitored regulatory process may be an important factor for a higher quality of regulation. Oversight bodies may be essential in enhancing regulatory quality by aiming to supervise, coordinate, and challenge regulators. Oversight bodies should have the capacity to supervise, coordinate, and challenge the regulator by holding sufficient authority to achieve the intended purposes.[295]

Effective self-regulation

Self-regulation should be incorporated into the overall regulatory frameworks as an essential component. Self-regulation is an effective and efficient regulatory mechanism to deal with the complex and dynamic capital markets. There can be some variables that serve as key success factors of SROs. In general, the objectives of SRO are the same with those of statutory regulator. By the nature, self-regulation has proven to be efficient and flexible, which means that SROs should be entitled with a greater flexibility in adapting disclosure requirements to respond to fast-changing markets. Statutory regulator's mission to appropriately oversight SROs would be challenging since it should *"strengthen the strengthen and make up for the weakness."* In 2000, IOSCO provided the "Model for Effective Regulation" that describes the effectiveness of self-regulation and explained some elements of effective self-regulation such as specialized knowledge, industry motivation, etc.[296] SRO's specialized knowledge about industry is an invaluable source of expertise. In other sense, SROs should have the expertise need to have qualified staffs to successfully accomplish their duty. SROs should encourage the industry to contribute to the compliance of requirements and standards. The basis of SROs is mainly a contractual relationship that can be less powerful than statutory regulator in respect of enforcement but can be more powerful and flexible in respect of adopting broader requirements that cannot be possible by statutory regulators. All members of an SRO are watching the decision of SRO, and therefore, they should be subject to pressure from other competing group in the industry, which can lead to a better compliance and transparent self-regulation. However, effective self-regulation does not come free of charge. An SRO should introduce and update transparent guidelines. In addition, to sustain the benefits of flexible self-regulation, the SRO should not be required to follow rigid procedures in review, approval, and legislation.

38. Socially Optimal Disclosure Regulation

It is sure that country-specific disclosure regulation have been developed not theoretically but historically according to market-specific environments. More theoretical model is demanded to measure the level of optimality and quality of disclosure regulation. A well-established economic model that is based on the "public interest theory" can provide profound understanding on the social optimality of disclosure regulation. It should include the externalities and main components of disclosure regulation, such as the nature of information and the behavior of manager, shareholder, and regulator.

In this regard, the model of Guttentag (2007) provides meaningful implications and considerations. Below is the summary of Guttentag (2007) (103).[75] The social utility of firm's disclosure policy deviates from the firms' private utility to the extent of inter-firm externality (λ). If the inter-firm externality ($0 \leq \lambda \leq 1$) equals 1, then there is no inter-firm externality. If λ is less than 1, then there is a positive inter-firm externality, meaning that the social disclosure cost is less than private disclosure cost.[76] A rational regulator will choose to mandate what the firm would not voluntarily choose to adopt. Therefore, regulator's mandatory disclosure policy (R*(a,g)) is calculated policy from the socially optimal disclosure policy (S*(a,g)) by subtracting the voluntary optimal disclosure (V*(a,g)).

$$R^*(a,g) = S^*(a,g) - V^*(a,g)$$

$$R^*(a,g) = \left\{ \left(\frac{1}{\sqrt{\lambda - k}} - \frac{1}{\sqrt{1 - k}} \right) \cdot \left(\sqrt{\tau \cdot (\delta \cdot \theta \cdot \epsilon^2 - \beta - 2 \cdot \sqrt{\gamma})} \right), 0 \right\}$$

The model of Guttentag (2007) provides meaningful implications in a concrete form. If the inter-firm externality is positive ($\lambda < 1$), it is optimal for regulator to mandate additional disclosure for accuracy information above the voluntary level (R(a, ~)>0). It is optimal to mandate disclosure so long as there is a higher probability of a liquidity shock (τ).[77]

Furthermore, the net social welfare gains from disclosure regulation (U_R) is calculated from the social utility ($U_S(S)$) by subtracting the firm's utility ($U_S(V^*)$) and the cost of disclosure regulation (C_R).

$$U_R = U_S(S^*(a,g)) - U_S(V^*(a,g)) - C_R$$

$$U_R = (1 - \theta) \cdot \left\{ \sqrt{\tau \cdot (\delta \cdot \theta \cdot \epsilon^2 - \beta - 2 \cdot \sqrt{\gamma})} \right\} \left\{ \frac{(\sqrt{\lambda - k} - \sqrt{1 - k})^2}{\sqrt{1 - k}} \right\} - C_R$$

So long as the inter-firm externalities are positive ($\lambda < 1$), and there are no significant regulation costs ($C_R \approx 0$), the net social welfare gains from disclosure regulation are positive. Hence, regulator need to pay attention to the disclosure requirements with a higher inter-firm externalities and lower regulation costs. In addition, so long as the disclosure of accuracy information reduces agency costs (i.e., k increases), the social welfare gains increase. The probability of a liquidity shock(τ) in this model provides additional implication on the criteria of disclosure regulation. All other things being equal, the social gains from disclosure regulation will be greater for firms with greater probability of liquidity shock, in other words firms with the investor's greater liquidity needs. Firms with higher liquidity needs should be subject to rigorous disclosure regulation.

4. DISCLOSURE ENFORCEMENT

41. Enforcement

42. Enforcement strategy

43. Disclosure review practices

41. Enforcement

411. Introduction

Concept

Enforcement refers to the application of social norms to ensure compliance with laws, rules, and regulations. It is mainly conducted through coercive measures and may be delegated to other entities. Major elements of enforcement procedures are detection, investigation, assessment, and taking measures. It is not only taking sanctions but also guiding the society to better practices. It is closely related to the legislation, supervision, surveillance, and monitoring that should be conducted in such a manner that gives a lead for offenders to quit similar offense. Public enforcement refers to the enforcement of the law by a government to detect non-compliance and impose sanctions. Private enforcement refers to the lawsuit initiated by an individual or entity to have a law court decision on the recovery of damages, which may be triggered in a stand-alone manner or be followed by public enforcement.

Disclosure review as an enforcement

Disclosure review may be viewed as a specific type of enforcement that is designed to deal with the informational issues of non-compliance effectively. Enforcement of disclosure can be defined as a function of examining and assessing the compliance with the relevant disclosure requirements, and taking appropriate measures when non-compliance or infringements are discovered. When non-compliances are detected, enforcers should also take appropriate actions and ensure that market participants are provided with accurate information.[297] The IAS Regulation emphasizes the importance of enforcement by describing that "*A proper and rigorous enforcement regime is key to underpinning investors' confidence in financial markets. Member States ... are required to take appropriate measures to ensure compliance ...*"[298] Enforcers are to establish consistent, efficient, and effective practices and ensure the consistent application of disclosure requirements by achieving a proper and rigorous enforcement regime for investors' confidence.[299]

Rationale of disclosure review

The traditional perfect competition model assumes a market with perfect information. As EMH assumes the existence of rational investor, frictionless market and information symmetry, market failure or inefficiency is inferred to be brought by the opposite conditions; irrational investor, information cost, and information asymmetry. For instance, Grossman &

Stiglitz (1980, p.405) argued that because the information is costly, prices cannot perfectly reflect the available information, and those who spent resources to obtain it would receive no compensation. (9) As a result, investors will not be fully incentivized to remedy the information failure by adopting private enforcement (e.g., lawsuit, settlement) at their own costs. Public enforcement of disclosure can be justified by its function to reduce the information cost of quality verification significantly. Such functions as "disclosure review," "disclosure scrutiny," or "disclosure examination" that is conducted by regulators or exchanges to verify the disclosure quality and ensure better compliance with disclosure requirements can be viewed as public enforcement of disclosure. Public enforcers are giving subsidy to investors by lowering the information verification cost.

Purpose of disclosure review

Investors need to have confidence in the disclosed information, or they would not want to play in such unlevel markets. Enforcer's action is an effective measure to enhance the investor's confidence. The objective of disclosure enforcement is to contribute to a consistent application of disclosure requirements for better disclosure relevant to an investor's investment decision making. Through enforcement actions, enforcers contribute to investors' protection and the promotion of market confidence as well as to the avoidance of regulatory arbitrage. Non-compliance may cause a significant loss of investor confidence unless it is detected and addressed. Even though serious misconduct is relatively uncommon, failure to detect it or to take action might magnify the harm. Market integrity is robust when misconduct is identified and dealt with quickly and fairly. The existence of vigorous enforcement sends the message that misconduct will be uncovered and penalized, and improved detection increases public confidence. Besides, the enforcement mechanism should fit with the overall transparency framework.

412. Enforcement Theories

Enforcement theory

They say that deterrence theory was first appeared in the 1760s and reappeared with a new form in the 1960s. The primary responsibilities of securities regulators or enforcers are to protect investors from a firm's non-compliance, contravention, or crime. *"The most common method of addressing crime, though, is through enforcement and punishment."*[300] The enforcement structure should be designed to make the value of punishment sufficiently outweigh the value of expected profits from offenses and to achieve the primary objectives of enforcement. Under the theory of rational behavior, people can be deterred from offending rules and regulations by establishing punishments for offenses or non-compliances. A potential offender compares the expected benefit of non-compliance with that of compliance. If enforcers sufficiently increase the cost of non-compliance, they will not offend.(433) Main points and considerations regarding public enforcement of law can be summarized in the light of the economic theory of optimal enforcement. When it is difficult for individuals to identify violators, it may be socially desirable to employ public enforcement. Public enforcement provides the force that may be needed to detect the violation, while private enforcement does not. Thus, every country conducts public enforcement on listed companies' disclosure to identify non-compliance.(434)

Deterrence factors

Researches have focused on the relationship between the severity, certainty, and the speed of punishment. Deterrence theory suggests that, when the potential offender estimates that the expected loss is greater than the expected benefit, three deterrence factors increase the costs of offense and deter violation: the certainty (likelihood of apprehension), celerity (speed of punishment), and the severity of punishment. The threat of severe punishment (severity) can be a meaningful deterrence only when the likelihood of apprehension (certainty) is high. An immediate punishment after an offense (celerity) is more effective than delayed punishment. Any measures to increase the severity, certainty, and celerity are expected to generate a deterrent effect in a diminishing manner. First, the severity of punishment has been the key deterrent upon which enforcers have relied. Increasing the severity of punishment during sudden financial scandals is well supported to deter violations. Second, the certainty of punishment is a more determining factor, but it requires more resources to increase certainty. A potential offender tends to rely more on the subjective certainty that is formed by the public or anecdotal information and personal experience. Third, the celerity refers to the speed of receiving punishment from enforcers for violating rules and regulations. Immediate punishment could generate a more deterrence effect than delayed punishment.(433)

Enforcement approaches: comprehensive vs selective

Two basic models of enforcement are suggested; comprehensive model and selective model. Under the comprehensive approach, enforcers investigate all possible violations that are suspected or detected. Under the strategic approach, enforcers detect and investigate the target that is selected in a predefined manner since the comprehensive model is too costly. A predefined selection criterion may include a random selection or a risk-based selection. The selective model can be termed as a strategic approach, as it uses a strategic selection criterion. Under the strategic approach, a violation can be detected, investigated, and enforced by the priority of disclosure deficiency risks. A strategic approach drives the worst violations first while supporting the enforcers with economized enforcement. Enforcers concentrate their resources and efforts exclusively on worst targets with a higher probability of detection and punishment. Under the strategic model, violations with below-average risks may be considered to be a second-priority case that may be tolerated. Conspicuous violations with higher risks are classified as first-priority cases that should be dealt with.(435) If an enforcer aims to detect and investigate all violations, then it will be a resource-consuming black hole. They might consume a huge amount of resources for just one unit of a marginal increase in enforcement performance. Instead, enforcers had better closely watch those firms of which disclosure is conspicuously deficient (e.g., disclosure quality is far below the lower limit). The strategic enforcement is the cost-effective one in achieving social benefits. Observing such a focused enforcement, other potential offenders will downscale their behaviors in order to avoid being as conspicuous as the worst offender.(435) When the comprehensive enforcement for all the non-compliance is impossible and unattainable, the partial and selective enforcement by priorities is inherent, necessary, and desirable. Therefore, even without a legal basis, enforcers should be able to allocate their limited resources pursuant to the priorities that are established on a reasonable basis. Such an approach is not in the dereliction of duty. If enforcers obstinately persist with comprehensive enforcement, they might create "enforcement pollution to society" or "enforcement overload to enforcers." Enforcers should not stop enforcement on the case of significant disclosure deficiency to detect a minor non-compliance.(435, 436) An enforcer that aims to attract the media spotlight might frequently focus on the minor non-compliance that is under the media spotlight.

Risk-based selection methods

a. Background

Enforcers have such finite resources that they cannot monitor all misbehaviors. They have to make decisions to allocate resources across a variety of regulatory risks efficiently. Enforcers, including securities market enforcers, seek the protection of public interest, facing a great number of potential offenders under limited resources. Enforcers should be equipped with various legal measures ranging from public censure to imprisonment to discourage deficient disclosure. Market participants are surely watching how enforcers handle non-compliant firms, which influences the likelihood of future non-compliance. McKinsey (2013) describes that a risk-based approach is becoming more important since market participants demand more transparent markets, while the regulatory environment is increasingly becoming more complex.[301]

b. Process

Many suggest various models for enforcement processes to better implement the risk-based approach. McKinsey (2013) suggests that an enforcement process may follow the process of *"definition of risk - estimation of risk - allocation of resources - conduct - evaluation."*[302]

c. Risk classification

Expected public harm from deficient disclosure may be defined as the product of the likelihood and severity of deficient disclosure. The degree of risk may be classified by the various combination of the likelihood and severity as below. The table below that is borrowed and modified from McKinsey (2013) can be a good example.[303]

Table 9) Risk classification - McKinsey (2013)

Severity				
High	Medium Risk	Medium High Risk	High Risk
	Medium Low Risk	Medium Risk	Medium High Risk
Low	Low Risk	Medium Low Risk	Medium Risk
	Low	Likelihood	High

d. Performance

The probability of finding an error or risk depends on the level of sophistication of enforcement targets. To achieve a given level of probability of finding an error or risk, enforcers do not need to allocate enforcement resources for unsophisticated targets in the same way with sophisticated targets. For sophisticated targets, enforcers should allocate more resources to identify a given level of the probability of error or risk. Sophisticated targets are firms that actively try to prevent detection, modify their practice in response to other firm's sanction, and spend more avoiding detection than enforcement agency spends detecting the targets.[304]

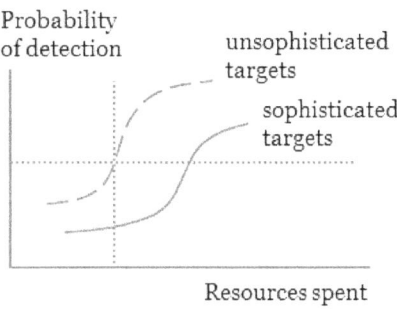

Figure 55 Unsophisticated targets

> Source of Figure 55) McKinsey & Company, "Risk-based resource allocation: Focusing regulatory and enforcement efforts where they are needed the most", February 2013, https://www.mckinsey.com/business-functions/risk/our-insights/risk-based-resource-allocation

413. Enforcement Procedure

Detection

Early detection of potential breach allows enforcers to take prompt and necessary action before the potential breach results in adverse consequences. The early detection that is associated with the celerity of punishment is key to preventing harm before it occurs and remediating quickly. Serious non-compliance is relatively uncommon, but delayed detect of failure to detect might magnify the harmful consequences. As severe sanctions alone are not enough to deter non-compliance, so enforcers must increase the likelihood of detection. Enforcers need to have various channels of gathering information for early detection, such as market surveillance and disclosure monitoring activities of the stock exchange or news media. Stock exchanges also supervise and monitor the firm's disclosure practices according to their listing rule. Therefore, most enforcers detect potential non-compliances in collaboration with SROs.(437)

Investigations

The purpose of an investigation is to find out whether there is serious non-compliance and to get a better understanding of the relevant facts so that enforcers can decide whether to take enforcement action and what kind of enforcement action may be necessary. MAS (2018) suggests that enforcers should respond with a formal investigation after careful consideration of a range of factors, including the seriousness of the misconduct, public interest, the availability of evidence.(437) An investigation can be initiated by either a reactive or proactive approach. A reactive investigation can be initiated from notification of market, referral by other institutions, and intelligence sources. A proactive investigation can be initiated from an enforcer's intelligence or contents analysis. The primary objective of the investigation process is to form the evidentiary basis for appropriate enforcement action. Thus, an investigation should be conducted objectively and effectively in accordance with internal standards.

Assessment of non-compliance

Not all breaches constitute serious non-compliance, and many breaches may be addressed by tools other than enforcement action, especially where breaches are technical or minor. Enforcers may consider many factors in assessing non-compliance. For example, they should consider the nature of non-compliance, the severity of the actual harm arisen from non-compliance, the potential harm that may arise from the non-compliance, the width, and the broadness of the harm from the non-compliance.

After investigation, enforcers assess the severity of non-compliance and the appropriate enforcement action to impose. All breaches do not constitute serious non-compliance, rather many breaches are technical or minor, which may be addressed and remedied without enforcement action. In assessing the severity of non-compliance or misconduct, enforcers have to use their own experience and judgment that should be consistently applied.

In assessing the severity, the enforcer may consider the economic losses due to non-compliance. A finance theory describes that the value of a firm equals the present value of future cash flows to shareholders. In an efficient market, the stock will reflect the firm value that is based on all publicly available information. Therefore, poor disclosure (e.g., misstatement and omission.) can potentially affect the stock price, even though it is deficient. The deficient disclosure may result in inflated or deflated stock price that is delineated from the true value. As a result, investors can experience a significant economic loss when the firm provides a corrective disclosure that reveals the truth. NERA (2019) describes that, in the process of public enforcement or private enforcement in many jurisdictions, they tend to use a statistical event study approach to estimate the economic loss and compensation, because they can isolate the stock price reactions caused by the corrective disclosure from those by other factors. For example, the compensation can be derived by the price difference between the last closing price "before" the corrective disclosure and the closing price on the date "of" the corrective disclosure after adjustment for other systematic effects. (438)

Sanction/Disciplinary action

Enforcers should aim to make sufficient sanctions to deter the non-compliant firm from repeated non-compliance and deter other firms from similar non-compliance. When enforcers take disciplinary action against a non-compliant firm, they should consider all possible sanctions. When enforcers assess the nature of the sanction, they should take into account all relevant circumstances. For example, enforcers should consider whether the con-compliant firm has taken to address the harm and how they cooperate with enforcers. A failure of a non-compliant firm in taking remedial steps to address harm or refusal to cooperate in the enforcement process may justify heavier sanctions. Many enforcers apply their already-established internal policy regarding decision making on sanctions (e.g., disciplinary committee).

Evaluation

Enforcers need to carry out a periodic evaluation on whether they have operated fairly and effectively in detection, investigation, and sanction. They have to consider a number of factors and segments when evaluating overall performance. Enforcers may also try to measure the deterrence effect. The impact of enforcement to the degree of deterrence can be measured with the non-compliance status such as the number or ratio of non-compliant cases, the number or ratio of severe cases, or the total amount of breached amount. On the other hand, they may choose to evaluate their functional performance by measuring the certainty, celerity, or severity of punishment.

414. Enforcement Actions

4141. Enforcement options

Enforcers can respond flexibly to changing environments when they have a wide range of enforcement options. Several theories are supporting various enforcement options. A sanction may be accompanied by other sanctions. First, denunciation theory suggests that punishing offenders publicly will attach social stigma on offenders and prevent others from committing similar offenses (e.g., suspension, informational sanction such as reprimand, censure, warning). Second, retributive theories suggest that intentional offenders should be punished so that the person can pay a debt to society (e.g., monetary penalty). Third, incapacitation theory suggests that holding offender in prison will prevent from committing additional crimes (e.g., jail, delisting, cancellation). Fourth, rehabilitation theories suggest that rehabilitation treatment or training programs will keep offenders from committing new offenses (e.g., conditions, special designation). (433)

4142. Denunciation: informational sanctions

Introduction

An information sanction such as warning, reprimand, or censure refers to issuing a clear statement of displeasure, disapproval, or criticism concerning the issuer's misbehavior. It is usually non-binding, and there are no other particular legal consequences. When an issuer is censured or reprimanded by an enforcer, it has no direct effect on the validity of listing or trading status. It most commonly takes the form of issuing a private letter or a public release. Informational sanctions can be appropriate for the unacceptable misbehaviors that should not happen again but are generating a lower level of concern. In representing the disapproval in relation to the misbehavior, SROs may use a sliding scale tone that may be reduced for those who offended technical requirements. SROs will consider whether the informational sanction provides an adequate level of investor protection. These may be appropriate for cases where there is a low possibility of recurrence. SROs should not use informational sanctions where the issuer or manager seriously lack insight.(439)

Warnings or letter of advice

The enforcers may issue to the offender a warning or letters of advice that are not generally published. In case, the historical record or prior warning may be taken into account in deciding future enforcement actions.

Reprimand

A reprimand is a warning that may include facts about breaches and concerns of enforcers. A reprimand may be issued publicly or privately. A reprimand used in the field of education provides some meaningful implications on how to increase the effectiveness of reprimanding policy. The regulator should correctly identify the target misbehavior. A reprimand should be clearly and firmly expressed in tone and content. The regulator should avoid inappropriate expression (e.g., implying damage limitation, an unfair comparison, hostile remarks). A reprimand should express the regulator's concern with the investor's harmed interests. A reprimand should emphasize what firms should do rather than complain about the non-compliance itself. A public reprimand is, at times, appropriate and necessary when there is a specific reason. The reprimanding policy should be consistent, and empty threats or reprimanding the whole participants should be avoided. However, keep in mind that reprimanding a legal entity is a different story at all from reprimanding human beings.

Public release of enforcement decision

Enforcers may choose to publish sanctions in a comprehensive or selective manner. When it comes to a selective public release, enforcers may decide to publish specific enforcement actions only where it is appropriate. Enforcers would consider various factors, including 1) whether it was willfully, intentionally, or dishonestly committed, 2) whether a public release is necessary for market confidence; 3) whether it is necessary to send a deterrent message to the industry.(437) Some enforcers only release the name of the offender or describe salient facts and summary, while other enforcers state a long story.

First, let us assume that enforcers have the policy to determine the publicity level based on the deterrent effect. If the deterrent effect from the public release of enforcement action is below the cost to the offender, then the public release will not be socially justified (left graph). Second, let us assume that enforcers have the policy to determine the publicity level based on the overall effects including the deterrent effect on other firms and confidence effect on investors. If the overall effect, including the deterrent effect on the offender and the externalities to other firms and investors, exceeds the cost to the offender, then a detailed public release is socially justified (right graph).

In general, enforcers' decisions on the degree of publicity influence the degree of the deterrent effect on the offenders and the externalities on other firms and investors. Consequently, rational enforcers will make the publicity decision, including the overall externalities and the costs to the offender. Firms would not consider the externality, but the enforcers do to achieve social welfare maximization.[305]

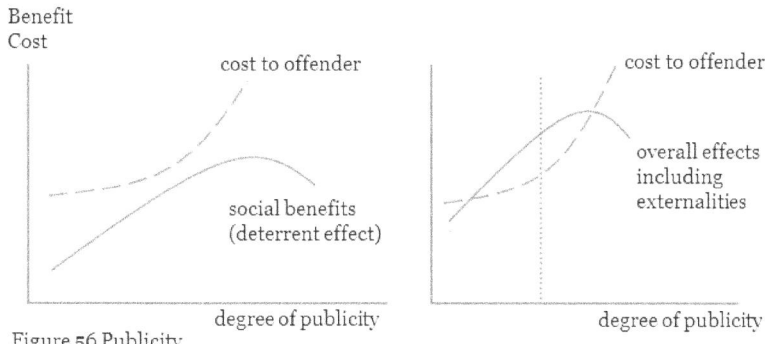
Figure 56 Publicity

Special designation

SROs may designate the securities issued by the non-compliant issuer as a special market segment or division. Such a special market segment may be composed of issues for which investors need to pay more skeptical attention. SROs may choose to exclude the issues of a special market segment from index calculation.

Suspension

SROs may consider market-based actions such as suspension of trading or listing status for a finite period of time. Suspension may be appropriate where a lighter sanction would not act as a sufficient deterrent. Suspension can yield a deterrent effect by sending a signal to the markets about the SRO's serious view of the misbehavior. The suspension will be appropriate where misbehavior is so serious that the issued stocks are incompatible with continued trading for a finite period. A suspension may be imposed where informational sanctions (e.g., publicity) or attaching conditions are not sufficient or appropriate.(439) SROs may suspend stock trading when it is necessary to protect investors from uninformed trading or sudden failure of fulfilling the attached conditions.

4143. Retributive: monetary sanctions

Some enforcers are empowered to impose monetary sanctions, such as fine or civil penalty in the provisions of law or regulation. Monetary sanction serves as an effective tool in deterring non-compliance. To achieve credible deterrence, it should be fair and proportionate by considering the severity of the offense and its impact. Enforcers had better refrain from imposing monetary sanctions when it is not serious. In determining the amount of civil penalty, enforcers would consider a wide range of factors, including the degree of market impact (e.g., loss, risk) and prior history of non-compliance (e.g., frequency, duration).

4144. Incapacitation/exclusion

If the issuer is unable to resolve the misbehavior and the recurrence risk, incapacitation such as delisting, cancellation, or revocation is inevitable. It is the last resort sanction to protect potential investors for the most serious, deliberate, dishonest, or persistent failures. Cancellation may be appropriate where any lighter sanctions would not generate enough deterrent effects but undermine investor's confidence. SROs should provide clear reasons for incapacitation. Factors that may be considered as reasonable in determining incapacitation may include fraud, dishonesty, concealing, willful failure, and falsification.

4145. Rehabilitation: improvement/condition

SROs may attach specific improvements or conditions to issuers where there is some risk but can be appropriately dealt with through the conditional sanctions. Attaching conditions might not be suitable for issuers involving dishonesty or abuse. Where misbehavior can be remedied, it may be appropriate to attach an improvement plan or condition. For example, the issuer can be mandated to get a special training course or modify current compliance procedures. Attaching conditions appear to provide a flexible means of addressing concerns. The conditions attached by the SROs should be appropriate, relevant, practicable, and sufficient to remedy the failure, but pose no risk of future harm. The conditions should be easily monitored by the SROs.(439) Some SROs such as the Japan Stock Exchange and Korea Exchange maintains a policy to attach improvement plans or conditions to non-compliant firms. Non-compliant issuers should submit an improvement plan and be monitored periodically.

4146. Criminal sanctions

EU Directive on criminal sanctions

The level of a sanction varies widely among the EU Member States, and the administrative sanction is not sufficient to ensure compliance with the rules. Thus, it is essential that enforcements be strengthened by criminal sanctions to demonstrate a stronger form of social disapproval for serious forms of offense.[306] EU adopted the Directive 2014/57/EU on criminal sanctions for market abuse (hereafter "CS MAD"). CS MAD requires that minimum rules should be established with regard to the definition of criminal offenses since the imposition of criminal sanctions will have an increased deterrent effect. Especially, *"Unlawful disclosure of inside information should be deemed to be serious in cases such as those where the impact on the integrity of the market is high."*[307] *"Member States shall take the necessary measures to ensure that unlawful disclosure of inside information constitutes a criminal offence at least in serious cases and when committed intentionally."*[308] *"Member States shall take the necessary measures to ensure ... effective, proportionate and dissuasive sanctions, which shall include criminal or non-criminal fines and may include other sanctions ... ."*[309]

Notification to relevant authority

When a breach is detected by the SROs, they are obligated to notify the fact to the relevant authorities such as criminal prosecutor.

42. Enforcement Strategy

421. Principles Of Enforcement

The purpose of imposing sanctions is to protect the investing public, to strengthen market integrity, and to maintain investor's confidence through cost-effective self-regulation. The primary purpose of sanction should not be the punishment itself but the protection of investing public, deterrence of misbehavior, and uphold high standards of transparency. To achieve such purposes, the self-regulatory organization must stand ready to discipline firms by imposing appropriate sanctions when necessary.

Enforcers had better establish principles, approaches, frameworks for a consistent and fair discipline, which may be integrated into a form of a guideline, including factors that should be taken into account in determining appropriate sanctions. Such a guideline that is not legally binding is expected to yield a meaningful indication in determining the appropriate sanction. Enforcers may establish a disciplinary guideline for internal use to achieve consistent and fair determination. On the other hand, enforcers may publish a reconstituted guideline so that issuers and other market participants may become more familiar with their disciplinary policy, which may generate a learning effect. Enforcers should be able to tailor sanctions to respond to the extraordinary and new type of misbehaviors to prevent future recurrence by other issuers. In determining the level of sanction, enforcers may consider other sanctions previously imposed by other regulators.

As the IOSCO has recognized that SROs may be a valuable regulator and enforcer in achieving the objectives of efficient securities regulation, most SROs are performing enforcement functions according to their rules.

422. Considerations Of Enforcement

General considerations

Enforcers will consider what sanction is appropriate by examining the findings, the issuer-specific circumstances, the aggravating or mitigating factors. In their guidance, institutions in various fields include major principles such as proportionality, factors, and dishonesty.

a. Proportionality: Regulators and exchanges should bear in mind that investor protection is always the primary concern. A rational regulator will weigh the interests of investing public with those of issuers.

b. Dishonesty: Dishonesty of issuer or manager is particularly serious as it undermines trust even though no direct and serious harm is likely to occur.

c. Determining Factors: Enforcers would consider aggravating factors and mitigating factors.

Determining factors

Enforcers will consider many aggravating and mitigating factors that should be relevant. Mitigating or aggravating factors are of particular significance in assessing the risk of misbehavior recurrence. Mitigating factors may include the evidence of overall adherence, efforts to address issues and prevent a recurrence, and good understanding. Aggravating factors may include poor compliance history, other breaches committed by management. For instance, Section 5 of the "Admission and disclosure standard" of LSE describes a number of factors.[310] USSC (2018) recommends that *"...In determining the type of sentence to impose, the sentencing judge should consider the nature and seriousness of the conduct, the statutory purposes of sentencing, and the pertinent offender characteristics..."*[311] Enforcers should provide the non-compliant with the opportunity of explaining their mitigating factors.

Determining methods

Every institution has its style of policy to determine the level of sanction. It might be classified by a pure sanction matrix approach and a full discretionary approach. A full discretionary approach that may evoke disaffection by issuers may not be appropriate in achieving the consistency of sanction. A monetary sanction more fits with the sanction matrix approach as the level of sanction can be finely designed. For instance, below is an example of how to establish a disciplinary sanction matrix by using the match table between the breached rule and the recommended disciplinary sanction.[312]

423. Considerations On Determining Factors

Self-reporting

In practice, non-compliant firms frequently make self-reporting to the authority of their non-compliance. In many countries, self-reporting is induced by lowering the sanction. Polinsky & Shavell (2007) explain why it is socially desirable and advantageous to create incentive mechanisms to encourage self-reporting. Self-reporting lowers enforcer's enforcement costs in the process of identification, detection, and investigation, reduces offender's risk by lowering sanction, and enables early detection that may also allow harm to be mitigated. In addition, other companies may follow the self-reporting firm.(434)

Repeat offenders

As FINRA recommends, *"sanction should be more severe for recidivists to prevent future misconduct by imposing progressively escalating sanctions on recidivists*." (440) In practice, repeat offenders are more severely sanctioned than first-time offenders. Imposing higher sanctions on frequent violators may be desirable for the purpose of deterrence. So far as frequent violators may be more likely to commit future violations, sanctioning based on offense history will create a deterrence effect.

Incapacitation / harm based

The threat of sanctions reduces harm by discouraging individuals from causing harm. However, incapacitation reduces harm by removing the offending firm from the positions in which the firm can cause harm. The optimal sanction is determined by comparing the expected net harm of non- incapacitation to the costs of imprisonment. If the offender were not incapacitated, then he might make an additional offense and social harm, which is the harm of non-incapacitation. If the expected net harm of non-incapacitation exceeds the costs of incapacitation, he should be put in incapacitation. In practice, the fact that a firm has already committed a serious harmful behavior would serve as a predictor for future violations. The low probabilities of detection that seem to be relatively prevalent in every enforcement arena can explain the higher or severe sanctions exceeding the harm. Sanctions in excess of harm are needed for sufficient deterrence when the probabilities of detection are significantly lower. Especially in circumstances where non-compliances are far less likely to be detected, an offender may significantly benefit from the non-compliance generating substantial harm to markets. As a result, severe sanctions would be desirable.(434)

Act-based sanctions

Act-based sanctions may be simpler to impose than harm-based sanctions. It is less difficult to determine whether the financial statement properly complies with the accounting standards than to detect whether the poor disclosure affected the market. In circumstances where the harm caused by an act is easily measured, harm-based sanctions may be more readily applied. In the market context, however, it is very difficult to distinguish the harm caused by misconduct from the harm caused by other factors.(434)

43. Disclosure Review Practices

431. United States

4311. Overview

Disclosure review

The mission of the capital market regulator is to protect investors by maintaining fair and efficient markets. A disclosure review, a specific type of enforcement regarding disclosure, is not intended to guarantee that firm's disclosure is complete and accurate but to preserve the integrity of disclosure quality. In spite of scrutiny, the firm's intrinsic responsibility for a complete and accurate disclosure is not be shifted to the regulator. As the accounting is analogized by a "communication" between firm and investor, a disclosure review is a "regulatory dialogue" between firm and regulator.

Comment letter

In the US, the "comment letter" is designed as a disclosure review to protect investors from misleading or inaccurate information. The "comment letter" refers to the letters that is issued by the SEC in response to filings of s registration statement or periodic reports.[313] The purpose of the comment letter is to enhance the firm's compliance with requirements and to make disclosure clear and free from deficiency. An enforcement mechanism such as comment letter is necessary because "... *appropriate oversight ... are important to protect the goals of transparency, relevance, and usefulness in financial reporting that are critical to the success of ... capital markets.*"(441) The SEC staff might ask a firm to revise or supplement information so that investors can better understand the firm's disclosure. Multiple rounds of comment letters could be exchanged for final resolution. The registration statement will become effective only after all facts have been resolved by the SEC.

Legal framework

Under the Securities Act of 1933 and the Securities Exchange Act of 1934, the SEC has operated the "letter of comment" process. The SEC has reviewed filings and issued comment letters to induce better compliance with applicable accounting principles and disclosure requirements.[314] Section 5 of the Securities Act of 1933 governs the registration statement.[315] There are no specifically stipulated provisions in the 1933 Act regarding the disclosure review process. However, in practice, the SEC staffs review the registration statement and periodic reports filed by firms to determine whether it is compliant with all requirements of the Act, regulations, and policies. After the comment procedure is resolved or it is determined not to be reviewed, the staff will declare that the registration statement is effective, and the firm can process the public offering procedures.[316] In case that the SEC adheres to such a formal process by suspending the effectiveness of the registration statement could invoke unexpected and excessive side effects. In spite of the provisions of the 1933 Act, the SEC devised an alternative and practical method to achieve the statutory purpose of full disclosure; comment letter. Issuers also have no incentive to risk the adverse consequences of SEC's formal procedure. Therefore, they will comply with comment letters.(442)

Selective review

The "Golden Age of Capitalism" resulted in the backlog of registration statements in the United States. In 1968, the SEC initiated a new procedure designed to decrease the disclosure review processing time. Based on the brief review for every registration statement, the SEC made one of the following decisions; 1) bedbug letter for filings with such a serious deficiency that will not be reviewed but withdrawn, 2) expedited treatment (i.e., cursory review) without comments, and 3) regular review.(443) In 1980, the SEC adopted a new procedure "selective review," under which a small percentage of periodic filings receive a full review. Such a risk-based process would help appropriate disclosure review under resource constraints. The selection criteria are not disclosed to make firms believe that they might be selected for a full review and thus prepare better filings.(374, 442, 444) In 2002, the Committee on Governmental Affairs United States Senate pointed out that SEC's discretionary-based selective review approach had failed to identify the Enron as worthy of a full review even though the Enron was rapidly growing, significantly changed in business with many subsidiary entities. (445)[317]

Mandated periodic review

The media focused on the fact that the SEC had not reviewed the filing of Enron since 1997. Consequently, the SOX of 2002 (i.e., Section 408 of the Securities Exchange Act) required the SEC to review periodic filings at least once every three years. In addition to the periodic review, the SOX of 2002 provides some indicators of the selective review. The indicators are aimed to enhance the quality of the prior risk-based review process. The SEC shall review the disclosure on a regular basis when the firm meets the "review criteria" stipulated in Section 408 of the Securities Exchange Act. The SOX supposedly assumes those review criteria as representing the characteristics of firms with deficient disclosure (e.g., restatement).(441)

Review process

The SEC focuses on screening disclosures that appear to be deficient in clarity or inconsistent with rules or standards. The SEC sets goals for disclosure review, select firms for review, and determines the scope of review. The following figure depicts the whole process of disclosure review.(446, 447) Firms may respond to a comment letter by amending a prior disclosure or agree to revise it in future filings. The SEC makes comment letters publicly available on EDGAR no sooner than 20 business days after completion. If a firm is selected for a review, the extent of review is determined by many factors that are set by Section 408 of the Sarbanes-Oxley Act and the SEC's selective review criteria. The scope of SEC's selective review includes 1) a full cover-to-cover review examining the entire filing; 2) a financial statement review examining the financial statements and related disclosure; 3) a targeted issue review examining the filing for specific items of disclosure for compliance with the applicable laws, regulations, standards, and requirements. A review process is closed when all comments are resolved, and the SEC sends a "no further comment."[318] Even though the comment letter process starts, it does not necessarily mean there are material issues that result from serious deficiency and, as a consequence, require a restatement. It is evidenced that only a very small percent of comment letters result in a restatement.(448, 449)

The amount of benefits of disclosure review depends on how regulators utilize disclosure review processes. Pincus, Holder, and Mock (1988) provide explanations that the SEC obtains enforcement investigation leads from several sources; 1) disclosure review (about 50%), 2) surveillances of exchanges, 3) public complaints, tips, and financial press.(450-452)

Evidentiary value

Even though the selective review is more strongly employed by the SEC, the resolution of the disclosure review process should not be accorded any evidentiary value. The SEC strictly refuse to accord any evidentiary value to the disclosure review. "*Notwithstanding the type of review applied to registration statements, ... the statutory burden of disclosure is on the issuer ... as a matter of law this burden cannot be shifted to the staff ...*" Courts also have been holding the same view with the SEC based on some rationale; SEC's review burden exceeds the ability of the SEC that cannot be completely updating facts about firms to assess the accuracy of the information, SEC's review does not reflect upon firms' compliance with laws. The disclosure review is a preventive mechanism but not concede any evidentiary values. (442)

4312. Public release

Transition to transparent regulation

Duro, Heese, and Ormazabal (2019) illustrate some policies that have been introduced to make regulatory oversight actions publicly available. For instance, regulators mandated the banking industry to disclose stress test results that contain information about financial risks. Such a transition to transparent regulation is based on the rationale that the public release of regulatory action will induce more active third-party monitoring behaviors and thus enhance the effectiveness of enforcement. The public release of regulatory action can guide market participants to exercise market discipline more actively. Managers who are concerned with the sharp downturn of investor's perception would choose to change their disclosure practice t0 meet the regulator's needs of transparency and compliance. The public release means public scrutiny. As the public release could badly affect regulators' reputation, regulators may exert more effort to maintain regulatory reputation by increasing "supervisory discipline."(453-455)

Public release in non-capital market

Goldstein & Sapra (2013) provide some examples of public release. First, many banks took on excessive risks of which information was not adequately disclosed, and, as a result, market discipline could not be properly exercised. The public release of stress test results may restore and boost investors' confidence in the banking sector. Second, it is argued that the US Savings and Loans crisis stemmed from the lack of information about sharply increasing interest rate gaps between the variable interest rates on deposit liabilities and the fixed rates earned on mortgage assets. If the market prices would have been publicly released to value mortgage assets, then the public information would have highlighted the hidden risks and activated market discipline much earlier.(453) Duro, Heese, and Ormazabal (2018) illustrates some researches on the public release of regulatory action in a non-capital market context that includes the ratings of school grade, restaurant hygiene grade, health plan. The public release of regulatory action is likely to mitigate information asymmetries.(454, 456)

Costs of public release

There can be unintended negative consequences from the public release of comment letter and its correspondences; proprietary cost and regulatory avoidance.

First, if the public release of comment letters can generate severe proprietary costs and damage firm value, it is unlikely to be justified by the small increase of social welfare. To mitigate the proprietary costs, the SEC rule (i.e., Rule 83 or 17 CFR 200.83) allows filing firms to request confidential treatment for their written response.(405, 453) The SEC rule (i.e., Rule 83 or 17 CFR 200.83) allows filing firms to request confidential treatment for their written response. Firms should submit a response letter using two separate versions; the redacted version excluding the confidential information and the confidential version, including the confidential information. The SEC release only the redacted version after some questions. Firms must provide an appropriate basis for the confidential treatment request.(405)

Second, Duro, Heese, and Ormazabal (2018) suggest that the public release of comment letters could weaken the positive effects. Peer firms in the market can infer the regulator's oversight priorities from the public release of a specific firm's comment letters, which allow peer firms to manage earnings in a way to avoid the focus of regulator.(454)

SEC's institutional background

Prior to 2004, analysts could have gathered the comment letter by requesting under the Freedom of Information Act (FOIA), which was very limited and burdensome. In 2004, due to the sharp increase of requests, the SEC announced: *"to expand the transparency of the comment letter process so that this information is available to a broader audience, free of charge."*(405, 454)

Trends

The number of comment letters issued has been continuously decreasing since 2010 for many consecutive years. Deloitte (2017) provides a report explaining that the average percentage of public companies that were subject to the SEC review each year is slightly over 50%. The number of disclosure reviews with comment letters and the total number of SEC comment letters issued have been declining.[319] Factors attributable to this trend include: externality (e.g., firms learn from other firm's comment letter), more frequent review after SOX 2002, SEC's more selective policy, less significant changes to rules, more effective communications, fewer filing (e.g., 10-K filing decreased 15% since 2013).(457, 458)

Commented area

Ernst Young (2018) provides the trends of comment letters to help managers improve disclosure practices. Management's discussion and analysis (MD&A) is in the top list of the most frequent area of the comment letter. The following table of Ernst Young (2018) summarizes the top 10 most frequent areas of comment letter in 2017 and 2018.(459)

Rank - Percentage - Comment area
- 1 - 43% - Management's discussion and analysis
- 2 - 47% - Non-GAAP financial measures
- 3 - 17% - Fair value measurements
- 4 - 15% - Segment reporting
- 5 - 13% - Revenue recognition
- 6 - 11% - Intangible assets and goodwill
- 7 - 12% - State sponsors of terrorism
- 8 - 12% - Income taxes
- 9 - 8% - Acquisitions and business combinations
- 10 - 6% - Contingencies

Note) Percentage: Comments as % of total registrants that received comment letters (2017 and 2018)

Source) Ernst Young (2018) - rearranged from the table.(459)

Firm Size & Rounds

Ernst Young (2018) provides a report that the majority of comment letters recipient is large public firms. Most registrants (i.e., 62%) receiving comment letters were large firms of which public floating size exceed 700 million US dollars. Most of the review (i.e., 78%) was completed in one letter, while 22% ended in over two letters. (459)

4313. Determinants or predictors

Mandatory selection criteria

Variables such as restatement history, volatility, size, earnings ratio, industry portion will naturally be found to be the well-explaining determinants because those are the "review criteria" stipulated in Section 408 of the Securities Exchange Act. For example, Chen, Johnston, and Ramnath (2010) find that firms tend to receive an SEC comment letter when they are restated in prior, less volatile, higher in price-earnings ratio, and larger in market capitalization or in industry revenue.(460) In addition to the determinants in the review criteria, suggested are other firm-level determinants as below.

Firm-level predictor

Firms with low profitability, weak governance, and contracted with small audit firms tend to receive more comment letters with a greater extent of comments.(448) Firms with CFOs who already experienced comment letters appear to process smoothly.(461) Firms with higher unexplained audit fees that can be are a measure of accounting quality are more likely to receive a comment letter.(462) Firms with lower profitability and low internal control are more likely to receive comment letters.(463) Conspicuous firms such as industry leaders are more likely to receive comment letters.(460)

Disclosure-level predictor

Firms with high complex disclosure tend to receive more comment letters with a eater extent of comments.(448) The SEC tends to make comment letters to firms that have been listed longer. Firms audited by large audit firms are more likely to have higher reporting quality and less likely to receive a comment letter.(460) Firms with poor quality (i.e., frequent restatement) are more likely to receive comment letters.(463)

Auditor style predictor

The term "auditor style" refers to the unique characteristics of individual audit firms in implementing audit standards and procedures. If an audit firm audits many firms, then the audited firms are more likely to have comparable accounting practices. As a result, the auditor style can also have an impact on the probability of receiving a comment letter. Firms with the same external auditor tend to have more similar patterns, which can be attributed to auditor's specific policies and procedures. In consequence, they tend to receive similar comment letters. Firms with long auditor tenure in common tend to receive more similar comment letter.(464)

4314. Opportunistic behaviors

Insider sales

Dechow, Lawrence, and Ryans (2015) provide strong evidence of insider sales in prior to the comment letter release. Insider sales prior to the public release of comment letters are pronounced for firms with financial and valuation issues. Stock price response was negative but delayed to the revenue recognition comment letters, especially when there are insider sales and acute comment issues. Stock return drift could be caused by investor's inattention, and insiders might profit from trading on material information about comment letters. In general, it is assumed that rational insiders will not take the risk of trading before the release of comment letters. However, the lack of investor's attention and the drift of negative stock price response to the release of comment letter would explain the pre-release insider sales. In addition, they suggest that a firm's insider trading policies are unlikely to include the prohibition of insider trading prior to the public release of comment which is released by the SEC.(465)

Compensation: strategic poor disclosure

Robinson, Xue, and Yu (2011) find that disclosure defects (i.e., comment letters) are positively associated with executives' compensation in the previous year, suggesting that managers exercise strategic discretion to omit disclosures that would reveal excess compensation. It is not evidenced that disclosure defects reduce excessive compensation in the following years. (466)

4315. Consequences

43151. Firm

Remediation cost

Cassell, Cunningham, and Lisic (2016) argue that the filing review process imposes substantial remediation costs on firms in terms of time and resources.(467) In addition to the direct cost (i.e., remediation costs), a comment letter have various types of real economic effects on firms in terms of executive turnover, auditor change, audit cost, accounting change, capital market transactions (e.g., M&A), and subsequent disclosure practices.

Executive's turnover

Regulatory actions can increase the likelihood of executive turnover. Gietzmann, Marra, and Pettinicchio (2016) find evidence that the firm's receipts of comment letter increase the likelihood of executives' replacement because executives (e.g., CFO) play a fundamental role in managing the reporting procedure and quality. The likelihood of CFO turnover is increasing with the number of the comment letter. Once a firm receives a severe comment letter, the likelihood of CFO turnover increases. (468)

IPO pricing

Li and Liu (2017) provide evidence that firms are likely to reduce the offer price when they receive a comment letter. The degree of price reduction is greater for firms with more rounds with the SEC.(469)

M&A outcomes

Periodic filings such as 10-K are selectively reviewed by the SEC, while the transactional filings such as mergers and acquisitions (i.e., Form S-4) are scrutinized without exception. When firms receive a comment letter from Form S-4, Johnson, Lisic, Moon, and Wang (2019) find that the M&A completion rate is significantly higher at the cost of prolonged process.(470)

Accounting change

Cunningham, Johnson, Johnson, and Lisic (2018) find that the issuance of comment letter induces firms to switch from accrual-based earnings management to real-activities-based earnings management. A comment letter that is not associated with estimates or accruals (e.g., classification, presentation and non-accounting issues) does not induce firms to change earnings management.(471)

Auditor resignation

Disclosure defects (e.g., restatement, comment letter) have significant implications for the relationships between the auditor and client firm. Huang and Scholz (2012) find that a restatement increases the likelihood of auditor-initiated switches (i.e., auditor resignation). Auditor resignations are costly to firms. Firms are less likely to contract with similar auditors but more likely to hire smaller auditors following a resignation.(472)

As restatements are associated with auditor changes, so might be a comment letter. Baldwin, Hurtt, and MacGregor (2013) conclude that the audit committee may perceive comment letter as a reporting failure that is likely to result in auditor resignation or dismissal. Auditor change is likely to increase with the number of the comment letter. Auditor change results regardless of the issue types (e.g., accounting or non-accounting) or filing types (e.g., 10-K or 10-Q). Such evidence implies that auditors need to be aware of the comment letter risk and take a more active role in reviewing all SEC filings.(473)

Audit fee

In response to the increases in regulation and litigation risk, auditors naturally consider whether the audit fee should be revised. A rational auditor would likely to have a risk-based pricing policy which charges more on firms with greater risks (e.g., firms received comment letter). Gietzmann and Pettinicchio (2014) find evidence that auditor tends to upwardly adjust the auditor fee for firms that received a comment letter. A significant increase in audit fees is evidenced to persist in future years. A comment letter works as a trigger that changes the firm's risk profile.(474)

Tax

Kubick, Lynch, Mayberry, and Omer (2014) find that firms received comment letter are likely to reduce the level of tax avoidance. If the costs from regulatory scrutiny are expected to exceed the benefits of tax avoidance, then firms are dis-incentivized to try tax avoidance. Thus, firms that received the tax-related comment letters are more likely to respond with changes in tax behavior.(475)

Legal system

Giamouridis, Koulikidou, and Leventis (2018) find that the negative language tone of comment letters issued to foreign firms listed on US stock exchanges produces significant investor reactions. Investors react more negatively to the comment letters issued to foreign firms domiciled in strong domestic enforcement countries (e.g., closer legal systems to the US). Evidence suggests that investors accept the comment letter of foreign firms domiciled in strong domestic enforcement as unexpected news.(476)

Disclosure

Duro, Heese, and Ormazabal (2019) argue that the public release of regulatory oversight (e.g., comment letter) can complement public enforcement. After the SEC changed its policy to disclose comment letters, market responses to earnings releases following comment letters increased significantly, implying that the public release of comment letters increases "market discipline." The public release increases managers' incentives to effectively remediate the issues and comply with regulatory requirements because the SEC's comment letter could more negatively affect market reputation. The increase of market responses is pronounced for firms with a higher proportion of institutional investors. (454)

Many pieces of literature generally find that comment letter improves disclosure quality. Johnson, Lisic, Moon, and Wang (2019) find that firms received comment letters and finished the M&A process are less likely to have goodwill impairment or a restatement in the next year of M&A, which means SEC's filing review improves disclosure quality.(470) Bozanic, Dietrich, and Johnson (2017) find that firms' disclosures following a comment letter are improved (i.e., more readable, less optimistic, and more forward-looking) and consequently lead to an increase in the intermediary following (e.g., analyst) and a reduction in litigation risk. In contrast, no improvement in disclosure was evidenced by firms that requested confidential treatment requests.(477) Bens, Cheng, and Neamtiu (2016) find that fair value related comment letters are associated with a significant reduction in the uncertainty about fair value estimates.(478) Duro, Heese, and Ormazabal (2019) show that the public release of comment letter enhances the effectiveness of the SEC's filing review. The public release of comment letter may incentivize firms to be more vigilant about disclosure practices and provide a higher quality of disclosure. As a result, in the long run, higher quality of disclosure that results from the comment letters could reduce the likelihood of substantive comment letter in the future. Firm's disclosure following the public release of comment letters exhibit higher quality of disclosure (e.g., fewer discretion, lower restatement, longer narratives).(454) However, Johnston & Petacchi (2017) find *"no evidence that comment letter firms in-*

crease the quantity or change the type of voluntary disclosure."(479)

43152. Investor

Abnormal returns

Dechow, Lawrence, and Ryans (2015) find the evidence of a delayed negative abnormal returns for revenue recognition comment letters.(465) Chen, Johnston, and Ramnath (2010) provide evidence that abnormal return volatility and trading volume significantly decreased around earnings announcements subsequent to the public release of comment letter. A decline of volume reactions is interpreted to indicate the improvement of information environment and higher consensus of firm value.(460) Edwards, Klassen, and Pinto (2018) focus on SEC's comment letters related with tax. The public releases of tax-related comment letters of tax aggressive firms show pronounced negative abnormal returns. Investors might expect higher reduction in future cash flows due to future tax payments. Tax aggressive firms with poorer disclosure quality experience stronger negative reactions to the public release of tax comment letters. (480)[320]

However, Johnson (2015) find that there are weak association between investor's responses and the public release of comment letter, and conclude that comment letter release provides little informational value to investors. One may assume that the complexity (e.g., more rounds of correspondence) of comment letter could influence the informativeness of comment letter and result in a stronger market reaction, however, positive evidence was not found. Besides, one may assume that the informativeness could be greater for firms with higher economic uncertainty (i.e., young, volatile revenues, forecast dispersion), however, weak evidence was found.(481) Ryans (2016) find some evidence of underreaction to comment letters which is possibly due to information processing costs and limited salience.(463) Investors might be inattentive or partially aware of the public release of comment letter due to the complexity of comment letter. Thus, investor's response could be selective or limited depending on the contents of comment letter.

Spread

Johnston & Petacchi (2017) find evidence that the resolution of the comment letter procedure enhances information asymmetry and liquidity because the adverse selection component of the bid-ask spread declines when the comment letter is resolved.(479) Ertimur and Nondorf (2006) find that firms that there is no association between the comment letters and liquidity (e.g., bid-ask spread, market depth).(461)

Rebalancing

Investigating the comment letters that question the application of US GAAP or IFRS, Gietzmann and Isidro (2013) finds that institutional investors react by rebalancing their portfolio. Institutional investors, especially low turnover institutional investors, are likely to reduce equity holdings.(482)

Analysts following

Bozanic, Dietrich, and Johnson (2017) find that firms' disclosures following a comment letter lead to an increase in the intermediary following (e.g., analyst).(477) Ryans (2018) point out that investors infrequently read comment letters due to the cost of searching and processing information, and, as a result, markets reaction to the public release of the comment letter is delayed or reduced, which can be generally interpreted to be uninformative. The comment letter is not widely identified as an essential information source by the analysis industry and financial media. (463)

Short seller

Grove, Johnsen, and Lung (2015), Ryans (2018) suggests a short seller as the most prominent users of comment letters. They are most incentivized to identify negative information especially prompted by an independent and reliable source such as the SEC.(463, 483)

43153. Regulator

Along with enhancing market discipline, Goldstein & Sapra (2013) suggest that the public release of the regulator's action (e.g., the bank's stress tests) also affects supervisory discipline. Disclosure could impact the credibility and reputation of regulators. By releasing stress-test results, regulators would be subject to greater scrutiny by outsiders and, as a result, regulators could be held more accountable. (453) Duro, Heese, and Ormazabal (2019) suggest that disclosure could facilitate more outside monitoring on the regulator's oversight process. The public release of the regulator's action may coerce regulators to efficiently allocate their restrained resources and, as a result, improve the level of regulatory effectiveness. The public release of the regulator's action can strengthen the effectiveness of public enforcement through increased market discipline and supervisory discipline.(454)

4316. Externality of disclosure review

Industry leader and peers: Learning & deterrence effect

Empirical evidence is mixed about various impacts of comment letters. There could be impacts less on shareholders but more on stakeholders who pay much attention to comment letters.(463) Investors of firms that did not receive comment letters from the SEC may be able to infer the SEC's concerns by reviewing comment letters addressed to peer firms. In addition, the public release of comment letters may generate subsequent learning effects to peer firms, which may educate firms and enhance disclosure practices.(484)

The public release of comment letters about industry leaders creates positive industry spillover in two ways; peer's disclosure response and investor's market reaction. Chen, Johnston, and Ramnath (2010) provide evidence on both spillovers. Industry leaders are more likely to receive a comment letter. Regarding peer's disclosure response, industry peers are likely to follow disclosure changes implemented by an industry leader that receive a comment letter. If the SEC reviews a specific industry intensely, then disclosure practices of industry peers are improved. Regarding investor's market reaction, investors of industry peers that did not received a comment letter benefit from the public release of comment letter about an industry leader. They do not find "... *any change in return volatility for industry peers, on average. However, in industries that receive greater attention from the SEC, peer firms do show a reduction in price reactions.*" (460)

Brown, Tian, and Wu Tucker (2018) provide evidence of the spillover effect of comment letters on qualitative disclosure (i.e., risk factor disclosure). After the industry leader or close industry peers receive a comment letter, firms that are not receiving any comment letter improved disclosure quality in the subsequent year and, in consequence of voluntary improvement, firms following industry leader or peers reduces their likelihood of receiving comment letter. (451)

The ultimate purpose of enforcement is to deter undesirable behaviors and outcomes with the most efficient mechanism. The spillover effect due to the public release of comment letters could generate the deterrence benefits similar to or better than regulatory enforcement. A rational manager will anticipate that they could have serious negative consequences when they receive a comment letter. Thus, they let another's shipwreck be their seamark. They may take another firm's failure to change their similar disclosure practices. The public release of comment letters enables firms to learn at another firm's cost. The spillover effect leads non-commented firms to better align with the objectives of the regulator. As a result, the regulator's resources can be leveraged.

Forensic analysis

Grove, Johnsen, and Lung (2015) suggest that, as comment letters serve as an independent source of relevant information about disclosure quality, so to forensic analysis. A comment letter will alert not only investors but also other external users (e.g., auditor). Some comment letters represent specific information not only useful to valuation but also forensic analysis. (483)

Loan analysis: Interest rate

Cunningham, Schmardebeck, and Wang (2017) find that banks are evidenced to use comment letters as a channel to obtain information about a borrower's creditworthiness. Banks are likely to charge higher interest rates on their borrowers that are under correspondence with the SEC regarding comment letters. The effect of comment letters on interest rates is more pronounced when the disclosure deficiencies are material, issues are related to valuation, and issues resulted in a restatement. Banks have the incentive to search for information about potential regulatory action for better evaluation of borrower's creditworthiness. As a due diligence process, banks generally have a procedure or checklist questioning about any ongoing regulatory investigation (e.g., comment letter). For specific questions, borrowers are generally forthcoming to avoid any adverse outcomes. As a result, banks can gain access to the comment letter correspondence prior to public release. They find that *"...banks charge even higher interest rates ... when comment letter correspondence is ongoing ... banks continue to charge borrowers higher interest rates following the resolution of the SEC's comments. Comment letters have a lasting impact on banks' pricing decision."* (449)

4317. Prevention & Remediation

Prevention

Some comment letters are likely to precede a formal investigation and an eventual enforcement action. Managers would consider the SEC comment letters as a potential trigger of enforcement. Thus, the proactive remediation at the comment letter stage can reduce the likelihood of subsequent enforcement action.(485) Industry leaders generate a spillover effect. For remembrance sake, industry peers had better check the disclosure of other firms frequently. Peers should let the industry leader's failure be a lesson to themselves. It is good to learn at other men's costs. Ernst Young (2018) provides best practices (Appendix D: SEC review process and best practices), noting that many firms resolve a comment without changing disclosures.(459) Some determinants of comment letter (e.g., complexity, size, profitability, auditor, and corporate governance) provide useful implications on how to prevent and resolve the issue. However, the firm cannot control most factors with ease in the short-term.

Readability

Cassell, Cunningham, and Lisic (2016) finds that the readability of the firm's comment review response is associated with better resolution (i.e., shorter response times, fewer rounds, and lower restatement) by using the Fog index. Disclosure review outcomes *"...are more favorable when the company's initial response is more readable."* The readability of response is an easy way to mitigate the remediation cost and can have a significant positive effect on regulators' reaction. Regulators, with resource constraints, can pay limited attention to individual comment letter case. Even though more readable responses are likely to be easier to process, managers are more likely to provide a less readable response when they want to conceal some information. Firms that responded with lower readability share some attributes in common (e.g., larger, less profitable, previously restated). Firms that have low readability with periodic report respond with low readability to the SEC.(467)

Expertise of CFO

Kwon, Lim, and Park (2019) find that the financial expertise of CFO improves the resolution of comment letters and enhances investors' perceptions of earnings. We cannot but highlight the role of CFO in complying with regulatory requirements and resolving regulatory issues.(461, 486)

External involvement

Ballestero & Schmidt (2019) find that auditor is more likely to be involved when there are many accounting issues. The involvement of an experienced partner of the auditor in the comment letter process have expedites the comment letter process. The involvement of an experienced partner is positively associated with improvements in the readability of the firm's responses to comment letters.(487) Firms are generally advised to include experienced auditors during the comment letter process so that it may not be delayed or hindered.(488) The issuance of the comment letter is more likely for firms that engage with non-Big four auditors.(448, 479) Determinants provide implications on how to remediate. Auditor change followed by the comment letter might be interpreted as "the day after the fair." (473) So far as it goes, some firms are evidenced to remediate via political connections proactively. Firms use their political connections to mitigate the likelihood of comment letter or the degree of enforcement actions. (489)

Governance

When received comment letter correspondence, firms must address the comments to satisfy the SEC's demands by increasing disclosure quality. Stronger governance may enable increased disclosure quality. Ertimur and Nondorf (2006) conclude that firms with stronger corporate governance are able to resolve comment letter concern more expediently.(461)

4318. Regulator's Limits

43181. Introduction

The public release of regulatory action emerged as a tool to increase the effectiveness of enforcement by complementing public enforcement with market monitoring. However, the disclosure review and its public release would not automatically yield sufficient performances. It is suggested that there are several regulatory concerns about the efficacy of enforcement activity; limited resource, capturing, inconsistency.(454) Regulators could often be operating with limited resources that are insufficient to achieve optimal performance(490), inconsistent in enforcement actions (485), or captured by firms(485, 489).

43182. Limited resource

The efficacy of the regulator's enforcement mechanism relies on the regulator's resources. The firm's disclosure behavior might be depending on the regulator's available resources and enforcement strategy. A resource-constrained regulator is more likely to investigate firms closer to regulators' office, and such firms might be less likely to commit a violation and more likely to employ conservative accounting practices. It is evidenced that the SEC is more likely to investigate firms located closer to its office and firms closer to the regulators' office are less likely to restate financial statements. (490)

43183. Inconsistency

Significance

Baugh, Kim, and Lee (2017) argue that the consistency of disclosure review yields investor's confidence. Thus, it can be mentioned as the key component of effective regulation. Similar violations should be sanctioned in equivalent ways to sustain public trust and regulatory confidence. Inconsistent enforcement or differentiated treatments might raise fairness concerns, and, as a result, resulting in non-compliance. (491)

Regulatory inconsistency

By synthesizing fragmented literature discussing the characteristics of top managers, Hambrick and Mason (1984) propose a more general "upper echelons theory," which suggests that *"organizational outcomes - strategic choices and performance levels - are partially predicted by managerial background characteristics."* Individual reviewers make decisions under the bounded rationality and, as a result, their decision can be influenced by their bounded environments (e.g., style, experience, knowledge, value), which have a substantial impact on outcomes (e.g., quality). Especially, the disclosure review is a complex mission that requires the reviewer's subjective assessment in which the reviewer's personal attributes can play an important role. In addition, some anecdotal or empirical evidence documents that enforcement actions can be inconsistent due to the differences in regulatory environments. For example, factors such as resource constraints (budget allocation), investigation costs (e.g., geographical proximity), and political connection can also create the inconsistency of enforcement. (489-492)

Baugh, Kim, and Lee (2017) show that reviewers' idiosyncratic style influences the filing review outcomes. The impact of reviewer style is persistent, and a stricter review style is likely to improve the quality of disclosure subsequent to a comment letter. Firms that are reviewed by a more demanding reviewer are more likely to restate reports during the review process and have fewer issues in the future.(491) As the SEC review process is individualized, review staff's personal style also matters. Do & Zhang (2018) find that the SEC reviewer exhibit unique personal styles of which effects on firms (e.g., remediation costs, reporting quality, etc.) are significant. (492)

Regulator's measures against inconsistency

To prevent and mitigate the side-effects that can be caused by individualized review, regulators have incentives to take all measures to ensure consistency among the reviewers. An introduction of organizational mechanisms such as standard procedures would limit reviewer's idiosyncratic choices to some degree. The SEC typically operates the review process that involves 'one examiner and one reviewer' and provide reviewers with guidance for qualified review. In addition, internal supervisory control activities would ensure uniform reviewing. The job requirements of the SEC would guide reviewers to be highly homogenous in educational and professional backgrounds, which might reduce the likelihood of inconsistency. Such measures are likely to reduce the idiosyncratic influences.(492)

43184. Capture

Regulatory capture

The capture theory hypothesizes that a firm's political connections are negatively associated with the likelihood of enforcement actions or penalties. By providing a negative relation between the firm's political connection and enforcement actions, some researchers suggest that the SEC is captured by politically connected firms.(489) It is evidenced that there is a significant difference in fraud detection ratio between firms. Fraudulent firms are likely to spend more on lobbying than non-fraudulent firms.(493) However, the results of Heese, Khan, and Ramanna (2017) indicate that politically connected firms are more likely to receive a comment letter. They argue that it is difficult to conclude that SEC is captured. Firms' political connections are more likely to have added scrutiny in the comment letter process, which is inconsistent with regulatory capture theory. (485)

Revolving door

The revolving door is a shift of personnel between regulators and industry. The revolving door is justified for some reason. Regulators need to hire industry professionals who already have enough experience in the industry, and the private sector also needs to hire professionals from regulating a position to seek more favorable enforcement action. However, one may claim that the relationship between the public sector and the private sector can be denatured into regulatory capture. As a result, a revolving door might be interpreted as evidence that regulators are less objective in enforcement and turn out to be an undermining door to the integrity of the regulator. DeHaan, Kedia, Koh, and Rajgopal (2012) suggest two conflicting explanations; human capital hypothesis vs. rent-seeking hypothesis. The human capital hypothesis refers to the positive behavior of the reviewer. A reviewer who expects future job opportunities in the private sector tends to increase the level of scrutiny to show personal expertise and, as a result, the revolving door will create a positive impact on the regulatory effort. A reviewer is likely to signal personal talent by making a tougher review rather than a lax review because the industry wants to employ talented reviewers. On the contrary, the rent-seeking hypothesis refers to the negative behavior of the reviewer. Reviewers could treat their prospective employers with leniency and relax enforcement. Evidence supports the human capital hypothesis. *"Enforcement efforts while at the SEC are higher for lawyers that leave and join law firms that are more likely to defend clients against the SEC."*(494)

Remedies for consistency

Many countries adopt legal frameworks to regulate the revolving door in order to enhance transparency and public interests. The ultimate purpose of such remedies should not be completely stopping the revolving door because the exchange of skilled experts can bring the innovation of process. Most countries seek to achieve a balance by preventing the abuse from unethical leverages but preserving the experts' freedom of mobility, which is to reduce or slow the opportunities for the conflicts of interest. In general, the target of revolving door regulation is mainly decision-makers because the industry is more likely to seek experts in a higher position. The most frequently used measure is mandating the "cooling-off periods" or "waiting periods," which is a period during which a former public official is prohibited from taking a position in the private sector that is related to the current regulatory position.

4319. Better Review

The evidence of Brown, Tian, and Tucker (2018) implies that reviewing the comment letter of industry leaders would create the externality. A regulator would expect more benefit by reviewing the industry leader or focusing attention on specific disclosures that can generate more externality or spillover effects.(495) The regulator needs to examine what determines the quality of disclosure review. Kubic (2017) find a positive association between the SEC's human capital allocation and detection rates. Without an accountant, the SEC is less likely to detect reporting errors. Incentives are less associated with the review performances. Benchmarks such as error detection ratio can be useful in monitoring the trends of SEC's ability to identify reporting errors. (496) Regulators need to examine their selection criteria for more efficient resource allocation periodically. Regulators should draw their attention to more substantive issues. A more simplified public release of comment letter correspondence might reduce complexity but generate more externalities. Regulators should enhance the credibility of enforcement by strictly following standard procedures.

432. Canada

Harmonized disclosure review

On July 16, 2004, the Canadian Securities Administrators (CSA) established a harmonized program for continuous disclosure reviews (CDR) program to improve the quality of continuous disclosure. Details regarding the CDR program can be found in "CSA Staff Notice 51-312 Harmonized Continuous Disclosure Review Program."(497) In 2009, this Notice was revised as the "CSA Staff Notice 51-312 (revised) Harmonized Continuous Disclosure Review Program."(498)[321] Under the CDR program, *"issuers deal only with staff of their principal regulator, and staff of other regulators rely on the staff of the principal regulator on matters related to reviews."* The principal regulator is responsible for reviewing the continuous disclosure and taking actions.[322] The CSA uses a risk-based approach in selecting issuers to review. The selection criteria are used as below;[323]

a. Full review: A full review covers many types of disclosure in broad scopes. Most recent financial statements, MD&A, and other types of documents, other information such as circulars, press releases, web sites, and public complaints about the issuer are gathered.

b. Issue-oriented review (IOR): An IOR is an in-depth review focusing on a specific issue (e.g., interim reports, compensation, particular industry).

In 2005, the CSA published "CSA Staff Notice 51-316 Continuous Disclosure Review of Smaller Issuers" to summarize some of the disclosure deficiencies of smaller issuers. It is to alert smaller issuers to avoid some common disclosure deficiencies. For instance, smaller issuers have not adopted new accounting requirements.[324] Pursuant to Section 11.5 of NI 51-102, the issuer must immediately correct material deficiencies identified by the CDR by refiling the applicable documents. If a material deficiency is identified, the issue may be publicized in the default lists, be issued a cease-trade order or be recommended enforcement actions.

Trends

The fiscal year of 2010 and 2011 was the peak for the number of issuers reviewed, showing the curved humpback trends. The percentage of "Full Review" is sharply decreasing, which might reduce the cost of disclosure review from the perspective of both regulators and issuers. The percentage of "Action" or "Refiling" does not show any marked trends.[325]

Fiscal year	2008	2009	2010	2011	2012	2013	2014	2015	2016	2018
Reviewed (#)	854	1094	1351	1351	1248	1336	991	1058	902	840
- Full review	442	465	527	436	453	368	221	280	280	160
- Issue-oriented-review	412	629	824	915	795	968	770	778	622	680
No action (%)	39	20	28	30	44	53	24	32	27	39
Education/Awareness (%)	0	14	9	10	9	2	16	9	11	10
Action (%)	61	66	63	60	47	45	60	59	62	51
- Prospective changes	36	48	43	40	28	26	37	30	31	25
- Refiling	19	13	16	16	17	14	14	21	23	18
- Cease trade order/ Referral to Enforcement/ Default list	6	5	4	4	3	5	9	8	8	8

Source) CSA Staff Notice 51-326, 329, 332, 334, 337, 339, 341, 344, 346, 355

Default list

The CSA introduced the "CSA 51-322 Reporting Issuer Defaults" that came into effect in December 2006 to provide a harmonized list of deficiencies that generally result in a "reporting issuer in default" of the securities laws. The circumstances under which issuers are considered to be in default are: 1) the reporting issuer has failed to file the continuous disclosure prescribed by securities laws (e.g., annual financial statements); 2) the financial statement does not comply with the requirements of National Instruments; 3) the reporting issuer has failed to pay a fee; 4) the issuer has failed to comply with any other requirements related to continuous disclosure.[326] The lists can be found on the websites of the securities regulatory authorities.

Review on forward-looking disclosure

The Ontario Securities Commission (OSC) of CANADA reviewed disclosures of forward-looking information in 2013 and provided guidance to improve forward-looking information disclosure. The report identified four main areas of improvement; 1) clear identification, 2) disclosure of material factor or assumptions, 3) updating previous disclosure, 4) comparison information.[327]

433. European Union

4331. ESMA

Guidelines on enforcement of financial information

In 2014, ESMA issued "Guidelines on Enforcement of Financial Information" (hereafter "GLEFI," ESMA/2014/1293) that applies to all competent authorities of the EU undertaking "enforcement of financial information."(499)[328] These principles-based guidelines describe objectives, scope, selection techniques, enforcement actions, and other aspects of enforcement methodology. Enforcers should ensure adequate independence from the government, issuers, and others.[329] By its nature, enforcement of financial information is normally an ex-post activity that starts from the publication of financial information. However, some enforcers have a pre-clearance system where enforcers may make an enforcement decision before disclosure. Guideline 4 describes some guidance of conditions for the pre-clearance.[330]

Types of examination

The GLEFI provides two types of examination under the "Definition." "Unlimited scope examination" of financial information refers to *"the evaluation of the entire content of the financial information in order to identify issues/areas that need further analysis and to assess whether the financial information is compliant with the relevant financial reporting framework."* "Focused examination" of financial information refers to *"the evaluation of pre-defined issues in the financial information and the assessment of whether the financial information is compliant with the relevant financial reporting framework in respect of those issues."*

Selection methods

Risk-based enforcement normally uses additional selection methods (e.g., random sampling, rotation). For a better selection, enforcer should consider *"the risk of a misstatement as well as the impact of a misstatement on the financial markets."* A pure risk-based approach might allow some loophole for some issuers that are continuously far beyond the risk-based selection criteria. Enforcers should design a well-developed selection method to achieve a loophole-free examination so that that *"there should always be a possibility of an issuer being selected for review."* Enforcers should take into consideration the probability of infringements (e.g., misstatement), the potential impact on markets, the complexity, the characteristics, experience of management, and the experience of the issuers' auditors. A larger issuer would face with more complexity, but a small issuer fewer resources.[331]

Types of enforcement actions

Whenever a material infringement is detected, the enforcer should take actions listed below: reissuance, corrective note[332], or correction in future financial statements. When taking action, enforcers should consider some factors. Choosing the action between a reissuance and a corrective note, whether the corrective note or reissuance provide users with sufficient clarity and adequate assessment should be the primary question. In choosing the action between the delayed correction and the earlier correction, the enforcer should consider the "timing of decision", "nature of decision", and "surrounding circumstances." For example, the enforcer could opt for a correction in future financial statements, where the market is already and sufficiently informed, or the infringements are just related to the presentation rather than the substance.[333]

Trends

ESMA publishes the "Enforcement and Regulatory Activities of European Accounting Enforcers" on an annual basis. Regarding the enforcement of financial information, the examination rate represented 19% in 2017 and 16% in 2018. An action ratio, a ratio of ex-post examinations resulted in actions, represented 32% in 2017 and 33% in 2018.(500) All national competent authorities (NCAs) examine ex-post annual consolidated financial statements. Most examinations are an ex-post basis, while a paucity of pre-clearance is conducted in 2018. Statistics by examination type in 2018 are below:[334]

Table 10) Disaggregation

2018	Disaggregation by type		Disaggregation by nature		
	Unlimited	Focused	Ex-post	IPO Prospectus	Pre-clearance
# of examinations (total: 947)	612	335	885	50	12

Note) "IPO Prospectus" means the Financial Statements contained in IPO Prospectus.

Source) summarized from the "Enforcement and Regulatory Activities of European Accounting Enforcers" in 2018 (Appendix IV – Number of examinations per country of IFRS financial statements)

Enforcement of financial information in prospectus

"Some NCAs apply the GLEFI on a voluntary basis for the review at financial statements contained in IPO prospectuses."[335] In addition, "… *majority of NCAs review financial statements contained in the prospectus in the wider context of the procedures to approve prospectuses set out by the Prospectus Regulation, and therefore not on the basis of the GLEFI…*"[336]

Enforcement of non-financial information

In 2018, EU enforcers expanded enforcement activities to include the non-financial information and the Alternative Performance Measures (APMs). In 2018, European enforcers examined about 31% of issuers with respect to non-financial information. However, different from the review of financial statements, the enforcement approach to disclosure reviews of non-financial information is not harmonized across the EU.(500)

Annual enforcement priorities for harmonization

ESMA publishes the "Public Statement on the European Common Enforcement Priorities" (the ECEP Statement) on an annual basis to promote consistent disclosure application, including disclosure review. "*Enforcers will continue to focus on material issues that are relevant for an individual issuer examined. Based on examinations performed, enforcers will take corrective actions whenever material misstatements are identified, and ESMA will report subsequently on their findings.*" For instance, the 2018 enforcement priorities reflect the new reporting standards and highlight the requirements to disclose nonfinancial information (i.e., environmental matters, climate changes). European enforcers will monitor the application of disclosure requirements, incorporate them into disclosure reviews and take corrective actions where appropriate.(501)

Public release of enforcement extracts

ESMA publishes some extracts from the confidential database of enforcement decisions on financial statements to strengthen supervisory convergence and provide relevant information for appropriate application of disclosure standards. In July 2019, ESMA published the 23rd Extract from the EECS's Database of Enforcement which contains eight decisions.(502)

4332. UK

Regulated market & AIM

Under Article 47 of the Markets in Financial Instruments Directive (2004/39/EC, MiFID), the Financial Conduct Authority (FCA) has been responsible for maintaining the list of "regulated market" in the UK. The Alternative Investment Market (AIM) has been excluded from the "regulated market" since it was self-regulated by the LSE Group rather than the United Kingdom Listing Authority (UKLA). However, under the Market Abuse Regulation, the scope of application was extended to the AIM.

Sanction by regulator

The FCA may impose a financial penalty or publish a censure statement if an issuer or a person has breached any of the disclosure requirements.[337] The "Enforcement Annual Performance Report" of the FCA indicates that disclosure issues maintain a focus by continuously opening and closing disclosure related cases.(438) After 2017, the FCA tends to open more investigation into disclosure issues, which continues to be a focus area.[338] For instance, in 2016, the FCA imposed a £70,000 fine against an AIM company for breaching the MAR by failing to make a prompt disclosure, which was the first case to impose fine on an AIM company for non-disclosure.[339]

AIM rules

"AIM Rules for Companies" describes that *"An AIM company must issue notification without delay of any new developments which are not public knowledge which, if made public, would be likely to lead to a significant movement in the price of its AIM securities. By way of example, this may include matters concerning a change in: its financial condition; its sphere of activity; the performance of its business; or tis expectation of its performance."*(Rule 11) Transaction-specific disclosures are described such as substantial transactions (Rule 12), related party transactions (Rule 13), reverse takeovers (Rule 14), fundamental changes of business (Rule 15). In addition, transactions completed during the twelve months prior to the date of the latest transaction must be aggregated (Rule 16). An AIM company must prepare a half-yearly report and publish annual audited accounts without delay and in any event not later than six months after the end of the financial year (Rule 18~19). Each AIM company must maintain a website, and the company information should be available free of charge (Rule 26). The company information includes business description, number of AIM securities in issue, directors, and the details of nominated adviser.

Disciplinary actions by LSE

Disciplinary actions and processes are described in Rule 42 (Sanction against an AIM company), Rule 44 (Disciplinary process), Rule 45 (Appeals). For instance, LSE announced a public censure and fine of 300,000 BGP on an AIM company which is related to (a) disclosure of misleading or incomplete information regarding the expected EBITDA and the progress of expansion plan; (b) disclosure failure with respect to related party transaction (i.e., consultancy payments); (c) director's delay in notification.[340] Sometimes LSE waives the fine but publishes details of the public censure to educate the market.[341]

By imposing disciplinary actions, stock exchanges seek to send a clear message to markets about their objectives that issuers take strong responsibility for ensuring robust procedures and enhanced transparency. LSE also aims to change the issuer's behaviors and maintain *"the integrity, orderliness, transparency and good reputation of its market."*[342] Where an issuer has contravened the "Admission and Disclosure Standards" of LSE (hereafter "Standards"), and it is appropriate to impose any sanctions, LSE will follow the disciplinary procedure set out in Section 5 of the Standards. LSE may impose one or more of the following actions: a) censure of the issuer and, in addition, the publication of such censure; b) a fine; and/or c) cancellation of the right of the issuer to have its securities traded on the Exchange's markets. An issuer may appeal against a decision of LSE. (Rule 4.20~22)

LSE may commence disciplinary action against issuers by which the "Standards" has been breached. LSE may issue a warning notice and/or refer disciplinary matters to either the Executive Panel or the Disciplinary Committee. LSE takes a number of factors into account when it takes disciplinary action, such as the seriousness, the size and nature of the breach, the actual or potential impact, the compliance history, and the consistent and fair application of the rule. Below summarizes the LSE disciplinary process and sanctions available.

a. Warning Notices

Normal Use = Rule breaches

(no hearing)

Available Sanctions = Formal record of action

b. Executive Panel (EP)

  Normal Use = Disciplinary matters

  Constitution = LSE staff

  Available Sanctions = One of: Private censure, Fine up to £100,000 per breach, Referral to Disciplinary Committee

c. Disciplinary Committee (DC)

  Normal Use = Disciplinary matters

  Constitution = Non-LSE staff

  Available Sanctions = One or more of: Private censure, Unlimited fine, Cancellation of right of the issue to have its securities traded on LSE

d. Appeals Committee

  Normal Use = Appeals against findings of EP/DC

  Constitution = Non-LSE staff

  Available Sanctions = Any sanction available respectively to the EP/DC

For example, For appeals against findings of Executive Panel (EP) or Discipliary Committee (DC), Appeals Committee that is constituted by Non-LSE stafff is processed, and any sanction available respectively to the EP/DC can be imposed.

Source) The above table is summarized from the tables of Section 5 of the "Standards."

4333. Germany

Under the Financial Reporting Enforcement Act (Bilanzkontrollgesetz-BilKoG) of 2004, financial reporting enforcement in Germany is conducted in two stages since 2005. The Financial Reporting Enforcement Panel (FREP), a government-appointed privately organized institution, is in charge of the first stage financial reporting enforcement of listed companies in Germany. The second stage of financial reporting enforcement is performed by the BaFin. Before the final decision, the FREP asks the company whether it accepts the suspected error, and most companies tend to accept it. The BaFin initiates one or three examinations per year when the companies refuse to accept the FREP's findings.[343]

The FREP initiates three types of examinations. It initiates an indication-based examination if there are specific indications of an infringement of financial reporting requirements, a request-based examination if the BaFin requests for examination, and an unlimited scope examination based on a random sampling method without any specific indication or request.[344] "Principles for Random Sampling" provides principles for unlimited scope examinations in accordance with the law. The sampling method of the FREP is based on the "Guidelines on Enforcement of Financial Information" of ESMA. The sample is stratified by two groups; Companies in the DAX/MDAX/SDAX are applied 4~6 years cycle, and other companies are applied 8~10 years cycle.[345]

The FREP conducts "Error Prevention Activities" by holding an event aimed at sharing experiences with the audit committee chairs. In addition, "*the FREP frequently makes recommendations to companies for future financial reporting purposes during the examination in order to eliminate weaknesses in future financial statements and improve the quality of financial reporting.*" The FREP publishes its enforcement priorities for the following calendar year.[346]

The FREP has published an annual "Activity Report," including summary and statistics of its financial reporting enforcement. From 2015 to 2018, examinations were completed in 8.4 months on average. Listed companies generally corrected identified errors in the subsequent financial statements.[347] The below table shows recent trends of financial reporting enforcement of the FREP.

Year   2006   2010   2015   2018

A	109	118	81	84	No. of examinations completed
B	19	31	12	134	No. of errors
B/A%	17	26	15	15	Percentage

Source) The above table is the summarized one from the "Activity Report" 2006~2018 of the FREP.[348]

434. Asia

4341. Japan

SESC

Within the FSA is established the Securities and Exchange Surveillance Commission (SESC) that consists of 6 divisions, including the Disclosure Inspection Division. Upon the adoption by the SESC deliberation, the recommendation for administrative disciplinary action shall be delivered to the Financial Services Agency (FSA). A summary of the recommendation shall be made public through the SESC website.[349] The SESC makes public the summary of "False Disclosure Statement" in the "SESC Latest Topics" every month.[350]

Registration statement & periodic reports

The SESC has the authority to conduct investigations for both criminal prosecution and administrative enforcement and may bring a case to the prosecutor or make recommendations to the FSA to impose administrative enforcements. The role of SESC is investigative and recommendatory. The FSA may issue a business improvement order, an improvement plan, and preventive measures. In Japan, there is no legal procedure of settlement between the governmental authority and the defendant in both criminal action and administrative action.(503)

The FSA is responsible for supervision and enforcement for disclosures required under the law. With respect to registration statements and periodic reports, the SESC carefully reviews filings to check whether issuers comply with the mandatory requirements. The SESC published the Annual Report including the number of cases where the SESC recommended the imposition of administrative penalties for violation of disclosure rules remains constant many years.(504)

Total	92~2012	2013	2014	2015	2016	2017	
192	164	3	6	8	7	4	Criminal charges
1028	704	70	66	59	91	38	Recommendations
101	71	9	8	6	5	2	Penalty (false statement)

Source) The above table is summarized from the SESC Annual Report of 2017/2018

Timely disclosure

Stock exchanges also conduct a review and impose a monetary fine for violating the listing agreement. Regarding examination on timely disclosure, JPX-R constantly monitors timely disclosure to maintain the quality of market transparency by examining whether disclosures are in line with the rules.[351] Disclosure examination shall be made to take necessary measures and thereby secure the appropriateness of corporate disclosure. Rule 28 (Subject of Disclosure Examination) of Business Regulations of JPX-R sets out that JPX-R shall conduct examination concerning timing, consistency, and appropriateness.[352]

In order to ensure compliance with the relevant requirements and rules, JPX-R may determine measures against the company that is deficient in compliance. Measures include a monetary fine, improvement measure, security on alert, security in question (Rule 30~34). The company may be required to submit an improvement report or designated as a "security on alert," depending on the severity of deficiency in the internal management system. If the company fails to complete the improvements within the specified period, it may be delisted. JPX announces the "Public Announcement Measure and Listing Agreement Violation Penalty" on its website.[353]

4342. Singapore

MAS

The Monetary Authority of Singapore (MAS) is an enforcer under the Monetary Authority of Singapore Act (MAS Act). It enforces the contravention of Section 203(2) of the Securities and Futures Act by failing disclosure as required by the Listing Rules.

SGX practice notes: risk-based disclosure review

Regarding continuing disclosure obligations, SGX aims to promote full and timely disclosure of all relevant information by issuers. In October 1998, SGX shifted from a merit-based regulatory regime to a disclosure-based regulatory regime. SGX may investigate whether there is an omission or misleading disclosure in the firm's announcements. SGX had reviewed every disclosure document prior to its issue to maintain the standard of disclosure, which was not to exercise merit judgment. From 2004, it adopted a more risk-based approach in disclosure review to pay greater regulatory attention to areas that pose significant risks. Regarding periodic reports, it had reviewed every document of every issuer but newly adopted the limited review for annual report and the selective review for other periodic reports. It conducts a limited review of every annual report by focusing on specific key issues that are strategically decided. It conducts the selective review by selecting issuers to review based on the risk factor such as the issuer's financial condition, the past incidence of non-compliance.

There is no disclosure review for other documents. Regulatory enforcement may be carried out according to the results of the disclosure review after the documents are issued. Some pre-vetting may be carried out where it is necessary to maintain the standard of disclosure.[354]

Disciplinary actions by SGX RegCo

SGX has established the Singapore Exchange Regulation Pte. Ltd (SGX RegCo) with effect from 15 September 2017. It is established and maintained by SGX as a ``ly-owned subsidiary to undertake all regulatory functions on behalf of SGX. It can require action to be taken by the subsidiaries of SGX Group.

Chapter 14 of the Mainboard Rule of SGX sets out the administrative and enforcement powers of SGX, the process for disciplinary actions, and the powers of the Disciplinary Committee and Appeals Committee. SGX may exercise "Administrative Powers" to issue public queries to issuers, require an issuer to make specified disclosures, place an issuer on the watchlist, halt or suspend trading, remove an issuer from the Official List (Rule 1405(1)). SGX may exercise "Investigative and Enforcement Powers" to take enforcement action, including the following: private warning, composition fines, education, or compliance program, independent review, approval or appointment of management (Rule 1405(3). Most of the disciplinary actions are public regulatory actions (i.e., public reprimand).

Fiscal year	'12	'13	'14	'15	'16	'17	'18
Composition fines	0	1	8	7	2	0	0
Private warnings/ Public regulatory actions	28	22	16	29	26	30	7
Referrals to disciplinary committees	3	0	2	2	1	6	3

Source) Regulation Statistics Report, SGX homepage[355]

Director watchlist

SGX RegCo has published a watchlist of names of directors and executive officers who have been reprimanded by SGX. If the proposed director or executive officers is on the watchlist, issuers or sponsors should consult SGX RegCo for guidance. SGX will assess the suitability of the proposed appointment. As of May 2018, SGX RegCo has put out a watchlist of 53 directors and executive officers.[356]

Disciplinary actions notified to MAS

Section 204 of the Securities and Futures Act 2002 set out penalties that the issuer who contravenes "continuous disclosure requirements" shall be guilty of an offense and shall be liable on conviction to a fine not exceeding $250,000 or to imprisonment for a term not exceeding seven years or to both.[357] SGX RegCo shall annually report to the MAS about its regulatory activities and may refer serious cases to the MAS. For instance, a certain company has admitted the contravention of Section 203(2) of the Securities and Futures Act by failing disclosure as required by the Listing Rules. The Company selectively disclosed information about future expected sales and earnings growth rate over the next 3 to 5 years. It was settled to pay the MAS SG$75,000 as a civil penalty with respect to the breach. The CEO has volunteered to personally bear the civil penalty on behalf of the Company. (505)

4343. Hong Kong

Overview

In most countries, disclosure review on periodic reports is performed by regulators but for Hong Kong. Below history may explain why HKEX undertakes the disclosure review program. The Securities and Futures Commission (SFC) was set up in 1989. Until 1991, both the SFC and the Stock Exchange of Hong Kong Limited (SEHK) were responsible for the securities listing. To avoid duplication, the SFC transferred its listing functions to the SEHK, which was contained in the "Memorandum of Understanding Governing Listing Matters" signed in 1991.(506) In 2000, the SEHK, Hong Kong Futures Exchanges Limited (HKFE), Hong Kong Securities Clearing Company Limited (HKSCC) were merged under a single holding company (HKEX) which listed itself on SEHK, and the MOU was amended. In 2003, SFC and SEHK signed the "Memorandum of Understanding Governing Listing Matters," which set out that *"SEHK has the legal functions under the Companies Ordinance, transferred from the SFC by statutory order ..."* and that *"SEHK ... shall; ensure ... the due and proper observance by listed companies, their directors as well as controlling shareholders ... of the provisions of the Listing Rules and of any obligations imposed ...; and maintain a suitable financial statement review program with a view to encourage high standards of financial disclosure and to detect instances of improper disclosure..."*[358]

Disclosure review

In discharging its responsibilities, SEHK maintains a disclosure review program to encourage high standards of disclosure by detecting instances of improper disclosure. The Listing Department of SEHK reviews and monitors issuer's reports by undertaking two types of review programs: 1) review on an annual report (AR), 2) financial statement review program (FSRP). Each review program has a different focus.[359]

Annual report review

SEHK has established an annual review program to review the issuer's annual report (AR). It provides detailed feedback, including findings and recommendations, in order to promote high-quality disclosure of the annual report. The AR review program focuses on rule compliance and disclosure of material events and developments. SEHK considers the disclosure in the annual report and various types of issuer's communications to monitor the consistency and materiality of the disclosure. The AR review program provides meaningful guidance to issuers and increases the issuer's awareness of the possible pitfalls in preparing periodic reports in relation to compliance with rules and regulations. In addition to these roles, SEHK may consider appropriate disciplinary action or referrals to other relevant regulatory agencies where staffs find any particular non-compliance with rules and regulations. SEHK considered the key findings in the last review, the market trends, and the major developments of issuers. Staffs consider whether issuers adopted the guidance issued from time to time. Where appropriate, SEHK may request issuers to make further disclosures by way of announcements or in subsequent reports.[360]

Financial statement review program

SEHK adopted a risk-based approach in selecting issuers for the financial statement review. In 2017, SEHK used four types of selection criteria: impact, probability, random, industry. Cases where an instance of major non-compliance by an issuer might adversely affect the reputation of the market as a whole are selected by meeting the criteria of "impact." Cases where there is a possible higher risk of misstatement or misapplication of accounting standards due to the existence of certain features (e.g., significant changes, newly listed) are selected by meeting the criteria of "probability." In 2017, SEHK reviewed 100 reports released by issuers, raised 540 enquires, and identified possible non-compliances with accounting and auditing standards in 6 cases and had referred to the relevant institutions. SEHK publishes the "Financial Statement Review Programme Report" every year, summarizing key findings from the review. The report describes both findings and recommendations.[361]

4344. Australia

ASIC: enforcement framework

ASIC is continuously pursuing the real-time oversight of corporate finance to focus on assessing the structure and disclosure of regulated transactions and reviewing ASX announcements.[362] ASIC pursues a variety of enforcement remedies considering the seriousness and consequences of the misconduct. It can take enforcement action designed for punishment, protection, preservation, correction (i.e., disclosures). ASIC classifies a variety of enforcement into punitive action, protective action, and corrective action. Punitive action seeks a remedy that punishes a violator from minor offenses (e.g. disclosure failure) to serious offenses (e.g., damage to market integrity). Examples of punitive actions includes imprisonment and financial penalties. Protective action, also known as 'administrative' actions, seeks a remedy that is designed to protect investors, rather than to punish violators. Examples of protective action includes disqualification from a management position, revocation, suspension, conditions, and public warning notices. For an administrative action, it is not necessary to go to court. Corrective action seeks a court order for corrective disclosure, which include corrective action for misleading or deceptive disclosure. ASIC may use negotiated resolution where it can achieve an effective outcome such as an improved, better, or quicker compliance program. In addition, "infringement notice" is an administrative action that can be issued by ASIC. For contraventions of the continuous disclosure obligations of the Corporations Act, the infringement notice can impose higher financial penalties. If an infringement notice is complied with, no further action can be taken. If it is not complied with, ASIC can bring a civil penalty action.(507)

ASIC: enforcement outcomes

ASIC publishes the "ASIC enforcement outcomes" semi-annually, including enforcement statistics and some distinctive case studies in each enforcement area. For instance, in 2017, the Federal Court of Australia declared that a company had failed to comply with its continuous disclosure obligations and ordered to pay a penalty of $650,000. The company admitted that it had not complied with its continuous disclosure obligations by failing to notify ASX that it was unlikely to achieve the forecast, as already stated in ASX announcements.[363] Directors of another company were disqualified for three years for breaching their duties regarding the continuous disclosure obligations. The Federal Court ordered each of the directors to pay the penalty. The share price was $0.02 before the announcement but hit a high of $0.052 cents between the announcement and a trading halt.[364]

ASX

"Guidance Note 8 Continuous Disclosing: Listing Rules 3.1~3.1B" explains which measures ASX can take for the non-compliant.[365] In case a complaint or allegation arguing that an entity has failed is raised by a third party, ASX usually inquires the entity. It there is a concern about disclosure, ASX typically issues an "aware letter" of which purpose is to enable entities to be in compliance with continuous disclosure obligations. The entity must respond to the letter according to the Listing rule 18.7. ASX reviews the response that will usually be published on the "ASX Market Announcement Platform" for investor's awareness. If an entity is suspected of committing a significant contravention of the Listing Rules or the Corporations Act, ASX notifies ASIC with details. ASX explains that *"Given the critical importance of timely disclosure ..., ASX will regards any contravention of Listing Rule 3.1 ... as a "significant" contravention ... and refer the matter to ASIC."*[366] If ASX considers that an entity is withholding information from the market, it may suspend trading.[367] In extreme case, it may remove the entity from the Official List. Official list is defined as a list of entities that ASX or ASIC has admitted and not removed. In addition, directors who repeatedly offend the disclosure requirement of listing rule are not likely to satisfy ASX Official Listing requirement under Listing Rule 1.1 Condition 20 which requires "good fame and character."[368]

5. DEMAND-SIDE APPROACHES

51. Overview

52. Information user

53. Bounded rationality

54. Information overload

55. Complexity

56. Literacy & education

51. Overview

511. Overlooking The Demand-Side

The supply-side approach focuses on the production, presentation, and dissemination of information, while the demand-side approach focuses on the interpretation and understanding. The demand-side approach has been overlooked for many reasons in the early days of the capital market.

First, the finance theory assumed rational investors who make the proper decisions based on the disclosed information, which guided regulators and researchers to mainly focus on the supply-side.

Second, investors, as a free-rider, tend to request more disclosure, which would keep themselves in stay with supply-side issues. Third, regulators also have paid less attention to demand-side issues since they have few options to handle such issues. It is not easy to study information user's responses since it is a psychological phenomenon that would include a great variety of individual strategies. Besides, no one would deny the idea that the demand-side approach is meaningless where there is lack of high-quality information.

512. Limits Of Supply-Side Approach

However, the limits of supply-side approach have emerged to be significant with the rapid growth of the capital markets.

Limits of the EMH

The efficient market hypothesis (EMH) emerged as a primary theoretical basis of the supply-side approach. Upon such a sound theoretical footing, regulators were persistently concerned with the supply-side issues and adopted strict disclosure regulation. In theory, investors are assumed to be rational and have perfect knowledge.

In reality, however, the informational environments surrounding investors are often imperfect, which hinders optimization but leads to the inaccurate valuation. The theory of "bounded rationality" adopts some limits to perfect rationality, which can be listed as below: a) uncertainty about the consequences of alternatives, b) incomplete information about alternatives, c) complexity in interpretation or computation.(508)

a. Uncertainty: Under the perfect rationality, the constraints of the demand and cost functions are assumed to be certain, and thus it is relatively easy to find the optimum. Under the bounded rationality, however, it is very difficult to find the optimum because the constraints are random variables.

b. Incompleteness: Under the bounded rationality, investors are assumed to have only incomplete information.

c. Complexity: Under the bounded rationality, the constraints are complex, which prevents investors from reaching the optimization. They inevitably economize in decision making by adopting heuristics and bear the cost of efforts to improve the approximation to optimization.

Bounded rationality

The demand-side approach provides both points of critical views. First, the EMH assumes that information users properly interpret the disclosed information. However, humans are cognitively limited, and there is the possibility of misinterpretation due to the investor's limited rationality. Second, the EMH assumes all the information is reflected in the stock price. In reality, however, investors do not consider all the information instead tend to ignore some types of information based on personal experiences. So far as investors ignore material information, the stock price does not reflect the true firm value, and thus the capital market is inefficient.(509)

Information overload

The supply-side approach is imperfect because it neglects how investors use the disclosed information. If investors are experiencing information overload, then a scale back policy to reduce disclosure requirements can enhance informational efficiency. The rigorous supply-side approach might be assessed as doing something but create severe side effects only for a scant supply of social welfare.

513. Conditions For Effective Disclosure

In light of conventional thoughts, more information would appear to result in more benefits to the capital market. Therefore, the basic question has been how to provide more information to markets. The disclosure-based regulatory regime that intends to be valid and effective requires two dimensions: a) information has to be disclosed; b) the users need to use the disclosed information effectively. The securities laws primarily focus on the first issue to mandate disclosure, while the second issue on how investors use the information is less known. If the users do not process information effectively, disclosure policy to mandate more information is of no use.(510)

As a result, we need to have a better understanding of the demand-side of disclosure to establish a more efficient capital market. The supply-side approach includes the production, format, and distribution of information. The demand-side approach includes investors' interpretation and decision making. Sometimes imperfect information might be caused from ignorance or uncertainty.

What investors need could not be the information itself but the effective investment decision to maximize their profit with reduced risk. Disclosure regulation should be a mechanism to support an effective investment decision. The information has power only when applied effectively and used properly. Even with the sufficient information, disclosure regulation would degenerate due to the lack of understanding.

Such an idea that full disclosure is enough to achieve the efficient market is reflected in the securities laws. However, it is "not enough" to lead investors to have access to more information in a timely manner because investors also need to understand the disclosed information fully and use it effectively. Macey (2003) argued that demand-side problems were the primary cause of the Enron scandal, and therefore we need to adopt a two-pronged approach (i.e., supply-side and demand-side) to achieve the efficient market.(511)

514. Initiatives Of Demand-Side Approach

Early stage

The demand-side approach, including the understandability of information users, has not been unmentioned. In the early stage of disclosure regulation, demand-side considerations have been commented sporadically in the practitioner's level. In 1934, right after the adoption of the Securities Act that was designed to supply relevant material information to investors, the chairman of SEC, William O. Douglas, already raised demand-side concerns over the investors' understandability of disclosure, by mentioning that *"...The Act presupposes that the glaring light of publicity will give the investors needed protection. But those needing investment guidance will receive small comfort from the balance sheets, contracts, or compilation of other data revealed in the registration statement. They either lack the training or intelligence to assimilate them and find them useful,..."*(512) From the early stage, they already noticed what investors need is not only information but also education and more guidance.

1970's Consumer protection movement

In 1975, the Citibank of New York voluntarily implemented a plain English policy as a persuasive communication tool for effective communication with consumers to capture more customers. Customer's response was very positive, and other banks followed.(513)

1980's Integrated disclosure system

In 1969, the Wheat Report mandated a prospectus, but it was argued to be too lengthy, complex, and burdening firms. In 1982, the integrated disclosure system was adopted. However, it was not aimed to reduce the investor's information load but to reduce the firm's disclosure cost.[369]

1990' Plain English disclosure

In 1993, the SEC tried a pilot program to implement a plain English project. It gave an incentive for expedited review when firms voluntarily adopt the pilot program. Some big firms answered that the cost of implementing plain English was not burdensome.(514) With the success of the pilot, the SEC enacted the "New Plain English Disclosure Rule (SEC proposed Rule 421(d))" in 1998.

52. Information User

521. Significance

In these days, the influence of information user is getting stronger, and, as a result, information users are more influencing firms, stock prices, and market efficiency. Recently, a variety of information intermediaries are emerging. They help information end-users to easily assimilate the disclosed information. The successful activities of intermediaries are the essential prerequisites of informational efficiency.

When a stricter disclosure regulation is going to be adopted, firms will respond with negative feedback, while information users will unanimously welcome because they are free-riders. When the regulator is going to remove a specific disclosure requirement, information users may respond with negative feedback for fear of losing free information even though they are not using the information. They might not have known the fact that the information has been mandated to disclose.

On the contrary, the capital market consists of a variety types of information users, and, as a result, investors' responses will not be concentrated but scattered. Not only the determinants of investors' investment decisions but also individual investor's ability to process information varies widely among investors, depending largely on their experience, investment approaches, and strategies. Furthermore, they also require different types of information.(515) An experienced expert who can make a conjecture without difficulty may not raise any issues for firm's non-disclosure, while lay investors pose serious issues. On the contrary, lay investors may not pay attention to the valuation-relevant information due to the lack of valuation knowledge, while experts request more information.

522. Classification Of Information Users

1) Various Classifications

Information user of the disclosed information ranges from internal stakeholders to external stakeholders. Disclosure is mainly aimed to address shareholders but can also be used by a plurality of stakeholders, such as employees, creditors, and competitors. Demands for specific information differ from users to users, and they respond differently to the disclosed information, which makes the disclosure decision more complicated. Notably, information user groups have different levels of understanding and bounded rationality.

Priority

It is an inevitable choice to prioritize information users because the disclosed information cannot satisfy all user's needs. In general, information users are classified into primary users and secondary users. The IASB identifies a group of "primary users" constituted by present and potential investors, creditors. The secondary users include customer, employee, partner, credit rating agency, and government. The primary purpose of disclosure is the provision of material information to investors, and thus, disclosure regulation should also consider the priority of information users. For example, it will be persuasive for regulators to increase the informativeness of primary users at the sacrifice of secondary users.[370]

Protection needs

Stakeholders, such as shareholders and creditors, have essential stakes in the firm and deserve to be firmly protected. Secondary users, such as analysts and media, do not have direct stakes in the firm, and thus regulators or firms that are solely interested in the stakeholder protection are not obliged to provide information to the secondary users. On the condition that analysts and media represent the interests of investors, paying special attention to such information users might be helpful to protect investors.

Professionality

Nonprofessional information users may not directly rely on the disclosed information but probably obtain the assimilated information through other nonofficial channels, such as analysts and media. These information intermediaries, an alternative source of information, work as a channel of information distribution.

2) **Venue/Context-based classification**

One may classify information users into internal users and external users. It is straightforward and involves a great significance regarding the issues of information asymmetry and insider trading. External users can be classified by two groups: capital market users and non-capital market users.

Internal user

A firm's manager is an information provider but sometimes becomes an information user for managerial decisions. Such a two-fold role of manager is related to the unique two-fold value that is provided by information: predictive value and feedback value. Besides, if manager's compensation is directly linked with the firm's performance, then they pay more attention to earnings and growth rates.(516) Employees are interested in evaluating the profitability and growth of their employers. They are interested in the information that is useful in assessing firm's ability to pay salaries and pensions. Labor union also requires financial information for salaries negotiation.

External user

a. Capital market users

External users are classified by two groups: capital market users and non-capital market users. Capital market users include shareholders, potential investors, creditors, financial analysts, brokers, exchanges, regulators, and financial media. Lay investors tend to rely on media, analysts prefer direct contact with firms. Sell-side analysts publish research reports on a firm in order to increase trading activities, and they are considered useful information intermediaries even though the probability of the conflicts of interest exists. Financial media aggregates and communicates information with a considerable degree of credibility.(517) The role of information intermediaries should not be considered as subordinate but essential in assimilating, aggregating, and widely distributing the disclosed information.

b. Non-capital market users

Non-capital market users include customers, tax bureau, and product market competitor. Creditors and debt instrument holders also provide capital to a firm. They are much interested in such information as future cash flows to find out the firms' ability to pay interests and principals. Business-related stakeholders, such as competitors, customers, and vendors, are interested in firms' information to judge the competitive advantage. A firm's managers sometimes become the external users of information that is produced by competitors. They might want to learn other firms' competitive advantage and follow the disclosure patterns of competitors. Other stakeholders, such as tax authorities and non-governmental organizations, can be users of the disclosed information. Such a widespread information demand might cause severe pressures on the disclosing firms and result in the deviation or misalignment from the capital market needs. The widespread demand and increasing number of external users imply that capital market regulators should be careful in establishing the priority of disclosure regulation.

523. Investor Categorization Policy

Purpose

In most countries, regulators adopt the investor categorization policy as an effort to protect investors. By limiting some types of investors who need regulatory protection, the categorization policy protects the bounded investors from any harms that might occur from the lack of understanding of a transaction. Even though the investor categorization policy does not explicitly aim to protect investors regarding the bounded rationality, we may interpret that the concept of bounded rationality is, at least, implicitly embedded in such policies. Meanwhile, investors who think they are overprotected may raise a complaint that they are not protected but regulated or restricted by the investor protection policy.

Sophistication requirement

The categorization policy pursues two types of protections; firm's disclosure and broker's certification. An offer of securities does not need disclosure if the offer is made to investors who are categorized as highly sophisticated. As a result, some investors who can assume the relevant risks are eligible to buy the pre-IPO issues that are exempted disclosure requirements (i.e., prospectus).

Categorization criteria

Many countries use various types of qualitative and quantitative tests to classify investors, such as an accredited investor, sophisticated investor, retail client, professional client, and elective professional client. Detailed criteria vary from country to country. To a certain degree, some of these criteria might be interpreted as a proxy of the investor's level of recognition, education, or rationality. As a result, the idea of protecting bounded investors is implicitly embedded in the investor categorization policy.

a. Qualitative test: expertise, knowledge, relation with issuer, experience in the relevant financial sector, and advised by experts.

b. Quantitative test: asset (e.g., total, net, or financial asset), annual income, history of significant transaction in size and amount, and investment portfolio.

United states

The concept of an "accredited investor" is defined in Rule 501 of Regulation D. As used in Rule 501(a) of Regulation D (17 CFR 230.501), accredited investor shall mean any person who comes within any of the stipulated categories, or who the issuer reasonably believes comes within any of the stipulated categories.[371] The 1933 Act provides firms with registration exemptions such as Rule 505 and 506 of Regulation D that allow firms to sell securities to "accredited investors" without registration. In short, accredited investors are eligible to buy the pre-IPO issues that are non-prospectus firms

53. Bounded Rationality

531. Concept

Background

One may assume that information users have a reasonable knowledge of a firm's business and the ability to interpret and analyze disclosure. Many theories assume perfect rationality, but imperfect rationality is prevalent in the real world. All humans are intendedly rational but inevitably limited. Thus, not only the properties of information, natures of disclosing firm, and attitudes of manager but also the characters of information users also matter in the effectiveness of investment decisions.

Simon (1957) seems to be the first to use the term "bounded rationality."(518) This notion has gained popularity in social science researches and sparked various analogous terms such as limited intelligence and limited rationality. These concepts are aimed to point out the vulnerable point of classical theory. Simon (1972, p.162) defines the bounded rationality as *"constraints on the information-processing capacities of the actor."*(508) Even though researches on the bounded rationality are becoming of great importance, there is still no comprehensive theory.

Theory

The assumption of perfect rationality is pervasive in economic theory. In the classical theory, the "objective" of economic behavior is an optimization (i.e., profit maximization) under the "constraints" of demand and cost functions. Information users are assumed to have perfect knowledge about the constraints. On the contrary, Simon (1972) suggested the theory of bounded rationality that information users are neither sufficiently rational because of the limited capabilities nor have perfect knowledge. The theory is constructed by adjusting the given objectives (i.e., satisficing) or by introducing some limits to the perfect rationality about the constraints.(508) Under the bounded rationality, investors will experience a U-shaped quality curve of information.(519-522)

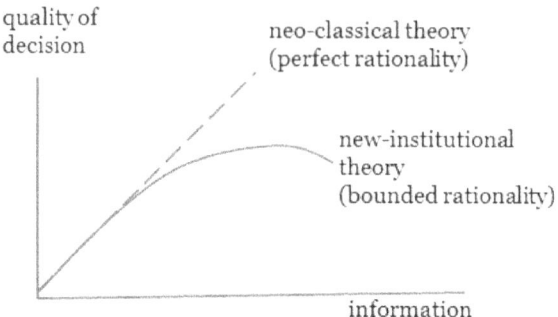
Figure 57 Bounded rationality

Counteracting measures: satisficing

In nature, information users seldom consider many alternatives. Some postulate different objectives from what is assumed in classical theories by replacing the optimization criteria with the satisfaction criteria. Most economic agents cannot concisely consider all possible alternatives.

Instead, they examine only simplified, filtered, or selected alternatives and make a decision as soon as their goal reaches the satisfactory level that was adjusted to meet reality. Under situations where complexity and uncertainty make it impossible to achieve the perfect rationality, such a satisficing strategy should be considered as a detour but a smart and practical approach. It does not mean abandoning the original objectives. For example, information users are satisfied with the disclosed information and make an investment decision when they are provided information over a "satisfactory level."

Most of the variant theories constructed by modifying the assumptions of constraints also call for the modification on the classical goals. Decision-makers who are facing cognitive limits are still goal-oriented but are satisfied with satisfactory level unavoidably or sometimes intentionally.(508, 510, 523) Under the bounded rationality, investors will experience the quality of decision making that is U-shaped curve.(519-522)

Not the theoretically attainable level of welfare, but the practicable level does make information users happy. The theory of bounded rationality explains the real-world decision very well. However, several reasons lead to the lack of objectivity: the level of satisfaction depends on individual users; unanimously agreed criteria of satisfaction level do not exist.

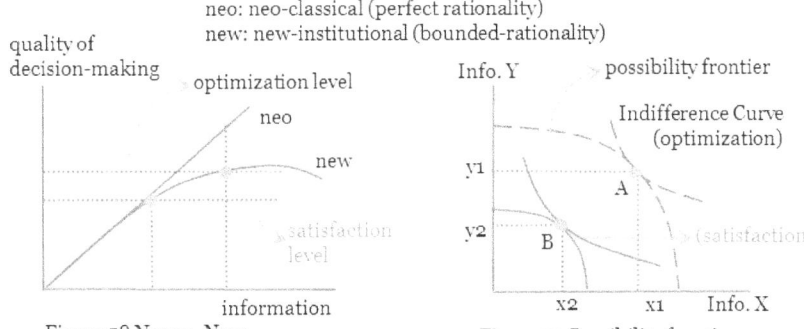

Figure 58 Neo vs. New   Figure 59 Possibility frontier

Due to the limited cognitive ability, investors tend to assimilate only some of the available information at the level of point B in Figure 59, even though full information is provided at point A. They are not optimized but satisfied for they achieved the level of satisfaction.

Issues of reduction in disclosure requirements

Be it so, is there serious inefficiency due to the bounded rationality? Let us say that regulators are mandating firms to provide information up to the optimization level (Figure 59, point A), but investors are satisfied at the level of point B. Then, do regulators have to reduce current disclosure requirement? The answer is not merely one-sided. It is quite sure that investors cannot assimilate all the available information, but no one would deny the idea that investor's preferences for specific information differ from investors to investors. Thus, the whole combination set of each information that is preferred by individual investors might be useful in analysis. As a result, regulators should not take advice of a specific information user group to reduce disclosure requirements merely based on the rationale of satisfaction.

Selective information seeking behavior

A human's cognitive ability is a limited resource that needs to be efficiently allocated for a better decision. People simplify complex tasks by eliminating or reducing the procedures of searching and processing information. As a result, information users sometimes seek direct communication with the source or filter information on a selective basis. Information users are likely to react strongly to a specific information type that they prefer.

Then, what determines information users' selective information-seeking behavior? Information-seeking behavior depends on the value of information that depends on the importance of information and the degree of information users' personal interests. The "Cognitive Consistency Theory" argues that information users tend to selectively accept information that is consistent with their current attitudes while rejecting inconsistent ones. People seek to perceive the information in a way that are simple. For example, newspaper readers who are interested in a specific issue might not pay attention to the whole contents but only to the title, when the article is too lengthy, complicated, or unrelated to the specific issue. Those affecting selective information-seeking behavior include the personal preference, degree of interest, level of difficulty, and cognitive attitudes. Besides, some demographical variables, such as age, sex, education, investment experience, also affect such selective behaviors.

532. Investors: Irrational Responses

Behavioral theory studies investor's decision-making and argues that the EMH is incomplete since investors often act irrationally due to cognitive biases. Many pieces of behavioral research in financial decision-making highlight the importance of designing investor education and financial literacy policy. IOSCO (2014, Appendix 2) illustrates behavioral responses in financial decision-making.(524) Evidence that support behavioral responses or rationale against the perfect rationality is too voluminous to illustrate.(523) Below is just a glimpse of them.

a. Over-reliance on third parties: Investors may have relied too heavily on a third party's opinion (e.g., underwriter, credit rating agency) in making an investment decision. For example, investors over-rely on the underwriter, but they do not scrutinize the prospectus to analyze risks.(525)

b. Incomplete information search: In general, humans do not consider all aspects of an investment decisions. Information users examine only relevant factors to make it manageable. If it is seemingly irrelevant to the factors of investment decisions, then they do not undertake information search thoroughly rather ignore some of available and material information. (523)

c. Framing: Due to the illusion and framing effect, even the identical alternatives that are presented in a different way often changes the decision. The "Prospect Theory" of Kahneman & Tversky (1983) provides a persuasive rationale that can explain the real-world investors' behaviors.(523, 526)

d. Over-confidence: A rational investor trades only when the expected gain exceeds the transactions costs. According to the experiment, however, an overconfident investor overestimates the precision of the information gathered and the expected gains of trading.(527)

533. Firms: Strategic Disclosure Decision

Lower disclosure by lower non-disclosure risk
Managers may make strategic decisions considering the degree of infor-

mation users' bounded rationality. Some studies suggest the hypothesis of limited attention, inattention, or investor's credulity. In the classic theory of voluntary disclosure, information users exhibit extreme skepticism about firms that do not disclose.

In reality, however, information users sometimes fail to update their opinion based upon the firm's disclosure or non-disclosure. They sometimes fail to update because a correct inference of a firm's non-disclosure requires much attention. Thus, due to the limitedness of attention and cognition, they are skeptical insufficiently.

Firms will determine whether to disclose or not based on the shapes of disclosure cost curve: indirect cost and non-disclosure cost. Non-disclosure cost is determined by the degree of investor's skepticism. Indirect cost is determined by the attitudes and responses of investors to the disclosed information (e.g., reputation, litigation).

Limited attention sometimes causes information users to fail in questioning the possibility of deliberate withholding. Such credulities of information users can lead to incomplete information by weakening the market pressure on firms to disclose. Firms already understand the fact that information users sometimes ignore the implications of non-disclosure. As a result, there can be non-disclosure even though disclosure cost is negligible. (528, 529)

Graphical explanation

Below is the graphical explanation of investor's bounded rationality.

Under the non-disclosure of both firm A and B, investors will voluntarily search and gather information at the optimal equilibrium E_1 (Figure 60). Under the voluntary disclosure of firm A, welfare-maximizing investors may move to E_2. At E_2, investors assimilate all the disclosure of firm A and make full efforts to search information for firm B. If firm B also subsequently provides voluntary information, rational investors might optimize at E4 (Figure 61).

However, if the investors who made voluntary information search for firm B could not noticed the voluntary disclosure of firm B due to the limited attention, then they cannot properly process the disclosed information of firm B. As a result, investors with limited attention to the disclosure of B will remain at E_2 that is far lower than E_4. If investors have selective information seeking behavior due to the cognitive limits, ignoring the material disclosure of firm B but seeking irrelevant or less-material information of firm A, then they may stay at E_3 of which welfare is lower than E_4. The investors could have benefitted the welfare of E_4 if he had been cautiously attentive to the disclosure of firm B.

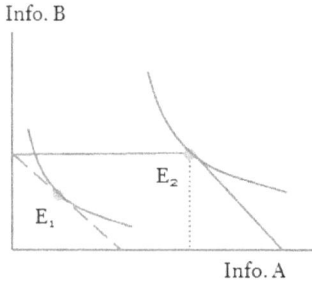
Figure 60 Voluntary disclosure (A)

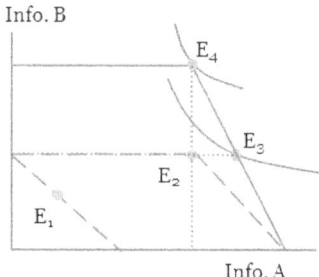
Figure 61 Voluntary disclosure (A+B)

Upon recognizing the investor's limited attention, firm B may interpret the investor's lack of interest as a signal that the disclosure cost, especially the litigation cost of non-disclosure, is negligible (Figure 62). The disclosure cost that is perceived by firm B decreases from 1 to 2 (Figure 63). As a result, manager may change the internal disclosure policy to scale back to the original level (Figure 63, $d_1 \rightarrow d_2$), which leads to firm's maximization of net disclosure benefit. If investors were skeptical, then firm B would have kept the original disclosure level at d_1.

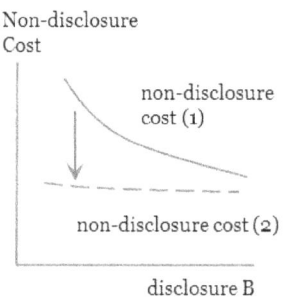
Figure 62 Non-disclosure cost

Figure 63 Disclosure cost

Some hypotheses explain the firm's increased benefits of non-disclosure decision.

a. Premium from silence: If the market is imperfect due to limited attention, the unraveling procedure will not maintain until the end. A lemon should remain silent (i.e., non-disclosure) and be treated as if it were a peach. Lemon's disclosure removes all premiums that could have been obtained from silence. So long as investors do not entirely doubt the quality of the non-disclosing firm, a lemon that is withholding bad news can benefit over-valuation.

b. False modesty: Unraveling model suggests that firms above the average criteria will choose to disclose any good news for a higher valuation. However, Harbaugh & To (2005) suggested that the unraveling model may not hold. The lemon with good news has the most incentive to disclose it, so firms that are disclosing good news may be treated as lemon. If a firm is already recognized as a high-type peach, the false modesty can be a state of equilibrium to withhold even good news that is easily attainable by mediocre firms. As a result, mandated disclosure mechanism can work as a way to reduce the "false modesty" behavior. (530)

Greater disclosure by lower trigger risk

In contrast, inattention or limited attention does not generate monotonous effects but may lead to firm's greater disclosure. Information users with limited attention can be insufficiently skeptical in scrutinizing the information that was already disclosed, generating relatively lower indirect cost than rational investors.

For example, due to investor's limited attention, firm B learns that the perceived indirect cost of disclosure (e.g., trigger risk) is lower than they have expected. As a result, disclosure cost moves from 1 to 3 due to the sharp decrease of the indirect cost (Figure 65). To maximize the net disclosure benefit, firm B provides greater disclosure ($d_1 \rightarrow d_3$). If investor who had been limited in attention but recently became very attentive due to the additional disclosure of firm B may reach the optimal level of welfare at E_5 that is higher than E_4 due to the more voluntary disclosure of firm B. However, inattentive investors still stay at E_3 (Figure 64). The poverty in abundance.

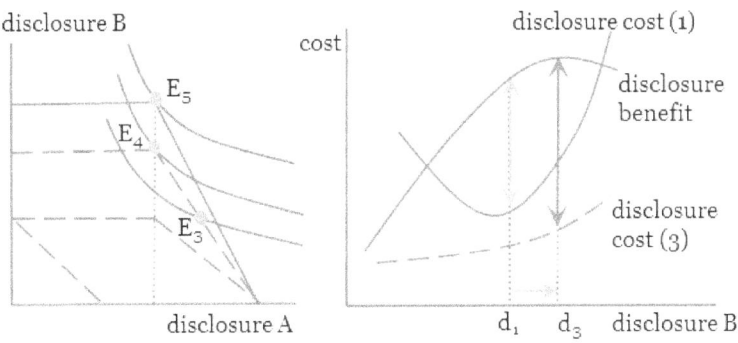

Figure 64 Inattentive investor   Figure 65 Disclosure cost

54. Information Overload

541. Overview

Background

Louis D. Brandeis (1914, p.92) emphasized the importance of disclosure; *"Publicity is justly commended as a remedy for social and industrial diseases. Sunlight is said to be the best of disinfectants; electric light the most efficient policeman."*(531) On the contrary, Paredes (2003) pointed out a drawback of heavy disclosure; *"... in addition to being a disinfectant, sunlight can also be blinding."*(510) Generally, more information is better. However, information can only empower investors if they can effectively understand it. An increase in the quantity of information has two different consequences: more information enables a higher quality; more information gives rise to a cognitive cost. More access to information with less ability often results in an inferior decision. Thus, the purpose of regulator and firm should be the provide more transparency, not just more information.

Information overload

The term "information overload" was grounded in cognitive psychology, but now it has evolved into numerous academic areas, including disclosure studies. The term is mentioned by Bertram Gross in 1964 and popularized by Alvin Toffler.(532, 533) According to Gross (1964), *"Information overload occurs when the amount of input to a system exceeds its processing capacity. Decision makers have fairly limited cognitive processing capacity. Consequently, when information overload occurs, it is likely that a reduction in decision quality will occur."*(533) Information overload refers to the difficulty in understanding information contents and making proper decisions caused by too much information.[372]

Investors will make worse decisions if they pay scant attention to the disclosed information. How information users process the information and make a decision is very important. After the information users figure out where to get what they need, they inevitably face the question of how to use it since the proper interpretation of information is key to investment decision making. More disclosure does not always mean effective disclosure. Overloaded disclosure could mean less effective disclosure. Besides, information overload occurs regardless of the nature of the information, and information producers also suffer a plurality of troubles: information overload, information search cost, disclosure cost, increasing noise, and even decreasing benefits of signaling.

Decision effectiveness; inverted-U shape

As investors are given more information, decision effectiveness initially increases. Nevertheless, once the quantity of information reaches a certain level, investors become overloaded with information, and decision effectiveness gradually decreases. Keller & Staelin (1987) empirically showed the functional relationship between information quantity and decision effectiveness to be an inverted U-shaped curve. Decision effectiveness first increases and then decreases as the percentage of information consumption. When people use most of the information available but not all, they appear to make more effective decisions.(509) Chewning & Harrell (1990) provided experimental findings that auditors and students exhibited an inverted-U relationship between information usage and information load.(519) Not only more disclosure but also higher-quality disclosure can cause information users to experience information overload. Altogether, an increase in quality can entice information users to use more of the available information.(70, 509)[373]

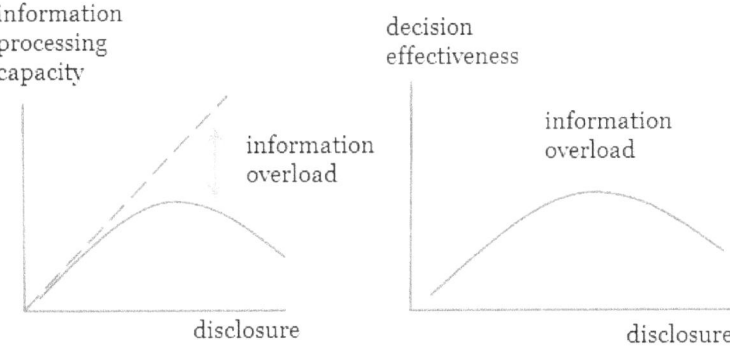

Figure 66 Processing capacity   Figure 67 Decision effectiveness

Disclosure overload

Johnson (1992) used the word of "disclosure overload" when describing that *"The sheer volume of those disclosures has led to concerns about disclosure overload and whether the more important disclosure information is being obscured by the marge amount of other information that is required."*(534)

Radin (2007) presented personal viewpoints and experiences regarding disclosure overload of financial statement and footnotes; *"Much of what is written is so long and so opaque that its usefulness is questionable. ... But as an investor looking at the number of pages that are boilerplate, redundant, immaterial, irrelevant, or overly fact-packed, I immediately suffer from MEGO - my eyes glaze over."*(535)

542. Causes Of Information Overload

Information overload occurs when the inflowing information exceeds the limits of processing capacity caused by limited cognitive ability. Consequently, information overload results in a reduction of decision effectiveness. Bounded rationality, such as processing limitations, is commonly thought to give rise to information overload. What information users face may not be a lack of information but rather an information overload. Not only information but also the information users' capability of attention can be the scare resource. A number of factors contribute to information overload.(510)

a. Provider (presentation): Investors tend to assimilate information more extensively if it is costless and easy to understand. Thus, how information is presented to users can affect the level of information overload, and a policy to simply provide more information is not enough to increase decision effectiveness. If managers present information in a way that is difficult for investors to digest, investors should suffer severe information overload.

b. Provider (number of stocks): An increasing number of listed firms can be directly related to an information user's behavior. The number of investment options offered in the capital market can be another source of information overload.

c. Provider (similarity): As the number of listed firms grows, firms in the same industry could be perceived to be more alike. As the similarity in the firm's business increases, so information overload would increase.

d. Information user (financial knowledge): Novice, who is less educated with financial knowledge, can be overwhelmed by an avalanche of information.

e. Information (increase): Due to the increasing demands, the amount of disclosure has been on the rise. Besides, financial media is driven to a tough competition that leads to more information. Especially, users can be overloaded even by a small amount of information that is in contradiction with other information.

543. Backgrounds Of Information Increase

A sharp increase in investment information that is the main derive of information overload is common within most markets over the world. The intrinsic nature of information users, producers, and regulators can explain why information has increased in the capital markets.

1) **Information user**

Free-rider

Information users, free-riders, will ask for more information since they bear no costs. Even though they well acknowledge their cognitive limits and the possibility of information overload, they do not hesitate to ask additional information.

Non-use value

The information generates a value when it is used; a use-value. While such a use-value comes from the direct use of information, a non-use value refers to the value that is assessed by information users even though they do not use it at that moment. Information users assign the non-use value when they think the information could be necessary for the future use. Information frequently provides users with a sense of psychological stability or comfort, even though the likelihood of using the information is very low. Information users who place a high value on the information that has non-use value can exert pressure on regulators not to reduce disclosure requirements. (510)

Real-time needs

The stock market collapse that is caused by financial scandals can increase an investor's demand for real-time information. Thus, regulators are more likely to advocate more strict and real-time based regulation to ensure timely, accurate, and continuous disclosure, which may result in information overload.

Financial media

Paredes (2003) argued that financial media plays a vital role with significant influence. The media works as a multiplier, accelerator, extender, and intensive analyzer of disclosed information.(510)

2) **Information producer**

Market punishment & litigation

Information users demand more and better information these days. They are quick to punish firms that are less transparent by selling stocks, suggesting "sell" recommendation, and raising litigation for skeptical disclosure. Firms often disclose more information not to inform investors, but to reduce their potential litigation risks.

Information technology

Besides, information technology is rapidly growing. The advent of information technology is ascribed as a primary reason for information overload due to its ability to provide more information at a lower cost. The association between information technology and information overload aroused many decades ago. Slovic (1972, p.779) remarks that *"Modern technology has contributed its share to the information explosion by making vastly greater quantities of elegant data readily available to the analyst, broker, and investor."*(536) Evaristo, Adams, and Curley (1995) indicated the conflicting impact of information technology on information overload: increase vs. mitigate. Once it is designed to simplify complex information environments and improve investors' decision, information technology will mitigate information overload and bring about effective investment decision.(537)

Increase in large-sized media

Additional disclosure requirements can be burdening firms by increasing disclosure costs, especially when financial media is small with limited resources. These days, with the help of large-sized financial media, firms can disseminate information at a lower cost.

3) Regulator

Low cost & efficient policy

Upon the outbreak of financial scandals, information users demand various additional regulations, including more rigorous disclosure requirements. For decades, regulators have turned to information as a useful regulatory tool because it is politically acceptable, cost-effective, and quickly implementable, while it minimizes the possibility of interference with firm's decision making and sustains firms' competitiveness. Such merits contributed to making disclosure regulation a popular choice.(70)

Limits of alternative devices

It is very limited for regulators to formulate other regulatory devices such as corporate governance. However, the procedure for establishing disclosure requirement is relatively simple. As a result, the disclosure requirements have continued to increase.

Materiality issue

A specific feature of securities regulation, such as "materiality," can be a source of information overload. Litigation averse managers are likely to disclose more.(510)

Regulatory overload

Concerns of information overload have steadily risen right after the adoption of substantive disclosure regulation. However, disclosure requirements are persistently increasing over the decades and might cause the "regulatory overload," which might generate an unintended consequence of information overload. The survey results of KPMG & FERF (2011) indicated that *"the complexity of financial standards and the volume of mandated disclosures are the most significant contributors to the issue of disclosure overload and complexity, and footnotes are the most significant source or cause of complexity."*(538)

Enforcements & litigation law

Even though regulators maintain disclosure requirements to the same level as before, firms inevitably disclose more information due to the vigorous enforcement and potential legal risks. The level of penalty and the likelihood of legal liability increases because of enforcement and litigation laws.

544. Arguments Of Information Overload

5441. Overview

Some make counter-arguments against information overload: a) information overload does not constitute a severe problem; b) individual investors can utilize expert filter mechanisms; c) information overload is not a major source of trouble for noise traders; d) information users or regulators have an alternative mechanism to evade from information overload.(510)

On the contrary, the advocates of information overload provides evidences and rationale: a) regulators need to find out how to overcome information overload since information overload is everywhere and severe; b) the extent of the expert filter is limited; c) noise traders are tiny; d) there are limited opportunities for individual investors to try free-riding.(510)

5442. Arguments

1) Non-capital market context

In the non-capital market context, many researchers have argued that overloaded information can lead to poor decisions because humans are cognitively limited.(509) For example, the number "seven" was suggested as a limit on human capacities. People can process about seven chunks of information at a time, and additional finer rating does not add much to the usefulness.(539) According to the experimental results, consumers are satisfied with more information but make poorer purchase decisions.(540, 541) Consumers (i.e., home-buyer) who were asked to choose among houses experienced a decrease in the accuracy of decision when the number of attributes or alternatives increased.(542) With simplified information, consumers are dissatisfied but can identify the best brand more accurately. (543)

On the contrary, the non-existence of information overload was also evidenced. Varying the amount of nutritional information provided to consumers on the point-of-purchase signs were unrelated to the purchase behavior.(544) There was no decrease in the accuracy of choice associated with the increases of information provided.(542)

2) Capital market context

Information provider

There was a significant increase in the length of earnings press releases. (545, 546) The cautionary language was quite brief in 1996, but it had increased dramatically by 2003. When managers disclose risk factors, they also elaborates substantively with technical, legal, or accounting terms. (216)

Information user

Numerous studies have identified information overload extensively in the capital market context also.(510)[374]

Regulator

Examining the stance of a regulator about the existence and degree of information overload will be meaningful since a rigorous disclosure regulation is a major cause of information overload. The SEC has also recognized that disclosure would not adequately protect investors with better investment decisions when they face cognitive limits.

After the Securities Act was adopted, William O. Douglas (1934), who later became the chairman of the SEC, raised concern with the overload by commenting that disclosure regulation will provide a certain extent of comfort to the individual investors who lack the cognitive ability to assimilate the disclosed information, indicating that no disclosure regulation would perfectly protect investors.(373, 512) The Wheat Report of 1969 concluded that prospectuses were too complex for investors to understand. (547) In 1996, the SEC formed the Task Force on Disclosure Simplification to make recommendations for understandable, complete, and timely disclosure.(548) In 1998, the SEC adopted plain English reporting requirements to make disclosure more understandable.(549)

Courts

Examining the stance of law court would contribute to confirming that the information overload is not just a theoretical, perceptional, or hypothetical argument but a more practical or realistic phenomenon. Paredes (2003) explained that the Supreme Court also recognized the information overload issues.(510) In the case of "TSC Industries, Inc. v. Northway, Inc.," the Court of Appeals defined material facts as "*...all facts which a reasonable shareholder might consider important...*" However, the Supreme Court judged that "*...an omitted fact is material if there is a substantial likelihood that a reasonable shareholder would consider it important...*" but rejected the view that a fact is material if an investor "might" find it important (426 U.S. 438 (1976)). The Supreme Court also mentioned the possibility of information overload as below.

> "*...the disclosure policy ... is not without limit. ... disclosure may accomplish more harm than good. ... if the standard of materiality is unnecessarily low, ... management's fear of exposing itself to substantial liability may cause it simply to bury the shareholders in an avalanche of trivial information – a result that is hardly conducive to informed decision making... the "might" formulation is "too suggestive of mere possibility, however unlikely..."*

Managers who are seized with fear of the strict materiality standard might provide an avalanche of information causing overload. The law court was concerned with the possible information overload that might be caused by the low threshold of materiality. There are many materiality tests adopted by the Court such as substantial likelihood test, probability magnitude test, substantial certainty text, and total mix test. Whatever tests are adopted, the purpose of the Supreme Court is to maintain the balance between the two conflicting goals; maximization of transparency and minimization of information overload.

Empirical evidences

KPMG & FERF (2011) published the "Disclosure overload and complexity: hidden in plain sight." To the question about what factors might cause immaterial disclosure, "*a significant majority (61 percent) of respondents indicated that potential objection*" by various regulators may cause managers to provide immaterial disclosure. Between the descriptive (essay) form disclosure and the more tabular presentation format, "*Nearly half say greater tabular presentation format for quantitative information disclosures will have a positive impact on preparer's burden*." A majority of respondents answered that "*SEC guidance concerning permissible cross-referencing of redundant data could help*" reduce disclosure overload and complexity. About 70 percent of respondents answered that disclosure preparers "*have little or no discretion on ability to reduce disclosures*." Astonishingly, many respondents answered that they have "*not taken specific steps to reduce disclosure complexity in their financial statements.*"(538)

Drake, Hales, and Rees (2019) surveyed a professional group who use financial statements. Many professional users answered that disclosure overload is not a problem but more information should be disclosed. The majority of professional users answered dissatisfied with the current disclosure. However, 21 percent of respondents answered disclosure overload is a problem. About 53 percent of respondents read less than half of footnotes, and "*there is a large amount of footnote disclosures that are left unread*". Some professional users "*do not appear to suffer from disclosure overload,*" but "*engage in directed search strategies and only read footnotes that pertain to a particular task.*" Only some "*sophisticated respondents appear to have a greater capacity to benefit from footnote disclosure.*"(550)

5443. Expert filters

54431. Roles of expert filters

Less overloaded

Many studies show that seasoned experts can more effectively filter and analyze a vast amount of information than non-experts like individual investors. They are trained to adopt a well-organized decision strategy ignoring less relevant information, focusing on more material information. The degree of negative effects of information overload depends on the degree of expert filters.(510)

Regulators' view

Regulators do not reject the idea that investors may rely on expert filters. For example, Douglas (1934), who became the SEC chairman in 1937, had mentioned that the information overload might have occurred by the 1934 Act, and expert filters can advise the investors who have limited cognitive ability.

"… *even though an investor has neither the time, money, nor intelligence to* assimilate the mass of information … The judgment of those experts will be reflected in the market price. Through them investors who seek advice will be able to obtain it." (512)

Mitigating information overload

Investors are not entirely rational, and the average individual investor cannot pay meticulous attention to all the details of the disclosed information. Instead, the useless or immaterial information is "filtered" by the long-experienced and well-educated market experts such as analyst, broker, fund-managers, and financial media. Besides, the individual investors can make use of the experts' abilities. For example, most investors invest through indirect investment vehicles (e.g., mutual funds) managed by expert managers, and they can rely on financial advisors or read the research reports. Hence, the expert filter might put worries of information overload to sleep.(510)

54432. Limits of expert filter

There are some reasons why non-experts cannot escape from information overload. Experts are also overloaded, they fall into overconfidence bias, they may fall into the trap of conflicts of interest, and they have different favorite stock picks from individual investors. Hence, the expert filter is not enough, and individual investors cannot completely escape from information overload even though they utilize the expert filter mechanisms such as indirect investment vehicles.(510)

Overloaded expert

It is more realistic to assume that even market experts have no choice but to experience information overload. Empirical results suggest that even experts experience information overload in the same manner with individual investors. Sometimes experts can be more confused than individual investors. Experts, as a human, can in part filter useless information but cannot be free from cognitive bias. Information overload is not a matter of existence but a matter of degree. Regardless of the level of expertise, everybody has limited cognitive abilities. Market professionals are subject to all sorts of cognitive biases that affect investment decisions. As a result, the degree of information overload may be eased but not eliminated by the expertise. The expert filter may weaken the extent of information overload to a certain degree, but cannot eliminate it all. Decision effectiveness is assumed to be an inverted-U curve. The decision effectiveness curve of an expert will turn down at a relatively higher level than that of non-experts, but it still curves down at some point.(18, 510)

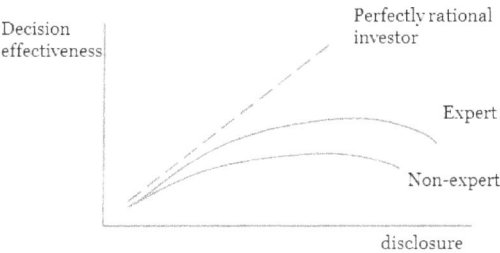

Figure 68 Decision effectiveness

Conflict of interests

Market experts carry out two conflicting roles; monitoring role vs. business opportunity. They monitor the management as a gatekeeper and also seek a business opportunity with firms. For example, financial intermediaries that hire analysts seek underwriting opportunities, and financial media that is an opaque-basher seeks advertisement opportunities from firms. An expert filter would not work effectively when market experts refuse its role as informational gatekeepers for fear of losing other business opportunities with listed firms.

Different stock picks

When the target firms that experts are willing to invest are different from the firms that individual investors prefer, then the mechanism of expert filter will be of little use to individual investors. Even though the expert filter is perfectly arranged, it may not work perfectly since the experts' favorite stock can be substantially different from individual investor's stock selection.

Overconfidence bias in expert filter

Many studies have reported the expert's overconfidence bias. Particularly experts who have been very successful might be overconfident. Seasoned experts often fall into the trap of the availability bias that makes them focus on readily available information only and deteriorate decision effectiveness.(551)

5444. Noise trader

The information overload will be regarded as a serious issue to information traders, but noise traders who use summarized information would pay less attention to voluminous information. As a result, information overload cannot be a serious issue when the portion of an information trader is shallow.

However, information overload can be critical in case that the trading portion of the noise trader is tiny while that of information trader is large. Even though the trading portion of an information trader is small, the impacts of an information trader that determines the level of market efficiency should not be treated as a light matter.(510) A little stone thrown on the water surface generates a wave.

5445. Free-riding

Individual investors basically cannot escape from information overload, but they can make an attempt to be a free-rider. Thus, some may argue that information overload is not a serious matter. According to the efficient market hypothesis, the uninformed traders can get a free ride on the market price that incorporates all the available public information of informed traders. On the contrary, many studies show evidence that semi-strong efficient market hypothesis is not valid. Thus, there can be scant opportunities for uninformed traders to get a free ride.(3, 510)

545. Overcoming Information Overload

Information overload can generate serious cognitive costs of information process that can induce a reduction in the rate of return from an investment. It is an extreme case, but investors can exit from the firm or market. No one would repudiate the idea that the information overload has risen from the supply side of information. By the way, it will not be an issue if information users are perfectly rational. Thus, the solution against information overload should be sought from both sides: supply and demand. Investor education for smart understanding may work well as a demand-side policy, while smart presentation and reduction of disclosure requirements would be a supply-side policy to ease the harmful effects of information overload.(510) As bounded rationality is unavoidable to humans, any mechanism such as expert filters, education cannot completely eliminate information overload.

5451. Smart presentation

Significance

Not more information, but better information is what information users want. Smart disclosure of a firm enables smart investment decisions of investors. The risk of information overload can be alleviated, and the accuracy of the decision can be improved when firms present information in an easier way for users to search, understand, evaluate, and compare among the alternatives. Thus, the purpose of disclosure regulation should be to provide better information in a practical and smart way. Disclosing firms should also study how to efficiently present information in an adequate way with various formats, such as text, number, percentage, trend, chart, and table.

Regulator

Regulators have made various attempts to guide firms to present information in a more accessible and understandable way, such as standardization, aggregation, and simplification. First, standard formats such as Form 10-K help users to reduce processing costs and compare across firms.

At the same time, regulators should consider the unexpected side-effect of standardization because all firms are not similar. Second, the aggregate information is easily assimilated than raw data. Without aggregation, overloaded raw data cannot be understood. Hence, most regulators require firms to aggregate or consolidate raw data in a standardized format (e.g., financial statements). Third, regarding simplification, in 1996, the Task Force on Disclosure Simplification recommended many ways to simplify disclosure. The "plain English" initiative is a good example of such attempts to improve how to present disclosure. The increased use of graphs, charts, and tables are recommended.(548)

The IR Society and researchers recommend firms that are interested in investor relation activities, which provide an analogy on how to present a firm's disclosure effectively. First, regulators sometimes consider a policy to require firms to use more understandable formats, such as graphical or tabular format and even oppose narrative presentations. Such intervention requires prudent thinking since it may interfere with managers' discretion to present the true state of individual firms fully. Second, separating key information from periodic reports and requiring real-time disclosure in Form 8-K is worthwhile. Once key information is separated, it would be highlighted and better communicated, promoting better understanding. Some countries are following such a real-time disclosure policy, and, from time to time, those are overlapped with the disclosure requirements of stock exchanges.[375] Third, requiring firms to disclose a summary of voluminous disclosure could allow a concise presentation, besides investors will not be harmed as the summary would not utterly replace the disclosure. Summarization can be viewed as an extension of aggregation. The regulator should consider a tiered or layered disclosure, requiring a summary in addition to complete statements. The summary could be hyperlinked to complete disclosure. The layered disclosure provides firms with the flexibility to disclose in multi-layers and allows investors to drill down from a big picture to the details. In many countries, firms are permitted or mandated to distribute a summary of financial statements. (356, 510, 552, 553)

KPMG & FERF (2011) provided some recommendation to prevent disclosure overload. For example, regulator should issue an interpretive release to address the permissibility of cross-referencing to avoid duplicate disclosures and the manner of addressing immaterial items. Summaries of detailed disclosure should not include a detailed description of immaterial matters but should conform to the guidance of regulator or standard setter. Disclosures should make maximum use of tables and graphics and avoid the use of long textual discussions.(538) On the contrary to the recommendation to use more tables, heavy reliance on tables might hinder the understandability of disclosure. For example, firms listed in the Korean Exchange traditionally provided annual reports including a lot of tables because it is more intuitive and more understandable. However, as investors information needs are getting more sophisticated, regulator tends to recommend firms to use more narrative disclosure.

Smart media

If firms present through new media, such as the Internet or SNS, information users may benefit from the reduced time and effort to search and evaluate the disclosed information. The Internet plays a vital role in making information users gather, compare, and process the information efficiently. Nevertheless, we have to be careful as the Internet has double-sided characters, helping investors to analyze versus aggravating information overload. Owing to the low-cost dissemination media, managers have the incentive to provide an avalanche of information to minimize litigation risk.

Limits

Information users frequently focus on the form, structure, and sequence of presentation that can have a different impact on decision making. As a result, managers need to exercise their discretion in presenting disclosure to a certain extent. However, firms' unlimited discretion in presenting disclosure might aggravate the decision effectiveness of investors by framing the investors' recognition and decision instead of maximizing the managers' private benefits. Such being the case, regulators may design a merited formatting policy. However, such a measure would restrict the managers' discretion of presenting firms' information in the best way to maximize the firm's net benefits of disclosure. Nevertheless, regulators do not know about what is the best presentation method, and no optimal format exists since one man's meat is another man's poison.

5452. Promoting expert filters

The role of experts in the capital market is significant. Even though they are small in number, experts are strong in analyzing information and influencing the market. Thus, how to enhance the expert's filtering mechanism is essential in enhancing market transparency. Not only regulators but also institutions that are hiring analysts may require professional and educational experiences as a minimum requirement. Establishing a well-functioning education institute is essential, and various types of incentive-compatible mechanisms should be adopted to promote the expert's credibility.

5453. Education for smart understanding

Decision-making strategies may differ across information users and depend upon many factors such as experience, training, and education. Long-experienced and well-trained information users may assimilate more information without overload. Without influencing the supply of information, decision effectiveness can be enhanced through education on how to filter and interpret the disclosed information.(554) Education can enhance investors' decision effectiveness by supporting them to assimilate more information effectively, filter or ignore less useful information, and deploy various investment strategies. As a result, most exchanges and regulators tend to arrange a variety of educational initiatives as those are prerequisites to foster rational investors and efficient markets. Such an education program suggests meaningful implications especially for a specific capital market that has a higher portion of individual investor. How to educate will be covered in the Chapter 365.

5454. Scale-back policy

As disclosure is costly, it is food for thought about disclosure requirements when the disclosed information is not in use. We could quickly think of an immediate reaction to shrinking disclosure requirements. A regulator might reduce disclosure requirements that are too stringent and less useful. For example, on May 2019, the SEC issued the proposal in Release No/33-10635 "Amendments to Financial Disclosures about Acquired and Disposed Businesses" that is *"to scale back disclosure requirements in order to reduce the complexity and costs of preparing financial information related to acquisitions and dispositions of other businesses despite opposition by some investor protection advocates."*[376]

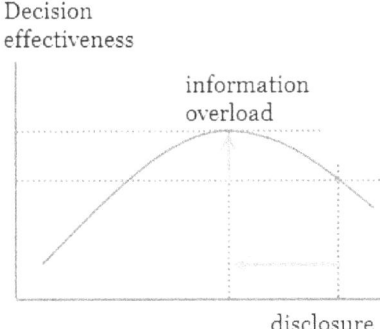

Figure 69 Disclosure reduction

As a consequence of such a reduction, firms may positively benefit from the reduced disclosure costs. As an additional consequence, the scale-back policy might enhance the effectiveness of investment decisions of bounded investors. The scale-back policy to reduce the quality or quantity of disclosure requirements might contribute to the information users' decision effectiveness when they are facing the declining phase of the inverted-U curve of decision effectiveness.(510)

546. Scale-Back Policy: Revisited

5461. Checking procedure

To draft a scaling back policy, regulators need to check whether investors are overloaded (e.g., degree of overload), whether they have solutions against overload (e.g., expert filters, heuristics), and which disclosure requirements should be deleted.(510) It is worth checking the degree of information overload because investors might cope a lot better with large amounts of information, and, as a result, no scale-back might be required. For example, heuristics can approximate the accuracy with substantial savings in the analysis efforts. As a result, they might make sound decisions using heuristics.(555)

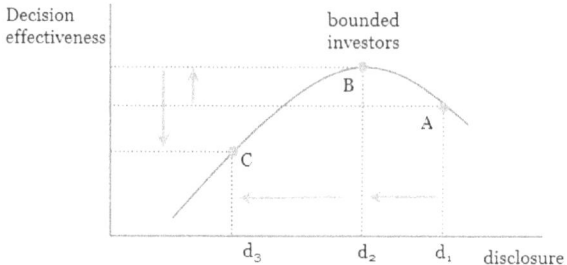

Figure 70 Disclosure scale-back policy

To get the correct answer to those questions above, regulators should have a better understanding of how investors process information and make investment decisions. In general, a disclosure policy to reduce information (Figure 70, $d_2 \to d_3$) will deteriorate decision effectiveness (B → C). However, if firms are currently providing the information at a sufficiently higher level (d_1), then a reduction of disclosure requirements ($d_1 \to d_2$) will enhance decision effectiveness (A → B). The benefit of reduction to investors is straightforward; less information promotes decision effectiveness.

5462. Conflicts: players

Experts vs. Non-experts

The regulator needs to find out what types of investors are overwhelmed by information overload. Disclosure reduction policy might positively affect the overloaded non-experts while negatively affect the non-overloaded experts. If only non-expert investors are overwhelmed by information overload, the scale-back policy will enhance the decision effectiveness of non-expert at the cost of the potential distortion of experts' decisions.

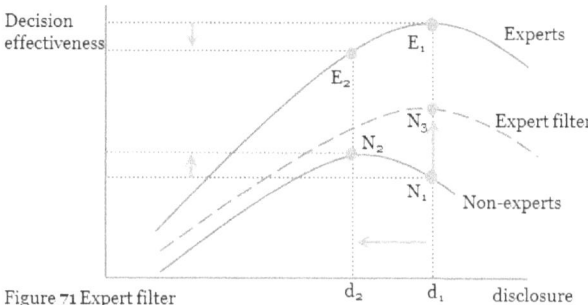

Figure 71 Expert filter

In such a conflicting situation between expert and non-expert, regulators may choose to scale-back for non-experts and leave experts to cope on their own (Figure 71, $d_1 \to d_2$, $N_1 \to N_2$, $E_1 \to E_2$). In contrast, if the expert filter is likely to provide non-experts with higher decision effectiveness, then regulators may choose to stand still (at d1) and strengthen the expert filter for non-experts to benefit ($N_1 \rightarrow N_3$).

Firms vs. Information users

The regulator should consider both impacts on the information users and providers. Disclosure scale-back will affect the information user's decision effectiveness, not alone the firm's disclosure benefit and cost. Thus, the regulator should precisely diagnose and consider both sides without losing a sense of balance.

The regulator should clearly define what the primary purpose of disclosure reduction is. Scale-back policy to mitigate information overload means supporting information users to optimize their decision effectiveness. However, deregulation approach to reduce the firm's disclosure burden on account of the supply-side theory can arrive at a completely different destination.

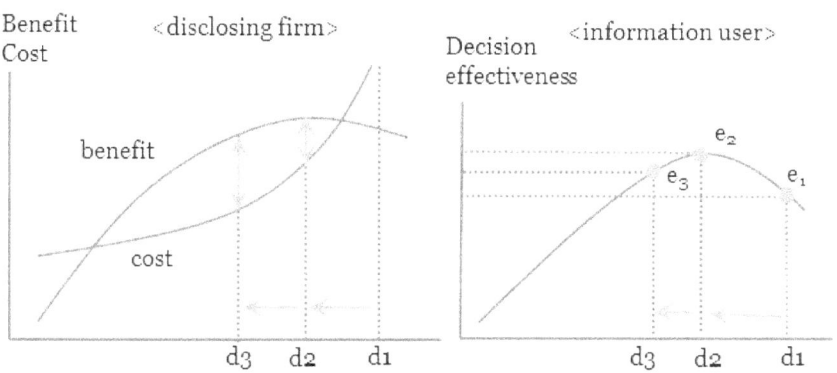

Figure 72 Disclosing firm   Figure 73 Information user

For example, let us suppose that a regulator reduced some of the disclosure requirements to alleviate firms' disclosure burdens. If the market is under severe information overload and disclosure cost (Figure 72 and 73, d_1), then disclosure deregulation policy can catch both hares. In the information user's point of view, decision effectiveness can be enhanced through the lowered information overload (Figure 73, $d_1 \rightarrow d_2$). In the disclosing firm's point of view, the firm's disclosure cost sharply decreases while disclosure benefits remain a similar level, eliminating a negative net benefit but generating a positive net benefit of disclosure (Figure 72, $d_1 \rightarrow d_2$).

However, if the market is situated at d2, then scale-back policy would support the disclosing firm by significantly decreasing disclosure cost and increasing the firm's net benefits of disclosure (Figure 72, $d_2 \rightarrow d_3$) at the cost of information users by decreasing the investor's decision effectiveness (Figure 73, $d_2 \rightarrow d_3$).

5463. Conflicts: regulatory goals

Multiple goals under securities regulation

Scale-back policy may be justified when it promotes information user's decision effectiveness by mitigating information overload. However, before drafting a scale-back policy, regulators need to consider the main goals of securities regulation that include promoting investor confidence, reducing agency costs, and supporting investor's decision making. The relative importance among the goals may change after the fashion of the time in the capital markets.

Agency problem

A reduction of agency cost is one of the primary purposes of the securities laws, and disclosure creates significant effects in deterring insiders from fraudulent or corrupt behaviors. Louis Brandeis expressed: *"Publicity is justly commended as a remedy for social and industrial diseases. Sunlight is said to be the best of disinfectants; electric light the most efficient policeman."*(510) When investors value a firm, they are evaluating the probability of fraudulent or corrupt behaviors also. Besides, all information creates both effects of price accuracy enhancement and agency cost reduction to a certain degree.

Thus, when it is adopted carelessly or imprudently, a scale-back policy might generate unexpected side-effects by sending the market with the wrong signal that fraud or misconduct can be acceptable or tolerated by regulators and investors. For example, firms might reduce internal resources that were allocated on a consistent base to monitor and prevent potential fraud or misconduct. It might even encourage managers to seek a chance of misconduct, increasing agency costs gradually.

Investor confidence

Financial frauds of the century attract the focus of public attention, harm investor confidence, and make investors hesitant from investing. Investor confidence is an essential element in maintaining the market thick and efficient. The policy to restore investor confidence generally includes regulating firms to provide more and better information. Disclosure policy is recognized as a relatively easy mechanism to introduce but also an effective measure to recover investor confidence that is occasionally ruined by frauds of the century.

By the way, the degree of investor's confidence is directly related to the degree of investor's belief on how much information they have access. If investors have the belief that current regulation provides investor protection above and beyond their expectations, then they will be more confident.

However, if investors interpret a scale-back policy as a significant deregulatory step, then it might undermine investor's confidence. It is particularly noteworthy that, even though an investor's "decision effectiveness" might be improved, investor "confidence" might be eroded due to the scale-back policy. Disclosure regulations adopted in many capital markets might not be assessed to have created substantive or effective consequences that are satisfying regulators and investors, but it could have played a leading role in restoring investor's confidence. In nature, disclosure scale-back policy could erode investor confidence. If restoring investor's confidence is one of the top objectives, then the disclosure reduction policy should be dropped from the agenda.(510)

Choices under multiple conflicts

In general, regulators might seek to promote all the goals simultaneously without conflicts. Nevertheless, when it comes to information overload, this is another pair of shoes. While promoting decision effectiveness, the scale-back policy might be contrary to other goals. Regulators should determine which policy substantively protects investors because investor protection is the most crucial goal of the securities laws. Scale-back policy designed to mitigate information overload may seriously harm other goals. The worst choice could be deteriorating all the goals.

Hypothetical case

We might think of hypothetical situations as below. The level of saturation points of each U-shaped curves in the below graph is just hypothetically assumed to explain the conflicts among various goals.

  a. stage A: Scale-back policy worsens all the goals.
  b. stage B: Scale-back policy helps decision effectiveness only.
  c. stage C: Scale-back policy worsens investor confidence only.
  d. stage D: Scale-back policy is helpful in achieving all the goals.

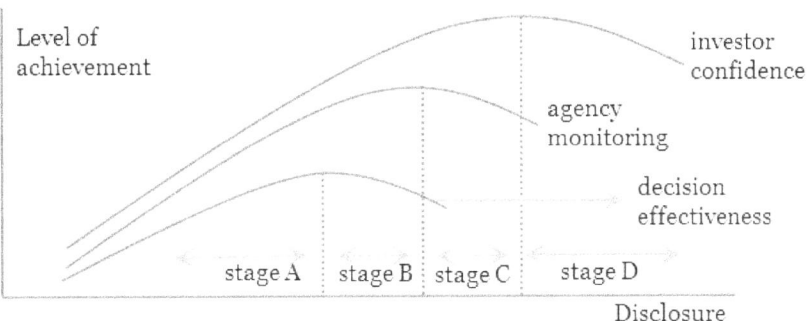

Figure 74 Stages

5464. Target information

There is an awaiting task to be solved that exists in disclosure policies, regardless of whether it is to add or reduce disclosure requirements. How much and what information are they using? What type of information should the investors have in order to make an effective decision? What kind of disclosure items should be removed from disclosure requirements?

Scale-back policy might be imprudent without a proper understanding of which information should be added or deleted. Misunderstanding can bring about more harm than good. If regulator mistakenly adopt scale-back policy for useful information, then investors might be worse off due to the lesser information.

To complicate matters further, every information user has different tastes for information. One man's meat is another man's poison. For example, the regulator may try to remove the disclosure requirement of the information that is not widely utilized. However, this approach might harm the market efficiency if the experts in specific areas heavily rely on the information that is to be removed.(510)

5465. Target audience

What type of information users should regulators target? This question has a significant meaning in drafting a scale-back policy because its impact may vary from users to users. Information users have a wide spectrum of interests, capability, experience, education, and strategies that are leading themselves to a different level of information overload. However, most security laws define "investor protection" in general terms only. Such a general definition is necessary to protect investors extensively but is not enough at working level. Consequently, regulators should have a policy to consider the potential responses of and impacts on each group of information users. (510)

When drafting a policy change, policymakers should choose the target audience because information users have different optimal choices. Regulators might choose to introduce the policy that is not targeting a specific audience but potentially result in vague or pointless outcomes. Paredes (2013) mentions some options on how to select target audience, which contain much food for thought.(510)

First, disclosure requirements could be tailored to "unsophisticated individual investors." This approach will be practical when the expert filter is inoperative. They can enhance investor confidence and evade the informational equality concerns that might be raised by the media or politician. Nevertheless, the regulator should be aware of possible information overload.

Second, disclosure regulation could be tailored to the "median investor group" that might be a good representative of all users. For example, regulator can choose a specific attribute of investor (e.g., experience, asset size) and design the new regulation targeting the median group.[377]

Third, disclosure requirements could be tailored to the "experts" whose decision is highly influential to the market. This idea may be aggressively supported, especially when the expert filter is up and running, but may put the informational equality concerns in the red-hot issue. It is inevitable to target the experts in adopting complex disclosure requirements.

Fourth, regulators seeking to catch two birds with one stone may design a "dual target approach," mixing one disclosure requirement available for experts and other requirements for individual investors. However, regulators should be aware of the risk of losing two birds.

5466. Implications of disclosure reduction

Parades (2003) and other researchers suggest many difficulties and complicating factors in the scale-back policy. First, it is tough to tell whether a certain group of investors is overloaded by the current level of disclosure requirements. Second, investors' investment decisions might be worsened when the regulator reduces disclosure requirements that are useful. Third, the regulator may face asymmetric responses from the market. Information users who suffered from information overload might not welcome the scale-back policy, but those who expect a severe suffer from the reduction will strongly resist. Besides, the information users' attitudes toward information may change from time to time. For example, shortly after the scale-back policy, a regulator may face an increasing demand from free-riders. Fourth, changes in disclosure requirements are subject to public pressures, and thus regulators should be ready for the risk of being criticized by the public. Furthermore, regulators should not forget the fact that regulators are neither free from bounded rationality. Scaling back can be more harm than good under the regulator's cognitive bias. At least, however, debates about the scale-back policy provide a bottom-line implication that regulators have to mandate additional disclosure requirements only after much thoughts because it is not easy to reduce.(510)

Regulators cannot correctly judge whether the current disclosure requirement exceeds the saturation point of investor's decision effectiveness. As a result, if the regulator is misled by arguments suggesting information overload, then a scale-back policy may badly affect the social welfare generating a dead-weight loss.

55. Complexity

551. Overview

Definition

Complexity is widely mentioned issues. As a result, the problem of complexity in a specific context, such as structured transactions, might have common issues to other contexts, such as the complex disclosure of a firm. (556) By the way, the complexity should not be defined in terms of the quality or quantity since a high-quality or large amount of disclosure can also be complicated and less understood when the firm's business is complex.

The complexity is generally used to characterize the qualitative attributes of information that negatively impact the understanding of information users. For example, Damodaran (2006) defined the complexity of disclosure as a status that includes *"both the absence of relevant information and the presence of extraneous information."*(107)

We may define the complexity of disclosure in terms of valuation model. Information should be disclosed in a more understandable manner for investors to apply to the valuation model as a meaningful input variable. If the disclosed information is complex, investors cannot avoid the difficulty in interpretation and evaluation. Considering the purpose of the information in the capital markets, the complexity might be defined as the difficulty of converting information to valuation inputs.

The complexity is in one sense subjective in other sense objective. If the complexity comes from the information or source, then it might be objective. It is subjective in nature because some may perceive certain information as a complex one, while others as a simple one. Non-experts may accept it as a complex one that can be perceived as a simple one by experts. Owing to such subjective nature of complexity, some rationale of information overload can also be applied to the complexity in a similar way.

Complexity and understandability

The firm's operational and financial activities must be disclosed in a manner that is easily understandable by information users who possess a reasonable level of knowledge. Understandability of disclosure is essential for information users. If the disclosed information is not easy for information users to understand, then this would undermine the reliability of the disclosed information.

Understandability has been frequently commented in the perspectives of supply-side; disclosing more understandable manner. On the contrary, the ability to understand the disclosed information is directly related to the demand-side theories. Compliance to disclosure requirements does not necessarily mean understandability. Even though the information is disclosed in compliance with the rules and standards, it could be complex or overloaded to lay investors.

The information has to be credible and usable to have value. Investors inevitably suffer from complexity due to the bounded rationality. Thus, disclosure should be available and accessible on a timely basis, but also be simple for investors to understand easily, meaning that the disclosed information should be in accordance with the availability, accessibility, and understandability. Complex information can be of help to a certain extent, but it can harm when the degree of complexity is over the saturation point.

Complexity and valuation

Investors cannot estimate the adequate input variables to the valuation model from the complex disclosure. For example, investors need the exact information on the size of cash flow. If firms included complex information in cash flow statements, investors cannot estimate the input accurately and thus, might discount the value of a complex firm because of the uncertainty.

Cause of financial crisis

The complexity of disclosure influences investors, generating the cognitive cost that can lead to market failure. The United States subprime mortgage crisis is frequently attributed to the conflicts of interest between firm and manager, investors' complacency, complexity of products information. Many expect the complexity to be the greatest financial-market challenge of the future.(525, 557, 558)

552. Sources And Determinants

5521. Behavioral vs. Structural source

Guay, Samuels, and Taylor (2015) suggests two views of complexity; behaviorism vs. structuralism. The behaviorism of managerial choice is that managers might go so far as to create complexity to obfuscate information and fool investors about firm value, and investors' inattention can lead the deceitful complexity to work. An alternative view of structuralism is that the complexity of disclosure instead reflects the complex nature of business mix and regulation, and managers attempt to minimize complexity.(559)

Behavioral sources

Firms may choose to make disclosure more difficult for information users to understand for some reason. The complexity of disclosure is directly linked to the complexity of the firm's managerial environments since disclosure decision is affected by managerial environments. It is not easy to extract relevant information from complex disclosure. Complex disclosure requires more costs, such as time, effort, cognitive ability, for information users to understand. Even professional analysts often fail to respond appropriately to the complex financial disclosure.(560, 561) If firms that want to delay or weaken the market reactions may have incentives to provide obfuscated disclosure. For example, firms with higher complexity have lower earnings performance, implying that managers create complexity to obfuscate poor performance.(346)

Structural sources

The complexity of disclosure can be attributed to disclosure itself or disclosure environment, such as the disclosing firm, regulatory authorities, and intermediaries.(107, 559) Note that a simple association cannot be found between the complexity and its structural sources. For example, even a firm with a monotonous business model can end up with very complex disclosure when it raises funds by using complex financial instruments. Conversely, disclosure of a firm with a complex business mix can be more understandable when it is free from managerial incentives.

5522. Firm-level Sources

Information may be disclosed in a less understandable manner by the firm. Because of the source dependent nature of information, the complexity of disclosure relies on firms' attributes and managerial incentives. Information can be disclosed in a complex way depending on the firm-side factors such as financing choice and business mix structure (e.g., consolidation). Disclosure is complex when the firm is complex. Some firm-specific factors (i.e., business mix, ownership structure, external growth strategy, and financing strategy) are suggested to give rise to the complexity of disclosure.(107)

Even though a lot of complexity is created from external sources, the internal source of complexity can be under firm's control. The fact that complexity comes from firm level attributes justifies the rationale that firms should make a voluntary effort to reduce complexity. However, according to the interviews of the biennial IBM Global CEO Study conducted with 1,541 CEOs and general managers from 60 countries. *"Only 49 percent of responding CEOs think their organizations are prepared to deal with a more complicated business environment."*[378]

Complex business mix

There are some reasons why firms diversify the business mix. Many firms have attempted to diversify business and reduce risk through mergers and acquisitions. A firm with a single business is more straightforward than a firm with multi-business. Firms that report a single-business will be easier to evaluate than firms that muddle up multi-business in a report. Like business, like disclosure! (107)

Complex holding structure

Firms pursue various types of benefits of a complex structure, such as tax benefits and hostile acquisition preemption. For example, managers might attempt to preempt hostile acquirer and gain effective control by structuring a business complexity. They can make it difficult for potential acquirers to detect whether the firm is undervalued. Besides, firms can reduce tax burdens by creating complex holding structures in tax havens. Complex structures allow firms to shift income or tax burden from one subsidiary to another. Creating subsidiaries or cross holdings with minimal shares would enhance the control at the price of the chaos of complexity. It aggravates the complexity problem, especially when subsidiaries are subject to different accounting standards. Some will be consolidated into a parent firm, while others reported by an equity method. Special purpose vehicles also lead to the complexity of structure and financial reporting.(107)

External growth strategy

Firms facing the limited opportunity of internal growth will try to grow through external growth strategies such as M&A, which seriously affect the complexity of disclosure. It is more than true that there is a big difference in the cost of complexity between simple firms and complex firms. The degree of difference in characteristics between a target firm and an acquiring firm influences the degree of complexity.(107)

Complex financing

Investment bankers have invented various types of hybrid securities, such as convertibles, warrants, asset-backed securities, and collateralized debt obligations that keep debt off the balance sheet to meet the needs of market participants who prefer the balance sheet with lower debt. They introduced complex securities to meet firms' needs of financing with favorable treatment (e.g., tax, accounting, and credit), which contributed to the competitiveness of investment bankers. Structured securities can add efficiency but also complexity, and, as a result, even sophisticated investors cannot understand such transactions. The competitiveness of one party does not come free but at the cost of the complexity of other parties.(556)

Firm's strategy, such as business mix and holding structure, provides firms with growth opportunity and the cost of complexity. Thus, the complexity of disclosure originated from a firm's business-mix strategy should be understood as a high price to pay for the growth and risk-reduction. As a result, firm's most important policy should be to set a clear vision and priority in dealing with complexity caused by firm's management strategy.

Firm's benefits

Firms with lower earnings tend to disclose their annual reports in a less readable format (i.e., lengthy, higher Fog index), while firms with persistent positive earnings tend to disclose it in a more readable manner.(346)

Information production cost: Language barrier, firm size, experience

Brochet, Naranjo, and Yu (2012) show evidence that "*Linguistic complexity is positively associated with the language barrier in the companies' home-country.*" The Non-US firms listed in US markets exhibit a higher degree of complexity in their disclosure and communication. Smaller firms have relatively higher costs of information communication than large firms, and they show a higher level of linguistic complexity. Firms that had more prior experience with English conference calls show a lower level of complexity because accumulated experience reduces the information communication cost.(562) Nelson and Pritchard (2008) provide evidence that firms tend to use more cautionary language in a more readable manner (e.g., low Fog Index) to reduce the expected litigation costs. However, they do not remove the cautionary language even though litigation risk seems to decrease.(216)

5523. Environmental sources

Even though the disclosed information is fully available and understandable, a firm's business mix can be too complex to understand. Regulatory environments, including accounting standards, can cause complexity. Thus, regulators or standard setters should pay attention to the possibility of generating complexity.

Regulatory framework: lax or tight regulation

Regulation might be the primary source of complexity. Disclosure can be complex due to lax regulation as well as tight regulation. The regulation-driven complexity may arise from numerous sources, such as ambiguously written regulation, interpretation left to firm's discretion, and frequent changes. There is an evidence of a strong country effect in the firm's disclosure policy, which implies that the legal framework and practice in a given country might be the main source of complexity rather than the firm-specific characteristics (e.g., financial performance).(123) The complexity of annual reports have increased due to strong regulation.(538)

Therefore, regulators also should pay more attention to the issues of complexity. For instance, in 2006, Christopher Cox, Chairman of U.S. SEC, admitted the regulation as a source of complexity. *"To more closely match the theory of a well-ordered market ... the SEC is currently pursuing a number of initiatives to improve the quality and usefulness of disclosure for individual investors ... These initiatives include 'Reducing the complexity of accounting rules and regulations.'"* (563)

Boilerplate disclosure

One may assume that the boilerplate disclosure practices is rooted in firms' poor disclosure decisions. However, the prevalence of similar boilerplate disclosure signifies that there is a benchmark model followed by firms. It might originate from managers' supposition that other firms' languages and tones that are already reviewed and accepted by the SEC staffs are more likely to be approved. Sometimes boilerplate disclosure may come from manager's optimization decisions. The manager's conservative attitudes to minimize the potential risk from disclosure (i.e., indirect costs) could naturally result in the uniform disclosure where firms share many attributes in common or where they use the consultation services of law firms. All the boilerplate disclosure might not be the real issue, but the boilerplate disclosure that is poor matters.

Accounting standards

Accounting standards are also responsible for the increasing complexity of financial statements. Accounting rules and the increasing level of details (e.g., footnotes) have complicated disclosure and often obscured the value-relevant information.(510) Firms are entitled to exercise the discretionary power in the measurement of accounting items (i.e., income, asset). The possibility of a discretionary decision that managers can adjust the numbers of assets and debts can add the complexity of financial reporting. While some firms use the leeway to provide information about their financial status, others use it to hide their weakness.

Language barriers

According to Brochet (2012), the complexity of a non-US firm is primarily driven by language barriers. *"The linguistic complexity is positively associated with the language barrier in the firms' home country."* The form of disclosure presentation can impose additional processing costs. Managers who resolve the language barrier by hiring a translator adds additional information production costs.(562)

5524. Information-level sources

Complexity depends on the nature of information, but one should not expect a uniform relation because the complexity is context-specific. For example, the Q&A in a conference call is more spontaneous than the staged and prepared disclosure that can be scrutinized ahead of release. Thus, the complexity of a conference call can have more substantial variations and more impacts than prepared disclosures.(562)

The idea in noteworthy that even simple information such as stock symbol or company name may create serious confusion even though they are operating in completely different industries: TSLA (Tesla) vs. TLSA (Tiziana Life Sciences); Twiter (TWTR) and Tweeter Home Entertainment (TWTRQ) that rose up 1500% when TWTR filed to go public; Zoom technologies (ZTNO) that had no sales vs. Zoom Video Communication (ZM) that is a rare unicorn. *"Eventually the SEC suspended trading in Zoom technologies because of confusion."*[379]

Qualitative information is more complex than quantitative information. Earnings forecast itself is very simple, but it can be very complicated when information users try to understand the detailed information about forecast assumptions and calculation process. Complexity can be created either by the absence of relevant information or the presence of irrelevant information. In order for electricity to flow, all the parts of a circuit must be connected to each other. If there is a broken path from a power source to a flashlight bulb, it cannot light up the bulb.

5525. Information users

The investors' request for more information and new securities might be a factor that drives complex disclosure. Schwarcz (2008) has pointed out that *"Complexity ... does not necessarily arise for complexity's sake, nor from a desire to obfuscate. Rather, it arises in response to demand by investors for securities that meet their investment criteria and their appetite for even higher yields and in order to facilitate the transfer and trading of risk to those who prefer to hold it, promoting efficiency."*(525, 564)

Investor's interpretation cost: investor type

The consequences of complexity are likely to be more pronounced among lay investors, but even the analysts or investors that are more sophisticated often fail to respond appropriately to complex disclosure. The prevalence of complexity suggests that the complexity cost is not trivial. The complexity of disclosure adversely affects lay investors, sophisticated investors, as well as information intermediaries. However, not large investors but small investors tend to interpret the information in a more diverse manner resulting in a decrease in consensus. More complex disclosure leads to lower trading volume, which will be more pronounced among smaller investors due to their limited expertise.(560, 565)

Foreign investor base

There is evidence of the relation between investors and complexity. The market response to complexity is more pronounced when the firm has a higher portion of its foreign investor base. Global investors tend to demand effective communication that is free of complexity. Thus, when the firm has a higher portion of the foreign investor base, it tends to face higher demands for the English conference calls that are free of complexity. (562)

Activeness of analysts

The market response to complexity is more pronounced when analysts are more active in asking questions during the call. Active information users push managers to disclose in a less complex manner and impose a heavy penalty on the complex firm.(562)

553. Measuring Complexity

Disclosure quantity

Damodaran (2006) suggested that the volume of disclosed information (i.e., disclosure quantity) can be a simple and effective measure of complexity. A voluminous report can indicate the complex structure of business and ownership and the manager's delicate attention on how to describe the firm's performance.

For example, simple indices such as the number of pages of annual reports or footnotes can be selected as a complexity index depending on the purpose of measurement. Multi-industry conglomerates tend to have

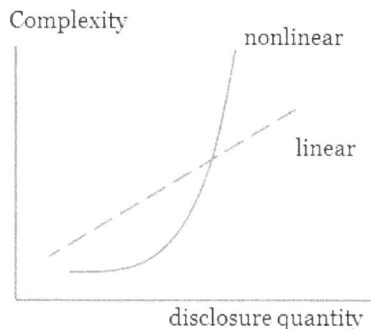

Figure 75 Complexity

longer reports.(107) It is noteworthy that the association between disclosure quantity and complexity might be a non-linear relation. If disclosure quantity increases over a certain threshold level, then the complexity might increase at an exponential rate.

Customized complexity index

There might be no consensus about the exact measure of complexity. A straightforward and simple measure of complexity will be the best measure. However, a single-dimensional index cannot truly represent the degree of complexity that is determined by multi-dimensional factors. To overcome the shortcomings of a single-dimensional measure, we may classify the sources of complexity and construct a customized complexity index. Considering the impacts of complexity on investor's valuation process, it is recommendable to construct a complexity index by using the factors that are related to the valuation model. For example, Damodaran (2006) suggested an information-based complexity index that is comprised of factors identified by the valuation inputs. Information users can construct a complexity score for each firm and adjust (e.g., discount) the firm value with the complexity index. For example, analysts may allocate higher complexity scores to a firm that has a complex business mix or heterogeneous subsidiaries since it is challenging to evaluate such firms.(107)

554. Consequences: Market Failure

Market failure

Complexity affects the market by increasing the information processing costs to information users. It limits the investors' ability to interpret information and reduces forecast precision, decreasing market demand. In a world of severe complexity, disclosure regulation would remain merely an information provision mechanism, not a measure to mitigate information asymmetry. When disclosure fails to help investors to understand the true state of a firm due to complexity, it means that disclosure is nothing but a defective mechanism in mitigating information asymmetry. Complex disclosure to escape from the potential litigation of non-disclosure is an appearance-only disclosure that is a troublemaker and fruitless labor. Largely, it is evidenced that an increase in complexity has negative consequences. (566)

Price, return, and volatility

In general, complex financial statements negatively affect the information environment by reducing price efficiency but increasing uncertainty.(566) The linguistic complexity affects the extent and speed to which the capital market reacts. *"Firms with more linguistic complexity in their conference calls show less trading volume and price movement following the information releases…the capital market's response to linguistic complexity is more pronounced when there is greater … demand for the English conference calls."*(562) Investors tend to underreact for firms with higher complexity in 10-K report.(567) Besides, *"individuals' returns are, on average, increasing in firms with more accessible and transparent disclosures."*(568)

Liquidity

It is evidenced that *"textual attributes are correlated with economic outcomes such as liquidity." "Liquidity, analyst following, and institutional ownership tend to be greater for firms whose annual reports are longer, contain less boilerplate and Fog…"*(569) The linguistic complexity is negatively associated with trading volume.(562) More complex (e.g., longer and less readable) disclosure have a larger impact on small investors reducing trading activity, but only a limited impact on large investors. Investors may stop processing the disclosed information that is complex due to higher cost, and some of them will cease trading activity. Thus, regulators need to pay attention to leveling the playing field across investor groups regarding the complexity.(565)

Dispersion, consensus

Analysts' behavior is related to a firm's disclosure choices, such as the readability of disclosure. It is costly for investors to interpret the disclosure when it is less readable, and investors will rely more on the expert filter. Thus, an investor's demand for the services provided by analysts will increase. As a result, analyst following will be greater for firms with higher complexity as measured by the Fog Index. Analysts who cover firms with less readable or complex disclosure exert themselves and take longer time to issue reports.(570)

There is evidence that 10-K report with fewer words tends to have lower analyst dispersion. Using the simple word count of disclosure can better capture the informativeness or complexity.(569) The complex and less readable 10-K is associated with low quality in analyst earnings forecasts: greater dispersion, lower accuracy, and greater uncertainty.(570) Less readable disclosures are associated with a less favorable and more dispersed bond rating and a higher cost of debt.(571)

555. Investors' Measures

Investors, managers, and regulators have incentives to cure the market failure caused by the complexity. Furthermore, there are many choices with which information users deal with the complexity to effectively reflect it in their valuation process. The adjustment approach to a valuation model can explain the firm's extreme choices from "ignoring complexity" to "ignoring the firm." The former means applying no adjustment to the input variables of the valuation model, while the latter means applying a full discount. All choices are positioned between both extremes.

Ignoring the complexity

In the conventional valuation models, there are no specific components with which investors can consider the complexity. The complexity has been considered to be irrelevant to the valuation because they assumed the significant diversification effect, trustworthy disclosure, and investor's rationality. Thus, there has been no reason for investors to consider the complexity but evaluate the firm as if the disclosure is transparent, and firms are simple.

However, the real market is mingled with the complex firms, opportunistic disclosures, bounded investors, and diluted diversification effects. Thus, investors' strategy of ignoring complexity is not a recommendable choice since it hurts the valuation. For example, it is frequently suggested that ignoring the complexity of Enron for a long time resulted in the fall of similar complex firms. In the real world, irrational information users tend to ignore undesired information. (107)

Ostriches are legendary animals for hiding their heads in the sand to avoid danger when they face the enemy. The "ostrich effect" is an attitude of ignoring the problem (e.g., complex disclosure) by disregarding the undoubted existence, hoping it might vanish automatically. Ignoring a minor error is rational, but ignoring the enemy does not mean an effective avoidance strategy.

Simplifying heuristics

Heuristics, such as a rule of thumb, is not an optimal method but a shortcut to achieve satisfying outcomes against bounded rationality. For example, even experts exercise simplifying heuristics like a credit rating. Many institutional investors tend to invest relying on the credit rating during the sub-prime crisis rather than utilizing complex information. Be sure to note that heuristics are generally effective but often causes bias and systematic error.

Expert filters

The arguments on the role of expert filters as a remedy for the information overload can be similarly applied to the complexity. Some complex information can be filtered by the experts and incorporated into the stock price. Thus, the role of an expert who can influence a manager's disclosure decision is very important.

Adjustment approach; complexity discount

The presence of disclosure complexity points to the need for investor's mechanism to deal with the complexity arising from many aspects. For example, investors need to incorporate the complexity into the valuation model to get a better result. We may define the valuation of a firm is a process of mapping the firm's value-relevant characteristics into a number (i.e., stock price). The complexity of the information about value-relevant characteristics inevitably affects the firm value. Investors can adjust the components of valuation model under the assumption that they exactly or, at least, stochastically know the degree and source of complexity.

Damodaran (2006) presented practical ways to adjust the components of the discounted cash flow valuation model; cash flows, discount rate, expected growth rate, and length of a growth period. To quantify the complexity discount, information users can use a complexity score to measure the complexity of disclosure and relate it to the individual components of the valuation model or directly to the estimated price.(107)

a. Cash flows: If the source of complexity is related to cash flow, investor may adjust the expected cash flows by haircutting with the degree of complexity.

b. Growth: Investor can adjust growth rate or growth period when the sources of complexity are related to growth rate or growth period

c. Discount rate: Investor may adjust discount rate by adding complexity risk premium to the traditional risk premium of the CAPM. Damodaran (2006) suggests three ways: increase beta; adjust the debt to equity ratio to include off-balance-sheet debts; adjust discount rate.

d. Complexity discount: Investor may evaluate a firm value by applying the complexity discount rate to the valuation result that is unadjusted.

In-tolerance: Ignoring the complex firm

Rational investors may refrain from analyzing disclosed information when the cost of information analysis exceeds the potential benefit. If the degree of complexity exceeds a threshold level, investors will even ignore the firm by excluding it from their favorites list.[380] When analysts adopt an ignoring strategy for the firms with complex disclosure, firms might have an incentive to minimize the complexity.(572)

For example, the optimizing managers would increase disclosure until they reach where they can maximize the net benefit of disclosure (Figure 77, $D_1 \rightarrow D_2$). By the way, investors who maximized their net benefit of information analysis at D_1 would not move to D_2 even though managers provide more information when it is complex (Figure 77, stay at D_1). If supplementary disclosure that is complex can be separated from the already disclosed information, rational investor may not use the complex part.

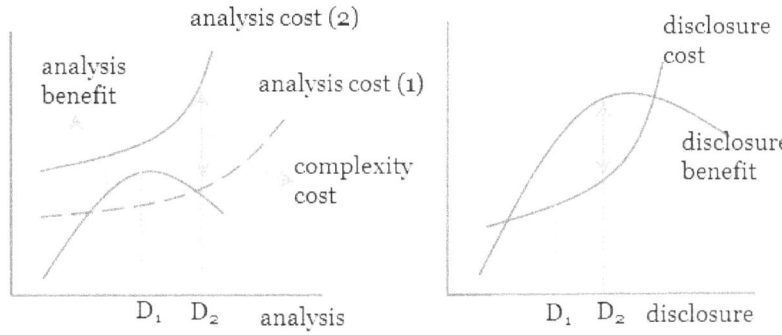

Figure 76 Information user   Figure 77 Disclosing firm

In general, however, one rotten apple spoils the barrel. The value of non-complete information is uncertain, and partial information may be worse than no information because separated or non-holistic information may be meaningless and distort all the contents. As a result, the complexity cost generated by more and complex disclosure might increase the overall cost of information analysis regardless of the level of disclosure, and thereby the investor's cost of analysis exceeds the benefit at all disclosure level, which guides investors to exclude the firm from their favorite list (Figure 76, analysis cost (1)→(2)). If firms optimize without considering the investor base effect as a significant disclosure benefit, then it may result in the investors' ignoring strategy.

Proactive responses

A skeptical and proactive investor may demand firms to keep the complexity below a certain level. If firms provide complex disclosure, then they ask more understandable disclosure to assimilate value-relevant information clearly. Guay (2015) found "… *a robust positive relation between financial statement complexity and subsequent voluntary disclosure. This relation is stronger … when firms have more outside monitors …* " External information users can scrutinize financial statements, discipline, or sometimes intimidate managers to mitigate the negative effects of complexity by providing adequate voluntary disclosure.(559)

556. Firms' Measures

Firms' voluntary introduction of effective measures to address complexity is necessary to better achieve market efficiency. First of all, firms should consider the sources of complexity before introducing measures against complexity. Many have examined how managers of complex firms respond to complexity. As the proverb says, "He that has a great nose thinks everybody is speaking of it." Managers have the incentive to reduce their complexity because they already know that they are complex. Investors would refuse to buy stocks issued by complex firms. Investors' persistent attitude to discount complex firms will drive firms to eliminate the complexity by way of establishing simple holding structures and providing more readable disclosure.

Simplified structure

A conglomerate discount can be attributed to the lack of focus in business, business inefficiencies, and complexity. Not only the number of business but also the mix of different business intensifies the complexity. Especially, the business mix between financial and non-financial business creates severe complexity. As a result, diversification to reduce the risk and increase firm value can incur an unexpected additional cost by complicating disclosure. With all efforts to enhance transparency, the conglomerate complexity cannot be completely eliminated unless the firm is split-up since such complexity is the price of the economies of scale. A break up can abate investors' suspicion about complexity by providing more simple disclosure for investors to understand easily. By the way, the firm could have structured a conglomerate with the idea that the value increase from risk diversification could compensate for the value decrease from complexity. After a breakup, firms will no longer have benefits coming from the economies of scale. Consequently, managers should compare the magnitudes of upsides and downsides of a breakup.

"...Tyco International Ltd.'s decision to abruptly reverse its strategic course from growth-through-acquisition to break up is aimed at boosting shareholder value, but it received a tepid welcome on Wall Street .... One weight on the stock has been investor questioning of Tyco's accounting, which has been complicated by the torrid pace of its acquisitions. Although Tyco insists that its books are solid, ... its share price fell sharply this year as the collapse of Enron made investors apprehensive about complex accounting structures..." (573)

Readable disclosure

Fight fire with fire; fight disclosure with disclosure. Managers have incentives to provide additional disclosure to improve investors' understandability. When they are planning to engage in complex transactions, rational managers could anticipate investors' difficulty in understanding the contents. In case investors raise questions or doubts, the stock price may decline. Anticipating investors' difficulties or observing investors' negative responses, managers may choose to make preemptive explanatory disclosure. They can supplement an ex-post disclosure not only to help investors but also to protect firm value.

In information user side, firm's explanatory or supplementary disclosure that is more readable mainly contributes to reduce the complexity cost by assisting investors to assimilate the disclosed information as a whole (Figure 78, analysis cost (1)→(2)). Besides, if the additional explanatory disclosure contribute to the increase of the overall analysis benefit, then the analysis benefit curve will move upward (Figure 78, analysis benefit (1)→(2)).

In firm's side, firm's policy to provide explanatory disclosure (Figure 79, $D_{11} \to D_{12}$) might be seemingly sub-optimal at the moment of disclosure if the disclosure benefit is assumed to be the same as DB(1) because the net benefit is reduced (NB(11)→NB(12)). However, disclosing firm can potentially experience more increased disclosure benefits (DB2) by the enhanced investor base effect compared to the complex disclosure context, which results in the increased net benefit ((NB(12)→NB(2))). In this regard, managers' optimal disclosure policy should be based on the long-term perspectives.

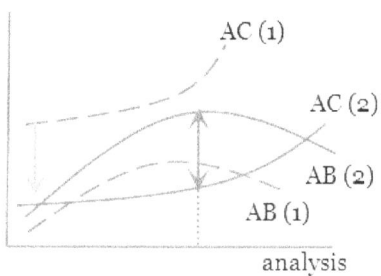

AB: analysis benefit
AC: analysis cost

Figure 78 Information user

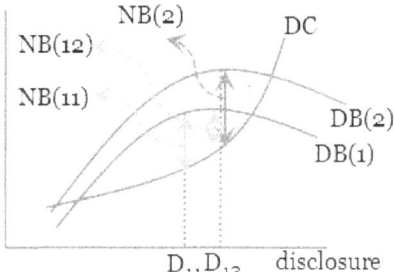

NB: net benefit of disclosure
DB: disclosure benefit

Figure 79 Disclosing firm

For example, Guay (2015) found that *"Managers use voluntary disclosure to mitigate the negative effects of complexity"* as a supplemental medium. In anticipation of complexity, firms could preempt the complexity by way of more frequent (e.g., the number of management forecasts) and immediate (e.g., the period between filing and forecast) voluntary disclosure before the filing. However, attempts to mitigate the complexity would likely occur after filing, since the prediction of complexity is not easy. (559)

a. Evidence

According to Guay (2015), there is a positive association between the complexity of financial statements and the voluntary disclosure disclosed immediately before and after the 10-K filing. Managers anticipate some of the complexity, and they use disclosure to manage the complexity.(559)

b. Determinants

Guay (2015) found determinants that influence the degree of relation between complexity and voluntary disclosure: performance, liquidity, and complex requirements. First, the association between the complexity and voluntary disclosure is positive but weaker when managers have lesser incentives to mitigate complexity (e.g., underperforms, loss, and large abnormal accruals). Second, managers likely provide more voluntary disclosure to achieve a target level of liquidity (e.g., illiquidity at the filing). Third, the association between complexity and voluntary disclosure is strongest after complex disclosure regulation (e.g., Regulation FD, the adoption of complex accounting standards).(559)

c. Intentional obfuscation and voluntary antidotes

One may assume that, when managers intend to create complexity to obfuscate information, they would provide investors with meaningful antidotes (e.g., more disclosure). However, the evidence suggests the opposite: managers intentionally choose to obfuscate disclosure and hesitate to prescribe antidotes.(559) Meanwhile, one may suggest a hypothesis that managers make an intentional choice for private benefits and also provide placebo antidotes that are aimed not to mitigate the complexity but to minimize the potential litigation risk. Managers might believe that crafty placebo antidotes protect themselves from the litigation without harming their private purpose. Kill two birds with one stone.

d. Aggregation, consolidation, segmentation

Managers likely provide aggregated disclosures to enhance the understandability by drawing investors' attention to summarized financial information.(295) Segment disclosure and consolidated financial statements are designed to attenuate the complexity to some degree but cannot be a complete resolution, or even might be worsening the complexity. One might blame these measures as suspected causes of complexity, but we should not be too hasty in blaming these measures so long as these are still mitigating the complexity to some extent, and any measures are far from being perfect antidotes. It is recommendable for regulators to minimize such unavoidable complexities by way of investor education or more simplified standards.

557. Regulators' Response

A wide variety of investors' responses are not always an optimal solution to mitigate complexity but survival techniques. Besides, listed firms' measures also have unavoidable limits due to its intrinsic nature of voluntary mechanism. Therefore, regulators need to pay more attention to implementing more efficient measures against complexity. Some regulators are already taking measures to mitigate the complexity to a greater or lesser extent, but none of them can find a perfect solution against the complexity.

Regulatory measures against the complexity, regardless of the sources of complexity (i.e., disclosure, business mix, securitization, derivatives), can be positioned between non-intervention and intervention. Non-intervention means a policy of toleration implying that complexity issues are not regulated by laws and regulations. Intervention policy might include restriction or proscription, disclosure policy, and simplifying regulation.

Restriction, proscription

In the history of the capital market, the scandal of the century is inevitably followed by legislative changes to impose restrictions on firms or industries to prevent the recurrence of such scandals. However, regulation is not without problems, and restrictions on financial innovation or business mix may reduce efficiency.(556)[381] Besides, it would be highly risky to proscribe firms from engaging in complex transactions or structures to reduce complexity because there are significant benefits from such complex transactions or structures, besides other firms might have some measures, albeit not perfect ones, to overcome the complexity.

The regulators should be careful because some firms may try to find or create a loop-hole to evade legislative changes that are designed to attenuate the complexity. Due to an adverse regulatory selection, only the compliant firm that provokes less complexity can be found to conform to the new regulation, but the less compliant firm that has more incentive of violation finds a look-hole. As a result, the legislative changes to attenuate the complexity might limit the effectiveness but leave the unintended side effects.

Simplifying accounting standards

In reality, firms have discretionary choices in choosing the accounting methods, and accounting information generates the most serious impacts on complexity. Besides, newly structured financial products proliferate. Regulators may reduce firms' discretionary choices to eliminate the complexity when it is generated by managerial choice. They may require firms to keep tax reports in concord with financial reporting purposes when the different accounting rules add serious complexity. They may require manufacturing firms with financial arms to provide a separate report that is complementary to the full report because mixing information of heterogeneous businesses into a report aggravates the complexity.(510)

Concise disclosure: disclosure on derivatives

In 1997, the US SEC issued Item 305 of SEC Regulation S-K, requiring firms to disclose information about derivatives risk exposure. Due to the intrinsic nature of derivatives trading, such disclosure requirements would create severe complexity. To address the expected complexity, Item 305 was drafted in pursuit of concise and brief information instead of a lengthy explanation of derivatives. However, some concerns arose since it did not seem to improve investors' understanding of derivative exposure. Investors could not get a clear understanding of the firm's complex derivatives trading even though the firm satisfied its disclosure obligations. Besides, Dozier (2000) suggested that Item 305 could divert investors' attention from more realistic risks to unlikely risks since it mandates disclosure of extreme worst-case scenarios.(574)

Plain language disclosure

Measures against demand-side issues, such as information overload and complexity, should not be limited to demand-side policies. Supply-side measures, such as better formatting and simple presentation, can help remedy demand-side issues.(510)

In a pilot program of "plain English," some big firms answered that the cost of implementing the "plain English" was not burdensome.(514)[382] In 1998, with the success of the pilot, the SEC enacted the "New Plain English Disclosure Rule" to increase the readability and understandability, (575)[383] which requires issuers to write the cover page, summary and risk factors sections of prospectus in Plain English.[384] Section 409 of Sarbanes-Oxley amended Section 12 of the Securities Exchange Act of 1934 to encourage the use of plain English.[385]

IOSCO (2010) also states that *"the information disclosed in periodic reports should be fairly presented ... Moreover, information disclosed in a periodic report should be presented in a clear and concise manner without reliance on boilerplate language."* (429) The Securities and Futures Commission (SFC) in Hongkong and Hongkong Stock Exchange (HKSE) also published many guidance.(576)[386]

One may argue that regulators should mandate the plain language disclosure for all types of reporting documents. Such a cover-all mandating would provide more readability and accessibility. However, in nature, the main portions of reporting document unavoidably include legal and technical jargon with lengthy sentences. Thus, the coverage of plain language disclosure policy would be generally limited due to its nature.

56. Literacy & Education

561. Disclosure Literacy

Significance

The aphorism "Knowledge is Power" implies the general importance of knowledge and literacy in decision making. The welfare benefits of the capital market depend on how effectively investors behave, but less-educated groups can make financial mistakes. Those who acknowledge their cognitive limitations can try to avoid the market, which may result in market failure or inequality among people.

Information overload and complexity can add challenges to financial literacy. What investors need is not only material information but also substantial knowledge to avoid making mistakes in assimilating the disclosed information. Thus, regulators need to make market participants well-equipped with adequate literacy for wise decision making.

For an efficient market, information provision is just a start line. Investor's literacy toward disclosed information determines the degree of market efficiency. Thus, financial literacy and disclosure literacy deserve much attention. To accomplish the highly literate capital market, regulators should pay attention to the demand-side policies, such as investors' education programs. Financial literacy and investor education are essential in achieving market efficiency, long-term growth, and equality. Researches on financial literacy provide many implications to the disclosure literacy that may be understood as a sub-component of financial literacy.

Evidence of Literacy

Most Americans are not making prudent financial decisions since they lack the knowledge, sophistication, and regulator's guidance.(577, 578) The OECD (2005) revealed the evidence that financial illiteracy is common even in developed countries.(579) Only 52 % of respondents correctly understand that holding a single company stock implies a riskier return than a stock mutual fund.(580) Therefore, many advanced countries have started to measure financial literacy.

Financial literacy

Literacy is a multi-layered concept, and its coverage depends on the scope of research. Thus, researchers have defined various concepts of literacy in many different ways. With the fast-growing financial market, a financial decision is becoming a matter of great importance. For instance, much attention has been paid to financial illiteracy in the 1990s because of the idea that financial illiteracy might have caused financial mistakes, such as the decreasing savings rate, increasing personal debts, and bankruptcy rate.

Financial literacy can be conceptualized with two dimensions; knowledge (e.g., analyze, understand) and use (e.g., application, manage).(581) Jump$tart Coalition defined "financial literacy" as *"The ability to use knowledge and skills to manage one's financial resources effectively for a lifetime of financial security"* (http://www.jumpstart.org). OECD (2011) defined financial literacy as *"a combination of awareness, knowledge, skill, attitude and behavior necessary to make sound financial decisions and ultimately achieve individual financial wellbeing."*(582)

Researchers have tried to make various operational definitions of financial literacy using the knowledge, ability, skill, financial behavior, mutual relationship, and experience.(583) Additionally, some researchers focused on sub-components of financial literacy, debt literacy, or risk literacy. For example, Lusardi and Tufano (2009, 2015) defined the "debt literacy" as the ability to make simple decisions regarding debt contracts, applying basic knowledge about interest compounding. The level of knowledge on fundamental concepts of debt is strikingly low, and there is a strong relationship between debt literacy and both financial experiences and debt loads. The debt illiteracy is severe among women, the elderly, and minorities. Individuals with lower levels of debt literacy tend to bear high costs.(584, 585) Lusardi, Schneider, and Tufano (2011) measured the "risk literacy" that refers to the ability to understand and evaluate risk in informed decision making. The level of risk literacy was evidenced to be very low.(586, 587)

Literacy, determinant of well-being

Huston (2010, Figure 2) shows the relationship between knowledge, education, literacy, behavior, and well-being. The level of endowed or attained human capital and the level of investor education influences the investor's financial literacy. Financial behaviors that are affected by other factors, such as cultural conditions and behavioral biases, determine the financial well-being (e.g., investment performance). By the way, investor's deficiency can be compensated by the available advice or tools (e.g., software).(581) Other influences, such as behavioral biases, can affect financial behaviors and well-being. Even a person who is highly literate with the ability to use sufficient knowledge may not exhibit higher well-being because of the negative impacts of other influences.

Information literacy

Some knowledge about information literacy will provide background understanding of disclosure literacy since the core natures of information also exist in disclosure. Information literacy is well defined by the American Library Association (ALA). ALA (1989) defines "information literacy" as *"the ability to recognize when information is needed and to locate, evaluate, and use effectively the needed information."*(588) Information literacy enables individuals to master information fully and make more self-directed decisions.

ALA suggests six competency standards of information literacy. The "competency standards of the ALA" might well contribute to the competency standards of disclosed information for a successful investment decision. (589)

a. Determine the extent of information needed.
b. Access the needed information effectively and efficiently.
c. Evaluate the information and its sources critically.
d. Incorporate selected information into one's knowledge base.
e. Use information effectively to accomplish a specific purpose.
f. Understand the issues surrounding the use of information. Access and use information ethically and legally.

Investor literacy

IOSCO paid attention to the concepts of investor education or financial literacy that have the potential to improve investment outcomes for investors. IOSCO (2014) identified the concept of "investor literacy" as the *"understanding ordinary investors have of market principles, instruments, organizations, and regulations."* (524)

Disclosure literacy

Researches in financial literacy have typically related individuals' knowledge of finance with financial decisions in the field of savings, retirement planning, or portfolio choice. They link financial literacy to specific types of transactions, such as saving behavior and portfolio choice.

Even though informational efficiency is essential in the capital markets, there is no literature on "disclosure literacy" because they are more focused on the literacy of credit borrowing and mortgages, and information users in the capital market are assumed to be rational with full literacy. Nevertheless, disclosure literacy deserves more attention considering a variety of evidence regarding the irrationalities.

As a subset of financial literacy, we need to develop a new concept of namely "disclosure literacy," which could be an important component of financial literacy. Considering the two dimensions of "understand and use," disclosure literacy could be defined as "the ability of how well an individual can understand and use the disclosed information." Disclosure literacy can be increasingly important in the contemporary environment of information overload, complexity. Disclosure education can also be useful in promoting informational efficiency.

Existence of disclosure literacy

The survey of SFC Hongkong in 2006 reveals that only 44.9% of IPO subscribers read the prospectus before subscription. Most of the respondents answered that they do not read the prospectus because it is too long, and they do not have time to read (82.3%), it is too legalistic (57.1%).(590) However, this survey indicates how investors use the disclosed information and the degree of disclosure overloaded but does not exactly mean disclosure literacy.

562. Measuring Literacy

Approaches

We need to measure and assess the degree of financial literacy in drafting a policy to improve investor's ability to make effective financial decisions. However, developing a standardized approach to measuring financial literacy is limited and unnecessary due to the multi-layered structure of financial literacy and the various measurement methods. Hastings, Madrian, and Skimmyhorn (2012) classified some measuring approaches into three types; self-assessment, test-based measure, outcome-based approach. The self-assessment approach is a subjective approach to measure an individual's level of financial knowledge or confidence in their financial abilities by self-scoring. The test-based measure is an objective approach to provide an accurate measure of actual financial literacy. There can be discrepancies between test results and actual outcomes. The outcomes-based approach is to measure the degree of financially sophisticated behavior (e.g., consistent refinancing a mortgage when interest rates fall).(591) Test-based and self-assessed measures are normally used in many literature. Those measures may provide implications when researchers try to measure disclosure literacy.

Self-assessment approach

In general, the self-assessment approach seems to be very useful in measuring financial literacy and analyzing behaviors. Confident respondents who are self-reporting high scores tend to record good scores on the objective measures. Such a positive relationship becomes even stronger when measured with advanced and sophisticated questions.(592, 593) The self-assessment approach often provides independent and predictive power for financial outcomes. Individuals with greater confidence were more likely to plan retirement financially and minimize fees successfully.(593)

In contrast, according to the OECD (2005, p.43~44), about 65% of US respondents answered that they are somewhat sure or very sure of their financial ability, but the scores of more confident were not much higher than those of less confident peers. About 67% of Australian respondents indicated they understand the concept of interest, but only 28% correctly answered the test.(579)

Such results suggest that survey respondents are unable to accurately judge how capable they are. Due to the unsupported over-confidence, the self-assessment approach might overestimate the level of financial literacy and thereby could result in the reduced demand for financial education. The quality of answers in the self-assessment approach also needs to be assessed.(594) Respondents can be framed by the questionnaire because they are sensitive to the format and language of questionnaire.(587, 595) With the help of the comparison between the subjective and objective approaches, individuals can learn the fact that they are often overly optimistic about how much they know, which could lead to the increased demand for financial education.

Test-based approach

It is evidenced that only 41%~46% of respondents have a financial literacy on the concept of interest compounding, inflation, and sales discounts in spite of the rapid increase in consumer borrowing in Russia.(596, 597) Only one-third of respondents knew when their debt amount doubles up.(585) Researchers may construct a financial literacy index to summarize the number of correct answers for the financial questions.(596) For example, the OECD developed a survey to capture financial literacy in a wide range of countries. The survey comprises financial literacy questionnaires that cover financial knowledge, behavior, and attitudes.(579)

Outcomes-based approach

Some researchers suggest an alternative measurement approach, namely an outcomes-based approach. They identify financially sophisticated behavior or financial mistakes and construct an index. For example, create a financial sophistication index from financial mistakes such as *"under-diversification, inertia in risk-taking, and the disposition effect in stock holding."*(591, 598, 599)

563. Determinants Of Literacy

Many researchers tried to identify factors that explain the level of individuals' financial literacy. The determinants of financial literacy might be close to the determinants of disclosure literacy. From the regulators' viewpoint, it may be helpful to identify the most vulnerable groups of financial consumers and thus concentrate their regulatory resources to improve the financial literacy of these specific groups.

General determinants

General determinants include economic upheaval, economic developments, and media.

a. Economic upheaval: Correct answers increased during the financial crisis, presumably because individuals pay more attention to finances that may affect their living conditions.(596) Information users might also present asymmetric patterns to the upturn and downturn; they can be presumed to pay more attention to disclosure in a sharp downturn.

b. Economic developments: Financial literacy is associated with economic developments. The percentage of individuals that correctly answered questions on interest compounding and inflation has a direct association with the economic development level. For instance, Netherlands 79%, US 72%, Indonesia 52%, Russia 46%, and rural India 34%.(596)

c. Media, information technology: The role, size, and number of financial media can have a serious association with overall financial literacy.

Socio-economic and demographic Determinants

Some socioeconomic and demographic variables are frequently chosen as determinants that are expected to be associated with the individuals' literacy level. Such variables include education, income, gender, age, race, marital status, region, religion, occupation, and the number of dependent family members. The below table is summarized from Potrich, Vieira, and Kirch (2015, table 2).(600)

a. Personal variables

- Gender: Men's literacy is higher than women's and increasing faster.

- Age: The middle-aged are more literate.

- Income: Low income is associated with low financial literacy levels.

- Occupation: The longer labor experienced have higher financial literacy.

- Education: The highly educated are higher in financial literacy levels.

b. Family variables

- Marital status: Singles are significantly more prone to have lower financial literacy levels than married individuals.

- Dependent: Individuals who have a child are less likely to have low financial literacy levels than those who have two or three children.

- Parental education: Individuals' financial literacy is uniformly related to parental educational levels.

Source) The above is summarized from Potrich, Vieira, and Kirch (2015)(600)

564. Consequences Of Literacy

5641. Market-level consequences

According to the panel survey of Russian individuals during the 2008 financial crisis, the high literates can contribute to a more efficient allocation of financial resources and to a more stable financial market. Rapid market growth coupled with low literacy is more dangerous.(596) Emerging market benefits more from financial education than developed markets.(601)

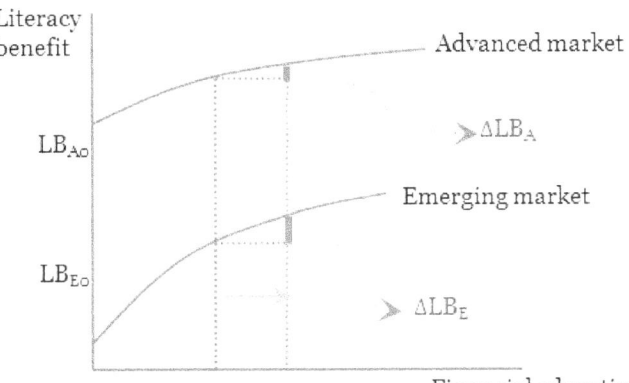

Figure 80 Market-level consequences

The marginal increase of literacy benefit from improved financial education in emerging market is greater than that in advanced market (Figure 80, $\Delta LB_A < \Delta LB_E$). Two rationale may explain why the literacy benefit of emerging markets are evidenced to be more sensitive to financial education. First, the literacy benefits from improved financial education may be increasing at a diminishing marginal rate, regardless of the capital market contexts. Second, the level of literacy benefit where there is no financial education may be higher in advanced markets owing to the widespread and already-accumulated general education. Literacy benefit curve of advanced market might be relatively flat, but the absolute level is higher (Figure 80, $LB_A > LB_E$ in all stage).

As a result, the evidence that developed markets are less sensitive to education should not lead to a quick interpretation that financial education is not essential in advanced markets. On the contrary, the above rationale may result in the opposite conclusion. The significance and impacts of financial literacy in advanced markets might be crucial. One unit of marginal increase in literacy benefit from financial education may have different meanings according to the characteristics of individual market contexts. Besides, to achieve one unit of marginal increase in literacy benefit, the required budget of financial education in advanced countries should be larger than that in emerging countries.

5641. Investor-level consequences

Many researchers tried to identify factors that explain the relationship between financial literacy and an investors' behaviors. Investors would follow the Plan-Do-See processes for a better choice and performance, to greater or lesser degrees. By the way, compared with the low literate, Hilgert (2003) finds that the highly literate are also *"more likely to engage in a wide range of recommended financial behaviors"* such as preparing an emergency.(602) As a result, the highly literate individuals are expected to behave differently from the low literate in each phase of the Plan-Do-See processes. For example, they are expected to exhibit smart behaviors, such as well-planning, well-doing, and well-seeing. Disclosure literacy matters especially in the Plan phase and See phase.

- Plan phase includes information search, strategy planning.
- Do phase includes stock picks, trading, allocation, risk management.
- See phase includes evaluation, monitoring.

1) Plan phase

Information sources

Most individuals, particularly those with low education, tend to rely on non-professional advice.(603) The low literate respondents tend to rely on informal sources of information, such as family, friends, and acquaintances, while the highly literate tend to rely on formal and expert third-party sources such as newspapers and financial magazines.(595)[387]

Advice

Insofar as financial advice or counseling is associated with substantial reductions in debt and delinquency rates, advice on information and disclosure might also be effective in improving informed decision especially to those who has the least ability to search information and assimilate the disclosed information.(604, 605)

Planning

The highly literate can be good planners who keep themselves responsive to the unexpected financial crisis and increase the possibility of wealth accumulation. It is evidenced that individuals who are likely to have a higher level of financial knowledge (e.g., older, better educated, and male) are more likely to be retirement planners.(580, 592) In the country where financial literacy has the strongest impact, the highly literate is associated with a relatively higher probability of planning.(606)

2) Do phase

Market participation

Financial literacy is significantly related to greater participation in the formal financial market but negatively related to the informal one. Financially unsophisticated individuals tend to avoid the stock market. The propensity to invest information-sensitive assets such as stocks is strongly associated with financial literacy or cognitive abilities.(595, 596, 607, 608) Financial sophistication measured by education predicts higher levels of market participation.(598) In order to enter the stock market, individuals need to spend a certain level of fixed "market participation costs" (e.g., time, money, and effort). Fixed cost rationale can explain why participation increases with wealth, education, and literacy.(609)

From this point of view, the fixed cost of market participation prevents the low literate from the market. The low literate might voluntarily choose to shun the risk of potential loss by staying out of the risky assets. Thus, a literacy enhancement policy needs to be designed as a way to motivate market participation by reducing the fixed cost of market participation. In contrast, if the fixed cost is mainly determined not by the literacy but by other factors such as wealth and income, then a literacy enhancement policy might not be an effective solution.

For investors to participate in the market, the expected benefits of market participation should exceed the expected costs that generally include fixed cost. The benefit and cost of market participation increases with literacy. Investors would not participate in the market when their literacy level is below the break-even point. By the way, the real market is not without the fixed cost of market participation that is determined by such factors as wealth, education, and literacy.

All investors face the limit of literacy of which level differs from investors to investors. Even though the illiterate might try to achieve higher net benefit of market participation without any literacy enhancement policy, the limit of literacy would frustrate his effort to achieve the BEP (right graph). The breakeven point (right graph, BEP_1) is not attainable because the limit of recognition is lower than the BEP. As a result, investors will not participate in the stock market.

By the way, a literacy enhancement policy such as financial education will reduce the fixed cost of market participation (Figure 81, $FC_1 \rightarrow FC_2$), which means that a literacy enhancement policy is a subsidy provided by a regulator to reduce the illiterate's fixed cost of market participation. Owing to the reduction in the fixed cost, the breakeven point is lowered, and the net benefit of market participation increases (Figure 82, $BEP_1 \rightarrow BEP_2$). As a result, the limit of literacy exceeds the breakeven point, and they can participate in the market.

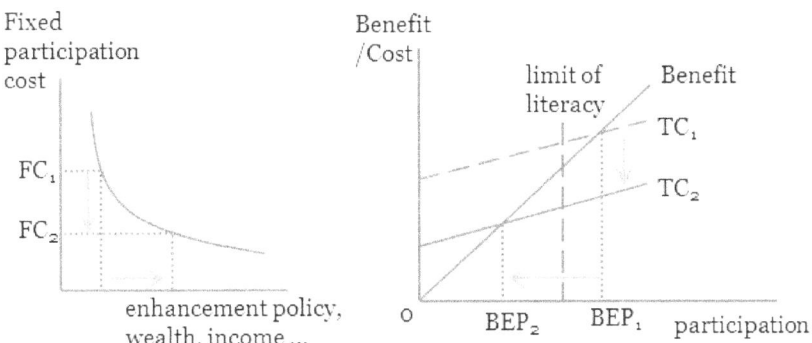

Figure 81 Fixed participation cost   Figure 82 Participation BEP

Diversification

The proxy of sophistication of literacy is associated with that of diversification. The more literate investors constitute portfolios closer to the ideal portfolio holdings, and they are better at managing portfolios.(610, 611) The financially low literates are suggested to have a less diversified portfolio.(612) On average, investors hold under-diversified portfolios. The degree of diversification increases with sophistication.(613) The degree of under-diversification is greater among less-sophisticated investors, and under-diversification is costly to most investors.(614)

3) See phase

The high literates may be assumed to be good in managing transaction costs and investment performance.

Cost

Lusardi & Tufano (2009, 2015) coin the term "the cost of ignorance" incurred by the illiteracy. The low literates are evidenced to pay a sizeable fraction of fees and charges; about a third of fees paid by the low literates are related to illiteracy. Financial literacy is evidenced to be costly.(584, 585)

Return

The low literates are less likely to participate in the stock market and, as a result, less likely to lose money because the low literates are more skeptical and thus stay out of the market to avoid loss. However, no association is evidenced between financial literacy and the size of loss. The low literates realized losses during financial crisis and did not participate during the market recovery.(615) The high literates are evidenced to generate higher expected returns.(606) A positive association is evidenced between intellectual ability and stock selection. High IQ investors have better skills in the stock selection by outperforming low IQ investors about 11% per year. (616)

Fraud/abuse monitoring

The low literates who are lack of the required financial knowledge might be susceptible to fraud and thus might be a cause of financial mistakes. Well-informed and highly literate investors may play an essential role in monitoring firms' fraud or market abuse.(596) Disclosure literacy might be an essential element in the See phase regarding fraud monitoring.

565. Education To Improve Literacy

1) Introduction

Concept

OECD (2005, p.26) defines "financial education" as *"the process by which ... investors improve their understanding of financial products and concepts and, through information, instruction and/or objective advice, develop the skills and confidence to become more aware of financial risks and opportun-*

ities, to make informed choices, to know where to go for help, and to take other effective actions to improve their financial well-being."(579) The objective of investor education to increase investor literacy is a public policy "*to improve welfare through better decision making.*"(581) Disclosure education can be considered as a subcomponent of a financial education mechanism to improve disclosure literacy.

Significance

An African proverb says, "You only see what you know." Rational investors would not be willing to invest a firm unless they understand the firm. Disclosure is to make investors fully informed. To make a sound investment decision, investors should have adequate financial and disclosure literacy to assimilate the disclosed information fully. Nowadays, investment environments require not only providing information but also educating investors. Investment education is necessary to ensure that investors fully acknowledge investment products and risks. Better informed and more educated investors are less vulnerable to the risk. Thus, improving financial and disclosure literacy contributes to the liquidity and competitiveness of capital markets. Well-designed financial education programs specifically to enhance literacy can be "*a good solution to mitigating financial problems.*"(581)

Regulators are paying attention to investment education to enhance the efficiency, stability, and competitiveness of the capital market and minimize the possibility of a financial crisis that may arise from the complexity or illiteracy. Lay investors who are less sophisticated are expected to benefit more from education.

Information overload & financial knowledge

Agnew & Szykman (2005) found that individuals with above-average financial knowledge are significantly less overload, but "*individuals with below average knowledge are simply overwhelmed by the investment decision in general.*" They provide experimental results on the relation between information overload and financial knowledge. "*Individuals with less than average knowledge were significantly more overwhelmed than those with above average knowledge. In addition, individuals presented with more choices experienced greater overload … This supports the notion that as the number of alternatives increases, participants begin to experience information overload.*" Moreover, "*the number of choices does have an impact on the reported overload for individuals with above average knowledge.*" However, individuals with below-average knowledge are overwhelmed regardless of the number of choices. Regulators should consider improving financial and disclosure education, especially for information users with below-average financial knowledge. (594) What investors need is not only an informed decision but also a wise decision. Financial education can play "*a critical role by equipping consumers with the knowledge required to make wise decisions.*" [388]

Role of disclosure education

In one sense, education to improve disclosure literacy can be meaningful under the assumption that disclosure affects the stock price; the market is not informationally perfect. If the market is informationally perfect and irrelevant to disclosure, then it is enough to promote education on how to establish an optimal portfolio. In the other sense, disclosure education will enable informed investment decision and contribute to the informationally perfect market. Disclosure education should make investors overcome the demand-side barriers and become rational investors.

2) **Educator**

Who should educate?

Fanto (1998) presented that many states in the United States have started investor education in high school and standardized materials are developed from the mid-1970s. Not only financial industry but also regulators have produced educational materials to educate students about how to invest and avoid financial fraud. Meanwhile, investor education became a commercial service provided by a private party. Regulators should ensure that pre-established standards are complied with, and encourage continued educational efforts, promote investors to use educational services, and prevent investor fraud or market abuse. Self-regulatory organizations also provide education services about fraud and market abuse.(575)

Governmental intervention; underproduction

One may raise questions on who should educate investors. Is there any need for public policy to improve financial literacy or should industry provide education services efficiently without governmental intervention? Where the externality exists, governmental role is justified to improve financial literacy through financial education. As education is a public good, industry may underproduce education services because of the inherent free-rider nature.(591)

3) **Consequences of education**

Positive consequences

Many empirical studies show the positive relationship between financial education and financial outcomes, supporting the usefulness of financial education.(606) Financial education can generate important benefits, such as greater literacy, strategic planning, savvier decisions, better management, higher participation, and greater wealth accumulation.(587) Investing in education to prevent financial illiteracy is costly but rewarding. Not only the individual economically vulnerable but also the society can stand to benefit from financial education.(606, 617) Financial education in high school is evidenced to enhance well-being. Financial knowledge is viewed as an investment in human capital. Poor literacy can lead to serious financial troubles of individual, family, and economy.(606) "*Financial education might help investors overcome suboptimal behavior,*" and "*more sophistication will bring investors closer to the economist's ideal portfolio hold-*

ings."(610) Sometimes a specific course of education program is mandated. A positive association between mandates and test scores was evidenced. (618) Financial education in personal finance for high schoolers improves financial knowledge.(619) In the United States, financial education that is mandated by the state government improved the credit scores and lowered the delinquency rates for young adults.(620)

Negative consequences

Mandell (2012) suggested that *"Unfortunately, there is little evidence that school-based financial education has had any durable effect ... At the primary level, there is some evidence that knowledge, attitudes, and even behavior appear to be most susceptible to intervention at an earlier age ... the mandated teaching of personal finance at the secondary level be strongly reconsidered..."*(621) Willis (2008) warned the meaningful possibility that *"... the pursuit of financial literacy poses costs that almost certainly swamp any benefits... financial education appears to increase confidence without improving ability, potentially leading to worse decisions."*(622)

4) Financial education policy

OECD recommendation

Financial markets are becoming more sophisticated, and investors assume more risk for their decisions while they have poor financial literacy. Financial education has been an important mechanism for investors to make efficient decisions and protect themselves from fraud.

In 2005, the OECD (2005) published the "Recommendation on Principles and Good Practices for Financial Awareness and Education" to promote financial education and awareness. Governments and institutions are recommended to implement the OECD principles and good practices for financial education and awareness. For implementation, careful considerations should be given to the issues of social, demographic, and cultural factors since those vary from country to country. To sum up, financial education should be provided in an unbiased manner as a life-time ongoing process, focusing on high priority issues depending on national circumstances. It should be designed to meet the needs and financial literacy level of target audience as a tool to promote economic growth, confidence, and stability. However, it should not be substituted for financial regulation. (579)

US: Financial literacy act

According to the "Fair and Accurate Credit Transactions Act of 2003" (abbreviated FACTA) that is the United State federal law, the "Financial Literacy and Education Commission" shall serve to improve financial literacy and education by developing a nation-wide strategy. The Commission shall take such actions to streamline, improve, or augment financial literacy and education programs.

5) How to Educate

One may say that financial education to improve financial literacy is an important priority, but we should keep in mind that it might take a longer time to benefit from financial education.

Opportunity

IOSCO (2014) suggested that providing investor education and financial literacy programs is compelling. To regulators, investor education program can be viewed as an additional and complementary tool available.(524) Improved disclosure literacy might lead to an increased investor confidence. As a result, a great many investors will participate in the markets and promote greater market efficiency.

Limitations

IOSCO (2001, 2014) warned that the investor education program does not guarantee that investors will make better decisions. It is just supporting information users and changing investment behavior. Investor education cannot replace but assist regulators in investor protection. Investors can better understand the regulator's role and protect themselves against fraud with the tool of education.(524, 623)

Challenges

The regulator should be ready to identify and utilize the effective methods of delivering investor education with standardized and customized materials that is no easy matter. Regulators must realize the one-size-fits-all program might be useless.(594) Financial education does not serve a single purpose. Education programs may be divided into many sub-categories, depending on the incentives and purposes of the organization.(575) No one would expect that a specific program will monotonously change investor's behavior. The fact that there are substantial differences among individual behavior implies that one-size-fits-all programs will not be enough, and thus educators need to prepare customized education programs targeting specific groups.(587, 617)

Evaluation

Fox, Bartholomae, and Lee (2005) suggest that *"Meaningful program evaluation is an essential and integrated element of successful programs."* Without careful evaluation, it is not guaranteed that financial education improves financial literacy. Thus, financial education should be implemented with evaluation as a necessary component, and the evaluation framework should provide flexibility.(624, 625) Researchers recommend educators to start financial education at a younger age because they are vulnerable to financial mistakes that can be lasting for life.(625) Education mechanisms should vary according to the types of information and investors to be educated.(623) With limited resources, regulators need to target investors who lack sophistication. Regulators should process in partnerships with SRO and industry to maintain investor confidence in the program.(623) Educators should provide investors with the knowledge of valuation, information search, and analysis, including how to interpret opportunistic disclosure and overcome psychological mistakes.(575) A sporadic or short-term education does not seem to be effective in improving investors' literacy or decision-making ability.

Investment as an education

Experience is the best and toughest teacher. Lessons learned from experience are the most lasting. Insofar as an investor wants to learn, not regulators but the market might be the best teacher. It is costly but also rewarding. Financial literacy affects market participation, information analysis, return, and diversification. Conversely, market participation can lead to improved financial literacy due to the learning-by-doing effect. Thus, investors with long-term investment experience are quite expected to have higher financial literacy.

When it comes to adults, investment should be a life-long process of decision and management. Thus, financial education should also be planned with a long-term perspective. *"Individuals with low financial literacy might be aware of their weakness and stay out of risky markets to avoid investment mistakes."*(615) Investors have an incentive to enhance their literacy, and thus present market participants have higher levels of financial literacy. Individuals who are instinctively indifferent to investment might have taken education programs reluctantly, which leads to lower outcome of financial education.(598)

Expert's advice

Expert's advice can be illustrated as an alternative to financial education for the low literates. However, whether financial literacy and financial advice are complements or substitutes is a matter of empirical question. (626) Expert advisors often induce individuals to make the worse decision such as shifting them to high-cost retirement funds. *"Bad financial decision-making can be due to a combination of lack of financial literacy and conflicted advice from advisers who know that many people are insensitive to differences in fees."*(627) Regarding disclosure literacy education, investors need to be educated how to filter the expert filters.

BIBLIOGRAPHY

1. Bachelier L, translated;, Davis M, Etheridge A. Louis Bachelier's Theory of Speculation: The Origins of Modern Finance: Princeton University Press; 2011. 192 p.
2. Fama EF. Random Walks in Stock Market Prices. University of Chicago Selected Papers. 1965;No.16.
3. Kratz OS. Frontier emerging equity markets securities price behavior and valuation: Springer Science & Business Media; 1999.
4. Shleifer A. Inefficient markets: An introduction to behavioral finance: Oxford university press; 2000.
5. Fama EF. Efficient capital markets: A review of theory and empirical work. The journal of Finance. 1970;25(2):383-417.
6. Fama EF, Fisher L, Jensen MC, Roll R. The adjustment of stock prices to new information. International economic review. 1969;10(1):1-21.
7. Jensen MC. The performance of mutual funds in the period 1945–1964. The Journal of finance. 1968;23(2):389-416.
8. Finnerty JE. Insiders and market efficiency. The Journal of Finance. 1976;31(4):1141-8.
9. Grossman SJ, Stiglitz JE. On the impossibility of informationally efficient markets. The American economic review. 1980:393-408.
10. Arrow KJ. Uncertainty and the welfare economics of medical care. The American economic review. 1963:941-73.
11. Akerlof GA. The market for" lemons": Quality uncertainty and the market mechanism. The quarterly journal of economics. 1970:488-500.
12. Bagehot W. The only game in town. Financial Analysts Journal. 1971;27(2):12-4.
13. Glosten LR, Milgrom PR. Bid, ask and transaction prices in a specialist market with heterogeneously informed traders. Journal of financial economics. 1985;14(1):71-100.
14. Copeland TE, Galai D. Information effects on the bid-ask spread. the Journal of Finance. 1983;38(5):1457-69.
15. Kyle AS. Continuous auctions and insider trading. Econometrica: Journal of the Econometric Society. 1985:1315-35.
16. Stoll HR. Inferring the components of the bid-ask spread: theory and empirical tests. The Journal of Finance. 1989;44(1):115-34.
17. Ferrell A. The case for mandatory disclosure in securities regulation around the world. Harvard Law and Economics Discussion Paper. 2004(492).
18. Braendle UC, Noll J. A fig leaf for the naked corporation. Journal of Management & Governance. 2005;9(1):79-99.
19. Stiglitz JE. The theory of" screening," education, and the distribution of income. The American Economic Review. 1975:283-300.
20. Jaffee DM, Russell T. Imperfect information, uncertainty, and credit rationing. The Quarterly Journal of Economics. 1976:651-66.
21. Stiglitz JE, Weiss A. Credit rationing in markets with imperfect information. The American economic review. 1981:393-410.
22. Carter R, Manaster S. Initial public offerings and underwriter reputation. The Journal of Finance. 1990;45(4):1045-67.

23. Beatty R. Auditor Reputation and the Pricing of Initial Public Offerings: Center for Research in Security Prices, Graduate School of Business, University of Chicago; 1989.
24. Ederington LH, Dewally M. A Comparison of Reputation, Certification, Warranties, and Information Disclosure as Remedies for Information Asymmetries: Lessons from the On-line Comic Book Market. Available at SSRN: http://ssrncom/abstract=351261 or http://dxdoiorg/102139/ssrn351261. 2002.
25. Diamond DW. Reputation acquisition in debt markets. The journal of political economy. 1989:828-62.
26. Huddart S, Hughes JS, Brunnermeier M. Disclosure requirements and stock exchange listing choice in an international context. Journal of Accounting and Economics. 1999;26(1):237-69.
27. Smith A. The theory of moral sentiments: Penguin; 1759.
28. Adam S. The wealth of nations: Aegitas; 1776.
29. De Geest G. The Death of Caveat Emptor. 2014.
30. Spence M. Job market signaling. The quarterly journal of Economics. 1973:355-74.
31. Leland HE, Pyle DH. Informational asymmetries, financial structure, and financial intermediation. The journal of Finance. 1977;32(2):371-87.
32. Ross SA. The determination of financial structure: the incentive-signalling approach. The Bell Journal of Economics. 1977:23-40.
33. Grossman SJ. The informational role of warranties and private disclosure about product quality. Journal of law and economics. 1981:461-83.
34. Milgrom PR. Good news and bad news: Representation theorems and applications. The Bell Journal of Economics. 1981:380-91.
35. Ross SA. Disclosure regulation in financial markets: Implications of modern finance theory and signaling theory. Issues in financial regulation. 1979;5:177-202.
36. Sletten E. The effect of stock price on discretionary disclosure. Review of Accounting Studies. 2012;17(1):96-133.
37. Lev B, Penman SH. Voluntary forecast disclosure, nondisclosure, and stock prices. Journal of Accounting Research. 1990:49-76.
38. Farrell J. Cheap talk, coordination, and entry. The RAND Journal of Economics. 1987;18(1):34-9.
39. Ajinkya BB, Gift MJ. Corporate managers' earnings forecasts and symmetrical adjustments of market expectations. Journal of Accounting Research. 1984:425-44.
40. Pownall G, Wasley C, Waymire G. The stock price effects of alternative types of management earnings forecasts. Accounting Review. 1993:896-912.
41. Kothari SP, Shu S, Wysocki PD. Do managers withhold bad news? Journal of Accounting Research. 2009;47(1):241-76.
42. Chambers AE, Penman SH. Timeliness of reporting and the stock price reaction to earnings announcements. Journal of accounting research. 1984:21-47.
43. Patell JM. Corporate Forecasts of Earnings Per Share and Stock Price Behavior: Empirical Test. Journal of Accounting Research. 1976;14(2):246-76.
44. Penman SH. An empirical investigation of the voluntary disclosure of corporate earnings forecasts. Journal of accounting research. 1980:132-60.
45. Waymire G. Additional evidence on the information content of management earnings forecasts. Journal of Accounting Research. 1984:703-18.
46. Skinner DJ. Why firms voluntarily disclose bad news. Journal of accounting research. 1994:38-60.
47. Arbel A, Carvell S, Strebel P. Giraffes, institutions and neglected firms. Financial Analysts Journal. 1983;39(3):57-63.
48. Merton RC. A simple model of capital market equilibrium with incomplete information. The journal of finance. 1987;42(3):483-510.
49. Coffee Jr JC. Market failure and the economic case for a mandatory disclosure system. Virginia Law Review. 1984:717-53.
50. Diamond DW. Optimal release of information by firms. The Journal of Finance. 1985;40(4):1071-94.

51. Verrecchia RE. Discretionary disclosure. Journal of accounting and economics. 1983;5:179-94.
52. Mingers JC. Information and meaning: foundations for an intersubjective account. Information Systems Journal. 1995;5(4):285-306.
53. Davis GB, Olson MH. Management information systems: conceptual foundations, structure, and development: McGraw-Hill; 1985.
54. Ackoff RL. From data to wisdom: Presidential address to ISGSR, June 1988. Journal of applied systems analysis. 1989;16(1):3-9.
55. Hirshleifer J. Where are we in the theory of information? The American Economic Review. 1973:31-9.
56. Kothari V. Securitization: The Financial Instrument of the Future: Wiley 1 edition; 2006.
57. Healy PM, Palepu KG. Information asymmetry, corporate disclosure, and the capital markets: A review of the empirical disclosure literature. Journal of accounting and economics. 2001;31(1):405-40.
58. Jevons WS. The theory of political economy: Macmillan and Company; 1879.
59. Womack R. Information intermediaries and optimal information distribution. Library & Information Science Research. 2002;24(2):129-55.
60. Blakeley N, Lewis G, Mills D. The Economics of Knowledge: What Makes Ideas Special for Economic Growth? : New Zealand Policy Perspectives Paper 05/05; 2005. Available from: http://www.treasury.govt.nz/publications/research-policy/ppp/2005/05-05.
61. Government N. Data and information quality management guide. 2018.
62. Hutton AP, Miller GS, Skinner DJ. The role of supplementary statements with management earnings forecasts. Journal of Accounting Research. 2003;41(5):867-90.
63. Hoskin RE, Hughes JS, Ricks WE. Evidence on the incremental information content of additional firm disclosures made concurrently with earnings. Journal of Accounting Research. 1986:1-32.
64. Han JC, Wild JJ. Stock price behavior associated with managers' earnings and revenue forecasts. Journal of Accounting Research. 1991:79-95.
65. Burk CF. InfoMap : a complete guide to discovering corporate information resources / Cornelius F. Burk, Jr. & Forest W. Horton, Jr. Horton FW, editor. Englewood Cliffs, N.J: Prentice-Hall; 1988.
66. Meyer HW. The nature of information, and the effective use of information in rural development. Information research. 2005;10(2):10-2.
67. OTAC U. Computer-based national information systems : technology and public policy issues: DIANE Publishing; 1981.
68. Birchler U, Bütler M. Information economics: Routledge; 2007.
69. Rocha LM, Schnell S. The Nature of Information(Luis). Lecture notes for I101–Introduction to Informatics School of Informatics, Indiana University. 2005.
70. Dalley PJ. The Use and Misuse of Disclosure as a Regulatory System. Fla St UL Rev. 2006;34:1089.
71. Kenneth A. information as an economic commodity. 2012.
72. Petersen MA. Information: Hard and soft. 2004.
73. Meek GK, Roberts CB, Gray SJ. Factors influencing voluntary annual report disclosures by US, UK and continental European multinational corporations. Journal of international business studies. 1995:555-72.
74. FASB. Improving Business Reporting: Insights into Enhancing Voluntary Disclosures 2001. Available from: http://www.fasb.org/.
75. Kanodia C. Effects of shareholder information on corporate decisions and capital market equilibrium. Econometrica: Journal of the Econometric Society. 1980:923-53.
76. Knight Frank H. Risk, uncertainty and profit. 1921.
77. Keynes JM. The general theory of employment, investment, and money. 1936.
78. Ibbotson RG, Sinquefield RA. Stocks, bonds, bills, and inflation: year-by-year historical returns (1926-1974). The Journal of Business. 1976;49(1):11-47.
79. Graham JR, Harvey CR. The theory and practice of corporate finance: Evidence from the field. Journal of financial economics. 2001;60(2):187-243.

80. Fama EF, French KR. The cross-section of expected stock returns. the Journal of Finance. 1992;47(2):427-65.
81. Banz RW. The relationship between return and market value of common stocks. Journal of financial economics. 1981;9(1):3-18.
82. Chan LK, Hamao Y, Lakonishok J. Fundamentals and stock returns in Japan. The Journal of Finance. 1991;46(5):1739-64.
83. Barry PJ. Capital asset pricing and farm real estate. American Journal of Agricultural Economics. 1980;62(3):549-53.
84. Chong J, Jin Y, Phillips M. The Entrepreneur's Cost of Capital: Incorporating Downside Risk in the Buildup Method. MacroRisk Analytics Working Paper Series, 2013.
85. Roy AD. Safety first and the holding of assets. Econometrica: Journal of the Econometric Society. 1952:431-49.
86. Markowitz HM. Foundations of portfolio theory. The journal of finance. 1991;46(2):469-77.
87. Estrada J. The cost of equity in emerging markets: a downside risk approach. 2000.
88. Estrada J. The cost of equity in emerging markets: A downside risk approach (II). Emerging Markets Quarterly. 2001;5:63-72.
89. Ang A, Chen J, Xing Y. Downside risk. Review of Financial Studies. 2006;19(4):1191-239.
90. Ross SA. The arbitrage theory of capital asset pricing. Journal of economic theory. 1976;13(3):341-60.
91. Roll R, Ross SA. An empirical investigation of the arbitrage pricing theory. The Journal of Finance. 1980;35(5):1073-103.
92. Chen N-F, Roll R, Ross SA. Economic forces and the stock market. Journal of business. 1986:383-403.
93. Committee J. Improving Business Reporting-A Customer Focus: Meeting the Information Needs of Investors and Creditors. Comprehensive Report of the Special Committee on Financial Reporting, American Institute of Certified Public Accountants; 1994.
94. Gigler F. Self-enforcing voluntary disclosures. Journal of Accounting Research. 1994:224-40.
95. Leuz C. Proprietary versus non-proprietary disclosures: Evidence from Germany. Available at SSRN 99861. 2003.
96. Blackwell D, editor Comparison of Experiments. Proceedings of the Second Berkeley Symposium on Mathematical Statistics and Probability; 1951 1951; Berkeley, Calif.: University of California Press.
97. Hayes RM, Lundholm R. Segment reporting to the capital market in the presence of a competitor. Journal of Accounting Research. 1996:261-79.
98. Berger PG, Hann R. Segment profitability and the proprietary costs of disclosure. SSRN Electronic Paper Collection. 2003.
99. Berger PG, Hann RN. Segment profitability and the proprietary and agency costs of disclosure. The Accounting Review. 2007;82(4):869-906.
100. Boone AL, Floros IV, Johnson SA. Redacting proprietary information at the initial public offering. Journal of Financial Economics. 2016;120(1):102-23.
101. Koh P-S, Reeb D. R&D Disclosures. Unpublished working paper, National University of Singapore. 2014.
102. Tang V. Proprietary costs and privately held firms' financing choice between public offerings and private placements. Working Paper, 2009.
103. Guttentag M. Accuracy Enhancement, Agency Costs, and Disclosure Regulation. Review of Law & Economics. 2007;3(2):611-41.
104. Mahoney PG. Mandatory disclosure as a solution to agency problems. The University of Chicago Law Review. 1995:1047-112.
105. Botosan CA. Disclosure level and the cost of equity capital. Accounting review. 1997:323-49.
106. Botosan CA. Disclosure and the cost of capital: what do we know? Accounting and business research. 2006;36(sup1):31-40.
107. Damodaran A. The Value of Transparency and the Cost of Complexity. Stern School of Business. 2006.
108. Graham JR, Harvey CR, Rajgopal S. The economic implications of corporate financial report-

ing. Journal of accounting and economics. 2005;40(1):3-73.
109. Healy PM, Hutton AP, Palepu KG. Stock performance and intermediation changes surrounding sustained increases in disclosure. Contemporary accounting research. 1999;16(3):485-520.
110. Botosan CA, Plumlee M. Disclosure level and expected cost of equity capital: An examination of analysts' rankings of corporate disclosure and alternative methods of estimating expected cost of equity capital. Social Science Research Network Electronic Paper Collection, http://papers ssrn com/paper taf. 2000.
111. Jog V, McConomy BJ. Voluntary disclosure of management earnings forecasts in IPO prospectuses. Journal of Business Finance & Accounting. 2003;30(1-2):125-68.
112. Schrand CM, Verrecchia RE. Information disclosure and adverse selection explanations for IPO underpricing. Available at SSRN 316824. 2005.
113. Easley D, Hvidkjaer S, O'hara M. Is information risk a determinant of asset returns? The journal of finance. 2002;57(5):2185-221.
114. Myers SC, Majluf NS. Corporate financing and investment decisions when firms have information that investors do not have. Journal of financial economics. 1984;13(2):187-221.
115. Milgrom PR, Weber RJ. A theory of auctions and competitive bidding. Econometrica: Journal of the Econometric Society. 1982:1089-122.
116. Hughes JS, Liu J, Liu J. Information asymmetry, diversification, and cost of capital. The Accounting Review. 2007;82(3):705-29.
117. Sengupta P. Corporate disclosure quality and the cost of debt. Accounting review. 1998:459-74.
118. Ziebart DA, Reiter SA. Bond ratings, bond yields and financial information. Contemporary Accounting Research. 1992;9(1):252-82.
119. Miller DP, Puthenpurackal JJ. The costs, wealth effects, and determinants of international capital raising: Evidence from public Yankee bonds. Journal of Financial Intermediation. 2002;11(4):455-85.
120. Glennerster R, Shin Y. Does Transparency Pay? IMF Staff Papers. 2008:183-209.
121. Choi FD. Financial disclosure and entry to the European capital market. Journal of Accounting Research. 1973:159-75.
122. Lang M, Lundholm R. Cross-sectional determinants of analyst ratings of corporate disclosures. Journal of accounting research. 1993:246-71.
123. Berglöf E, Pajuste A. What do firms disclose and why? Enforcing corporate governance and transparency in Central and Eastern Europe. Oxford Review of Economic Policy. 2005;21(2):178-97.
124. Gao P. Disclosure quality, cost of capital, and investor welfare. The Accounting Review. 2010;85(1):1-29.
125. Diamond DW, Verrecchia RE. Disclosure, liquidity, and the cost of capital. The journal of Finance. 1991;46(4):1325-59.
126. Demsetz H. The cost of transacting. The quarterly journal of economics. 1968:33-53.
127. Amihud Y, Mendelson H. Asset pricing and the bid-ask spread. Journal of financial Economics. 1986;17(2):223-49.
128. Tinic SM. The economics of liquidity services. The Quarterly Journal of Economics. 1972:79-93.
129. Amihud Y, Mendelson H. Dealership market: Market-making with inventory. Journal of Financial Economics. 1980;8(1):31-53.
130. Ho T, Stoll HR. Optimal dealer pricing under transactions and return uncertainty. Journal of Financial economics. 1981;9(1):47-73.
131. Easley D, O'hara M. Price, trade size, and information in securities markets. Journal of Financial economics. 1987;19(1):69-90.
132. George TJ, Kaul G, Nimalendran M. Estimation of the bid-ask spread and its components: A new approach. Review of Financial Studies. 1991;4(4):623-56.
133. Welker M. Disclosure Policy, Information Asymmetry, and Liquidity in Equity Markets. Contemporary accounting research. 1995;11(2):801-27.
134. Heflin F, Shaw KW, Wild JJ. Disclosure quality and market liquidity. Available at SSRN 251849.

2000.

135. Leuz C, Verrecchia RE. The economic consequences of increased disclosure. Journal of accounting research. 2000:91-124.

136. Coller M, Yohn TL. Management forecasts and information asymmetry: An examination of bid-ask spreads. Journal of accounting research. 1997;35(2):181-91.

137. Coval JD, Moskowitz TJ. Home bias at home: Local equity preference in domestic portfolios. The Journal of Finance. 1999;54(6):2045-73.

138. Huberman G. Familiarity breeds investment. Review of financial Studies. 2001;14(3):659-80.

139. Easley D, O'hara M. Information and the cost of capital. The journal of finance. 2004;59(4):1553-83.

140. Rock K. Why new issues are underpriced. Journal of financial economics. 1985;15(1):187-212.

141. Lambert R, Leuz C, Verrecchia RE. Accounting information, disclosure, and the cost of capital. Journal of Accounting Research. 2007;45(2):385-420.

142. Bowman RG. The theoretical relationship between systematic risk and financial (accounting) variables. The Journal of Finance. 1979;34(3):617-30.

143. Jorgensen BN, Kirschenheiter MT. Disclosure, betas and information quality. Unpublished, available in URL: http://www Olinwustl edu/fs/acadseminars/down-load pdf. 2003.

144. Barry CB, Brown SJ. Differential information and security market equilibrium. Journal of Financial and Quantitative Analysis. 1985;20(04):407-22.

145. Klein RW, Bawa VS. The effect of estimation risk on optimal portfolio choice. Journal of Financial Economics. 1976;3(3):215-31.

146. Kalymon BA. Estimation risk in the portfolio selection model. Journal of Financial and Quantitative Analysis. 1971;6(1):559-82.

147. Coles JL, Loewenstein U. Equilibrium pricing and portfolio composition in the presence of uncertain parameters. Journal of Financial Economics. 1988;22(2):279-303.

148. Coles JL, Loewenstein U, Suay J. On equilibrium pricing under parameter uncertainty. Journal of Financial and Quantitative Analysis. 1995;30(03):347-64.

149. Clarkson PM, Thompson R. Empirical estimates of beta when investors face estimation risk. The Journal of Finance. 1990;45(2):431-53.

150. Barry CB. Portfolio analysis under uncertain means, variances, and covariances. The Journal of Finance. 1974;29(2):515-22.

151. Frost PA, Savarino JE. An empirical Bayes approach to efficient portfolio selection. Journal of Financial and Quantitative Analysis. 1986;21(3):293-305.

152. Brown S. The effect of estimation risk on capital market equilibrium. Journal of Financial and Quantitative Analysis. 1979;14(02):215-20.

153. Handa P, Linn SC. Arbitrage pricing with estimation risk. Journal of Financial and Quantitative Analysis. 1993;28(01):81-100.

154. Reinganum MR, Smith JK. Investor preference for large firms: new evidence on economies of size. The Journal of Industrial Economics. 1983:213-27.

155. Clarkson P, Guedes J, Thompson R. On the diversification, observability, and measurement of estimation risk. Journal of Financial and Quantitative Analysis. 1996;31(01):69-84.

156. Beyer A, Guttman I. Voluntary disclosure, disclosure bias and real effects. Journal of Accounting Research. 2010.

157. Fishman MJ, Hagerty KM. Disclosure decisions by firms and the competition for price efficiency. The Journal of Finance. 1989;44(3):633-46.

158. Kanodia C, Mukherji A, Sapra H, Venugopalan R. Hedge disclosures, future prices, and production distortions. Journal of Accounting Research. 2000:53-82.

159. Verdi RS. Financial reporting quality and investment efficiency. 2006.

160. Dye RA. Mandatory versus voluntary disclosures: The cases of financial and real externalities. Accounting Review. 1990:1-24.

161. Dye RA, Sridhar SS. The allocational effects of the precision of accounting estimates. Journal of Accounting Research. 2007;45(4):731-69.

162. Dontoh A. Voluntary disclosure. Journal of Accounting, Auditing & Finance.

1989;4(4):480-511.
163. Fombrun C, Shanley M. What's in a name? Reputation building and corporate strategy. Academy of management Journal. 1990;33(2):233-58.
164. Espinosa Blasco M, Trombetta M. The Reputational Consequences of Disclosure. 2004.
165. Cao Y, Myers JN, Myers LA, Omer TC. Company reputation and the cost of equity capital. Review of Accounting Studies. 2015;20(1):42-81.
166. Wurgler J. Financial markets and the allocation of capital. Journal of financial economics. 2000;58(1):187-214.
167. Bloomfield T, Leftwich R, Long JB. Portfolio strategies and performance. Journal of Financial Economics. 1977;5(2):201-18.
168. Campbell JY, Lettau M, Malkiel BG, Xu Y. Have individual stocks become more volatile? An empirical exploration of idiosyncratic risk. The Journal of Finance. 2001;56(1):1-43.
169. Lintner J. Security prices, risk, and maximal gains from diversification. The journal of finance. 1965;20(4):587-615.
170. Jin L, Myers SC. R 2 around the world: New theory and new tests. Journal of financial Economics. 2006;79(2):257-92.
171. Richardson M, Smith T. A test for multivariate normality in stock returns. Journal of Business. 1993:295-321.
172. Sheikh AZ, Qiao H. Non-Normality of Market Returns: A Framework for Asset Allocation Decision Making. Journal of Alternative Investments. 2010;12(3):8-35.
173. Regulation) CCoCM. The Competitive Position of the U.S. Public Equity Market 2007. Available from: http://capmktsreg.org/press/the-competitiveness-position-of-the-u-s-public-equity-market/.
174. Leuz C, Wysocki PD. The Economics of Disclosure and Financial Reporting Regulation: Evidence and Suggestions for Future Research. Preliminary. 2015.
175. Prencipe A. Proprietary costs and voluntary segment disclosure: evidence from Italian listed companies. SDA BOCCONI, Research Division Working Paper. 2002(02-75).
176. Sanders J, Sherman A, Clark S. New segment reporting: Is it working? Strategic Finance. 1999;81(6):35.
177. Coates JC. The goals and promise of the Sarbanes-Oxley Act. The Journal of Economic Perspectives. 2007:91-116.
178. US.SEC. Proposed Rule: Form 8-K Disclosure of Certain Management Transactions 2002. Available from: http://www.sec.gov/rules/proposed/33-8090.htm.
179. Coates JC, Srinivasan S. SOX after ten years: A multidisciplinary review. Accounting Horizons. 2014;28(3):627-71.
180. EU. Guidelines on materiality, proprietary and confidentiality and on disclosure frequency. 2013.
181. Dye RA. Disclosure of nonproprietary information. Journal of accounting research. 1985:123-45.
182. Scott TW. Incentives and disincentives for financial disclosure: Voluntary disclosure of defined benefit pension plan information by Canadian firms. Accounting Review. 1994:26-43.
183. Porter ME. Creating and Sustaining Superior Performance. New York, NY: Free press; 1985.
184. Almazan A, Suarez J, Titman S. Stakeholder, transparency and capital structure. National Bureau of Economic Research, 2003.
185. GUO RJ, Lev B, Zhou N. Competitive costs of disclosure by biotech IPOs. Journal of Accounting Research. 2004;42(2):319-55.
186. Nichols C, editor Proprietary costs and other determinants of nonfinancial disclosures2010: AAA.
187. Clinch G, Verrecchia RE. Competitive disadvantage and discretionary disclosure in industries. Australian Journal of Management. 1997;22(2):125-37.
188. Ellis JA, Fee CE, Thomas SE. Proprietary costs and the disclosure of information about customers. Journal of Accounting Research. 2012;50(3):685-727.
189. Darrough MN, Stoughton NM. Financial disclosure policy in an entry game. Journal of Accounting and Economics. 1990;12(1-3):219-43.

190. Clarkson PM, Kao JL, Richardson GD. The voluntary inclusion of forecasts in the MD&A section of annual reports. Contemporary Accounting Research. 1994;11(1):423.
191. Prencipe A. Proprietary costs and determinants of voluntary segment disclosure: evidence from Italian listed companies. European Accounting Review. 2004;13(2):319-40.
192. Verrecchia RE, Weber J. Redacted disclosure. Journal of Accounting Research. 2006;44(4):791-814.
193. Bradbury ME. Voluntary disclosure of financial segment data: New Zealand evidence. Accounting & Finance. 1992;32(1):15-26.
194. Mitchell JD, Chia CW, Loh AS. Voluntary disclosure of segment information: Further Australian evidence. Accounting & finance. 1995;35(2):1-16.
195. Porter ME. How competitive forces shape strategy. 1979.
196. Cohen DA. Financial reporting quality and proprietary costs. Available at SSRN 592001. 2002.
197. Dedman E, Lennox C. Perceived competition, profitability and the withholding of information about sales and the cost of sales. Journal of Accounting and Economics. 2009;48(2):210-30.
198. Harris MS. The association between competition and managers' business segment reporting decisions. Journal of Accounting Research. 1998:111-28.
199. Bamber LS, Cheon YS. Discretionary management earnings forecast disclosures: Antecedents and outcomes associated with forecast venue and forecast specificity choices. Journal of Accounting Research. 1998:167-90.
200. Shin Y-C. The effect of product market competition on corporate voluntary disclosure decisions. Available at SSRN 338361. 2002.
201. Kirby AJ. Trade associations as information exchange mechanisms. The RAND Journal of Economics. 1988:138-46.
202. Ettredge M, Kwon S, Smith D. Competitive harm and managers' attitude towards SFAS No. 131. Journal of Accounting, Auditing, and Finance. 2002;17(2):93-109.
203. IOSCO. Principles for Ongoing Disclosure and Material Development Reporting by Listed Entities 2002. Available from: https://www.iosco.org/library/pubdocs/pdf/IOSCOPD132.pdf.
204. SEC US. Report on Review of Disclosure Requirements in Regulation S-K 2013. Available from: https://www.sec.gov/news/studies/2013/reg-sk-disclosure-requirements-review.pdf.
205. Lobo GJ, Kwon SS, Ndubizu GA. The impact of SFAS No. 14 segment information on price variability and earnings forecast accuracy. Journal of Business Finance & Accounting. 1998;25(7‐8):969-85.
206. Ettredge M, Kwon SY, Smith DB. The effect of SFAS No. 131 on numbers of reported business segments. Available at SSRN 208549. 2000.
207. Berger PG, Hann R. The impact of SFAS No. 131 on information and monitoring. Journal of Accounting Research. 2003;41(2):163-223.
208. Herrmann D, Thomas WB. An analysis of segment disclosures under SFAS No. 131 and SFAS No. 14. Accounting Horizons. 2000;14(3):287-302.
209. Kinney WR. Predicting earnings: entity versus subentity data. Journal of Accounting Research. 1971:127-36.
210. Collins DW. Predicting earnings with sub-entity data: Some further evidence. Journal of Accounting Research. 1976:163-77.
211. Balakrishnan R, Harris TS, Sen PK. The predictive ability of geographic segment disclosures. Journal of Accounting research. 1990:305-25.
212. Francis J, Philbrick D, Schipper K. Shareholder litigation and corporate disclosures. Journal of accounting research. 1994:137-64.
213. Clearinghouse TSCA. Securities Class Action Filings 2014 Year in Review 2014.
214. Noe CF. Voluntary disclosures and insider transactions. Journal of Accounting and Economics. 1999;27(3):305-26.
215. Amel-Zadeh A, Lev B, Meeks G. The Benefits and Costs of Managerial Earnings Forecasts in Mergers and Acquisitions. Available at SSRN 2198958. 2013.
216. Nelson KK, Pritchard AC, editors. Litigation risk and voluntary disclosure: The use of meaningful cautionary language. 2nd Annual Conference on Empirical Legal Studies Paper; 2007.
217. Rogers JL, Van Buskirk A. Shareholder litigation and changes in disclosure behavior. Journal

of Accounting and Economics. 2009;47(1):136-56.
218. Butler HN, Ribstein LE. The Sarbanes–Oxley Debacle: What We've Learned. How to Fix ItAEI Press, Washington, DC. 2006.
219. Miller GS, Piotroski JD. Forward-looking earnings statements: Determinants and market response. Available at SSRN 238593. 2000.
220. Johnson MF, Kasznik R, Nelson KK. The impact of securities litigation reform on the disclosure of forward-looking information by high technology firms. Journal of Accounting Research. 2001:297-327.
221. Field L, Lowry M, Shu S. Does disclosure deter or trigger litigation? Journal of Accounting and Economics. 2005;39(3):487-507.
222. Waymire G. Earnings volatility and voluntary management forecast disclosure. Journal of Accounting Research. 1985:268-95.
223. Kasznik R, Lev B. To warn or not to warn: Management disclosures in the face of an earnings surprise. Accounting review. 1995:113-34.
224. Skinner DJ. Earnings disclosures and stockholder lawsuits. Journal of Accounting and Economics. 1997;23(3):249-82.
225. Trueman B. Managerial Disclosures and Shareholder Litigation. Review of Accounting Studies. 1997;2(2):181-99.
226. Watts RL, Zimmerman JL. Towards a positive theory of the determination of accounting standards. Accounting review. 1978:112-34.
227. Watts RL, Zimmerman JL. Positive accounting theory: a ten year perspective. Accounting review. 1990:131-56.
228. Raffournier B. The determinants of voluntary financial disclosure by Swiss listed companies. European accounting review. 1995;4(2):261-80.
229. Klumpes PJ. Incentives and disincentives for voluntary disclosure by pension funds: international evidence. Accounting and Business Research. 2000;30(4):287-98.
230. Herrmann D, Thomas WB. Geographic segment disclosures: theories, findings, and implications. The International Journal of Accounting. 1997;32(4):487-501.
231. Wagenhofer A. Voluntary disclosure with a strategic opponent. Journal of Accounting and Economics. 1990;12(4):341-63.
232. Buzby SL. Company size, listed versus unlisted stocks, and the extent of financial disclosure. Journal of accounting research. 1975:16-37.
233. Cerf AR. Corporate reporting and investment decisions: Public Accounting Research Program, Institute of Business and Economic Research, University of California; 1961.
234. Shehata NF. Theories and determinants of voluntary disclosure. Accounting and Finance Research (AFR). 2014;3(1).
235. Cooke TE. Voluntary corporate disclosure by Swedish companies. Journal of International Financial Management & Accounting. 1989;1(2):171-95.
236. Singhvi SS, Desai HB. An empirical analysis of the quality of corporate financial disclosure. Accounting review. 1971:129-38.
237. Ahmed K, Courtis JK. Associations between corporate characteristics and disclosure levels in annual reports: a meta-analysis. The British Accounting Review. 1999;31(1):35-61.
238. Wallace RO, Naser K. Firm-specific determinants of the comprehensiveness of mandatory disclosure in the corporate annual reports of firms listed on the stock exchange of Hong Kong. Journal of Accounting and Public policy. 1995;14(4):311-68.
239. Ng EJ, Koh HC. An agency theory and probit analytic approach to corporate non-mandatory disclosure compliance. Asia-Pacific Journal of Accounting. 1994;1(1):29-44.
240. Craswell AT, Taylor SL. Discretionary disclosure of reserves by oil and gas companies: an economic analysis. Journal of Business Finance & Accounting. 1992;19(2):295-308.
241. Depoers F. A cost benefit study of voluntary disclosure: Some empirical evidence from French listed companies. European Accounting Review. 2000;9(2):245-63.
242. Hossain M, Perera MHB, Rahman AR. Voluntary disclosure in the annual reports of New Zealand companies. Journal of International Financial Management & Accounting. 1995;6(1):69-87.

243. Brennan N. Voluntary Disclosure of Profit Forecasts by Target Companies in Takeover Bids. Journal of Business Finance & Accounting. 1999;26(7-8):883-917.
244. Patel SA, Dallas G. Transparency and disclosure: Overview of methodology and study results- United States. Standard and Poor's Corporation; 2002.
245. Atiase RK. Predisclosure information, firm capitalization, and security price behavior around earnings announcements. Journal of Accounting Research. 1985:21-36.
246. Brown LD, Richardson GD, Schwager SJ. An information interpretation of financial analyst superiority in forecasting earnings. Journal of Accounting Research. 1987:49-67.
247. Jensen MC, Meckling WH. Theory of the firm: Managerial behavior, agency costs and ownership structure. Journal of financial economics. 1976;3(4):305-60.
248. Malone D, Fries C, Jones T. An empirical investigation of the extent of corporate financial disclosure in the oil and gas industry. Journal of Accounting, Auditing & Finance. 1993;8(3):249-73.
249. Imhoff Jr EA. The representativeness of management earnings forecasts. Accounting Review. 1978:836-50.
250. Ruland W. The time series of earnings for forecast reporting and nonreporting firms. Journal of Business Finance & Accounting. 1979;6(2):187-201.
251. Belkaoui A, Kahl A. Corporate Financial Disclosure in Canada, Research Monograph No. 1 of Canadian Certified General Accountants Association. Vancouver; 1978.
252. McNally GM, Eng LH, Hasseldine CR. Corporate financial reporting in New Zealand: An analysis of user preferences, corporate characteristics and disclosure practices for discretionary information. Accounting and business research. 1982;13(49):11-20.
253. Shleifer A, Vishny RW. Large shareholders and corporate control. Journal of political economy. 1986;94(3, Part 1):461-88.
254. Agrawal A, Mandelker GN. Large shareholders and the monitoring of managers: The case of antitakeover charter amendments. Journal of Financial and Quantitative analysis. 1990;25(2):143-61.
255. McKinnon JL, Dalimunthe L. Voluntary disclosure of segment information by Australian diversified companies. Accounting & Finance. 1993;33(1):33-50.
256. Ben Ali C, Gettler-Summa M, Trabelsi S. Disclosure quality and ownership structure: evidence from the French Stock Market. 2007.
257. Gelb DS. Managerial ownership and accounting disclosures: an empirical study. Review of Quantitative Finance and Accounting. 2000;15(2):169-85.
258. Ho SS, Shun Wong K. A study of the relationship between corporate governance structures and the extent of voluntary disclosure. Journal of International Accounting, Auditing and Taxation. 2001;10(2):139-56.
259. Chau GK, Gray SJ. Ownership structure and corporate voluntary disclosure in Hong Kong and Singapore. The International Journal of Accounting. 2002;37(2):247-65.
260. Cormier D, Magnan M, Van Velthoven B. Environmental disclosure quality in large German companies: economic incentives, public pressures or institutional conditions? European accounting review. 2005;14(1):3-39.
261. Bushee BJ, Noe CF. Corporate disclosure practices, institutional investors, and stock return volatility. Journal of Accounting Research. 2000:171-202.
262. Haniffa RM, Cooke TE. Culture, corporate governance and disclosure in Malaysian corporations. Abacus. 2002;38(3):317-49.
263. Forker JJ. Corporate governance and disclosure quality. Accounting and Business research. 1992;22(86):111-24.
264. Chen CJ, Jaggi B. Association between independent non-executive directors, family control and financial disclosures in Hong Kong. Journal of Accounting and Public policy. 2000;19(4-5):285-310.
265. Cooke TE. The impact of size, stock market listing and industry type on disclosure in the annual reports of Japanese listed corporations. Accounting and business research. 1992;22(87):229-37.
266. Givoly D, Palmon D. Timeliness of annual earnings announcements: Some empirical evi-

dence. Accounting review. 1982:486-508.
267. Karaoglu E, Sandino T, Beatty RP, editors. Benchmarking Against the Performance of High Profile'Scandal'Firms2007: AAA.
268. Balakrishnan K, Cohen DA. Competition and financial accounting misreporting. Available at SSRN 1927427. 2013.
269. Li X. The impacts of product market competition on the quantity and quality of voluntary disclosures. Review of Accounting Studies. 2010;15(3):663-711.
270. Guadalupe M, Pérez-González F, editors. Competition and private benefits of control. AFA 2007 Chicago Meetings Paper; 2010.
271. Giroud X, Mueller HM. Does corporate governance matter in competitive industries? Journal of Financial Economics. 2010;95(3):312-31.
272. Barako DG. Determinants of voluntary disclosures in Kenyan companies annual reports. African Journal of Business Management. 2007;1(5).
273. Sidgwick H. The scope and method of economic science. 1885.
274. Pigou AC. The economics of welfare, 1920. McMillan&Co, London. 1932.
275. Jorion P, Zhang G. Information transfer effects of bond rating downgrades. Financial Review. 2010;45(3):683-706.
276. Jorion P, Zhang G. Credit contagion from counterparty risk. The Journal of Finance. 2009;64(5):2053-87.
277. Hertzel MG, Li Z, Officer MS, Rodgers KJ. Inter-firm linkages and the wealth effects of financial distress along the supply chain. Journal of Financial Economics. 2008;87(2):374-87.
278. Jarrow RA, Yu F. Counterparty risk and the pricing of defaultable securities. the Journal of Finance. 2001;56(5):1765-99.
279. Xu T, Najand M, Ziegenfuss D. Intra-industry effects of earnings restatements due to accounting irregularities. Journal of Business Finance & Accounting. 2006;33(5-6):696-714.
280. Erwin GR, Miller JM. The Intra-Industry Effects of Open Market Share Repurchases: Contagion or Competitive? Journal of Financial Research. 1998;21(4):389-406.
281. Lang LH, Stulz R. Contagion and competitive intra-industry effects of bankruptcy announcements: An empirical analysis. Journal of financial economics. 1992;32(1):45-60.
282. Slovin MB, Sushka ME, Polonchek JA. An analysis of contagion and competitive effects at commercial banks. Journal of Financial Economics. 1999;54(2):197-225.
283. Foster G. Intra-industry information transfers associated with earnings releases. Journal of accounting and economics. 1981;3(3):201-32.
284. Laux P, Starks LT, Yoon PS. The relative importance of competition and contagion in intra-industry information transfers: An investigation of dividend announcements. Financial Management. 1998;27(3):5.
285. Firth M. Dividend changes, abnormal returns, and intra-lndustry firm valuations. Journal of financial and Quantitative Analysis. 1996;31(2):189-211.
286. Gleason CA, Jenkins NT, Johnson WB. The contagion effects of accounting restatements. The Accounting Review. 2008;83(1):83-110.
287. Goldman E, Peyer U, Stefanescu I. Fraudulent earnings manipulation and its impact on rivals. Working paper, Indiana University and INSEAD. 2009.
288. Collin-Dufresne P, Goldstein R, Helwege J. Are jumps in corporate bond yields priced? Modeling contagion via the updating of beliefs. University of California Berkeley Working Paper. 2003.
289. Chen SS, Ho LC, Shih YC. Intra-lndustry Effects of Corporate Capital Investment Announcements. Financial Management. 2007;36(2):1-21.
290. Brander JA, Lewis TR. Bankruptcy costs and the theory of oligopoly. Canadian journal of economics. 1988:221-43.
291. Goldman E, Peyer U, Stefanescu I. Financial misrepresentation and its impact on rivals. Financial Management. 2012;41(4):915-45.
292. Jorion P, Zhang G. Good and bad credit contagion: Evidence from credit default swaps. Journal of Financial Economics. 2007;84(3):p.860~83.
293. Rogers JL. Disclosure quality and management trading incentives. Journal of Accounting Research. 2008;46(5):1265-96.

294. Einhorn E, Ziv A. Biased voluntary disclosure. Review of Accounting Studies. 2012;17(2):420-42.
295. D'Souza J, Ramesh K, Shen M. Disclosure of GAAP line items in earnings announcements. Review of Accounting Studies. 2010;15(1):179-219.
296. Gibbins M, Richardson A, Waterhouse J. The management of corporate financial disclosure: opportunism, ritualism, policies, and processes. Journal of accounting research. 1990:121-43.
297. Subramanyam K. The pricing of discretionary accruals. Journal of accounting and economics. 1996;22(1):249-81.
298. Healy PM. The effect of bonus schemes on accounting decisions. Journal of accounting and economics. 1985;7(1):85-107.
299. Gray SJ, Gordon PD, Roberts CB. Making corporate reports valuable: a survey of corporate reporting practices by major UK companies. [Edinburgh]: Institute of Chartered Accountants of Scotland; 1991. 2 v. p.
300. Sudarsanam S, City U, Business S, Centre for Empirical Research in F, Accounting. Defensive strategies of target firms in UK contested takeover bids : a survey: City University, Business School, Centre for Empirical Research in Finance and Accounting; 1994.
301. Trueman B. Why do managers voluntarily release earnings forecasts? Journal of accounting and economics. 1986;8(1):53-71.
302. Zamora VL. Do Managers Benefit from Superior Forecasting? Available at SSRN 1324204. 2009.
303. Weisbach MS. Outside directors and CEO turnover. Journal of financial Economics. 1988;20:431-60.
304. Warner JB, Watts RL, Wruck KH. Stock prices and top management changes. Journal of financial Economics. 1988;20:461-92.
305. Patell JM, Wolfson MA. Good news, bad news, and the intraday timing of corporate disclosures. Accounting Review. 1982:509-27.
306. Cao Y, Wasley CE, Wu JS. Soft-talk management cash flow forecasts: Verifiability, credibility and stock price effects. 2007.
307. Schrand CM, Walther BR. Strategic benchmarks in earnings announcements: The selective disclosure of prior-period earnings components. The Accounting Review. 2000;75(2):151-77.
308. Lerner J. Patent protection and innovation over 150 years. National Bureau of Economic Research, 2002.
309. Coughlan AT, Schmidt RM. Executive compensation, management turnover, and firm performance: An empirical investigation. Journal of Accounting and Economics. 1985;7(1):43-66.
310. Murphy KJ, Zimmerman JL. Financial performance surrounding CEO turnover. Journal of Accounting and Economics. 1993;16(1):273-315.
311. Aboody D, Kasznik R. CEO stock option awards and the timing of corporate voluntary disclosures. Journal of accounting and economics. 2000;29(1):73-100.
312. Botosan CA, Stanford M. Managers' motives to withhold segment disclosures and the effect of SFAS No. 131 on analysts' information environment. The Accounting Review. 2005;80(3):751-72.
313. Bens DA, Berger PG, Monahan SJ. Discretionary disclosure in financial reporting: an examination comparing internal firm data to externally reported segment data. The Accounting Review. 2011;86(2):417-49.
314. King RR. Reputation formation for reliable reporting: An experimental investigation. Accounting Review. 1996:375-96.
315. Hodge FD, Hopkins PE, Pratt JH. The credibility of accounting classification: Determinants and consequences. Available at SSRN 391140. 2003.
316. Bernard VL, Skinner DJ. What motivates managers' choice of discretionary accruals? Journal of Accounting and Economics. 1996;22(1):313-25.
317. Baiman S, Verrecchia RE. The relation among capital markets, financial disclosure, production efficiency, and insider trading. Journal of accounting research. 1996:1-22.
318. Nagar V, Nanda D, Wysocki P. Discretionary disclosure and stock-based incentives. Journal of Accounting and Economics. 2003;34(1):283-309.
319. Bettis JC, Coles JL, Lemmon ML. Corporate policies restricting trading by insiders. Journal of

Financial Economics. 2000;57(2):191-220.
320. FASB. Statement of Financial Accounting Concepts No.8 2010. Available from: https://www.fasb.org/resources/ccurl/515/412/Concepts%20Statement%20No%20208.pdf.
321. Metzger MJ, Flanagin AJ, Eyal K, Lemus DR, McCann RM. Credibility for the 21st century: Integrating perspectives on source, message, and media credibility in the contemporary media environment. Communication yearbook. 2003;27:293-336.
322. Hellmueller L, Trilling D, editors. The Credibility of Credibility Measures: A Meta-Analysis in Leading Communication Journals, 1951 to 2011. Comunicación presentada en el WAPOR 65th Annual Conference in Hong Kong; 2012.
323. Frost CA. Disclosure policy choices of UK firms receiving modified audit reports. Journal of Accounting and Economics. 1997;23(2):163-87.
324. Koch AS. Financial distress and the credibility of management earnings forecasts. 2002.
325. Park JC. Essays on mandatory and voluntary disclosure: The stock market reaction to mandatory segment reporting changes and the credibility of voluntary management forecasts: Carnegie Mellon University; 2006.
326. Grant EB. Market implications of differential amounts of interim information. Journal of Accounting Research. 1980:255-68.
327. Jennings R. Unsystematic security price movements, management earnings forecasts, and revisions in consensus analyst earnings forecasts. Journal of Accounting Research. 1987:90-110.
328. Williams PA. The relation between a prior earnings forecast by management and analyst response to a current management forecast. Accounting Review. 1996:103-15.
329. Pownall G, Waymire G. Voluntary disclosure credibility and securities prices: Evidence from management earnings forecasts, 1969-73. Journal of Accounting Research. 1989:227-45.
330. Ng J, Tuna İ, Verdi R. Management forecast credibility and underreaction to news. Review of Accounting Studies. 2013;18(4):956-86.
331. Hassell JM, Jennings RH, Lasser DJ. Management Earnings Forecasts: Their Usefulness as a Source of Firm‐Specific Information to Security Analysts. Journal of Financial Research. 1988;11(4):303-19.
332. Wang RY, Strong DM. Beyond accuracy: What data quality means to data consumers. Journal of management information systems. 1996;12(4):5-33.
333. Andrus RR. Approaches to information evaluation. MSU business topics. 1971;19(3):40-6.
334. Hassan O, Marston C. Disclosure measurement in the empirical accounting literature-a review article. Available at SSRN 1640598. 2010.
335. Bose DC. Principles of management and administration: PHI Learning Pvt. Ltd.; 2002.
336. CFAI. Segment Disclosures: Investor Perspectives 2018. Available from: https://www.cfainstitute.org/en/research/survey-reports/segment-disclosures-survey-report.
337. Beattie V, McInnes B, Fearnley S. A methodology for analysing and evaluating narratives in annual reports: a comprehensive descriptive profile and metrics for disclosure quality attributes. Accounting Forum. 2004;28(3):205-36.
338. Lang MH, Lundholm RJ. Corporate disclosure policy and analyst behavior. Accounting review. 1996:467-92.
339. Barron OE, Kile CO, O'Keefe TB. MD&A quality as measured by the SEC and analysts' earning forecasts. Contemporary Accounting Research. 1999;16(1):75.
340. Beretta S, Bozzolan S. Quality versus quantity: the case of forward-looking disclosure. Journal of Accounting, Auditing & Finance. 2008;23(3):333-76.
341. Gill A, Ltd CLS. Corporate Governance in Emerging Markets: Saints & Sinners ; Who's Got Religion?: Credit Lyonnais Securities (Asia) Limited; 2001.
342. Krishnamurti C, Šević A, Šević Ž. Voluntary disclosure, transparency, and market quality: Evidence from emerging market ADRs. Journal of Multinational Financial Management. 2005;15(4):435-54.
343. Nagar V, Nanda D, Wysocki PD, editors. Compensation policy and discretionary disclosure. JAE Boston Conference June; 2001.
344. Lang MH, Lundholm RJ. Voluntary Disclosure and Equity Offerings: Reducing Information Asymmetry or Hyping the Stock? Contemporary accounting research. 2000;17(4):623-62.

345. Chen S, Miao B, Shevlin TJ. A New Measure of Disclosure Quality: The Level of Disaggregation of Accounting Data in Annual Reports. Available at SSRN 2475624. 2014.
346. Li F. Annual report readability, current earnings, and earnings persistence. Journal of Accounting and Economics. 2008;45(2–3):221-47.
347. Loughran T, McDonald B. Measuring readability in financial disclosures. The Journal of Finance. 2014;69(4):1643-71.
348. Mohan S. Disclosure quality and its effect on litigation risk. Available at SSRN 956499. 2006.
349. Tetlock PC. Giving content to investor sentiment: The role of media in the stock market. The Journal of finance. 2007;62(3):1139-68.
350. Lang MH, Lins KV, Miller DP. ADRs, analysts, and accuracy: Does cross listing in the United States improve a firm's information environment and increase market value? Journal of Accounting Research. 2003;41(2):317-45.
351. Bailey W, Andrew Karolyi G, Salva C. The economic consequences of increased disclosure: Evidence from international cross-listings. Journal of Financial Economics. 2006;81(1):175-213.
352. Irani AJ, Karamanou I. Regulation fair disclosure, analyst following, and analyst forecast dispersion. Accounting Horizons. 2003;17(1):15-29.
353. Bushee BJ, Leuz C. Economic consequences of SEC disclosure regulation: evidence from the OTC bulletin board. Journal of Accounting and Economics. 2005;39(2):233-64.
354. Clarkson PM, Kao JL, Richardson GD. Evidence that management discussion and analysis (MD&A) is a part of a firm's overall disclosure package. Contemporary accounting research. 1999;16(1):11.
355. Juran JM. Managerial breakthrough: A new concept of the manager's job: McGraw-Hill Companies; 1964.
356. Society I. Best practice guidelines for annual reports 2013. Available from: http://www.irs.org.uk/resources/best-practice-guidelines.
357. Botha H, Boon J. The information audit: principles and guidelines. Libri. 2003;53(1):23-38.
358. Buchanan S, Gibb F. The information audit: Role and scope. International journal of information management. 2007;27(3):159-72.
359. Downs CW. Communication Audits: Scott, Foresman; 1988.
360. IOSCO. Objectives and Principles of SEcurities Regulation. 1998.
361. Hicks JW. Securities Regulation: Challenges in the Decades Ahead. Ind LJ. 1992;68:791.
362. Zalaghi H, Khazaei M. The role of deductive and inductive reasoning in accounting research and standard setting. Asian Journal of Finance & Accounting. 2016;8(1):23-37.
363. Wilson J. Essentials of business research: A guide to doing your research project: Sage; 2014.
364. Pellissier R. Business research made easy: Juta and Company Ltd; 2008.
365. Babbie ER. The basics of social research: Cengage learning; 2013.
366. Godfrey J, Hodgson A, Tarca A, Hamilton J, Holmes S. Accounting theory2010.
367. Bernard HR, Bernard HR. Social research methods: Qualitative and quantitative approaches: Sage; 2012.
368. Lodico MG, Spaulding DT, Voegtle KH. Methods in educational research: From theory to practice: John Wiley & Sons; 2010.
369. Riahi-Belkaoui A. Accounting Theory: Harcourt Brace Jovanovich; 1981.
370. Ford CL. Principles-Based Securities Regulation 2009. Available from: http://www.rotman.utoronto.ca/-/media/Files/Programs-and-Areas/CMI/2009-papers/Principles-Based-Securities-Regulation---Ford_English.pdf?la=en.
371. Hellman N, Carenys J, Moya Gutierrez S. Introducing More IFRS Principles of Disclosure–Will the Poor Disclosers Improve? Accounting in Europe. 2018;15(2):242-321.
372. Fleming RA. 100 years of securities law: Examining a foundation laid in the Kansas blue sky. Washburn LJ. 2010;50:583.
373. Loss L, Seligman J. Securities Regulation: Little Brown & Co Law & Business; 1991.
374. Loss L. Fundamentals of securities regulation: Aspen Publishers Online; 1983.
375. Jarrell GA. The economic effects of federal regulation of the market for new security issues. Journal of Law and Economics. 1981:613-75.
376. KansasMoney.gov. "Blue Sky Laws" Originated in Kansas 2016. Available from: https://kansas-

money.gov/posts/blue-sky-laws.
377. Society KH. Kansas Blue Sky Laws 2016. Available from: http://www.kshs.org/kansapedia/kansas-blue-sky-laws/18618.
378. Mahoney PG. The origins of the blue-sky laws: a test of competing hypotheses. Journal of Law and Economics. 2003;46(1):229-51.
379. Hohenstein K. Chasing the Devil Around the Stump: Securities Regulation, the SEC and the Courts 2011. Available from: http://www.sechistorical.org/museum/galleries/ctd/index.php.
380. Sargent MA. Report on State Merit Regulation of Securities Offerings. Bus Law. 1986;41:785, 93.
381. Campbell Jr RB. An Open Attack on the Nonsense of Blue Sky Regulation. J Corp L. 1984;10:553.
382. Seligman J. The Historical Need for a Mandatory Corporate Disclosure System. J Corp L. 1983;9:1.
383. Mulvey T. Certified securities. The American Economic Review. 1914;4(3):588-601.
384. Agrawal AK. The impact of investor protection law on corporate policy: Evidence from the Blue Sky laws. 2009.
385. Mahoney PG. Wasting a Crisis: Why Securities Regulation Fails: University of Chicago Press; 2015.
386. Macey JR, Miller GP. Origin of the Blue Sky laws. Tex L Rev. 1991;70:347.
387. Rajan R, Zingales L. Saving capitalism from the capitalists: New York: Crown Business; 2003.
388. Makens HH. Who Speaks for the Investor? An Evaluation of the Assault on Merit Regulation. University of Baltimore Law Review. 1984;13(3):2.
389. Mofsky JS, Tollison RD. Demerit in Merit Regulation. Marq L Rev. 1976;60:367.
390. US.SEC. Report on the Uniformity of State Regulatory Requirements for Offerings of Securities That Are Not "Covered Securities" 1997. Available from: https://www.sec.gov/news/studies/uniformy.htm.
391. NASAA. A Century of Investor Protection 2011. Available from: http://www.nasaa.org/wp-content/uploads/2011/07/100_Years_Commemorative_FINAL.pdf.
392. La Porta R, Lopez-de-Silanes F, Shleifer A, Vishny RW. Legal determinants of external finance. Journal of finance. 1997:1131-50.
393. La Porta R, Lopez-de-Silanes F, Shleifer A, Vishny RW. Agency problems and dividend policies around the world. The journal of finance. 2000;55(1):1-33.
394. Shleifer A, Wolfenzon D. Investor protection and equity markets. Journal of Financial Economics. 2002;66(1):3-27.
395. Reed RR, Washburn LH. Blue Sky Laws: Analysis and Text: Clark Boardman Company Limited; 1921.
396. Goodkind CG. Blue Sky Law: Is There Merit in the Merit Requirements. Wis L Rev. 1976:79.
397. Mofsky JS. Blue Sky Restrictions on New Business Promotions. Duke LJ. 1969:273.
398. Karmel RS. Blue-Sky Merit Regulation: Benefit to Investors or Burden on Commerce. Brook L Rev. 1987;53:105.
399. Posner RA. Economic analysis of law. 1973.
400. Braisted CH. State Registration of Securities: An Anachronism No Longer Viable. Wash ULQ. 2000;78:401.
401. Brach GE. The Blue Sky Law. Marq L Rev. 1918;3:142.
402. Grundfest J, Perino MA. Securities Litigation Reform: The First Year's Experience a Statistical and Legal Analysis of Class Action Securities Fraud Litigation Under the Private Securities Litigation Reform Act of 1995. Available at SSRN 10582. 1997.
403. Seligman J. Fundamentals of securities regulation: Aspen Publishers Online; 2004.
404. Leuz C, Triantis A, Yue Wang T. Why do firms go dark? Causes and economic consequences of voluntary SEC deregistrations. Journal of Accounting and Economics. 2008;45(2):181-208.
405. US.SEC. SEC staff to publicly release comment letter and responses. SEC Press Release No. 2004-89 2004. Available from: https://www.sec.gov/news/press/2004-89.htm.
406. Veil R. European capital markets law: Bloomsbury Publishing; 2017.
407. Segre C. The development of a European capital market. Report of a Group of Experts ap-

pointed by the EEC Commission. November 1966 1966. Available from: http://aei.pitt.edu/31823/.
408. ESMA. ESMA Guidelines on Alternative Performance Measures 2016.
409. Commission E. Revamping the prospectus, the gateway to European capital markets 2015. Available from: https://europa.eu/rapid/press-release_MEMO-15-6198_en.pdf.
410. EFAMA. Position Paper: Proposal for regulation on a prospectus to be published when securities are offered to the public or admitted to trading. 2016. Available from: https://efama.org/Publications/Public/EFAMA%20Position%20Paper%20on%20Prospectus.pdf.
411. Commission E. Consultation on the Review of the Prospectus Directive 18/02/2015~13/05/2015 - Feedback statement on the public online consultation -. 2015.
412. Watkins L. EU Prospectus Regulation: New Format and Content Requirements 2019. Available from: https://www.latham.london/2019/05/eu-prospectus-regulation-new-format-and-content-requirmenets/.
413. ESMA. Consultation Paper-Draft technical advice on format and content of the prospectus 2017.
414. ESMA. Consultation Paper: Draft technical advice on scrutiny and approval of the prospectus. 2017.
415. ESMA. Consultation Paper: Draft technical advice on content and format of the EU Growth prospectus 2017. Available from: https://www.esma.europa.eu/document/draft-technical-advice-content-and-format-eu-growth-prospectus.
416. Commission E. Commission Delegated Regulation (EU) 2019-980 as regards the format, content, scrutiny and approval of the prospectus 2019.
417. Commission E. Commission Delegated Regulation (EU) 2019-979 regard to regulatory technical standards on key financial information in the summary of a prospectus 2019.
418. ESMA. Questions and answers- Transparency Directive (2004-109-EC) 2019.
419. MAZARS. Transparency Directive Assessment Report - Study on the application of selected obligations of directive 2004/109/EC on the haronisation of transparency requirements in relation to information about issuers whose securities are admitted to trading on a regulated market 2009. Available from: https://ec.europa.eu/info/system/files/report-application-annexes--26012011_en.pdf.
420. Commission E. Commission Staff Working Document - The review of the operation of Directive 2004-109-EC- emerging issues 2010. Available from: http://ec.europa.eu/smart-regulation/evaluation/search/download.do?documentId=4511.
421. Demarigny F. An EU-listing Small Business Act - Establishing a proportionate regulatory and financial environment for Small and Medium-sized Issuers Listed in Europe (SMILEs) 2010. Available from: http://www.eurocapitalmarkets.org/sites.default/files/eulistingsbaenfinal.pdf.
422. Committee UHoCT. Banking Crisis: reforming corporate governance and pay in the City. London: The Stationery Office Limited. 2009.
423. ESMA. Guidelines on the Market Abuse Regulation - market soundings and delay of disclosure of inside information 2016. Available from: https://www.fca.org.uk/publication/forms/delayed-disclosure-form-guide.pdf.
424. IOSCO. Statement on Disclosure of ESG Matters by Issuers 2019. Available from: https://www.iosco.org/library/pubdocs/pdf/IOSCOPD619.pdf.
425. IOSCO. Objectives and Principles of Securities Regulation. 2017.
426. IOSCO. Methodology for Assessing Implementation of the IOSCO Objectives and Principles of Securities Regulation. 2017.
427. IOSCO. International Disclosure Standards for Cross-Border Offerings and Initial Listings by Foreign Issuers. 1998.
428. IOSCO. International Disclosure Principles for Cross-Border Offerings and Listings of Debt Securities by Foreign Issuers. 2007.
429. IOSCO. Principles for Periodic Disclosure by Listed Entities 2010. Available from: https://www.iosco.org/library/pubdocs/pdf/IOSCOPD317.pdf.
430. IOSCO. General Principles Regarding Disclosure of Management's Discussion and Analysis of Financial Condition and Results of Operations 2003. Available from: https://www.iosco.org/library/pubdocs/pdf/IOSCOPD141.pdf.

431. OECD. OECD Guiding Principles for Regulatory Quality and Performance 2005. Available from: https://www.oecd.org/fr/reformereg/34976533.pdf.
432. Coglianese C. Measuring regulatory performance evaluating the impact of regulation and regulatory policy. 2012.
433. Johnson B. Do Criminal Laws Deter Crime?: Deterrence Theory in Criminal Justice Policy: A Primer: MN House Research; 2019.
434. Polinsky AM, Shavell S. The theory of public enforcement of law. Handbook of law and economics. 2007;1:403-54.
435. Lemos MH, Stein A. Strategic Enforcement. Minn L Rev. 2010;95:9.
436. Tieger JH. Police discretion and discriminatory enforcement. Duke LJ. 1971:717.
437. MAS. Enforcement 2018. Available from: https://www.mas.gov.sg/-/media/MAS/News-and-Publications/Enforcement-Actions/Enforcement-Monograph.pdf?la=en&hash=5046D3B907B29F7E46CB147E1C0C6DFBB3E1CED.
438. NERA. Trends in Regulatory Enforcement in UK Financial Markets 2019. Available from: https://www.nera.com/content/dam/nera/publications/2019/Trends%20in%20Regulatory%20Enforcement%20in%20UK%20Financial%20Markets%202020 2018-19%20Mid-Year%20Report.pdf.
439. PSI. Guidance to sanctioning - PSI.
440. FINRA. Sanction Guidelines 2019. Available from: https://www.finra.org/sites/default/files/Sanctions_Guidelines.pdf.
441. Lawrence J, Lei G, Smith DB. SEC comment letters and financial statement restatements. Available at SSRN 1575389. 2010.
442. Poliakoff AD. SEC Review: Comfort or Illusion. U Balt L Rev. 1987;17:40.
443. Owens HF. The SEC registration process and some practical problems involved 1970. Available from: https://www.sec.gov/news/speech/1970/042570owens.pdf.
444. US.SEC. SEC News Digest Issue 80-222 1980.
445. Senate CoGAUS. Financial oversight of enron the sec and private sector watchdogs 2002. Available from: https://www.govinfo.gov/content/pkg/CPRT-107SPRT82147/html/CPRT-107SPRT82147.htm, https://www.gpo.gov/fdsys/pkg/CPRT-107SPRT82147/pdf/CPRT-107SPRT82147.pdf.
446. SEC US. Evaluation of the Division of Corporation Finance's Disclosure Review and Comment Letter Process, Report No. 542 2017.
447. GAO U. Management Has Enhanced Supervisory Controls and Could Further Improve Efficiency 2016. Available from: https://www.gao.gov/assets/690/680352.pdf.
448. Cassell CA, Dreher LM, Myers LA. Reviewing the SEC's review process: 10-K comment letters and the cost of remediation. The Accounting Review. 2013;88(6):1875-908.
449. Cunningham LM, Schmardebeck R, Wang W. SEC comment letters and bank lending. Available at SSRN 2727860. 2017.
450. Feroz EH, Park K, Pastena VS. The financial and market effects of the SEC's accounting and auditing enforcement releases. Journal of accounting research. 1991;29:107-42.
451. Brown SV, Tian X, Wu Tucker J. The spillover effect of SEC comment letters on qualitative corporate disclosure: Evidence from the risk factor disclosure. Contemporary Accounting Research. 2018;35(2):622-56.
452. Pincus KV, Holder WW, Mock TJ. Reducing the incidence of fraudulent financial reporting: The role of the Securities and Exchange Commission: School of Accounting, University of Southern Calfiornia [sic]; 1987.
453. Goldstein I, Sapra H. Should banks' stress test results be disclosed? An analysis of the costs and benefits. Foundations and Trends in Finance, forthcoming. 2013.
454. Duro M, Heese J, Ormazabal G. The effect of enforcement transparency: Evidence from SEC comment-letter reviews. The Review of Accounting Studies. 2019.
455. Djankov S, Glaeser E, La Porta R, Lopez-de-Silanes F, Shleifer A. The new comparative economics. Journal of comparative economics. 2003;31(4):595-619.
456. Jin GZ, Leslie P. The effect of information on product quality: Evidence from restaurant hygiene grade cards. The Quarterly Journal of Economics. 2003:409-51.

457. analytics A. Trends in SEC Non-GAAP Comment Letters 2016~2018. 2018.
458. Deloitte. SEC Comment Letters – Including Industry Insights, Nov 2017 2017. Available from: https://www2.deloitte.com/content/dam/Deloitte/us/Document/audit/ASC/us-aerssec-comment-letters-including-industry-insights-2017.pdf.
459. Young E. SEC Comments and Trends: An Analysis of Current Reporting Issues. Ernst & Young New York, NY; 2018.
460. Chen R, Johnston R, Ramnath S. The effect of regulator oversight on firms' information environment: Securities and Exchange Commission comment letters. Working paper. Massachusetts Institute of Technology and Purdue University, 2010.
461. Ertimur Y, Nondorf M. IPO firms and the SEC comment letter process. Workingg Paper (July, 2006). 2006.
462. Hribar P, Kravet T, Wilson R. A new measure of accounting quality. Review of Accounting Studies. 2014;19(1):506-38.
463. Ryans J. Textual classification of SEC comment letters. Available at SSRN 2474666. 2018.
464. Baugh M, Schmardebeck R. Auditor Style and Common Disclosure Deficiencies: Evidence from SEC Comment Letters. Available at SSRN 3368511. 2019.
465. Dechow PM, Lawrence A, Ryans JP. SEC comment letters and insider sales. The Accounting Review. 2015;91(2):401-39.
466. Robinson JR, Xue Y, Yu Y. Determinants of disclosure noncompliance and the effect of the SEC review: Evidence from the 2006 mandated compensation disclosure regulations. The Accounting Review. 2011;86(4):1415-44.
467. Cassell CA, Cunningham LM, Lisic LL. The consequences of writing not so readable responses to SEC comment letters. Working paper; 2016.
468. Gietzmann M, Marra A, Pettinicchio A. Comment letter frequency and CFO turnover: A dynamic survival analysis. Journal of Accounting, Auditing & Finance. 2016;31(1):79-99.
469. Li B, Liu Z. The oversight role of regulators: evidence from SEC comment letters in the IPO process. Review of Accounting Studies. 2017;22(3):1229-60.
470. Johnson BA, Lisic LL, Moon JS, Wang M. SEC Comment Letters and M&A Outcomes. Available at SSRN 3335390. 2019.
471. Cunningham LM, Johnson BA, Johnson ES, Lisic LL. The switch up: An examination of changes in earnings management after receiving SEC comment letters. Available at SSRN 2760638. 2018.
472. Huang Y, Scholz S. Evidence on the association between financial restatements and auditor resignations. Accounting Horizons. 2012;26(3):439-64.
473. Baldwin J, Hurtt D, MacGregor J. The Relationship between SEC Comment Letters and Subsequent Auditor Change. Citeseer, 2013.
474. Gietzmann MB, Pettinicchio AK. External auditor reassessment of client business risk following the issuance of a comment letter by the SEC. European Accounting Review. 2014;23(1):57-85.
475. Kubick TR, Lynch DP, Mayberry MA, Omer TC. The effects of increased financial statement disclosure quality on tax avoidance: An examination of SEC Comment Letters. 2014.
476. Giamouridis D, Koulikidou K, Leventis S. The Power of Words in Capital Markets: SEC Comment Letters on Foreign Issuers and the Impact of Domestic Enforcement. 2018.
477. Bozanic Z, Dietrich JR, Johnson BA. SEC comment letters and firm disclosure. Journal of Accounting and Public Policy. 2017;36(5):337-57.
478. Bens DA, Cheng M, Neamtiu M. The impact of SEC disclosure monitoring on the uncertainty of fair value estimates. The Accounting Review. 2015;91(2):349-75.
479. Johnston R, Petacchi R. Regulatory oversight of financial reporting: Securities and Exchange Commission comment letters. Contemporary Accounting Research. 2017;34(2):1128-55.
480. Edwards A, Klassen KJ, Pinto K. Investor Response to Tax Related SEC Comment Letters. 2018.
481. Johnson BA. The impact of SEC comment letter releases: Short window evidence on information content and changes in information asymmetry: The Ohio State University; 2015.
482. Gietzmann MB, Isidro H. Institutional investors' reaction to SEC concerns about IFRS and US

GAAP reporting. Journal of Business Finance & Accounting. 2013;40(7-8):796-841.
483. Grove H, Johnsen T, Lung P. SEC comment letters: an unlikely secret weapon for forensic accountants, short sellers, and other financial statement users. Short Sellers, and Other Financial Statement Users (December 19, 2015). 2015.
484. Duro Rivas M. The Role of Public Disclosure in Regulatory Oversight: Evidence from SEC Comment Letters: Columbia University; 2015.
485. Heese J, Khan M, Ramanna K. Is the SEC captured? Evidence from comment-letter reviews. Journal of Accounting and Economics. 2017;64(1):98-122.
486. Kwon SY, Lim J-H, Park J. The Impact of Chief Financial Officers' Financial Expertise on Securities and Exchange Commission Comment Letters. Available at SSRN. 2019.
487. Ballestero R, Schmidt JJ. Does Auditor Involvement Expedite SEC Comment Letter Resolution? Available at SSRN 3350730. 2019.
488. ErnstYoung. SEC Reporting Update-2018 trends in SEC comment letters 2018.
489. Correia MM. Political connections and SEC enforcement. Journal of Accounting and Economics. 2014;57(2-3):241-62.
490. Kedia S, Rajgopal S. Do the SEC's enforcement preferences affect corporate misconduct? Journal of Accounting and Economics. 2011;51(3):259-78.
491. Baugh M, Kim K, Lee K. The Effect of SEC Reviewers on Comment Letters and Financial Reporting Quality. KAIST College of Business Working Paper Series. 2017(2017-021).
492. Do TP, Zhang H. Styles of regulators: Evidence from the SEC's comment letters. Huai, Styles of Regulators: Evidence from the SEC's Comment Letters (October 14, 2018). 2018.
493. Yu F, Yu X. Corporate lobbying and fraud detection. Journal of Financial and Quantitative Analysis. 2011;46(6):1865-91.
494. DeHaan E, Kedia S, Koh K, Rajgopal S, editors. Does the revolving door affect the SEC's enforcement outcomes. American Accounting Association Annual Meeting Presentation Available at http://papers ssrn com/sol3/papers cfm; 2012.
495. Brown SV, Tian XS, Tucker JW. The spillover effect of SEC comment letters on qualitative corporate disclosure: Evidence from the risk factor disclosure. Jenny Wu, The Spillover Effect of SEC Comment Letters on Qualitative Corporate Disclosure: Evidence from the Risk Factor Disclosure (January 18, 2015). 2015.
496. Kubic M. Examining the Examiners: SEC Error Detection Rates and Human Capital Allocation. Available at SSRN 3078689. 2017.
497. CSA. CSA Staff Notice- 51-312 Harmonized Continuous Disclosure Review Program 2004. Available from: https://www.osc.gov.on.ca/document/en/Securities-Category5/csa_20040716_51-312_harm-con-dis.pdf.
498. CSA. CSA Staff Notice- 51-312 (Revised) Harmonized Continuous Disclosure Review Program 2009. Available from: https://www.osc.gov.on.ca/document/en/Securities-Category5/csa_20090714_51-312_harm-con-dis.pdf.
499. ESMA. FINAL REPORT ESMA Guidelines on enforcement of financial information 2014. Available from: https://www.esma.europa.eu/document/final-report-esma-guidelines-enforcement-financial-information.
500. ESMA. ESMA Report Enforcement and Regulatory Activities of European Accounting Enforcers in 2018.
501. ESMA. PUBLIC STATEMENT European common enforcement priorities for 2018 annual financial reports. Available from: https://www.esma.europa.eu/document/european-common-enforcement-priorities-2018-annual-financial-reports.
502. ESMA. ESMA's 23rd Extract from the EECS's Database of Enforcement 2019. Available from: https://www.europa.eu/press-news/esma-publishes-23rd-extract-eecs-database.
503. Savitt W. The Securities Litigation Review, Edition 4 - Japan PDF 2018.
504. SESC_annualreport2018. Available from: https://www.fsa.go.jp/sesc/english/reports/report/.htm.
505. Tjio H. Enforcing Corporate Didsclosure. Singapore Journal of Legal Studies. 2009:332-64.
506. Kotewall RG, Kwong GCK. Report of the Panel of Inquiry on the Penny Stocks Incident 2002. Available from: https://www.info.gov.hk/info/pennystock-e.htm.

507. AU-ASIC's approach to enforcement. Available from: https://asic.gov.au./about-asic/asic-investigations-and-enforcement/asic-s-approach-to-enforcement/.
508. Simon HA. Theories of bounded rationality. Decision and organization. 1972;1(1):161-76.
509. Keller KL, Staelin R. Effects of Quality and Quantity of Information on Decision Effectiveness. Journal of Consumer Research. 1987;14(2):200-13.
510. Paredes TA. Blinded by the light: Information overload and its consequences for securities regulation. Wash ULQ. 2003;81:417.
511. Macey JR. A Pox on Both Your Houses: Enron, Sarbanes-Oxley and the Debate Concerning the Relative Efficacy of Mandatory versus Enabling Rules. Wash ULQ. 2003;81:329.
512. Douglas WO. Protecting the investor. Yale L Rev. 1934;23:522, 4.
513. Felsenfeld C. Plain English Movement, The The Plain English Movement: Panel Discussion. Can Bus LJ. 1981;6:408.
514. Serafin AT. Kicking the Legalese Habit: The SEC's Plain English Disclosure Proposal. Loy U Chi LJ. 1997;29:681.
515. Abdul Rahman AB. Disclosure of corporate financial information in Malaysia. 1998.
516. Hirshleifer D, Teoh SH. Limited attention, information disclosure, and financial reporting. Journal of Accounting and Economics. 2003;36(1):337-86.
517. Dyck A, Zingales L. The right to tell: The role of the media in development. World bank. 2002;in R. Islam ed. The right to tell: The role of the Media in Development, The World Bank, Washington DC, 2002.
518. Simon HA. Models of man; social and rational. 1957.
519. Chewning EG, Harrell AM. The effect of information load on decision makers' cue utilization levels and decision quality in a financial distress decision task. Accounting, Organizations and Society. 1990;15(6):527-42.
520. Stocks MH, Harrell A. The impact of an increase in accounting information level on the judgment quality of individuals and groups. Accounting, Organizations and Society. 1995;20(7):685-700.
521. Simnett R. The effect of information selection, information processing and task complexity on predictive accuracy of auditors. Accounting, Organizations and Society. 1996;21(7):699-719.
522. Tuttle B, Burton FG. The effects of a modest incentive on information overload in an investment analysis task. Accounting, Organizations and Society. 1999;24(8):673-87.
523. Jones BD. Bounded rationality. Annual review of political science. 1999;2(1):297-321.
524. IOSCO. Strategic Framework for Investor Education and Financial Literacy 2014. Available from: https://www.iosco.org/library/pubdocs/pdf/IOSCOPD462.pdf.
525. Schwarcz SL. Protecting financial markets: Lessons from the subprime mortgage meltdown. Minn L Rev. 2008;93:373.
526. Kahneman D, Tversky A. Choices, values, and frames. American psychologist. 1983;39(4):341.
527. Barber BM, Odean T. Boys will be boys: Gender, overconfidence, and common stock investment. Quarterly journal of Economics. 2001:261-92.
528. Hirshleifer DA, Lim SS, Teoh SH. Disclosure to an audience with limited attention. Available at SSRN 604142. 2004.
529. Basu RS, Pierce S, Stephan A. The Effect of Investor Inattention on Voluntary Disclosure. Available at SSRN 3071399. 2019.
530. Harbaugh R, To T. False modesty: When disclosing good news looks bad. 2005.
531. Brandeis LD. Other People's Money and How the Bankers Use It. Chapter V: What Publicity Can Do" Accessed December. 1914;21:2006.
532. Speier C, Valacich JS, Vessey I. The influence of task interruption on individual decision making: An information overload perspective. Decision Sciences. 1999;30(2):337-60.
533. Gross BM. The managing of organizations: The administrative struggle: [New York]: Free Press of Glencoe; 1964.
534. Johnson LT. Research on disclosure. Accounting Horizons. 1992;6(1).
535. Radin AJ. Have we created financial statement disclosure overload? The CPA Journal. 2007;77(11):6.

536. Slovic P. Psychological study of human judgment: Implications for investment decision making. The Journal of Finance. 1972;27(4):779-99.
537. Evaristo R, Adams C, Curley S. Information load revisited: A theoretical model. ICIS 1995 Proceedings. 1995:18.
538. FERF K. Disclosure overload and complexity: hidden in plain sight 2011. Available from: http://www.kpmg.com/us/en/issuesandinsights/articlespublications/pages/disclosure-overload-complexity.aspx.
539. Miller GA. The magical number seven, plus or minus two: some limits on our capacity for processing information. Psychological review. 1956;63(2):81.
540. Jacoby J, Speller DE, Kohn CA. Brand choice behavior as a function of information load. Journal of Marketing Research. 1974:63-9.
541. Jacoby J, Speller DE, Berning CK. Brand choice behavior as a function of information load: Replication and extension. Journal of consumer research. 1974:33-42.
542. Malhotra NK. Information load and consumer decision making. Journal of consumer research. 1982:419-30.
543. Scammon DL. Information load and consumers. Journal of consumer research. 1977:148-55.
544. Muller TE. Buyer response to variations in product information load. Journal of Applied Psychology. 1984;69(2):300.
545. Francis J, Schipper K, Vincent L. Expanded disclosures and the increased usefulness of earnings announcements. The Accounting Review. 2002;77(3):515-46.
546. Davis AK, Piger JM, Sedor LM. Beyond the numbers: An analysis of optimistic and pessimistic language in earnings press releases. Federal Reserve Bank of St Louis Working Paper Series. 2006(2006-005).
547. Commission USSE. Disclosure to Investors: A Reappraisal of Federal Administrative Policies Under the '33 and '34 Acts: The Wheat Report 52-53. 1969.3.27.
548. US.SEC. Report of the Task Force on Disclosure Simplification 1996. Available from: http://sec.gov/news/studies/smpl.htm.
549. Commission USSE. Plain English Disclosure 1998.10.1. Available from: http://www.sec.gov/rules/final/33-7497.txt.
550. Drake MS, Hales J, Rees L. Disclosure Overload? A Professional User Perspective on the Usefulness of General Purpose Financial Statements. Contemporary Accounting Research. 2019;36(4):1935-65.
551. Esgate A, Groome D, Baker K. An introduction to applied cognitive psychology: Psychology Press; 2005.
552. Society I. Best practice guidelines for online presentations 2013. Available from: http://www.irs.org.uk/resources/best-practice-guidelines.
553. Society I. Best practice guidelines for websites 2013. Available from: http://www.irs.org.uk/resources/best-practice-guidelines.
554. Payne JW, Bettman JR, Johnson EJ. The adaptive decision maker: Cambridge University Press; 1993.
555. Johnson EJ, Payne JW. Effort and accuracy in choice. Management science. 1985;31(4):395-414.
556. Schwarcz SL. Rethinking the disclosure paradigm in a world of complexity. U Ill L Rev. 2004:1.
557. Schwarcz SL. Disclosure's Failure in the Subprime Mortgage Crisis. Utah L Rev. 2008:1109.
558. Schwarcz SL. Systemic risk. Georgetown Law Journal. 2008;97(1).
559. Guay WR, Samuels D, Taylor DJ. Guiding through the fog: Financial statement complexity and voluntary disclosure. Available at SSRN 2564350. 2015.
560. Hirst DE, Hopkins PE. Comprehensive income reporting and analysts' valuation judgments. Journal of Accounting Research. 1998;36:47-75.
561. Bloomfield RJ. The incomplete revelation hypothesis" and financial reporting. Accounting Horizons. 2002;16(3):233-43.
562. Brochet F, Naranjo P, Yu G. Causes and consequences of linguistic complexity in non-US firm conference calls. Harvard Business School Research Paper. 2012(2154948).
563. Cox C. Improving Financial Disclosure for Individual Investors 2006.5.3. Available from:

http://www.sec.gov/news/testimony/ts050306cc.htm.
564. Schwarcz SL. Regulating complexity in financial markets. Wash UL Rev. 2009;87:211.
565. Miller BP. The effects of reporting complexity on small and large investor trading. The Accounting Review. 2010;85(6):2107-43.
566. Bushee BJ, Gow ID, Taylor DJ. Linguistic Complexity in Firm Disclosures: Obfuscation or Information? Available at SSRN 2375424. 2016.
567. You H, Zhang X-j. Financial reporting complexity and investor underreaction to 10-K information. Review of Accounting studies. 2009;14(4):559-86.
568. Lawrence A. Individual investors and financial disclosure. Journal of Accounting and Economics. 2013;56(1):130-47.
569. Lang M, Stice-Lawrence L. Textual analysis and international financial reporting: Large sample evidence. Journal of Accounting and Economics. 2015;60(2-3):110-35.
570. Lehavy R, Li F, Merkley K. The effect of annual report readability on analyst following and the properties of their earnings forecasts. The Accounting Review. 2011;86(3):1087-115.
571. Bonsall SB, Miller BP. The impact of narrative disclosure readability on bond ratings and the cost of debt. Review of Accounting Studies. 2017;22(2):608-43.
572. Downs A. An economic theory of political action in a democracy. The journal of political economy. 1957:135-50.
573. JOHANNES L. Tyco Hopes to Increase Shareholder Value With Breakup, but Wall Street Is Skeptical 2002. Available from: http://www.wsj.com/articles/SB1011755656584867200.
574. Dozier MH. Note, Barings's Ghost, Item 305 in SEC Regulation SK and" Market Risk" Disclosures of Financial Derivatives, 34 Ga. L Rev. 2000;1417.
575. Fanto JA. We're All Capitalists Now: The Importance, Nature, Provision and Regulation of Investor Education. Case W Res L Rev. 1998;49:105.
576. HKEX. Guide on Producing Simplified Listing Documents Relating to Equity Securities for New Applications. 2017.
577. Bernheim D. Do households appreciate their financial vulnerabilities? An analysis of actions, perceptions, and public policy. Tax policy and economic growth. 1995;3:11-30.
578. Bernheim DD. Financial illiteracy, education, and retirement saving. Wharton School Pension Research Council, University of Pennsylvania, 1998.
579. OECD. Improving financial literacy: analysis of issues and policies: Organisation for Economic Co-operation and Development; 2005.
580. Lusardi A, Mitchell OS. Financial literacy and planning: Implications for retirement well-being. Michigan Retirement Research Center Research Paper No WP. 2005;108.
581. Huston SJ. Measuring financial literacy. Journal of Consumer Affairs. 2010;44(2):296-316.
582. OECD-INFE. Measuring Financial Literacy: Questionnaire and Guidance Notes for conducting an Internationally Comparable Survey of Financial Literacy. Periodical Measuring Financial Literacy: Questionnaire and Guidance Notes for conducting an Internationally Comparable Survey of Financial Literacy. 2011.
583. Hung A, Parker AM, Yoong J. Defining and measuring financial literacy. 2009.
584. Lusardi A, Tufano P. Debt literacy, financial experiences, and overindebtedness. Journal of Pension Economics and Finance. 2015;14(04):332-68.
585. Lusardi A, Tufano P. Debt literacy, financial experiences, and overindebtedness. National Bureau of Economic Research, 2009.
586. Lusardi A, Schneider DJ, Tufano P. Financially fragile households: Evidence and implications. National Bureau of Economic Research, 2011.
587. Lusardi A, Mitchell OS. The economic importance of financial literacy: Theory and evidence. National Bureau of Economic Research, 2013.
588. Association AL. Presidential Committee on Information Literacy: Final Report. 1989.
589. Association AL. Information literacy competency standards for higher education. 2000.
590. Lai I. Role of Disclosure in Complementing Financial Literacy Campaigns 2006.
591. Hastings JS, Madrian BC, Skimmyhorn WL. Financial literacy, financial education and economic outcomes. National Bureau of Economic Research, 2012.
592. Lusardi A, Mitchell OS. How ordinary consumers make complex economic decisions: Finan-

cial literacy and retirement readiness. National Bureau of Economic Research, 2009.
593. Parker AM, Bruin WB, Yoong J, Willis R. Inappropriate confidence and retirement planning: Four studies with a national sample. Journal of Behavioral Decision Making. 2012;25(4):382-9.
594. Agnew JR, Szykman LR. Asset allocation and information overload: The influence of information display, asset choice, and investor experience. The Journal of Behavioral Finance. 2005;6(2):57-70.
595. Van Rooij M, Lusardi A, Alessie R. Financial literacy and stock market participation. Journal of Financial Economics. 2011;101(2):449-72.
596. Klapper LF, Lusardi A, Panos GA. Financial literacy and the financial crisis. National Bureau of Economic Research, 2012.
597. Klapper L, Lusardi A, Panos GA. Financial literacy and its consequences: Evidence from Russia during the financial crisis. Journal of Banking & Finance. 2013;37(10):3904-23.
598. Calvet LE, Campbell JY, Sodini P. Down or out: Assessing the welfare costs of household investment mistakes. National Bureau of Economic Research, 2007.
599. Calvet LE, Campbell JY, Sodini P. Measuring the financial sophistication of households. National Bureau of Economic Research, 2009.
600. Potrich ACG, Vieira KM, Kirch G. Determinants of Financial Literacy: Analysis of the Influence of Socioeconomic and Demographic Variables. Revista Contabilidade & Finanças. 2015;26(69):362-77.
601. Bose U, MacDonald R, Tsoukas S. The role of financial education in international portfolios during the recent financial crisis. 2010.
602. Hilgert MA, Hogarth JM, Beverly SG. Household financial management: The connection between knowledge and behavior. Fed Res Bull. 2003;89:309.
603. Lusardi A. Saving and the effectiveness of financial education. Pension Research Council WP2003-14. 2003.
604. Elliehausen G, Christopher Lundquist E, Staten ME. The impact of credit counseling on subsequent borrower behavior. Journal of Consumer Affairs. 2007;41(1):1-28.
605. Hirad A, Zorn PM. A little knowledge is a good thing: Empirical evidence of the effectiveness of pre-purchase homeownership counseling: Joint Center for Housing Studies of Harvard University Cambridge, MA; 2001.
606. Mitchell OS, Lusardi A. Financial Literacy and Economic Outcomes: Evidence and Policy Implications. Available at SSRN 2568732. 2015.
607. Christelis D, Jappelli T, Padula M. Cognitive abilities and portfolio choice. European Economic Review. 2010;54(1):18-38.
608. Yoong J. Financial illiteracy and stock market participation: Evidence from the RAND American Life Panel. Financial literacy: Implications for retirement security and the financial marketplace. 2011;76.
609. Campbell JY. Household finance. The Journal of Finance. 2006;61(4):1553-604.
610. Kimball M, Shumway T. Investor sophistication, and the participation, home bias, diversification, and employer stock puzzles. Ann Arbor: Unpublished Manuscript, University of Michigan. 2006.
611. Kimball MS, Shumway T. Investor sophistication and the home bias, diversification, and employer stock puzzles. Diversification, And Employer Stock Puzzles (January 29, 2010). 2010.
612. Guiso L, Jappelli T. Financial literacy and portfolio diversification. 2008.
613. Goetzmann WN, Kumar A. Why do individual investors hold under-diversified portfolios? Yale School of Management, 2005.
614. Goetzmann WN, Kumar A. Equity portfolio diversification. Review of Finance. 2008;12(3):433-63.
615. Bucher-Koenen T, Ziegelmeyer M. Who lost the most? Financial literacy, cognitive abilities, and the financial crisis. 2011.
616. Grinblatt M, Keloharju M, Linnainmaa J. Do smart investors outperform dumb investors. Chicago Booth Research Paper. 2009;9(33):46.
617. Lusardi A, Michaud P-C, Mitchell OS. Optimal financial knowledge and wealth inequality. National Bureau of Economic Research, 2013.

618. Tennyson S, Nguyen C. State curriculum mandates and student knowledge of personal finance. Journal of Consumer Affairs. 2001;35(2):241-62.
619. Walstad WB, Rebeck K, MacDonald RA. The effects of financial education on the financial knowledge of high school students. Journal of Consumer Affairs. 2010;44(2):336-57.
620. Brown A, Collins JM, Schmeiser MD, Urban C. State mandated financial education and the credit behavior of young adults. 2014.
621. Mandell L. School-Based Financial Education: Not Ready for Prime Time. 2012.
622. Willis LE. Against financial literacy education. Iowa Law Review. 2008;94:08-10.
623. IOSCO. Discussion Paper on the Role of Investor Education in the Effective Regulation of CIS and CIS Operators: Report of the Technical Committee of the International Organization of Securities Commissions 2001. Available from: https://www.iosco.org/library/pubdocs/pdf/IOSCOPD117.pdf.
624. Fox J, Bartholomae S, Lee J. Building the case for financial education. Journal of consumer affairs. 2005;39(1):195-214.
625. Wagner J. An analysis of the effects of financial education on financial literacy and financial behaviors. 2015.
626. Stolper OA, Walter A. Financial literacy, financial advice, and financial behavior. Journal of Business Economics. 2017;87(5):581-643.
627. Turner JA, Klein BW, Stein NP. Financial illiteracy meets conflicted advice: The case of Thrift Savings Plan rollovers. The Journal of Retirement. 2016;3(4):47-65.

FOOTNOTES

[1] Liquidity is closely related to the price, and thus bid-ask spread is generally used to measure the degree of liquidity empirically. The quoted bid-ask spread is the difference between the ask price quoted and the bid price quoted. The realized bid-ask spread is the average difference between the ask price traded and the bid price traded. Quoted spreads can be measured in dollars or as a percent of the price.

[2] "The New Palgrave: A Dictionary of Economics" (1987, p.549) defines "moral hazard" as "actions of economic agents in maximizing their own utility to the detriment of others, in situation where they do not bear the full consequences or, equivalently, do not enjoy the full benefits of their actions due to 1) uncertainty and 2) incomplete or restricted contracts which prevent assignment of full damages (benefits) to the agent responsible."

[3] By comparing the effects of many signaling strategies in an on-line comic book market, Dewally and Ederington (2002) found that book certification by trusted third-party results in "a higher price regardless of the seller's reputation." They also emphasize the importance of considering alternative strategies when analyzing signaling strategies. Without certification, money-back guarantees and book seller's reputation matter, but "rational buyers apparently tend to question why a seller chose a less effective strategy."

[4] The term is said to originate from a meeting between a French minister and a group of businessmen in 1681. When the merchants are asked how the government could be of service, they replied "Laissez- faire." (Investopia, Jim Chappelow, Jul25, 2019, https://www.investopia.com/terms/l/laissezfaire.asp)

[5] Spence (1973) defined "indices" as an unalterable attribute, "signals" as an alterable one. *"For example, education is something that the individual can invest in at some cost in terms of time and money"*, while race and sex are not generally alterable. Individuals are assumed to signal so as to maximize the difference between signaling benefits and costs. In the job market, employers are ready to scrutinize job applicant's attributes to overcome information asymmetry regarding the job applicant's capabilities. Job applicants who are already cognizant of the employer's screening strategy will make voluntary signals. There is an essential assumption that *"a signal will not effectively distinguish one applicant from another unless the costs of*

signaling are negatively correlated with" productivity. Signaling costs of the more productive applicant is lower than that of the less productive one. If this condition does not hold, everyone will make same signal so that nobody can be distinguished. If a specific signaling strategy is productive relative to the costs, everyone will heavily invest in the signaling, and it may lose the signaling effect. For example, systematic over-investment in education can be a distinct possibility of social inefficiency.

[6] For example, fiddler crab can be a good example of the cheating signaler. Female fiddler crab has symmetric claws, but male fiddler has asymmetric claws. Male fiddler crab is known to make a fighting signal against an enemy and enticing signal for female crab with its enlarged claw. It shows off strong claws but hides weak claws. If such a cheating signal is found out by its predator, it may cause the signaling system to totally collapse and put all the fiddler family in danger of extinction by its predator. A dishonest signal can make information asymmetry even worse off than before.

[7] Such concepts as budget line, welfare function, indifference curve, equilibrium, or optimization that are used in this chapter are fundamental in microeconomic theory or welfare economics.

[8] When it comes to commodity production, the average cost is high when the production unit is low, but it decreases as the production unit increases because of fixed cost, and it increases as variable cost increases with the increased production.

[9] "Voluntary disclosure" is more generally used in the capital market to compare with mandated or regulated disclosure. There is a tendency to use "discretionary disclosure" to focus on the behaviors of managers who exercise discretion in disclosure decisions.

[10] Researchers can explain the firm-specific risk premium (e.g., size effect) by using the build-up model.

[11] Liquidity risk may be cited as an example of firm-specific risk. In a thinly traded market, investors will not pay the full value of assets instead require compensation for potential loss that depends on investor's perception of liquidity risk.

[12] Benefits and costs from the perspective of 'economy or society' are essential in understanding the principles of "disclosure regulation." However, only benefits and costs of "disclosing firm" will be a matter of grave concern of voluntary disclosure because rational firm-value-maximizing managers will not pay attention to the benefits and costs of the economy or society (e.g., efficient capital allocation, investor protection, meritless lawsuits).

[13] Many factors push managers into voluntary disclosure of more information than required by the rule, which is frequently named as disclosure factors, disclosure benefits, determinants, and disclosure motives. In this book, "disclosure benefit" is defined as positive effects or consequences of disclosure to the disclosing firm, not to the manager. Disclosure benefit provides incentives for the firm to make voluntary disclosure when it exceeds disclosure cost. To differentiate from disclosure benefit, "disclosure mo-

tives" in this book is defined as effects "to the manager," not to the disclosing firm. Thus, when it comes to disclosure benefit, managers are assumed to act entirely on behalf of shareholders' interests.

[14] "...the variance of the firm's cash flow ... increases if and only if the adjustment cost of new investment is sufficiently low..."

[15] Relative spread: The relative spread is the dollar spread divided by the average of the bid and ask prices.

[16] Share turnover: Share turnover is trading volume scaled by shares outstanding

[17] The firms with low disclosure rankings (i.e., bottom third) showed 50 percent higher bid-ask spread than the firms with high rankings (i.e., top third).

[18] Healy, Hutton and Palepu (1999) examined that firms of which AIMR disclosure scores increase show a decline in relative spreads.

[19] They also find that *"the effects of higher quality disclosures in reducing adverse selection risk are most pronounced for large trades relative to quoted depth."*

[20] Forecasting firms experience an increase in bid-ask spread prior to the forecast but show a significant decrease after the forecast, which suggests that information asymmetry may prompt management to issue a forecast, and it results in more liquidity.

[21] Easley & O'hara (2004) dictates that *"The asset structure ... in some asset specific risks being less than completely diversifiable. ... What allows those risks and the information risk ... is simply that agents must be compensated for risk, and the asset structure is not sufficient to remove the risk."*

[22] Rule 10b-5: Employment of Manipulative and Deceptive Practices": It shall be unlawful for any person, ..., (a) ..., (b) ... to omit to state a material fact necessary in order to make the statements made, in the light of the circumstances under which they were made, not misleading, or, or (c) ..., in connection with the purchase or sale of any security."

[23] On the other hand, some managers can be hesitant about disclosing with the worries of a potential lawsuit by litigator who finds a hole from the disclosed information (i.e., the indirect cost of disclosure). One man's meat is another man's poison. Such indirect cost of the disclosure will be covered in the chapter of disclosure cost.

[24] A residual variance is a difference in asset returns from the security market line. A residual variance contributes to measuring unsystematic volatility.

[25] With an increase in the number of firms in a large economy, the average "firm's own variance" of returns disappears because the firm's own variance term only appears once and is divided by the number of firms. Whereas average "covariance with other firms" is not diversified away, because the number of covariance terms also increases with the number of firms. (The two formula is copied from Lambert, Leuz, and Verrecchia (2007).)

[26] ATC: average total cost, AVC: average variable cost, AFC: average fixed cost

[27] Merriam Webster, https://www.merriam-webster.com/dictionary/proprietary

[28] Confidential treatment request can be made pursuant to the SEC Rule 24b-2 of the 1934 Act, the SEC Rule 406 of the 1933 Act, and the SEC's Rules of Practice (17 CFR 201.190), which describe the procedure of the nondisclosure of information. Besides, the SEC Rule 83 provides a procedure by which issuer may request withholding under the Freedom of Information Act (FOIA).

[29] Damodaran (2006) warns that *"...In fact, there is the possibility that the perception that a firm is in trouble can create a death spiral, where customers stop buying the firm's products and employees abandon ship, thus creating even more financial trouble, until it becomes a self-fulfilling prophecy."*

[30] According to Clinch (1997), *"...Knowledge about aggregate demand affects a firm's choice of an optimal level of production. Knowledge also affects a firm's disclosure policy since disclosing what a firm knows privately influences the production schedules of competing firms. For example, since anticipated high aggregate demand stimulates production across firms, while low demand curtails production, a firm may be inclined to disclose evidence of low demand so as to discourage overproduction. Similarly, a firm may be inclined to withhold evidence of high demand so as to exploit underproduction by competitors...."*

[31] Information about major customer is useful for investors to assess the risk of losing a significant customer. For instance, the degree of concentration in a customer base is informative to investors. Hence, SEC Regulation S-K requires the publicly traded firms to report the identity of any major customer that comprises more than 10% of consolidated revenues. Losing such customers would have a material adverse effect. According to Ellis, Fee, and Thomas (2012), the identity of a major customer tends to be concealed for firms with high proprietary cost (e.g., R&D expenditures, intangible assets, advertising expenditures, profit persistence, and less competitive industries).

[32] Under SEC Rule, any firm filing reports may make an objection to its public disclosure and request 'confidential treatment' for competitively sensitive information contained in material agreements. The firm can request such 'redaction' for specific contents.

[33] As a proxy of entry barriers, Leuz (2003) used the capital intensity that is measured as the ratio of net property, plant, and equipment divided by total assets.

[34] For example, the Herfindahl index (i.e., HHI) calculated as the sum of the squared market share of each firm in a particular industry group. An increase in HHI indicates the decrease in competition and the increase in market power, concentration, and competitiveness.

[35] In a perfect competition market where many firms are competing, post-entry competition is fierce, but they have less to lose from the disclosure of proprietary information. As a matter of fact, there might be little chance of holding proprietary information. On the contrary, one might assume that a

high market share concentration can be a powerful entry barrier, and, as a result, the dominating firm might not be reluctant to disclose proprietary information. Actually, market share concentration may be an entry barrier to a certain degree. As the market share concentration is quarry or prey, the dominating firm have much to lose from the disclosure of proprietary information. In the real world, as a result, *"Poor and liberal, rich and covetous."*

[36] The relative importance of competitive forces differs by industry. For example, even though the rivalry is fierce in an industry, however, the competition or rivalry may be irrelevant to profitability, rather other factors may be influencing profitability. Rivalry may be important in an industry, while the power of resource suppliers is important in other industries.

Many researchers try to adopt various proxies for industry competition. One may adopt the "structural proxies" that represent industry structure (e.g., number of competitors, concentration ratio, entry barrier) to proxy the degree of industry competition, while others consider the "behavioral proxies" that is focusing on the interrelation and strategies adopted by the rivalry. Depending on the strategic behaviors of competitors, the proprietary cost of a market can be far different in magnitude from other markets even though they are similar in market structures. Thus, a behavioral approach would be researcher's another option to find out the meaningful determinants of proprietary cost.

[37] The product market level disclosure benefit generated by the disclosure of proprietary information could be named by "proprietary benefit."

[38] Any information publicly available will not be treated as proprietary. Thus, firms must treat information as confidential in order to receive confidential treatment and prove that disclosure of proprietary information will give the firm a competitive disadvantage. Relevant SEC rules are 17 CFR 230.406 and 17 CFR 240.24b-2.

[39] The Standard Industrial Classification (SIC) is an industry classification system established in the United States in 1937.

[40] Rule 10b-5 : Employment of Manipulative and Deceptive Practices *"It shall be unlawful for any person, …, (a) …, (b) To make any untrue statement of a material fact or to omit to state a material fact necessary in order to make the statements made, in the light of the circumstances under which they were made, not misleading, or, or (c) …, in connection with the purchase or sale of any security."*

[41] To measure the aggregate loss for all filings, Cornerstone Research, Inc. developed the "Disclosure Dollar Loss (DDL) Index" which is the change in dollar value of the defendant firm's market capitalization. The report emphasizes that the *"DDL should not be considered as an indicator of liability or a measure of potential damages"* but an estimate of *"the impact of all information revealed"* during the class period.

[42] Securities class action filings in 2014 are below; technology (1,117 cases, 28.1%), services (798 cases, 20.1%), and financial (750 cases, 18.9%). (Source; Stanford Securities Class Action Clearinghouse, Securities Class Ac-

tion Filings 2014 Year in Review, Figure 6)

[43] In general, the non-disclosure risk of bad news is greater than that of good news, which leads managers to make more disclosure that is optimal, for a given disclosure benefit (left graph). For a given threshold level, the non-disclosure risk of bad news is sharply increasing with delay, which leads to preemptive disclosure (right graph).

[44] The impact of firm size is multi-faceted. Regarding direct cost, larger firm tends to have relatively lower information production cost, thus firm size is positively associated with voluntary disclosure. Regarding indirect cost, larger firm tends to face lower competitive harm from disclosure, and thus firm size is positively associated with voluntary disclosure. Regarding disclosure benefit, large firms have more capital needs than small firms. Consequently, they are willing to provide voluntary disclosure.

[45] Social information includes information about directors, employee, social responsibility, and value-added disclosure.

[46] FASB, https://www.fasb.org/summary/stsum158.shtml

[47] Stanford Encyclopedia of Philosophy, Winter 2009 Edition, https://plato.stanford.edu/archives/win2009/entries/determinism-causal

[48] https://en.wikipedia.org/wiki/Free_will

[49] For example, in the short run, smoking can provoke lung cancer, but the converse does not hold. In the long run, however, the inverse may hold when the patient well-cured from prior lung cancer is determined to quit smoking.

[50] The length of the listing period may be relevant in explaining the extent of disclosure. Investors are more risk aversive to the newly listed firms. When firms fail to provide adequate disclosure, they can be stigmatized as a lemon. Thus, the newly listed firms will disclose more information to reduce skepticism and enhance investors' confidence. Especially, a recently listed firm are more likely to raise additional capital compared to the already listed firms that are matured and rely more on internal funds.

[51] With more resources, larger firms can provide less costly but more accurate disclosure. They disclose already-gathered information at a lower cost since they require more information than small firms for internal purposes.

[52] Large firms have a stronger position in the product market, and they are less vulnerable to competition. However, voluntary disclosure of small firms may endanger a competitive position against large firms in the same industry.

[53] On the contrary, small-firm investors are provided with a larger amount of "unexpected" information by disclosure, which may lead a higher degree of unexpected stock price changes. Firm size should be inversely related to the price effect of disclosure.

[54] Firms with diffused shareholdings might be voluntarily disclosing even under the low disclosure pressure when managers or controlling shareholders think they have nothing to lose from public disclosure.

[55] In general, the "contagion effect" refers to a phenomenon that mostly

bad news (e.g., bankruptcy, downgrade, or restatement) affect other firms' stock price negatively. The contagion effect is also used in the researches of international financial crisis.

[56] The confidential treatment will be covered in the Chapter 44.

[57] According to the Bankruptcy Code of the United States, Chapter 11 is referred to as "reorganization or rehabilitation" code, while Chapter 7 provides for "liquidation." Under Chapter 7, a variety of assets is sold/liquidated to repay debts, while debtors negotiate with creditors to change the terms of debt financing without liquidation under Chapter 11.

[58] Oscar Wilde, Act 1 of "The Importance of Being Earnest."

[59] Gibbins, Richardson, and Waterhouse (1990) describes that "...*The ritualistic ... is described as a propensity toward uncritical adherence to prescribed norms for the measurement and disclosure of financial information. Norms are the formal or informal rules, procedures, and standards believed by the firm's managers to apply to a particular disclosure issue...*"

[60] For example, if talented managers designed and disclosed firms' new strategy, then copycat competitors in the job market can easily learn and establish similar or better strategies to overtake the disclosing manager. Such a copycat may find a way to outperform the originator; in result, the copycat may attain better renown. This may be termed as the "managerial proprietary cost."

[61] Cao, Wasley, and Wu (2007) defines "soft-talk" forecasts as certain types of cash flow forecasts that are disclosed in equivocal items without a precise GAAP definition and far from a verifiable GAAP cash flow number. About 20% of cash flow forecasts are argued to be "soft-talk".

[62] Merriam Webster

[63] Statement of Financial Accounting Concepts) No. 8 Appendix: Basis for Conclusions for Chapter 3 "*BC3.44 Transparency, high quality ... and credibility have been suggested as desirable qualitative characteristics of financial information. However, ... Credibility is similar but also implies trustworthiness of a reporting entity's management.*"

[64] As the credibility includes the quality, researches of the disclosure quality can be classified as a special dimension of credibility.

[65] The New Testament in Matthew 7:17 (NIV)

[66] In general, various types of market penalties, such as reputational harm, legal cost, and potential job opportunity loss, will deter the manages from making intentionally biased or opportunistic forecasts. However, such penalties are less effective for the managers of the distressed firm. They have a greater incentive to release biased good news forecasts but pay less attention to enforcements or penalties that may be imposed later owing to the inaccurate forecasts. Learning out such attributes of the distressed firms, information users will make a skeptical response to the disclosure made by the distressed firms.

[67] Investors of large firms tend to have more sources of information than investors of small firms since analysts and press have a tendency to follow

large firms and provide enough analysis. Thus, the importance of the EPS growth pattern in determining the credibility of disclosure declines with firm size.

[68] Andrus' four types of utility:
- Form utility: Information will be more valuable if the form of information closely matches information user's demand. A consistent and understandable format is more valuable.
- Time utility: Information will be more valuable if it is available when needed.
- Place utility: Information will be more valuable if it can be delivered easily.
- Possession utility: The person who owns information influences its value by controlling its dissemination to others.

[69] Hierarchical framework:
- Intrinsic quality: accuracy, objectivity, believability, reputation.
- Contextual quality: relevancy, value-added, timeliness, completeness, appropriate amount.
- Representational quality: interpretability, ease of understanding, representational consistency, concise representation.
- Accessibility: accessibility, access security.

[70] The Gunning Fog Index is calculated with the following formula; 1) add the average sentence length and the percentage of complex words which has three or more syllables, 2) multiply the above result by 40%. The index indicates the number of years of formal education that an intended audience would need to understand the text. Thus, a higher score indicates a less readable disclosure. The Fog index is sometimes used as a measure of complexity of disclosure. (https://en.wikipedia.org/wiki/Gunning_fog_index)

Gunning Fog Index=0.4*(words per sentence + percent of complex words)

[71] 1. Trading venue: Cross-listing in advanced markets is a commitment to follow stronger enforcements, higher standards, and more stringent scrutiny from investors. Thus, cross-listing or the issuance of ADR is often used as a proxy of disclosure quality. Firms listed in developed markets are assumed to provide better disclosure than firms listed in emerging markets.

2. Analysts following: Greater analyst following indicate a better disclosure.

3. Forecasts: Analysts' forecasts are more accurate for firms that disclose better because better disclosure enables analysts to forecast earnings better. Firms with better disclosure have less dispersion in analysts' forecasts and less volatility in forecast revisions.

4. Special events: Special events can be a good proxy to measure the disclosure. For example, the eventual change of accounting standard from local standard to global standard, mandating OTC firms to follow requirements under the 1934 Act.

[72] Consequently, some researchers may develop a self-constructed market-based index and call it "disclosure index," under the assumption that the market-based index is strongly associated with the disclosure quality, and

thus it is a good proxy of the disclosure quality. However, such measures are still an indirect approach that is a market-based disclosure measure.

[73] PDCA cycle:
- Plan: Establish objectives and processes that are required to deliver the desired goal.
- Do: Enact the plan.
- Check/study: The results gathered from the DO phase are evaluated. Gap analysis can be used to check. Issues, problems, inefficiencies are identified.
- Act/adjust: By solving problems, a process is improved and have better standards.

[75] Voluntary disclosure model of Guttentag (2007) is summarized in the Chapter 223.

[76] The function of the socially optimal disclosure policy (S(a,g)) is quite similar to the function of the voluntarily optimal disclosure policy (V(a,g) in Chapter 223, but that divisor is (λ-k) instead of (1-k). Voluntarily disclosure can be said to be a specific case of a general model where there is no inter-firm externality (λ=1). The variable k signifies the extent to which the disclosure of accuracy information (a) reduces agency costs.

[77] In this model, no significant inter-firm externalities are assumed to arise from the disclosure of agency information for simple analysis. As a result, the extent of agency information (g) that is additionally mandated is zero in R*(a,g), meaning that regulator have no reason to intervene to mandate additional disclosure of agency information. However, if we adjust the original assumption to reflect real world, then mandatory disclosure of agency information would generate quite inter-firm externality in terms of utility or cost. For example, disclosure of agency information by a firm with poor governance may impact other similar firms.

[78] Joseph N. Dolley explained the story behind the blue sky law in the Topeka State Journal. *"That name goes back to the drought of the nineties. ... Even water for domestic use was disappearing. ... So we raised the necessary money and contracted with some Chicago slicker to supply us with the necessary quantity of moisture. ... They set up their equipment on a platform ... But there was no sign of rain. The fifth day our committee visited the rain-makers plant, to discover that the rain makers had disappeared, leaving their equipment behind. ... When I appeared before the judiciary committee of the Kansas house ..., remembering our experience with the blue sky artists in trying to make rain, I suggested "the blue sky law.""*

[79] *"The name ... indicates the evil at which it is aimed ... to use the language of a cited case, speculative schemes which have no more basis than so many feet of blue sky;"* or ... *"to stop the sale of stock in fly-by-night concerns ... and other like fraudulent exploitations."* - (Hall v. Geiger-Jones Co., 242 U.S. 539, 550 (1917))

[80] In 1912 and 1913, ten states adopted statutes similar to the Kansas merit review.

[81] The Kansas Uniform Securities Act of 2015 includes a similar language under 17-12a306(a)(7)(c) as a ground for stop orders. *"The administrator may issue a stop order denying effectiveness to, or suspending or revoking the effectiveness of, a registration statement if the administrator finds that the stop order is in the public interest and that ... the offering ... is being made on terms that are unfair, unjust, or inequitable."*

[82] First, urban states with larger financial markets might have experienced less abuse than farming states because large institutional investors and stock exchanges operating in urban states might be keeping more close eyes on the issuer's misbehavior. Thus, the social cost of securities fraud in large city-states might be lower than that in farming states, which lead to delayed adoption.

Second, once issuers in farming state were relatively smaller and weaker in internal control, the social cost of securities fraud in farming state could be greater. As a result, early adopters could be assumed to be serious states, which support the public interest approach.

Third, all regulators are operating under limited budget, and they experience the economies of scale in fraud detection. However, there might be dis-economies of scale if the market size of urban states exceeds a certain level. If the degree of regulation exceeds the minimum point of the average fraud detection cost, and then the average cost will rise.

[83] Uniform Securities Act of 1956

"Sec.306. (Denial, Suspension, and Revocation of Registration) (a) The Administrator may issue a stop order denying effectiveness to, or suspending or revoking the effectiveness of, any registration statement if he finds...

  (2) that ...

    (E) the offering is being made on terms that are unfair, unjust or inequitable.

    (F) the offering has been or would be made with unreasonable amounts of underwriters' and sellers' discounts, commissions, or other compensation, or promoters' profits or participation, or unreasonable amounts or kinds of options;"

[84] California Corporations Code 25140.

"(d) ..., the commissioner shall not have authority to issue any stop order or to refuse to issue or to suspend or revoke any permit ... where the security is being publicly offered for cash pursuant to a registration statement under the Securities Act of 1933 and the offering is the subject of a firm commitment underwriting by an underwriter ... registered under the Securities Exchange Act of 1934 ..." (Amended by Stats. 1990, Ch. 1035, Sec. 2.)

[85] NASAA (2011), "A Century of Investor Protection", http://www.nasaa.org/wp-content/uploads/2011/07/100_Years_Commemorative_FINAL.pdf, *"In the 18 months following the enactment of the Kansas law, more than 1,500 companies applied for permission to do business in the state. Of these, 75 percent "were mining, oil, gas and stock selling schemes of a fraudulent nature in which there could be no possible return for the money invested.*

Of the remaining 25 percent, about half were companies with highly speculative propositions and not at all bona fide investment opportunities," according to noted political scientist Clarence Addison Dykstra."

[86] Wall Street Journal, "Apple Computer Set to Go Public Today; Massachusetts Bars Sale of Stock as Risky", 12 Dec 1980, http://online.wsj.com/public/resources/documents/AppleIPODec12_1980_WSJ.pdf

[87] CNBC, "If you invested $1,000 in Apple at its IPO, here's how much money you'd have not", 1 November 2018, https://www.cnbc.com/2018/11/01/how-much-a-1000-dollar-investment-in-apple-at-its-ipo-would-be-worth-now.html

[88] Section 18 State Control of Securities of the 1933 act sets out that *"Nothing in this title shall affect the jurisdiction … of any State …."* and Section 28(a) of the 1934 act sets out that *"Nothing in this title shall affect the jurisdiction … of any State … insofar as it does not conflict with the provisions of this title …."*

[89] *USA Sec. 101. (Sales and Purchases) It is unlawful for any person, in connection with the offer, sale or purchase of any security, directly or indirectly*

(1) to employ any device, scheme, or artifice to defraud,

(2) to make any untrue statement of a material fact or to omit to state a material fact necessary in order to make the statements made, in the light of the circumstances under which they are made, not misleading, or

(3) to engage in any act, practice, or course of business which operates or would operate as a fraud or deceit upon any person

[90] The Uniform Sales of Securities Act of 1930 was promulgated in 1930, enacted by only five states, and dropped from the Uniform Act list in 1943. Meanwhile, the National Conference of Commissioners on Uniform State Laws (NCCUSL) developed the Uniform Securities Act ("USA") of 1956 by substantially revising the 1930 Act. Finally, the Act was successfully adopted by 37 states, and revised again in 1985, and replaced by the USA of 2002. The Act earned broad supports from representatives of government and private sectors and became the standard model for many states to follow after being endorsed by many organizations such as NYSE, NASAA, NASD, SIA, as a result.

[91] Examples of exempt securities include such as securities listed securities, and examples of transactional exemptions include such as any transaction pursuant to an offer to a small number of persons during a short period.

[92] Registration by notification requires a notice filing with the state. It is for mature issuers with relatively sound profits. Registration by coordination is available where there is the registration under the federal Securities Act. The review process is coordinated with the SEC. Registration by qualification requires a full review by the state. It is required if an offering is not registered under the Securities Act, such as an offering exempt from registration under the Securities Act but not exempt from state registration requirements.

[93] NASAA, Model Accredited Investor Exemption, 27 Apr 1997, https://www.nasaa.org/wp-content/uploads/2011/07/24-Model_Accredited_Investor_Exemption.pdf, (*"Any offer or sale of a security by an issuer in a transaction that meets the requirements of this rule is exempted from [Sections requiring registration and filing of advertising materials]."*)

[94] For instance, issuers seeking registration under the guideline must not be a development stage company that either has no specific business plan or purpose, or has indicate that its business plan is to merge with or acquire an unidentified company. (III-E of the Statement of Policy)

[95] For instance, the issuer must file with the Administrator and provide to investor annual financial statements, certified by the issuer's chief executive officer. (V-A of the Statement of Policy)

[96] For instance, unless the Administrator determines that it is not necessary to disqualify an offering, registration is not available to an issuer if the issuer, within the last five years, has filed an application for registration which is subject of stop order, or has been convicted of any felony, or is subject to court-imposed sanctions, etc. (VI-A of the Statement of Policy)

[97] NASAA, Small Company Offering Registrations (SCOR) Statement of Policy, 19 May 2019, https://www.nasaa.org/wp-content/uploads/2019/05/Amended-SCOR-Statement-of-Policy.pdf

[98] *SEC. 18. (Exemption from State Regulation of Securities Offerings) (a) Scope of Exemption - ... no law, rule, regulation of any State ... 1) ...with respect to registration or qualification of securities... shall apply to a security that is a covered security..., or 2) shall prohibit, limit, or impose any conditions upon the use of any offering document..., or 3) shall prohibit, limit, or impose conditions, based on the merits of such offering or issuer, upon the offer or sale of any security that is a covered security.*

[99] A security is a "covered security" if such security is 1) nationally traded securities (e.g., NYSE, Nasdaq NMS), 2) a security of the same issuer that is equal or senior in seniority to the listed security (Section 18(b)(1)). Securities issued by an investment company that is registered, etc. A security is a covered security with respect to the offer or sale to qualified purchasers. The "qualified purchasers" are defined by the SEC rule. (Section 18(b)(3)). In addition, certain federal exempt offerings are included. A security is a covered security with respect to a transaction that is exempt from federal registration pursuant to some provisions of Section 3 and Section 4 of 1933 Act (e.g., government securities, bank securities and commercial paper) (Section 18(b)(4)).

[100] The securities commission of any State shall retain jurisdiction to investigate and bring enforcement actions with respect to fraud, deceit, or unlawful conduct.

[101] The securities commission of any State shall not be prohibited from requiring the filing of any document filed with the SEC *"solely for notice purposes and the assessment of any fee."*

[102] Filing or registration fees shall continue to be collected in amounts determined pursuant to State law.

[103] The securities commission of any State shall not be prohibited from suspending the offer or sale within such State as a result of the failure to submit any filing or fee required under law.

[104] Section 16 (Additional Remedies; Limitation on Remedies) of the Securities Act of 1933.

"... (b) Class Action Limitation. - No covered class action based upon the statutory of any State or subdivision thereof may be maintained in any State or Federal court by any private party alleging – (1) an untrue statement or omission of a material fact in connection with the purchase or sale of a covered security; or (2) that the defendant used or employed any manipulative or deceptive device or contrivance in connection with the purchase or sale of a covered security.

(c) Removal of Covered Class Actions. - Any covered class action brought in any State court involving a covered security, as set forth in subsection (b), shall be removable to the Federal district court for the district in which the actions is pending, and shall be subject to subsection (b). ...

(d) ... (e)

(f) Definitions. ... (2) Covered Class Action. –

(A) In general. – The term "covered class action" means – (i) any single lawsuit in which – (I) damages are sought on behalf of more than 50 persons ... ; or (II) one or more named parties seek to recover damages ...; or (ii) any group of lawsuits filed in or pending in the same court and involving common questions of law or fact, ..."

[105] "Registration by Notification" was adopted in the Section 302 of USA but were little used and it was removed in Section 302 of RUSA.

[106] For instance, required information includes the information of significant subsidiary, information of director and officer, capitalization of long-term debt, and such information as the Administrator requires by rules or order.

[107] https://www.sec.gov/rules/final/2016/33-10238.pdf

[108] States should agree to participate in the CER program. In 1997, NASAA (1997) indicates that 37 states of the 43 states that require the review of non-exempt equity offerings have joined the CER program. (https://www.sec.gov/news/studies/uniformy.htm)

[109] The issuer sends registration materials and one-page of the CER application form to the states in which it intends to offer its securities, which is submitted to the program administrator (Arizona Securities Division). The program administrator designates one state for a merit review and another state for full disclosure review. The non-lead states have ten days to comment on the application. The two lead states gather comments from all the states and issue review letter. The lead states resolve outstanding comments with the issuer.

[110] A private offering is made only to a limited number of investors who are informed of the company's material information, and, as a result, the com-

pany does not need to follow legal procedures.

[111] Section 2(a) Definitions. –
"When used in this title, unless the context otherwise requires – ...
(3) The term "sale" or "sell" shall include every contract of sale of disposition of a security or interest in a security, or value. The term "offer to sell", "offer for sale", or "offer" shall include every attempt or offer to dispose of, or solicitation of an offer to buy, a security or interest in a security, for value."

[112] Section 5 (Prohibitions Relating to Interstate Commerce and the Mails)
> *"(a) Unless a registration statement is in effect as to a security, it shall be unlawful for any person, directly or indirectly*
>> *(1) to make use of any means or instruments of transportation or communication in interstate commerce or of the mails to sell or offer to buy such security through the use or medium of any prospectus or otherwise; or*
>> *(2) to carry or cause to be carried through the mails or in interstate commerce, by any means or instruments of transportation, any such security for the purpose of sale or for delivery after sale."*

[113] Section 3 (Exempted Securities)
"(a) Except as hereafter expressly provided, the provisions of this title shall not apply to any of the following classes of securities: ...
(b) Additional Exemptions.
(1) Small Issues Exemptive Authority. - The Commission may ... add any class of securities to the securities exempted ..., if it finds that the enforcement ... is not necessary in the public interest and for the protection of investors by reason of the small amount involved or the limited character of the public offering; ..."

[114] Section 4 (Exempted Transactions)
"(a) The provisions of section 5 shall not apply to - ... (2) transactions by an issuer not involving any public offering."

[115] SEC v. Ralston Purina Co., 102 F. Supp. 964 (E.D. Mo. 1952), https://casenext.com/case/securities-exchange-comm-v-ralston-purina

[116] SEC v. Ralston Purina Co., 346 U.S. 119 (1953), https://caselaw.findlaw.com/us-supreme-court/346/119.html

[117] SEC v. Ralston Purina Co., 346 U.S. 119 (1953), https://caselaw.findlaw.com/us-supreme-court/346/119.html, (Due to the amendment, "*...the application of 4(1)...*" should be understood as "*...the application of 4(a)(2) ...*")

[118] SEC, Final Rule: Nonpublic Offering Exemption, November 6, 1962, https://www.sec.gov/rules/final/33-4552.htm

[119] The SEC requires the companies to print the preliminary prospectus with red ink on the left side of the cover, which resulted in the name of "red herring." It should include a bold-type and red-color disclaimer on the cover containing that it is incomplete and subject to change.

[120] EY, Trends in US IPO registration statements, November 2018, https://www.ey.com/publication/vwluassetsdld/iporegistrationstatements_04688-181us_30october2018/$file/ipregistrationstatements_04688-181us_30october2018.pdf

[121] *"Section 6. Registration of securities*
(e) Emerging Growth Companies
(1) In General
   Any emerging growth company … may confidentially submit to the Commission a draft registration statement, for confidential nonpublic review …
(2) Confidentiality
   Notwithstanding any other provision of this subchapter, the Commission shall not be compelled to disclose any information provided or obtained by the Commission pursuant to this subsection …"

[122] Under disclosure context, "gun jumping" or "jumping the gun" refers to issuer's offering before the approval of registration statement. Investor should be able to make investment decision based on full disclosure. If a company is in violation of the disclosure rule, the company is guilty of "jumping the gun" or "gun jumping."

[123] PWC, Update on Emerging Growth Companies and the JOBS Act, April 2018, https://www.pwc.com/us/en/deals/assets/pwc-deals-update-on-the-JOBS-act.pdf

[124] EY, Trends in US IPO registration statements, November 2018, https://www.ey.com/publication/vwluassetsdld/iporegistrationstatements_04688-181us_30october2018/$file/ipregistrationstatements_04688-181us_30october2018.pdf

[125] Section 13 Periodical and Other Reports
"(a) Every issuer of a security registered pursuant to section 12 of this title shall file with the Commission, in accordance with such rules and regulations as the Commission may prescribe as necessary or appropriate for the proper protection of investors and to insure fair dealing in the security –"

[126] The SEC mandated the public companies to file annual reports in 1934, and the mandate expanded to semiannual report in 1955 and to quarterly report in 1970. In almost every twenty years, additional reports have been mandated.

[127] Annual Report on Form 10-K should be disclosed within 90 days of the end of its fiscal year, including an audited financial statement. A Form 10-K is substantially similar to a Form 10 (General form for registration of securities). Quarterly Report on Form 10-Q should be disclosed within 45 days of the end of each of its fiscal quarters, including unaudited financial statements. Current Report on Form 8-K should be disclosed within four business days after the occurrence of the event.

[128] Public floating means an aggregated worldwide market value of the noting and non-voting common equity held by its non-affiliates.

[129] SEC, Statement at Open Meeting on a Concept Release on the Business and Financial Disclosure Required by Regulation S-K, April 13, 2016, https://www.sec.gov/news/statement/stein-statement-1-041316.html

[130] SEC, Report on Review of Disclosure Requirements in Regulation S-K, December 2013, https://www.sec.gov/news/studies/2013/reg-sk-disclosure-requirements-review.pdf ("The staff recommends that a comprehen-

sive approach should be used to review and revise the disclosure requirements. A comprehensive approach is to review and update requirements on a wholesale basis, taking into account the appropriateness of substantive requirements as a whole as well as presentation and delivery issues.")

[131] SEC, SEC proposes to Modernize Disclosures of Business, Legal Proceedings, and Risk Factors Under Regulation S-K, https://www.sec.gov/news/press-release/2019.148

[132] Section 14 (Proxies)
"(a) It shall be unlawful for any person, ..., in contravention of such rules and regulations as the Commission may prescribe as necessary or appropriate in the public interest or for the protection of investors, to solicit or to permit the use of his name to solicit any proxy or consent or authorization in respect of any security ... registered pursuant to section 12 of this title."

[133] SEC Schedules 14A is commonly used to provide securities holders with sufficient information in making an informed vote. Schedule 14A. Information required in proxy statement, https://www.law.cornell.edu/cfr/text/17/240.14a-101

[134] SEC, Fast Answers: Form 8-K, https://www.sec.gov/fast-answers/answersform8khtm.html

[135] SEC, Form 8-K, https://www.sec.gov/files/form8-k.pdf
(*"Section 1 Registrant's Business and Operations*
Section 2 Financial Information: Item 2.01 ... 2.06
Section 3 Securities and Trading Markets
Section 4 Matters Related to Accountants and Financial Statements
Section 5 Corporate Governance and Management
Section 6 Asset-Backed Securities
Section 7 Regulation FD
Section 8 Other Events.")

[136] NASDAQ requires advance notice under the NASDAQ Marketplace Rule 5250 and IM-5250-1 "Disclosure of Material Information" and NYSE under NYSE Listed Company Manual Section 202.06 "Procedure for Public Release of Information; Trading Halts."

[137] DORSEY, "Going Dark - Voluntary Delisting and Deregistration under the Securities Exchange Act of 1934 - The Attractions of the Dark Side," Mar 17, 2009, https://www.dorsey.com/newsresources/publications/2009/03/going-dark--voluntary-delisting-and-deregistrati__

[138] Rule 13e-3 Going private transactions by certain issuers or their affiliates.
"(b) Application of section to an issuer (or an affiliate of such issuer) subject to section 12 of the Act.
(1) It shall be a fraudulent, deceptive or manipulative act or practice, in connection with a Rule 13e-3 transaction, for an issuer which has a class of equity securities registered pursuant to section 12 of the Act ..., or an affiliate of such issuer, directly or indirectly
  (i) To employ and device, scheme or artifice to defraud any person;

(ii) To make any untrue statement of a material fact or to omit to state a material fact necessary in order to make the statements made, in light of the circumstances under which they were made, not misleading; or

(iii) To engage in any act, practice or course of business which operates or would operates as a fraud or deceit upon any person.

(c) Application of section to an issuer (or an affiliate of such issuer) subject to section 15(d) of the Act.

(1) It shall be unlawful as a fraudulent, deceptive or manipulative act or practice for an issuer ...

(2) ... .

(d) Material required to be filed. The issue or affiliate engaging in a Rule 13e-3 transaction must file with the Commission:

(1) A Schedule 13E-3, including all exhibits;

(2) An amendment to Schedule 13E-3 reporting promptly any material changes in the information set forth in the schedule previously filed; and

(3) A final amendment to Schedule 13E-3 reporting promptly the results of the Rule 13e-3 transaction."

[139] DORSEY, "Going Dark - Voluntary Delisting and Deregistration under the Securities Exchange Act of 1934 - The Attractions of the Dark Side," Mar 17, 2009, https://www.dorsey.com/newsresources/publications/2009/03/going-dark--voluntary-delisting-and-deregistrati__

[140] Rule 12d2-2 Removal from listing and registration.

"Preliminary Notes:

1. The filing of the Form 25 by an issuer relates solely to the withdrawal of a class of securities from listing on an national securities exchange and/or from registration under section 12(b) of the Act, and shall not affect its obligation to be registered under section 12(g) of the Act and/or reporting obligations under section 15(d) of the Act.

2. Implementation. The rules of each national securities exchange must be designed to meet the requirements of this section ... .

(a) A national securities exchange must file with the Commission an application on Form 25 to strike a class of securities from listing on a national securities exchange and/or registration under section 12(b) of the Act within a reasonable time after the national securities exchange is reliably informed that any of the following conditions exist with respect to such a security:

(1) The entire class of the security as been called for redemption ...

(4) All rights pertaining to the entire class of the security have been extinguished; ... ."

[141] SEC, Release No. 34-55540, March 27, 2007, https://www.sec.gov/rules/final/2007/34-55540.pdf, https://www.sec.gov/files/form15f.pdf

[142] § 240.12h-6 – Certification by a foreign private issuer regarding the termination of registration of a class of securities under section 12(g) or the duty to file reports under section 13(a) or section 15(d).

"(a) A foreign private issuer may terminate the registration of a class of securities under section 12(g) of the Act, or terminate the obligation under section

15(d) of the Act to file or furnish reports required by section 13(a) of the Act with respect to a class of equity securities, or both, after certifying to the Commission on Form 15F that: ...

(4) (i) The average daily trading volume of the subject class of securities in the United States for a recent 12-month period has been no greater than 5 percent of the average daily trading volume of that class of securities on a worldwide basis for the same period; or

(ii) ... a foreign private issuer's subject class of equity securities is either held of record by ... Less than 300 persons ... ."

[143] DORSEY, "Going Dark - Voluntary Delisting and Deregistration under the Securities Exchange Act of 1934 - The Attractions of the Dark Side," Mar 17, 2009, https://www.dorsey.com/newsresources/publications/2009/03/going-dark--voluntary-delisting-and-deregistrati__

[144] DORSEY, Going Dark - Voluntary Delisting and Deregistration under the Securities Exchange Act of 1934 - The Attractions of the Dark Side, Mar 17, 2009, https://www.dorsey.com/newsresources/publications/2009/03/going-dark--voluntary-delisting-and-deregistrati__

[145] Douglas S. Ellenoff, Going Dark: What Companies Need to Know, https://www.otcmarkets.com/files/ellenoff-going-dark.pdf

[146] The SEC Rule 24b-2 of the 1934 Act, the SEC Rule 406 of the 1933 Act, and the SEC's Rules of Practice (17 CFR 201.190) describe the procedure of confidential treatment requesting the nondisclosure of information filed with the Commission.

Rule 24b-2 Nondisclosure of information filed with the Commission and with any exchange.

"(a) Any person filing any registration statement, ... or other document ... pursuant to the Act may make written objection to the public disclosure of any information contained therein in accordance with the procedure set forth below. The procedure provided in this rule shall be the exclusive means of requesting confidential treatment of information required to be filed under the Act.

(b) ... the person shall omit from material filed the portion thereof which it desires to keep undisclosed ... . In lieu thereof, it shall indicate at the appropriate place in the material filed that the confidential portion has been so omitted and filed separately with the Commission."

[147] "Rule 83 Confidential treatment procedures under the Freedom of Information Act.

... (c) Written request for confidential treatment to be submitted with information

(1) Any person who ... submits any information ... to the Commission, which information is entitled to confidential treatment and for which no other specific procedure exists ..., may request that the Commission afford confidential treatment under the Freedom of Information Act to such information for reasons of personal privacy or business confidentiality ... and should take all steps reasonably necessary to ensure ... that at the time the information is first received by the Commission (i) it is supplied separated from information for which con-

fidential treatment is not being requested, (ii) it is appropriately marked as confidential, and (iii) it is accompanied by a written request for confidential treatment which specifies the information as to which confidential treatment is requested."

[148] SEC, "New Rules and Procedures for Exhibits Containing Immaterial, Competitively Harmful Information", April 1, 2019, https://www.sec.gov/corpfin/announcement/new-rules-and-procedures-exhibits-containing-immaterial

[149] FindLaw, "Obtaining Confidential Treatment for Information Furnished to the SEC", https://corporate.findlaw.com/litigation-disputes/obtaining-confidential-treatment-for-information-furnished-to-the.html

[150] Final Report of the Committee of Wise Men on the Regulation of European Securities Markets, 15 February 2001 (https://www.esma.europa.eu/sites/default/files/library/2015/11/lamfussy_report.pdf)

[151] *"3. The content and scope of the disclosure and information rules ... should be harmonized ... : the model prospectus proposed ... might be a suitable basis for such harmonization ...*

8. ... Although the practice of providing a continuous flow of information has been spreading in recent years, it is doubtful whether it will do so sufficiently unless it is made compulsory. This suggests ... that the law will have to step in .... Given the fears of business firms that more exhaustive disclosure ... would weaken their competitive position unless their rivals were obliged to be equally forthcoming, ... there must be no discrimination on grounds of nationality. ...

49. ... 2) ... To this end the Group recommends:

a) Any discriminatory provisions ... should be removed, and disclosure requirements and the procedures for admission to quotation should be harmonized..."

[152] EUROPA, https://europa.eu/european-union/law/treaties_en

[153] European Parliament homepage, http://www.europarl.europa.eu/factsheets/en/sheet/7/the-principle-of-subsidiarity

[154] EUROPA homepage (https://europa.eu/european-union/law/treaties_en) and European Parliament homepage (http://www.europarl.europa.eu/factsheets/en/sheet/7/the-principle-of-subsidiarity)

[155] European Union homepage (https://europa.eu/european-union/law/treaties_en)

[156] EUR-Lex (https://eur-lex.europa.eu/legal-content/EN/TXT/?url=celex:12016E288#document1, "To exercise the Union's competences, the institutions shall adopt regulations, directives, decisions, recommendations and opinions.") and "Secondary legislation" (https://eur-lex.europa.eu/legal-content/EN/

TXT/?url=LEGISSUM:ai0032)
[157] European Union homepage (https://ec.europa.eu/info/law/law-making-process/types
-eu-law_en) and EUR-Lex (https://eur-lex.europa.eu/summary/nonlegislative_acts.html)
[158] Article 290 of TFEU (http://eur-lex.europa.eu/eli/treaty/tfeu_2012/oj)
[159] Article 291 of TFEU (http://eur-lex.europa.eu/eli/treaty/tfeu_2012/oj)
"1. Member States shall adopt all measures of national law necessary to implement legally binding Union acts.
2. Where uniform conditions for implementing legally binding Union acts are needed, those acts shall confer implementing powers on the Commission, or, in duly justified specific cases and in the cases provided for Article 24 and 26 of the Treaty on European Union, on the Council
3. For the purpose of paragraph 2, the European Parliament and the Council, acting by means of regulations in accordance with the ordinary legislative procedure, shall lay down in advance the rules and general principles concerning mechanisms for control by Member States of the Commission's exercise of implementing powers.
4. The word 'implementing' shall be inserted in the title of implementing acts."
[160] ESMA homepage (https://ec.europa.eu/info/business-economy-euro/banking-and-finance/finance-reforms-and-their-progress/regulatory-process-financial-services/regulatory-process-financial-services_en)
[161] The Lamfalussy architecture is composed of four levels as below;

Level 1 (Directives & Regulations): The EU Parliament and Council adopt high level legislation to establish the principles that are focused on the enactment of directives or regulations.
Level 2 (Delegated acts & Implementing measures): The Commission enacts delegated or implementing measures regarding the framework legislations.
Level3 (Guidelines & Recommendations): For a consistent interpretation, an independent authority (ESMA) develops guidelines and recommendations directed to the national supervisory authorities. These are not binding but providing a significant interpretational help.
Level 4 (Supervision of the Enforcement by Member States): The ESMA monitors and evaluates the enforcement of the EU rules based on the ESMA Regulation in order to achieve supervisory convergence.

[162] European Parliament homepage (http://www.europarl.europa.eu/factsheets/en/sheet
/8/supranational-decision-making-procedures), The European Parliament has the power to approve EU legislation together with the Council that consists of EU countries' governments. European Commission is the executive branch of the European Union, which is the only institution empowered to initiate legislation. The Commission proposes legislation, implement decisions, and manages the business of the EU. Once legislation is passed,

the Commission ensures it to be implemented. The Commission is assisted by committees when drafting or adopting the technical measures. The Commission drafts a proposal, assesses the potential consequences, and prepares a 'Impact assessments' which describe the advantages and disadvantages of policy options. The Commission consults interested parties. The European Parliament and the Council review proposals prepared by the Commission and propose amendments. The Parliament and the Council can propose amendments and have the power to block the proposed legislation if they cannot agree. If both institutions agree on amendments, the proposed legislation is adopted.

[163] https://eur-lex.europa.eu/legal-content/EN/ALL/?uri=CELEX:61990CJ0006 ("…

THE COURT,… hereby rules: 1. The provisions of Council Directive 80/987/EEC of 20 October 1980 on the approximation of the laws of the Member States relating to the protection of employees in the event of the insolvency of their employ which determine the rights of employees must be interpreted as meaning that the persons concerned cannot enforce those rights against the State before the national courts where no implementing measures are adopted within the prescribed periods; 2. A member State is required to make good loss and damage caused to individuals by failure to transpose Directive 80/987/EEC.)

[164] Article 16 of Regulation (EU) 1095/2010, EUR-Lex (https://eur-lex.europa.eu/legal-content/EN/TXT/?uri=celex%3A32010R1095)

[165] "Guidelines for persons receiving market soundings (13/07/2016 2016/1130)" is related with Article 11(11). "Guidelines on legitimate interests of issuers to delay disclosure of inside information and situations in which the delay of disclosure is likely to mislead (13/07/2016 2016/1130)" is related with Article 17(11). "Guidelines on MAR - information relating to commodity derivatives markets or related spot markets for the purpose of the definition of inside information on commodity derivatives (30/09/2016 2016/1412)" is related to Article 7(5).

[166] Examples of distinct Paragraphs include:

Paragraph 21. Issuers or persons responsible for the prospectus should disclose the definitions of all APMs used, in a clear and readable way.

Paragraph 22. APMs disclosed should be given meaningful labels reflecting their content and basis of calculation in order to avoid conveying misleading messages to users.

Paragraph 41. The definition and calculation of an APM should be consistent over time. In exceptional circumstances where issuers or persons responsible for the prospectus decide to redefine an APM, the issuer should: i) explain the changes; ii) explain the reasons why these changes result in reliable and more relevant information on the financial performances, and; iii) provide restated comparative figures.

[167] paragraph 3~4 of Prospectus Regulation

[168] Article 6 (The prospectus) the Regulation (EU) 2017/1129

[169] Article 3 (Obligation to publish a prospectus and exemption) of Prospectus Regulation
[170] Article 12(1~3) of Prospectus Regulation
[171] Article 24(1) of Prospectus Regulation
[172] Paragraph 8 of Prospectus Regulation
[173] The URD is similar to a shelf-registration in the United States.
[174] Paragraph 39 of Regulation (EU) 2017/1129
[175] Paragraph 40 of Regulation (EU) 2017/1129
[176] Paragraph 43 of Regulation (EU) 2017/1129 and Article 9 (The universal registration document) of Regulation (EU) 2017/1129
[177] Paragraph 54 of Prospectus Regulation
[178] Article 16 (Risk factors) of the Regulation (EU) 2017/1129
"1. The risk factors featured in a prospectus shall be limited to risks which are specific … and … material …, as corroborated by the content of the registration document and the securities note. … the issuer … shall assess the materiality of the risk factors based on the probability of their occurrence and the expected magnitude of their negative impact. Each risk factor shall be adequately described, explaining how it affects the issuer. … The assessment of the materiality of the risk factors … may also be disclosed by using a qualitative scale of low, medium or high. The risk factors shall be presented in a limited number of categories depending on their nature. In each category the most material risk factors shall be mentioned first …"
[179] Paragraph 29 of the Regulation (EU) 2017/1129 explains that *"The presentation of risk factors in the summary should consist of a limited selection of specific risks which the issuer considers to be of most relevance to the investor when the investor is making an investment decision. The description of the risk factors in the summary should be of relevance to the specific offer and should be prepared solely for the benefit of investors and not give general statements on investment risk, or limit the liability of the issuer, offeror or any persons acting on their behalf…"*
Article 7 (The prospectus summary) of Regulation (EU) 2017/1129
*"1. The prospectus shall include a summary that provides the key information that investors need in order to understand the nature and the risks of the issuer ….
2. The content of the summary shall be accurate, fair and clear and shall not be misleading…
3. The summary shall be drawn up as a short document written in a concise manner and of a maximum length of seven sides of A4-sized paper when printed. The summary shall: (a) be presented and laid out in a way that is easy to read…; (b) be written … in language that is clear, non-technical, concise and comprehensible for investors. (4.~9. are omitted)
10. The total number of risk factors … shall not exceed 15."*
[180] Paragraph 33 of Regulation (EU) 2017/1129
[181] Paragraph 67 of Regulation (EU) 2017/1129.
[182] Article 1 of Regulation (EU) 2017/1129

[183] Article 1(4) of Regulation (EU) 2017/1129
[184] Paragraph 13 and Article 3 (Obligation to publish a prospectus and exemption) of Regulation (EU) 2017/1129
[185] Paragraph 12 of Regulation (EU) 2017/1129
[186] Point (g) was added in Article 7(2) of Directive 2010/73/EU; "*(g) a proportionate disclosure regime shall apply to offers of shares by companies whose shares of the same class are admitted to trading on a regulated market or a multilateral trading facility as defined in Article 4(1)(15) of Directive 2004/39/EC, which are subject to appropriate ongoing disclosure requirements and rules on market abuse, provided that the issuer has not disapplied the statutory pre-emption rights.*"
[187] recital 49~50 of Regulation (EU) 2017/1129
[188] Article 14 (Simplified disclosure regime for secondary issuances) of Regulation (EU) 2017/1129
"1. The following persons may choose to draw up a simplified prospectus under the simplified disclosure regime for secondary issuances, in the case of an offer of securities to the public or of an admission to trading of securities on a regulated market: ...
2. By way of derogation from Article 6(1), and without prejudice to Article 18(1), the simplified prospectus shall contain the relevant reduced information which is necessary to enable investors to understand: ..."
[189] EFAMA (European Fund and Asset Mnagement Association), Position Paper: Proposal for regulation on a prospectus to be published when securities are offered to the public or admitted to trading., 2016, https://efama.org/Publications/Public/EFAMA%20Position%20Paper%20on%20Prospectus.pdf ("*In the case of SMEs, the prospectus is one of the few sources of information for an asset manager, which makes its relevance even higher. Reducing the amount of required information in the prospectus will lead to lower (visible) regulatory burden, but not necessarily to lower overall burdens for the issuing company. In the future, many prospective buyers of the issued financial instrument are likely to ask questions pertaining to information that is not in the (lighter) prospectus anymore, but is relevant to institutional investor's investment analysis and thus their decision. In these cases, a lighter prospectus may well lead to a lower regulatory burden, but also to additional efforts from the issuer to answer non-standardised questions by prospective investors.*")
[190] European Commission homepage, https://ec.europa.eu/growth/sme/business-friendly-environment/sme-definition_en
[191] Article 2 (Definitions) of Regulation (EU) 2017/1129
"*For the purposes of this Regulation, the following definitions apply: ...
(f) 'small and medium-sized enterprises' or 'SMEs' means any of the following:
    (i) companies, which, according to their last annual or consolidated accounts, meet at least two of the following three criteria: an average number of*

employees during the financial year of less than 250, a total balance sheet not exceeding EUR 43 000 000 and an annual net turnover not exceeding EUR 50 000 000;

(ii) small and medium-sized enterprises as defined in point (13) of Article 4(1) of Directive 2014/65/EU."

[192] point (13) of Article 4(1) of MiFiD II (Directive 2014/65/EU)

[193] Paragraph 51 and Article 15(1) of Prospectus Regulation

[194] Paragraph 52 of Regulation (EU) 2017/1129

[195] Paragraph 53 of Regulation (EU) 2017/1129

[196] Article 15 (EU Growth prospectus) of Regulation (EU) 2017/1129

"1. The following persons may choose to draw up an EU Growth prospectus under the proportionate disclosure regime ... in the case of an offer of securities to the public provided that they have no securities admitted to trading on a regulated market:

(a) SMEs;

(b) issuers, other than SMEs, whose securities are traded or are to be traded on an SME growth market, provided that those issuers had an average market capitalisation of less than EUR 500 000 000 ...;

(c) issuers, other than those referred to in points (a) and (b), where the offer of securities to the public is of a total consideration in the Union that does not exceed EUR 20,000,000 ..., and provided that such issuers have no securities traded on an MTF and have an average number of employees ... of up to 499;

(d) offerors of securities issued by issuers referred to in points (a) and (b)."

[197] According to the Prospectus Regulation and MiFID II, "SME growth market" means a multilateral trading facility (MTF) that is registered as an SME growth market in accordance with Article 33 of MiFID II. See, Recitals 132~135 of Regulation (EU) 2017/1129 and Article 2 (Definitions) of Regulation (EU) 2017/1129.

Article 4 (Definitions) of the Directive 2014/65/EU

"1. For the purposes of this Directive, the following definitions apply: ...

(12) 'SME growth market' means a MTF that is registered as an SME growth markets in accordance with Article 33;"

[198] Article 6(3) of Prospectus Regulation

[199] recital 56 of Prospectus Regulation

[200] recital 58~59 of Prospectus Regulation

[201] Article 7(11) (The prospectus summary) of Prospectus Regulation

[202] Article 19 of Prospectus Regulation

[203] Article 21 of Prospectus Regulation

[204] Commission Delegated Regulation (EU) 2019/980 of 14 March 2019 supplementing Regulation (EU) 2017/1129 as regards the format, content, scrutiny and approval of the prospectus to be published when securities are offered to the public or admitted to trading on a regulated market. This repeals Commission Regulation (EC) NO 809/2004. Commission Delegated Regulations (EU) 2019/979 of 14 March 2019 supplementing Regulation (EU) 2017/1129 with regard to regulatory technical standards on key finan-

cial information in the summary of a prospectus applies from 21 June 2019.
[205] Article 23 of Prospectus Regulation
[206] Paragraph 41 of Prospectus Regulation
[207] Paragraph 60 of Prospectus Regulation
[208] Article 20 of Prospectus Regulation
[209] Article 9 of Regulation (EU) 2017/1129
[210] Article 9 and Article 44 of Prospectus Regulation
[211] ESMA, "ESMA Guidelines on risk factors under the Prospectus Regulation," Oct 10, 2019, https://esma.europa.eu/sites/default/files/library/esma31-62-1293_gideline_on_risk_factors_under_the_prospectus_regulation.pdf
[212] Paragraph 7 of Transparency Directive of 2004
[213] Regulation (EC) No 1606/2002 of the European Parliament and of the Council of 19 July 2002 on the application of international accounting standards.
[214] Directive 2004/109/EC Chapter 2
[215] Paragraph 10~12 of Transparency Directive of 2004
[216] Paragraph 16 of Transparency Directive of 2004
[217] Article 4(1), point 14, of Directive 2004/39/EC (aka. MiFiD)
[218] Regulated information is defined in Article 2(1)(k) of Transparency Directive of 2004.
Member states can adopt Member-level regulated information according to Article 3 of Transparency Directive of 2004. *"1. The home Member State may make an issuer subject to requirements more stringent than those laid down in this Directive. The home Member State may also make a holder of shares, or a natural person or legal entity referred to in Articles 10 or 13, subject to requirements more stringent than those laid down in this Directive."*
[219] ESMA homepage provides hyperlink to the national database of regulated information at https://www.esma.europa.eu/access-regulated-information
[220] Article 21 of Transparency Directive of 2004
[221] MAZARS (2009), p.48, Annex B-Statistics 122. Impact of the Directive on listing on a Regulated Market
[222] MAZARS (2009), p.91, Annex B-Statistics 231. Experience of difficulties with the publication deadlines, 232. Timing of disclosure depending on the size of listed companies
[223] MAZARS (2009), p.83, Annex B-Statistics 215. Compliance cost
[224] Demarigny (2010), p.5, *"On average, 93% of listed companies that are not in the largest market capitalizations benefit from less than 7% of the liquidity."*
[225] Regarding the notification requirement of major holdings, ESMA published the "Standard Form for Major Holdings" and "Practical Guide: National rules on notifications of major holdings under the Transparency Directive." ESMA homepage (https://www.esma.europa.eu/document/

standard-form-major-holdings); EUR-Lex homepage (https://www.eur-lex.europa.eu/legal-content/EN/ALL/?uri=CELEX%3A32013L0050).

[226] EUR-Lex homepage (https://www.eur-lex.europa.eu/legal-content/EN/ALL/?uri=CELEX%3A32013L0050)

[227] Paragraph 2~5 of Transparency Directive of 2013

[228] Article 2(1) of MAR

[229] Article 17(1) of MAR

[230] Article 7(1) of MAR

[231] Article 8 of MAR

[232] Article 14 of MAR

[233] Article 10 of MAR

[234] Article 9(1) of MAR, ("*An issuer ... may, on its own responsibility, delay disclosure to the public of inside information provided that all of the following conditions are met: (a) immediate disclosure is likely to prejudice the legitimate interests of the issuer ...; (b) delay of disclosure is not likely to mislead the public; (c) the issuer ... is able to ensure the confidentiality of that information ... Where an issuer ... has delayed the disclosure of inside information ..., it shall inform the competent authority ... immediately after the information is disclosed to the public.*")

[235] Article 12 of MAR set forth the scope of market manipulation in detail. Market manipulation shall comprise such activities as a) entering into a transaction or placing an order which i) gives false or misleading signals; or ii) secures the price at an abnormal or artificial level; b) entering into any other activity which affects the price; c) disseminating information which gives false or misleading signals or is likely to secure the price, including the dissemination of rumours.

[236] Article 17(4) of MAR

[237] Paragraph 50 of MAR

[238] ESMA homepage, https://www.esma.europa.eu/sites/default/files/library/2015/11/06_562.pdf

[239] Article 7(5) of MAR ("*ESMA shall issue guidelines to establish a non-exhaustive indicative list of information which is reasonably expected or is required to be disclosed in accordance with legal or regulatory provisions ...*")

[240] EUR-Lex homepage, https://eur-lex.europa.eu/legal-content/EX/TXT/uri=CELEX%3A32013L0034

[241] EUR-Lex homepage. https://eur-lex.europa.eu/legal-content/EX/TXT/uri=CELEX%3A32014L0095, Article 19a (Non-financial statement) of Accounting Directive

"*1. Large undertakings which are public-interest entities exceeding ... the criterion of the average number of 500 employees ... shall include in the management*

report a non-financial statement containing information to the extent necessary for an understanding of the undertaking's development, performance, position and impact of its activity, relating to, as a minimum, environment, social and employee matters, respect for human rights, anti-corruption and bribery matters …"
Article 29a (Consolidated non-financial statement)
"1. Public-interest entities which are parent undertakings of a large group exceeding … the criterion of the average number of 500 employees … shall include in the consolidated management report a consolidated non-financial statement containing information to the extent necessary for an understanding of a group's development …"

[242] European Commission, Communication from the Commission – Guideline on non-financial reporting (methodology for reporting non-financial information), https://ec.europa.eu/info/publications/non-financial-reporting-guidelines_en

[243] https://publications.parliament.uk/pa/cm201415/cmselect/cmtreasy/881/881.pdf

[244] https://www.londonstockexchange.com/companies-and-advisors/main-market/companies/sfs/faqs/faqs.htm

[245] https://www.londonstockexchange.com/home/guide-to-listing.pdf

[246] FCA homepage, "Guide to submitting a notification of delayed disclosure of inside information via the FCA website", https://www.fca.org.uk/publication/forms/delayed-disclosure-form-guide.pdf

[247] Primary Information Provider (PIP) disseminates regulatory information, such as information disclosed in the Listing Rule and DTR, to news vendors, such Secondary Information Providers (SIPs). The FCA has authorized some services providers as PIPs such as RNS, Business Wire, etc. RNS is an RIS approved by the FCA and operated by the LSE. Secondary Information Provider (SIP) is news vendors that get information from RIS to process and distribute it to retail investors or other media.

[248] London Stock Exchange homepage (https://www.londonstockexchange.com/companies-and-advisors/main-market/documents/admission-and-disclosure-standards-news2018.pdf

[249] The Main Market of LSE is an EU regulated market. The regulatory requirements for a Main Market may vary depending on the segment. The ongoing obligations differ depending on the listing route. Some standards apply to all publicly quoted companies regardless of market classification.

[250] SIX Exchange Regulation, https://www.six-exchange-regulation.com/en/home/regulation/issuer.html

[251] SIX Regulation homepage, https://www.six-exchange-regulation.com/en/home/publications/explorer/sanction-decisions.html#c=/content/ser/global/en/taxonomy/ business-topic/obligations/ad-hoc-publicity

[252] SIX Exchange Regulation, Listing Rule, https://www.six-exchange-regulation.com/en/

home/regulation/issuer.html,

"Art. 61 (Sanctions)

One or more of the following sanctions may be imposed on issuers and guarantors. Where appropriate, these sanctions may be imposed cumulatively:

1. reprimand;

2. fine of up to CHF 1 million (in case of negligence) of CHF 10 million (in case of wrongful intent);

3. suspension of trading;

4. delisting or reallocation to a different regulatory standard;

5. exclusion from further listings;

6. withdrawal of recognition. ...

In considering the sanction to be imposed, the competent body will take into consideration, in particular, the severity of the breach and the degree of fault. When setting the level of fines, the competent body will take into account the impact of the sanction on the party concerned."

[253] SIX Exchange Regulation homepage, https://www.six-exchagne-regulation.com/en/
home/publications/explorer/sanction-decisions.html

[254] Disclosure-related law or regulation includes such as the Securities and Exchange Law, Ministerial Ordinance with respect to the disclosure of corporate information and the rule of TSE (Rules a Timely Disclosure of corporate information by issuer of listed securities and the like).

[255] Rule 28 (Subjects of Disclosure Examination) of Business Regulation

[256] JPX-R homepage, http://www.jpx.co.jp/english/regulation/ensuring/listing/compliance/index.html

[257] Rule 30 (Designations as Securities on Alert) of Business Regulation

[258] Rule 31 (Request for Improvement Report) of Business Regulation

[259] Rule 32 (Designations as Disclosure In Question Security) of Business Regulation

[260] Rule 33 (Public Announcement Measure) and Rule 34 (Imposition of Listing Agreement Violation Penalty) of Business Regulation

[261] Section 203 of Securities and Futures Act 2002

"(1) A person to whom this subsection applies must not intentionally, recklessly or negligently fail to notify the approved exchange of such information as is required to be disclosed by the approved exchange under the listing rules or any other requirement of the approved exchange, if the person is required by the approved exchange under the listing rules or any other requirement of the approved exchange to notify the approved exchange of information on specified events or matters as they occur or arise for the purpose of the approved exchange making that information available to an organised market operated by the approved exchange.

(2) (omitted)

(3) Despite section 204 or 335, a contravention of subsection (1) is not an offence unless the failure to notify is intentional or reckless."

[262] The SGX Mainboard Rule provides the Corporate Disclosure Policy in Appendix 7.1 and the Practice Note 7.1 (Continuing Disclosure) that should be observed by issuers.
Rule 703 (Disclosure of Material Information) of the Mainboard Rule
"(1) An issuer must announce any information known to the issuer concerning it or any of its subsidiaries or associated companies which:
(a) is necessary to avoid the establishment of a false market in the issuer's securities; or
(b) would be likely to materially affect the price or value of its securities."
[263] Paragraph 8 (Some Events Requiring Disclosure Under Rule 703) of Appendix 7.1 Corporate Disclosure Policy
[264] Rule 703 (Disclosure of Material Information) of the Mainboard Rule
(2) Rule 703(1) does not apply to information which it would be a breach of law to disclose.
(3) Rule 703(1) does not apply to particular information while each of the following conditions applies.
  Condition 1: a reasonable person would expect the information to be disclosed;
  Condition 2: the information is confidential; and
  Condition 3: one or more of the following applies:
    (a) the information concerns an incomplete proposal or negotiation;
    (b) the information comprises matters of supposition or is insufficiently definite to warrant disclosure;
    (c) the information is generated for the internal management purposes of the entity;
    (d) the information is a trade secret.
[265] Paragraph 10 and 14 of Appendix 7.1 Corporate Disclosure Policy of the Mainboard Rule
[266] Paragraph of Appendix 7.1 Corporate Disclosure Policy of the Mainboard Rule
[267] Article 25 of Corporate Disclosure Policy (Appendix 7.1 of the Mainboard Rules)
[268] Paragraph 5 of the Appendix 7.1 Corporate Disclosure Policy of the Mainboard Rule
[269] Singapore Corporate Awards, https://www.scawards.com.sg/index.html
[270] Section 675 describes continuous disclosure requirement of other disclosing entities. Section 676 describe when information is generally available. Section 677 defines "material effect on price or value." Section 678 set out that the Criminal Code applies to an offence based on subsection 674(2), 674(5) or 675(2).
[271] Section 677 (material effect on price or value) of the Corporations Act as of 1 January 2018:
"For the purpose of sections 674 and 675, a reasonable person would be taken to expect information to have a material effect on the price or value of ED securities of a disclosing entity if the information would, or would be likely

to, influence persons who commonly invest in securities in deciding whether to acquire or dispose of the ED securities." Section 111AC of the Corporations Act defines a disclosing entity as a corporation that issues Enhanced Disclosure (ED) securities.

[272] Listing Rule 3.1

[273] Note of Listing rule 3.1

[274] ASX, Continuous Disclosure: an Abridged Guide, https://www.asx.com.au/documents/about/abridged-continuous-disclosure-guide-clean-copy.pdf,

"Listing rule 3.1 does not apply to particular information while each of the following is satisfied in relation to the information.

3.1A.1 One or more of the following 5 situations applies:
- *It would be a breach of a law to disclose the information;*
- *The information concerns an incomplete proposal or negotiation;*
- *The information comprises matters of supposition or is insufficiently definite to warrant disclosure;*
- *The information is generated for the internal management purposes of the entity; or*
- *The information is a trade secret; and*

3.1A.2 The information is confidential and ASX has not formed the view that the information has ceased to be confidential; and

3.1A.3 A reasonable person would not expect the information to be disclosed."

[275] Listing Rule 3.1

[276] Chapter 5 of Listing rule

[277] Listing rule 4.7B and Appendix 4C

[278] Chapter 5 of Listing rule

[279] https://www.asx.com.au/documents/rules/Guidance_Note_8.pdf

[280] ASX, Continuous Disclosure: an Abridged Guide, https://www.asx.com.au/documents/about/abridged-continuous-disclosure-guide-clean-copy.pdf

[281] The Preamble of IOSCO By-Laws states its objectives that securities administrators resolve; a) to cooperate in promoting adherence to international standards in order to protect investors, maintain fair, efficient and transparent markets, and seek to address systemic risks; b) to enhance investor protection and promote investor confidence; and c) to exchange information on experiences in order to implement appropriate regulation.

[282] Other entities include; Auditors, Credit Rating Agencies, and other information providers, Collective Investment Schemes, Market Intermediaries, Secondary and Other Markets, Clearing and Settlement.

[283] 1. The responsibilities of the Regulator should be clear and objectively stated.

2. The Regulator should be operationally independent and accountable in the exercise of its functions and powers.

3. The Regulator should have adequate powers, proper resources and the capacity to perform its functions and exercise its powers.

4. The Regulator should adopt clear and consistent regulatory processes.
5. The staff of the Regulator should observe the highest professional standards, including appropriate standards of confidentiality.
6. The Regulator should have or contribute to a process to identify, monitor, mitigate and manage systemic risk, appropriate to its mandate.
7. The Regulator should have or contribute to a process to review the perimeter of regulation regularly.
8. The Regulator should seek to ensure that conflicts of interest and misalignment of incentives are avoided, eliminated, disclosed or otherwise managed.

[284] Methodology for Assessing Implementation of the IOSCO Objectives and Principles of Securities Regulation
[285] "APEC-OECD Integrated Checklist on Regulatory Reform", p.33, https:www.oecd.org/regreform/34989455.pdf
[286] Box 1. Central Definitions of the "APEC-OECD Integrated Checklist on Regulatory Reform", p.34, https:www.oecd.org/regreform/34989455.pdf
[287] OECD, Appendix (Background Note to the OECD Reference Checklist for Regulatory Decision-Making), Recommendations of the Council on Improving the Quality of Government Regulation, http://www.oecd.org/officialdocuments/publicdisplaydocumentpdf/?doclanguage=en&cote=OCDE/GD(95)95
[288] OECD, Mar 9, 1995, Recommendations of the Council on Improving the Quality of Government Regulation, http://www.oecd.org/officialdocuments/publicdisplaydocumentpdf/?doclanguage=en&cote=OCDE/GD(95)95
[289] OECD, https://www.oecd.org/regreform/regulatory-policy/recommendations-guidelines.htm
[290] OECD, https://www.oecd.org/gov/regulatory-policy/2012-recommendation.htm
[291] OECD homepage, https://www.oecd.org/regulatory-policy/1_coglianese%20web.pdf
[292] OECD homepage, www.oecd.org/gov/regulatory-policy/measuring-regulatory-performance.htm
[293] World Bank, https://info.worldbank.org/governance/wgi
[294] World Bank, https://info.worldbank.org/governance/wgi/pdf/rq.pdf
[295] http://www.oecd.org/mena/goverrnance/38403668.pdf
[296] IOSCO, 2000, Model for Effective Regulation
[297] Preamble paragraph 21 of the ESMA Guidelines on enforcement of financial information
[298] Preamble paragraph 16 of the Regulation (EC) No 1606/2002 of the European Parliament and of the Council of 19 July 2002 on the application of International Accounting Standards
[299] Paragraph 6 of the ESMA Guidelines on enforcement of financial information
[300] https://www.house.leg.state.mn.us/hrd/pubs/deterrence.pdf

[301] McKinsey & Company, "Risk-based resource allocation: Focusing regulatory and enforcement efforts where they are needed the most", February 2013, https://www.mckinsey.com/business-functions/risk/our-insights/risk-based-resource-allocation

[302] McKinsey & Company, "Risk-based resource allocation: Focusing regulatory and enforcement efforts where they are needed the most", February 2013, https://www.mckinsey.com/business-functions/risk/our-insights/risk-based-resource-allocation

[303] McKinsey & Company, "Exhibit 3. Expected loss is the product of likelihood and severity of an event" of the "Risk-based resource allocation: Focusing regulatory and enforcement efforts where they are needed the most", February 2013, https://www.mckinsey.com/business-functions/risk/our-insights/risk-based-resource-allocation

[304] McKinsey & Company, "Exhibit 5. Exhibit 5. For sophisticated targets, conduct deeper inspections." of the "Risk-based resource allocation: Focusing regulatory and enforcement efforts where they are needed the most", February 2013, https://www.mckinsey.com/business-functions/risk/our-insights/risk-based-resource-allocation

[305] The degree of externality will depend on the degree of similarity or relatedness among firms (refer the Chapter 2633 and Chapter 5316).

[306] Preamble paragraph 4-7 of CS MSD

[307] Preamble paragraph 11 of CS MAD

[308] Article 4(1) of CS MAD

[309] Article 9 of CS MAD

[310] Section 5 (Compliance Procedures) of the "Admission and disclosure standard"

"… There are a number of factors which the Exchange takes into account when considering what disciplinary action to take in relation to a rule breach. These are set out below:
  - The seriousness, size and nature of the rule breach
  - How the rule breach came to light
  - The actual or potential market impact of the rule breach, and any likely repercussions
  - The general compliance history of the issuer, and specific history regarding the rule breach in question
  - Consistent and fair application of the rules (any precedents of previous similar rule breaches)
  - The responsiveness and conduct of the issuer in relation to the matter under investigation…"

[311] United States Sentencing Commission, Guidelines Manual 2018, Chapter Five Determining the Sentence, Introductory Commentary, https://www.ussc.gov/guidelines/2018-guidelines-manual

[312] Enforcers may adopt a multi-tiered adjustment procedure. For example, enforcers determine an initial sanction based on the basic nature of misbehavior and then adjust the initial sanction based on additional

circumstances and factors. Enforcers may determine to lower the sanction level when the misbehavior was occurred even though good faith efforts to comply with requirements were made.

[313] There are two types of filings that are reviewed: registration statements and periodic reports. Periodic reports which represent the ongoing disclosure obligations under the Securities Exchange Act of 1934 include 10-K, 10-Q, 8-K, and proxy statements. Registration statements (aka. transactional filings) are filed under the Securities Act of 1933 (e.g., IPO Form S-1, M&A Form S-4).

[314] SEC, Evaluation of the Division of Corporation Finance's Disclosure Review and Comment Letter Process, Report No. 542, Sep 13, 2017, SEC homepage (https://www.sec.gov/oig/reports-and-publications/evalation-division-corporation-finance-disclosure-review-and-comment)

[315] 15 U.S.C. § 77e, Securities Act of 1933, section 5

[316] Section 8(a) of the 1933 Act states that a registration statement will become effective automatically 20 days after it is filed with the Commission. Under section 8(b) of the 1933 Act the SEC may not approve the effectiveness of a registration statement when it is incomplete or inaccurate in any material respect. Even though the registration statement has already become effective, the SEC may suspend the effectiveness if there is a material untrue statement or failure to state a material fact.

[317] "Securities law experts ... suggested a couple of factors that should have at least triggered the SEC's interest in these reports, including Enron's astonishingly rapid growth ... and the significant change in the nature of its business (from energy to trading) ... The sheer number of Enron-related entities ... also should have raised suspicions ... the SEC's selective review process did not identify Enron's later annual reports ... as worthy of review. One reason for this was that, under the Commission's priority system, Enron was not "due"' to have its annual report reviewed until 2002 ... the SEC staff confirmed that Enron's 2000 Form 10-K would not have been flagged for review under their remaining screening criteria."

[318] SEC homepage (https://www.sec.gov/divisions/corfin/cffilingreview.htm)

[319] Deloitte (2017) illustrates SEC staff's note that "...whereas approximately 70 percent of filing reviews resulted in a comment letter in the early 2000s, only about 35 percent of filing reviews resulted in a comment letter in 2015."

[320] Tax aggressive firms are proxied as firms with the cash effective tax rates below the sample median, and firms with poorer disclosure quality are proxied as firms with reporting lags above the sample median.

[321] Until 2004, some members of the Canadian Securities Administrators (CSA) had maintained a continuous disclosure review program of their own. Meanwhile, to harmonize continuous disclosure obligation across Canada by replacing local requirements, the CSA introduced the "National Instrument 51-102 Continuous Disclosure Obligation," which came into force on March

30, 2004.

[322] https://www.osc.gov.on.ca/en/SecuritiesLaw_csa_20090724_51-312_harm-con-dis.htm

[323] CSA Staff Notice 51-312 (Revised) Harmonized Continuous Disclosure Review Program, 2010, OSC homepage (https://www.osc.gov.on.ca/documents/en/Securities-Category5/csa_20090724_51-312_harm-con-dis.pdf)

[324] CSA Staff Notice 51-316 Continuous Disclosure Review of Smaller Issuers, 2005, BCSC home page (https://www.bcsc.bc.ca/Securities_Law/Policies/Policy5/51-316_Continuous_Disclosure_Reivew_of_Smaller_Issuers_CSA_Staff_Notice_/)

[325] On July 27, 2017, the CSA announced in "CSA Staff Notice 51-351 Continuous Disclosure Review Program Activities for the fiscal year ended March 31, 2017" that a CSA Staff Notice detailing the results of the CDR program will be published every two years instead of annually.

[326] https://www.osc.gov.ca/en/SecuritiesLaw_csa_20070105-322_reporting-default.jsp

[327] Ontario Securities Commission Forward-looking Information Disclosure, Jun 13, 2013 (https://www.osc.gov.on.ca/documents/en/Securities-Category5/sn_20130613_51-721_forward-looking,pdf) ; OSC Staff Notice 51-721 Forward-looking Information Disclosure, Jun 13, 2013 (https://www.osc.gov.on.ca/en/SecuritiesLaw_sn_20130613_51-721_fordward-looking.htm)

[328] Paragraph 21~22 of "ESMA Guidelines on enforcement of financial information", ("Enforcement of financial information" is defined as "examining the compliance of financial information with the relevant financial reporting framework, taking appropriate measures where infringements are discovered ... and taking other measures relevant for the purpose of enforcement." The examination of financial information is "to assess whether it is in accordance with the relevant financial reporting framework. In order for enforcement of financial information to be effective, enforcers should also take appropriate actions in accordance with these guidelines, ..., to ensure that ... the market participants are provided with accurate information compliant with the relevant financial reporting framework.")

[329] Guideline 3 (paragraph 39) of "ESMA Guidelines on enforcement of financial information"

[330] In 2018, EU enforcers conducted pre-clearances for 12 cases according to the "Enforcement and Regulatory Activities of European Accounting Enforcers in 2018." Paragraph 43~46 of "ESMA Guidelines on enforcement of financial information" set out details of pre-clearance as below:

Pre-clearance

43. Guideline 4: Where pre-clearance is permitted, it should be part of a formal process, and provided only after the issuer and its auditor have finalised their position on the accounting treatment concerned.

44. Enforcement of financial information normally takes published finan-

cial information as its starting point. Hence, by nature, it is an ex-post activity which is carried out according to the examination procedures ...
45. However, some enforcers have a well-developed pre-clearance system where issuers are able to secure an enforcement decision ex-ante... These guidelines provide that certain conditions should be in place when enforcers are using pre-clearance. In particular, the issuer and its auditor should have determined the accounting treatment to be applied based on all specific facts and circumstances as this will enable pre-clearance decision to be based on the same level of information as an ex-post decision. This will avoid pre-clearance decisions becoming general interpretations.
46. Pre-clearance should be part of a formal process, meaning that a proper decision is taken by the enforcer in a way similar to that in which ex-post decisions are taken. This implies that the enforcer should not be able to reverse its position after the financial information has been published unless facts and circumstances have changed ... or there are other substantial grounds for doing so...

[331] Guideline 5 (paragraph 47~49) of "ESMA Guidelines on enforcement of financial information" describes the selection methods.

[332] A corrective note is to issue a note making public a material misstatement with respect to the already disclosed items and the corrected information. ("Definition" of "ESMA Guidelines on enforcement of financial information")

[333] Guideline 7 (paragraph 57~61) and the paragraph 14 of "Appendix I – Description of the enforcement process" in the "Enforcement and Regulatory Activities of European Accounting Enforcers in 2018" describes the types of enforcement actions

[334] Appendix IV (Number of examinations per country of IFRS financial statements) in the "Enforcement and Regulatory Activities of European Accounting Enforcers in 2018"

[335] Paragraph 2 of the Appendix IV (Number of examinations per country of IFRS financial statements)

[336] footnote 55 of the Appendix IV (Number of examinations per country of IFRS financial statements)

[337] Disclosure and Transparency Rule (DTR) 1.5.3 (Sanctions), FCA homepage (https://www.handbook.fca.org.uk/handbook/DTR.pdf)

[338] FCA homepage, (https://fca.org.uk/publication/corporate/annual-report-2018-19-enforcement-performance.pdf)

[339] Financial Conduct Authority homepage, "AIM Investment Company fined for failing to disclose inside information as soon as possible", available at https://www.fca.org.uk/news/press-releases/aim-investment-company-fined-failing-disclose-insideinformation-soon-possible and https://www.fca.org.uk/news/press-release/aim-investment-company-fined-failing-disclose-inside-information-soon-possible

[340] LSE homepage, For companies & advisers/Advisers/AIM Notices (Notice

[340 cont.] #AD21, https://www.londonstockexchange.com/companies-and-advisors/aim/advisors/aim-notices/ad21.pdf)

[341] LSE homepage, For companies & advisers/Advisers/AIM Notices (Notice #AD22, https://www.londonstockexchange.com/companies-and-advisors/aim/advisors/aim-notices/ad22.pdf)

[342] https://www.londonstockexchange.com/companies-and-advisors/main-market/documents/admission-and-disclosure-standards-new2018.pdf

[343] DPR-FREP, Homepage (https://www.frep.info/index_en.php); "Information on the examination process of the Financial Reporting Enforcement Panel (FREP)", (https://www.frep.info/docs/prueferfahren/info)ablauf_pruefverfahren_en.pdf)

[344] DPR-FREP, "Information on the examination process of the Financial Reporting Enforcement Panel (FREP)" p.2, (https://www.frep.info/docs/prueferfahren/info/ablauf_pruefverfahren_en.pdf)

[345] DPR-FREP, "Principles for Random Sampling (15.11.2018)", (https://www.frep.info/pruefverfahren/verfhrensregelungen_en.pdf)

[346] DPR-FREP, Activity Report 2018, 24 January 2019, https://www.frep.info/docs/jahresberichte/2018/2018_tb_en.pdf

[347] DPR-FREP, Activity Report 2018, 24 January 2019, https://www.frep.info/docs/jahresberichte/2018/2018_tb_en.pdf

[348] DPR-FREP Homepage, https://www.frep.info/presse/taetigkeitsberichte_en.php

[349] SESC, Basic Guideline on Disclosure Statement Inspection, August 30, 2013, https://www.fsa.go.jp/sesc/english/guideline/disclosure.pdf

[350] SESC Latest Topics, https://www.sesc.go.jp/sesc/english/topics/index.htm

[351] Japan Exchange Group, Inc. (JPX) was established as a business combination between Tokyo Stock Exchange Group and Osaka Securities in January 2013. According to the Financial Instruments and Exchange Act (FIEA), Japan Exchange Regulation (JPX-R) was also established as an independent self-regulatory body under JPX. JPX-R specializes in listing examination, listed company compliance, market surveillance based on entrustment by the exchanges pursuant to the Articles of Incorporation. Exchanges take disciplinary action based on recommendations of JPX-R.

[352] Business Regulations, JOX-R homepage (https://www.jpx.co.jp/english/rules-participants/rules/regulations/bv22ga0000001bkf-att/jpxr_business_regulations_20180401.pdf)

[353] To illustrate an "Improvement Report" case, a company disclosed an investigation report of the third-party committee concerning inappropriate accounting treatment and corrected past earnings reports. This case was in violation of the listing rules due to the disclosure containing false statements. TSE implemented the public announcement measure. The deficiencies came from the organizational structure for timely disclosure, and improvements to the organizational structure were deemed highly ne-

cessary. TSE requires the Company to submit an improvement report. (JPX homepage, Listed Companies/Market Alerts)

[354] Practice Notes 1.2 (Oversight of Issuers) of the Mainboard rules of SGX, SGX homepage Rulebook, (rulebook.sgx.com/en/display/display_main.html?rbid=3271&element_id=4830)

[355] SGX homepage (Regulation-Resources & Reports-Reports, https//www2.sgx.com/regulation/reports

[356] SGX homepage (Director's and Executive Officers' Watchlist, https//www.sgx.com/regulation/directors-and-executive-officers-watchlist)

[357] Section 204 of Securities and Futures Act 2002

(1) Any person who contravenes any of the provisions of this Division shall be guilty of an offence and shall be liable on conviction to a fine not exceeding $250,000 or to imprisonment for a term not exceeding 7 years or to both.

(2) No proceedings shall be instituted against a person for an offence in respect of a contravention of any of the provisions of this Division after -

  (a) a court has made an order against him for the payment of a civil penalty under section 232; or

  (b) the person has entered into an agreement with the Authority to pay, with or without admission of liability, a civil penalty under section 232(5), in respect of that contravention

[358] Memorandum of Understanding Governing Listing Matters, Jan 2003, HKEX homepage (https://www.hkex.com.hk/-/media/HKEX-Market/Listing/How-We-Regulate/Overview/mou_28jan03.pdf?la=en)

[359] "Exchange's Review of Issuer's Annual Disclosure" are available in the "Listing - Rules and Guidance – Other Resources - Listed Issuers -Review of Issuer's Annual Report Disclosure" in the HKEX homepage. (https://www.hkex.hk/Listing/Rules-and-Guidance/Other-Resources/Listed-Issuers?sc_lang=en)

[360] Review of Issuer's Annual Report Disclosure Report 2018, Jan 2019, HKEX homepage (https://www.hkex.com.hk/-/media/HKEX-Market/Listing/Rules-and-Guidance/Other-Resources/Exchanges-Review-if-Issuers-Annual-Disclosure/rdiar_2018.pdf)

[361] Financial Statement Review Programme Report of 2017, June 2018, HKEX homepage (https://www.hkex.com.hk/-/media/HKEX-Market/Listing/Rules-and-Guidance/Other-Resources/Exchange-Review-of-Issuers-Annual   -Disclosure/frm_17.pdf?la=en)

[362] ASIC, https://asic.gov.au/what-we-do/our-role/asics-corporate-plan-2019-23/

[363] ASIC, "ASIC enforcement outcomes July to December 2017"

[364] ASIC, "ASIC enforcement outcomes July to December 2016"

[365] "8.8 Other enforcement action by ASX" of "Guidance Note 8 Continuous Disclosure Listing rules 3.1 - 3.1B"

[366] "8.7 Referrals to ASIC" of "Guidance Note 8 Continuous Disclosing: Listing Rules 3.1~3.1B", According to the Corporations Act and the MOU between ASX and ASIC, ASX makes referral to ASIC as soon as practicable if it suspects that a person is related with a significant contravention of its operating rules or the Corporations Act.

[367] Listing rule

17.3 ASX may at any time suspend an entity's securities, or a class of them, from quotation if in ASX's opinion any of the following applies.

17.3.1 The entity is unable or unwilling to comply with, or breaks, a listing rule.

17.3.2 It is necessary to suspend quotation to prevent a disorderly or uniformed market.

17.3.3 ASX's rules require the suspension.

17.3.4 It is appropriate for some other reason.

[368] Listing rule 1.1 (requirements for ASX Listing)

For an entity to be admitted to the official list as an ASX Listing, the following conditions must be met to ASX's satisfaction. ...

Condition 20. The entity must satisfy ASX that each director or proposed director of the entity at the date of listing is of good fame and character...

[369] SEC, http://www.sec.gov/news/studies/capform/capffull.txt

[370] ISAB Discussion Paper, BC1.14-BC1.17

[371] "*The issuer shall take reasonable steps to verify that purchasers are accredited investors by reviewing documentation such as wage and tax statement, tax returns, bank statements, etc. The stipulated categories are below.*

(1) Any bank, or other institution whether acting in individual or fiduciary capacity; any broker or dealer; any insurance company; any investment company; any employee benefit plan if the investment decision is made by a plan fiduciary (e.g., bank, etc.), if total asset is in excess of $5,000,000 or, if a self-directed plan, with investment decisions made solely by accredited investors;

(2) Any private business development company as defined in the Investment Advisers Act of 1940;

(3) Organization, corporation, etc. with total assets in excess of $5,000,000;

(4) Any director, executive officer, or general partner of the issuer, etc.;

(5) Any natural person whose net worth exceeds $1,000,000;

(6) Any natural person who had an income in excess of $200,000, etc.;

(7) Any trust, with total assets in excess of $5,000,000 whose purchase is directed by a sophisticated person; and

(8) Any entity in which all of the equity owners are accredited investors."

[372] Information overload is also known as infobesity, information glut, data smog, and info pollution. Especially, information pollution refers to the state of information contaminated by irrelevant, redundant, useless, and undesirable information that can have a detrimental effect on information users. (https://www.beckley.va.gov/wholehealth/Surroundings.pdf)

[373] The concept of information overload may differ depending on the purpose of analysis. If one is interested in the difficulty in understanding

information contents, he may define it as the gap between the amount of information provided and the processing capacity (left graph). If one is interested in whether investors decision effectiveness is maximized or enhanced, he may define it as the decrease in decision effectiveness (right graph).

[374] Paredes (2003) indicated the limits of empirical study to measure the degree of information overload. To learn about how severely they are overloaded, we need to measure the gap. For example, we should measure the accuracy and effectiveness of each decision and then compare the effectiveness of the overloaded decisions with that of non-overloaded decisions (i.e., optimized decision). However, measuring the extent of overload is challenging since neither the effectiveness of the decision nor the optimum level of information cannot be precisely measured.

[375] In the United States, in addition to filing periodic reports, listed firms must report certain material events on a more current basis. Form 8-K is the "current report" that firms must file with the SEC to announce major events. Such events include bankruptcy, change in control, shutting down a plant, and signing material agreements.

[376] Thomson Reuters, Divided SEC Scale Back Disclosure for Business Combination, May22, 2020, https://tax.thomsonreuters.com/news/divided-sec-scales-back-disclosure-for-business-combination/

[377] Many countries adopt qualitative and quantitative tests to classify investors. Some criteria are proxies of the investor's rationality. Such investor categorization policy can be useful in the scale-back policy. Chapter 323 (Investor categorization policy) covers more.

[378] Paul Krill, IBM survey: CEOs say they can't handle growing business complexity, InfoWorld, May 18, 2010, https://www.infoworld.com/article/2626736/ibm-survey--ceos-say-they-can-t-handle-growing-business-complexity.html

[379] Al Root, Tesla Hit a New High. No, It Was TLSA. Confused?, Jul 15, 2020, https://barrons.com/articles/tesla-stock-symbol-confusion-biotech-tiziana-51594852166?siteid=yhoof2&yptr=yahoo; Jonathan Garber, A company called Zoom Technologies is surging because people think it's Zoom Video Communications (ZOOM, ZM), Apr 18, 2019, https://markets.businessinsider.com/news/stocks/publicly-listed-zoom-video-communications-traders-buying-zoom-technologies-2019-4-1028122561#; Steve Kovach, A Stock Called 'TWTRQ' was up as much as 1,500% Because People Thought it was Twitter, Oct 5, 2013, https://businessinsider.com/twtr-stock-up-1500-percent-2013-10

[380] Chapter 234 (Investor base effect) explains the Merton's investor's recognition hypothesis that may provide conceptual understandings on the ignoring strategy.

[381] If regulators proscribe firm's choice (e.g., complex accounting due to structured security) where information asymmetry exceeds a threshold

level, not only the firm but also all markets would shrink. For example, structured security is widely issued because of efficiency in achieving a variety of benefits. It also transfers investment risk to expertise investors who are willing to take it. Therefore, regulator's proscription policy might reduce efficiency significantly.

[382] In 1993, the U.S. SEC established the Office of Investor Education and Assistance and tried a pilot program to implement a "plain English" project. It gave an incentive, such as expedited review, when firms voluntarily adopt the pilot program.

[383] SEC Rule 421(d) "Presentation of information in prospectuses"

[384] Further guidance was followed to support preparing a prospectus in a "clear, concise and understandable" manner.

[385] 17CFR§240.13a-20 "Plain English presentation of specified information" describes detailed standards. The SEC has continuously increased the use of plain English in various filings which range from the registration statement to MD&A. The SEC extended plain English to various items and provided standards for the issuers to use short sentences, everyday language, tabular presentations, but avoid the jargon and multiple negatives in preparing the disclosures. The failure of observing rules of plain English disclosure could result in a comment letter.

[386] In 1998, the Securities and Futures Commission (SFC) in Hongkong published a "How to create a clear prospectus" guide. HKSE published a number of guidance on disclosure in listing documents included under the title "Simplification Series." In 2016, Hongkong Stock Exchange (HKSE) announced the "Guide on Producing Simplified Listing Documents Relating to Equity Securities for New Applications," of which objective is to improve investors' ability to understand the information in listing documents necessary to make properly informed assessments of applicants. Some of the listing documents submitted to HKSE should be presented in plain language format by simplifying the language and layout, avoiding defined terms and technical jargon.

[387] The tendency of the low literate investor relying on informal information sources might be creating the irrationality.

[388] Testimony of Chairman Alan Greenspan, Financial literacy Before the Committee on Banking, Housing, and Urban Affairs, U.S. Senate, February 5, 2002 (https://www.federalreserve.gov/boarddocs/testimony/2002/20020205/default.htm)

ABOUT THE AUTHOR

Yungwan Suh

Yungwan, Suh earned his Bachlor's degree in Economics from Korea University and Master's degrees in Finance from Michigan State University. He is working for Korea Exchange in disclosure department.

www.ingramcontent.com/pod-product-compliance
Lightning Source LLC
Chambersburg PA
CBHW070615220526
45466CB00001B/7